# BARRON'S

# 1100 WORDS
# You Need to Know

SIXTH EDITION

**MURRAY BROMBERG**
PRINCIPAL EMERITUS
ANDREW JACKSON HIGH SCHOOL
QUEENS, NEW YORK

**MELVIN GORDON**
READING SPECIALIST
NEW YORK CITY SCHOOLS

*All inquiries should be addressed to:*
Barron's Educational Series, Inc.
250 Wireless Boulevard
Hauppauge, NY 11788
**www.barronseduc.com**

*Library of Congress Catalog Card No. 2012938495*

ISBN: 978-1-4380-0166-1


PRINTED IN THE UNITED STATES OF AMERICA

9 8 7 6 5 4 3 2 1

# CONTENTS

Full Pronunciation Key . . . . . . . . . . . . . . . . . . . . . . . . . . . . . . . . . . . . . . . . . . . . . . .iv

WEEKS 1–46 . . . . . . . . . . . . . . . . . . . . . . . . . . . . . . . . . . . . . . . . . . . . . . . . . . . . .1

Buried Words . . . . . . . . . . . . . . . . . . . . . . . . . . . . . . . . . . . . . . . . . . . . . . . . . .290

Words in Context . . . . . . . . . . . . . . . . . . . . . . . . . . . . . . . . . . . . . . . . . . . . . . .294

Answers . . . . . . . . . . . . . . . . . . . . . . . . . . . . . . . . . . . . . . . . . . . . . . . . . . . . . .295

Final Review Test . . . . . . . . . . . . . . . . . . . . . . . . . . . . . . . . . . . . . . . . . . . . . . .315

Panorama of Words . . . . . . . . . . . . . . . . . . . . . . . . . . . . . . . . . . . . . . . . . . . . .323

Bonus Weeks . . . . . . . . . . . . . . . . . . . . . . . . . . . . . . . . . . . . . . . . . . . . . . . . . .371

VOC/QUOTE . . . . . . . . . . . . . . . . . . . . . . . . . . . . . . . . . . . . . . . . . . . . . . . . . . .385

The Lighter Touch 100 . . . . . . . . . . . . . . . . . . . . . . . . . . . . . . . . . . . . . . . . . . .392

Index . . . . . . . . . . . . . . . . . . . . . . . . . . . . . . . . . . . . . . . . . . . . . . . . . . . . . . . . .400

# INTRODUCTION

The study of the English language has spread all over the world, and high school and college students everywhere have come to realize that language mastery depends on the possession of a comprehensive vocabulary. This is just what *1100 Words You Need to Know* has been offering through the five earlier editions and continuing on this sixth one.

We are proud that Amazon.com has rated this book as the number one best seller in its category. In addition to the various exercises that help readers learn challenging vocabulary, we have now added a section called "The Lighter Touch 100," which shows that vocabulary can be taught with a sense of humor. By investing a mere 15 minutes with this new book, you will soon see a dramatic improvement in your vocabulary.

*Murray Bromberg*
*Melvin Gordon*

# FULL PRONUNCIATION KEY

| | | | | | |
|---|---|---|---|---|---|
| a | bat, trap | j | just, enjoy | u̇ | bull, pull |
| ā | rage, lace | k | kin, talk | ü | dual, sue |
| ä | jar, farther | l | lose, hurl | | |
| | | m | mice, cram | v | vast, have |
| b | bag, sob | n | not, into | w | wish, wood |
| ch | chill, such | ng | song, ring | y | youth, yes |
| d | done, said | | | z | zoo, zest |
| | | o | rot, cot | zh | pleasure, treasure |
| e | met, rest | ō | tow, blow | | |
| ē | ease, see | ô | cord, lord | ə | stands for: |
| er | fern, learn | oi | toil, boil | | a in around |
| | | ou | mouse, bout | | e in waken |
| f | feel, stiff | | | | i in cupid |
| g | gone, big | p | pest, cap | | o in demon |
| h | him, hold | r | red, art | | u in brush |
| | | s | see, best | | |
| i | inch, pin | sh | crush, crash | | |
| ī | ivy, hive | t | time, act | | |
| | | th | this, math | | |
| | | ŦH | they, booth | | |

iv

# WEEK 1 ❖ DAY 1

**NEW WORDS**

**voracious**
və rā´ shəs

**indiscriminate**
in´ dis krim´ ə nit

**eminent**
em´ ə nənt

**steeped**
stēpt

**replete**
ri´ plēt´

## READING WISELY

The youngster who reads *voraciously*, though *indiscriminately*, does not necessarily gain in wisdom over the teenager who is more selective in his reading choices. A young man who has read the life story of every *eminent* athlete of the twentieth century, or a coed who has *steeped* herself in every social-protest novel she can get her hands on, may very well be learning all there is to know in a very limited area. But books are *replete* with so many wonders that it is often discouraging to see bright young people limit their own experiences.

**Sample Sentences** On the basis of the above paragraph, try to use your new words in the following sentences. Occasionally it may be necessary to change the ending of a word; e.g., *indiscriminately* to *indiscriminate*.

1. The football game was _____ with excitement and great plays.

2. The _____ author received the Nobel Prize for literature.

3. My cousin is so _____ in schoolwork that his friends call him a bookworm.

4. After skiing, I find that I have a _____ appetite.

5. Modern warfare often results in the _____ killing of combatants and innocent civilians alike.

**Definitions** Now that you have seen and used the new words in sentences, and have the definitions "on the tip of your tongue," try to pair the words with their meanings.

6. voracious _____    **a.** of high reputation, outstanding

7. indiscriminate _____    **b.** completely filled or supplied with

8. eminent _____    **c.** choosing at random without careful selection

9. steeped _____    **d.** desiring or consuming great quantities

10. replete _____    **e.** soaked, drenched, saturated

---
### TODAY'S IDIOM

*to eat humble pie*—to admit your error and apologize

After his candidate had lost the election, the boastful
campaign manager had *to eat humble pie.*

---

ANSWERS ARE ON PAGE 295

**abound**
ə bound´

**technology**
tek nol´ ə jē

**prognosticate**
prog nos´ tə kāt

**automaton**
ô tom´ ə ton

**matron**
mā´ trən

## SOLVING THE SERVANT PROBLEM

The worlds of science-fiction *abound* with wonders. Yet modern *technology* progresses so rapidly that what may be today's wild dream may be next year's kitchen appliance. A British scientist has *prognosticated* that within ten years every suburban *matron* will have her own robot servant. One task this domesticated *automaton* will not have to contend with will be scouring the oven because even today the newest ranges can be "programed" to reduce their own baked-on grime to easily disposed of ashes.

**Sample Sentences** Now that you've seen the words used in context, and—hopefully—have an idea of their meanings, try to use them in the following sentences. Remember that a word-ending may have to be changed.

1. The mayor refused to _____ as to his margin of victory in the election.

2. The time is approaching when human workers may be replaced by _____.

3. A clever salesman will always ask a _____ if her mother is at home.

4. The western plains used to _____ with bison before those animals were slaughtered by settlers.

5. Man may be freed from backbreaking labor by the products of scientific _____.

**Definitions** Test yourself now by matching the new words with the definitions. If you are not sure of yourself, cover the top half of this page before you begin.

6. abound _____ a. an older married woman

7. technology _____ b. branch of knowledge dealing with engineering, applied science, etc.

8. prognosticate _____ c. a robot; a mechanical "person"

9. automaton _____ d. to exist in great numbers

10. matron _____ e. to predict or foretell a future event

─── **TODAY'S IDIOM** ───

*a pig in a poke*—an item you purchase without having seen; a disappointment

The mail order bicycle that my nephew bought turned out to be *a pig in a poke,* and he is now trying to get his money back.

ANSWERS ARE ON PAGE 295

### NEW WORDS

**paradox**
par´ ə doks

**realm**
relm

**annals**
an´ nəlz

**compound**
kom pound´

**tinge**
tinj

## IT'S A MAN'S WORLD

How *paradoxical* that the world's greatest chefs have all been men! Cooking would clearly seem to be a field that lies exclusively within women's *realm*, yet the *annals* of cookery are replete* with masculine names: Brillat Savarin, Ritz, Diat, Larousse. To *compound* the puzzle, there has rarely been a *tinge* of rumor or scandal casting doubts on the masculinity of these heroes of cuisine.

(*replete—if you've forgotten the meaning, see page 1)

**Sample Sentences** Try your hand now at using your new words by writing them in their correct form (change endings if necessary) in these sentences:

1. His gloom was now _____ by the failing mark on his geometry test.

2. The _____ of sports are replete* with the names of great black athletes.

3. One of the great _____ of American life is that though minority groups have suffered injustices, nowhere in the world have so many varied groups lived together so harmoniously.

4. A _____ of garlic is all that's necessary in most recipes.

5. The cruel king would not allow the prince to enter his _____ , restricting him to the forest, which abounded* with wild animals.

   (*abounded—studied previously, see page 2)

**Definitions** If you are having trouble in picking the right definitions, it may be best *not* to do them in the order given, but to do the ones you are surest of first.

| | | | |
|---|---|---|---|
| 6. paradox | _____ | **a.** | a trace, smattering, or slight degree |
| 7. realm | _____ | **b.** | a statement that at first seems to be absurd or self-contradictory but which may in fact turn out to be true |
| 8. annals | _____ | **c.** | to increase or add to |
| 9. compound (v.) | _____ | **d.** | historical records |
| 10. tinge (n.) | _____ | **e.** | special field of something or someone; kingdom |

---

### TODAY'S IDIOM

*a flash in the pan*—promising at the start but then disappointing

The rookie hit many home runs in spring training, but once the season began he proved to be *a flash in the pan.*

---

ANSWERS ARE ON PAGE 295

badger
baj´ər

implore
im plôr´

drudgery
druj´ ər ē

interminable
in ter´ mə nə bəl

perceive
pər sēv´

# WEEK 1 ❖ DAY 4

## HOW NOT TO GET YOUR WAY

It is difficult to change someone's opinion by *badgering* him. The child who begs his mother to "get off his back" when she *implores* him for some assistance with the household *drudgery*, may very well plead *interminably* for some special privilege when he wants something for himself. How paradoxical* that neither is able to *perceive* that no one likes being nagged.

(* paradoxical—studied previously, see page 3)

**Sample Sentences** Getting the hang of it? Now go on to use the five new words in the following sentences—remember, past tenses may be required.

1. She does her homework on Fridays to save herself from the _____ of having to do it during the weekend.

2. The teacher continually _____ the pupil for the missing assignments.

3. The eminent scientist _____ difficulties in putting the invention into practice.

4. The sick child's mother _____ the doctor to come immediately.

5. I listened to the boring lecture for what seemed an _____ fifty minutes.

**Definitions** Pick the letter of the definition that matches your new word and write it in the answer space.

6. badger (v.)    _____    a. unpleasant, dull, or hard work

7. implore    _____    b. unending

8. drudgery    _____    c. to plead urgently for aid or mercy

9. interminable    _____    d. to understand, know, become aware of

10. perceive    _____    e. to pester, nag, annoy persistently

---
**TODAY'S IDIOM**
---

*to pour oil on troubled waters*—to make peace, to calm someone down

When I tried to *pour oil on troubled waters*, both the angry husband
and his wife stopped their quarrel and began to attack me.

---

ANSWERS ARE ON PAGE 295

# WEEK 1 ❖ DAY 5                                    REVIEW

You have accomplished something worthwhile this week. In learning twenty useful words and four idioms, you have taken a step toward a greater mastery of our language. As a result of today's lesson, you will become aware of those words that require greater study on your part for complete success in these first lessons.

Take the following quiz by matching the best possible definition with the word you have studied. Write the letter that stands for that definition in the appropriate answer space.

## REVIEW WORDS

_____ 1. abound
_____ 2. annals
_____ 3. automaton
_____ 4. badger
_____ 5. compound
_____ 6. drudgery
_____ 7. eminent
_____ 8. implore
_____ 9. indiscriminate
_____ 10. interminable
_____ 11. matron
_____ 12. paradox
_____ 13. perceive
_____ 14. prognosticate
_____ 15. realm
_____ 16. replete
_____ 17. steeped
_____ 18. technology
_____ 19. tinge
_____ 20. voracious

## DEFINITIONS

a. to be completely soaked in something
b. to be able to tell what will happen in the future
c. someone's special field
d. to continually nag
e. carelessly chosen
f. related to science of engineering
g. to add to
h. beg for assistance
i. of outstanding reputation
j. a mature woman
k. small amount of
l. dull, difficult work
m. desiring huge amount
n. existing in great number
o. historical records
p. to come to have an understanding of
q. completely filled with
r. machine that behaves like a person
s. seemingly self-contradictory situation
t. unending

## IDIOMS

_____ 21. to eat humble pie
_____ 22. a pig in a poke
_____ 23. a flash in the pan
_____ 24. to pour oil on troubled waters

u. a blind item; poor purchase
v. admit to defeat
w. a star today, a flop tomorrow
x. to try to make peace

Now check your answers on page 295. Make a record of those words you missed. You can learn them successfully by studying them and by using them in your own original sentences. If you neglect them, then the effort you have put into your vocabulary building campaign up to this point will have been wasted.

## WORDS FOR FURTHER STUDY          MEANINGS

1. _____   _____

2. _____   _____

3. _____   _____

4. _____   _____

5. _____   _____

# SENSIBLE SENTENCES?
## (From Week 1)

❖ Underline the word that makes sense in each of the sentences below.

1. The huge football player had a *(voracious, replete)* appetite.

2. After a seemingly *(interminable, indiscriminate)* wait, the surgeon came to give us the news.

3. Without a *(paradox, tinge)* of evidence, the coroner could not solve the murder.

4. In the *(realm, annals)* of the blind, the one-eyed man is king.

5. We invited the *(eminent, steeped)* engineer to address our club.

6. In the Catskill Mountains, the woods *(abound, implore)* with deer.

7. I cannot *(perceive, prognosticate)* why people voted for the corrupt senator.

8. Night and day my kid brother *(badgers, compounds)* me for money.

9. Science fiction movies usually feature *(annals, automatons)*.

10. With his expertise in *(drudgery, technology)*, my uncle is able to earn a good salary.

❖ Do these sentences make sense? Explain why.

11. The rookie was amazing during spring training but he turned out to be *a flash in the pan.*

12. I complained to the salesperson because he had sold me *a pig in a poke.*

13. When I tried *to pour oil on troubled waters*, I only made matters worse.

14. After the election, when my candidate conceded his loss, I had *to eat humble pie.*

**6**

ANSWERS ARE ON PAGE 295

# WORDSEARCH 1

❖ Using the clues listed below, fill in each blank in the following story with one of the new words you learned this week.

## *Reggie the Con Man*

In the ①_____ of crime, there are few scoundrels who could match the exploits of Reggie Hayes, who also used the names of Reginald Haven, Ricardo Hermosa, Father Harris, and dozens of other aliases. Reggie's police record, principally in Chicago and Baltimore, is ②_____ with scams that he perpetrated upon gullible people. Generally, his favorite target was a ③_____ who should have known better.

Dressed as a priest ("Father Harris"), he was most convincing, however. His method of operation was to "find" a wallet stuffed with hundred dollar bills outside a supermarket and then ④_____ an unsuspecting woman to share his good fortune, since there was no identification in the wallet. But first, to establish her credibility, his victim had to put up a sum of money as a testimonial to her good faith. Mrs. Emma Schultz, age 72, tearfully told the police that she had withdrawn $14,000 from her bank and placed it in a shopping bag supplied by the helpful priest. He told her to hold onto the bag while he went next door to a lawyer's office to make the sharing of their good fortune legal.

After a seemingly ⑤_____ wait, Mrs. Schultz discovered to her chagrin that the heartless thief had skipped out the back way, leaving her "holding the bag"—a switched bag containing shredded newspaper—while he made his getaway with her life savings.

## Clues

① 3rd Day
② 1st Day
③ 2nd Day
④ 4th Day
⑤ 4th Day

## NEW WORDS

**laconic**
lə kon´ ik

**throng**
thrŏng

**intrepid**
in trep´ id

**accost**
ə kôst´

**reticent**
ret´ ə sənt

## TO THE POINT

Calvin Coolidge, our thirtieth president, was named "Silent Cal" by reporters because of his *laconic* speech. One Sunday, after Mr. Coolidge had listened to an interminable* sermon, a *throng* of newsmen gathered around him. An *intrepid* reporter *accosted* the Chief Executive: "Mr. President, we know that the sermon was on the topic of sin. What did the minister say?" "He was against it," the *reticent* Coolidge replied.

(*interminable—see page 4. *Each review word will be followed by an asterisk—you will find the first use of the word by consulting the Index at the back of the book.*)

**Sample Sentences**  Use the new words in the following sentences:

1. His speech was usually rambling, but this time I found it brief and _____ .

2. If a surly panhandler should _____ you, keep on walking.

3. Even under repeated questioning, the witness remained _____ .

4. A howling _____ of teenage girls surrounded the rap artists.

5. The corporal received the Silver Star for his _____ deeds in combat.

**Definitions**  Match the new words with their dictionary meanings.

6. laconic  _____  a. expressing much in few words

7. throng  _____  b. brave

8. intrepid  _____  c. to approach and speak to

9. accost  _____  d. crowd

10. reticent  _____  e. silent

---

### TODAY'S IDIOM

*the sword of Damocles*—any imminent danger
(a king seated one of his subjects underneath a sword that was
hanging by a hair, in order to teach him the dangers a king faces)

Although the president of the company seemed quite secure, he always
complained that there was a *sword of Damocles* hanging over his head.

---

8

ANSWERS ARE ON PAGE 295

NEW WORDS

**furtive**
fėr´ tiv

**felon**
fel´ ən

**plethora**
pleth´ ə rə

**hapless**
hap´ lis

**irate**
ī´ rāt   or   ī rāt´

# WEEK 2 ❖ DAY 2

## IF I HAD THE WINGS OF AN ANGEL

Casting a *furtive* glance over his shoulder, the *felon* slipped out the main prison gate to be swallowed up in the British fog. A *plethora* of escapes from supposedly secure prisons embarrassed the *hapless* wardens. To compound* their problems, the officials were badgered* by *irate* citizens who accused the guards of accepting bribes from convicts whose motto was: "Stone walls do not a prison make, nor iron bars a cage."

(*compound—see page 3; *badgered—see page 4)

**Sample Sentences**  Use the new words in the following sentences.

1. The _____ contest winner was unable to locate the lucky ticket.

2. My uncle was _____ when the drunken driver swerved in front of us.

3. In a _____ manner she removed her shoes and tiptoed up to her room.

4. When the teacher asked why the homework had not been done, he was greeted by a _____ of incredible alibis.

5. Since the boss learned that Bob associated with a known _____ , he fired him.

**Definitions**  Match the new words with their meanings.

6. furtive _____ **a.** angry, incensed

7. felon _____ **b.** a person guilty of a major crime

8. plethora _____ **c.** unfortunate

9. hapless _____ **d.** excess

10. irate _____ **e.** secret, stealthy

---
### TODAY'S IDIOM
---

*Pyrrhic victory*—a too costly victory
**(King Pyrrhus defeated the Romans but his losses were extremely heavy)**

In heavy fighting the troops managed to recapture the hill,
but it could only be considered a *Pyrrhic victory*.

## NEW WORDS

**pretext**
prē´ tekst

**fabricate**
fab´ rə kāt

**adroit**
ə droit´

**gesticulate**
je stik´ yə lāt

**vigilant**
vij´ ə lənt

## DR. JEKYLL OR MR. HYDE?

Under the *pretext* of being a surgeon he gained entry to the hospital. When interviewed by the director, he had to *fabricate* a tale of his medical experience, but he was so *adroit* at lying that he got away with it. It was not until the phony "doctor" began to *gesticulate* wildly with his scalpel, that a *vigilant* nurse was able to detect the fraud. In the annals* of medical history there have been a number of such cases.

**Sample Sentences** Use the new words in the following sentences.

1. The shootings at Columbine High School made educators much more

   _____ ,

2. My nephew is quite _____ at making model airplanes.

3. Most fishermen can _____ a story about the size of the one that got away.

4. Her _____ of being tired did not fool us for an instant.

5. I often marvel as I watch the traffic officer _____ at the onrushing cars.

**Definitions** Pick the letter of the definition that matches your new word and write it in the answer space.

6. pretext        _____    a. to lie; to construct

7. fabricate      _____    b. skillful

8. adroit         _____    c. an excuse

9. gesticulate    _____    d. watchful

10. vigilant      _____    e. move the arms energetically

---

**TODAY'S IDIOM**

*a wet blanket*—one who spoils the fun

Everyone wanted the party to go on, but Ronnie,
*the wet blanket*, decided to go home to bed.

---

ANSWERS ARE ON PAGE 295

# WEEK 2 ❖ DAY 4

**NEW WORDS**

**avid**
av´ id

**cajole**
kə jōl´

**rudimentary**
rü´ də men´ tə rē

**enhance**
in hans´

**nuance**
nü äns´

## YOU'VE GOT TO BE A FOOTBALL EXPERT

As an *avid* football fan, I try to see every game the Jets play. Whenever I can *cajole* my father into accompanying me, I try to do so. He has only a *rudimentary* knowledge of the game, and since I am steeped* in it, I enjoy explaining its intricate details to him. It certainly does *enhance* your appreciation of football when you are aware of every *nuance* of the sport.

**Sample Sentences** Use the new words in the following sentences. You may have to change the ending of a word.

1. Since my grasp of algebra is _____ , I cannot solve the problem.

2. The parakeet refused to be _____ into entering her cage.

3. It will _____ your enjoyment of an opera if you know what the plot is about in advance.

4. In reading the satires of Jonathan Swift, one must be vigilant* in order to catch each _____ .

5. Bill Clinton is an _____ student of the social media and is listed on Facebook.

**Definitions** Match the new words with their meanings.

6. avid _____ a. eager

7. cajole _____ b. slight variation in meaning, tone, etc.

8. rudimentary _____ c. coax

9. enhance _____ d. intensify, heighten

10. nuance _____ e. elementary

---
**TODAY'S IDIOM**

*to beard the lion in his den*—to visit and oppose a person on his own grounds

Having decided *to beard the lion,* I stormed into the manager's office to ask for a raise.

---

Keep adding to your vocabulary, as it is one of the most useful tools a student can possess. Let's go over the twenty new words and four idioms you studied during this week.

In the following quiz, match the best possible definition with the word you have studied. Write the letter that stands for that definition in the appropriate answer space.

## REVIEW WORDS

_____ 1. accost
_____ 2. adroit
_____ 3. avid
_____ 4. cajole
_____ 5. enhance
_____ 6. fabricate
_____ 7. felon
_____ 8. furtive
_____ 9. gesticulate
_____ 10. hapless
_____ 11. intrepid
_____ 12. irate
_____ 13. laconic
_____ 14. nuance
_____ 15. plethora
_____ 16. pretext
_____ 17. reticent
_____ 18. rudimentary
_____ 19. throng
_____ 20. vigilant

## DEFINITIONS

a. uncommunicative
b. enthusiastic
c. alert
d. overabundance
e. courageous
f. to greet first
g. an excuse
h. unlucky
i. angry
j. criminal
k. basic, elementary
l. clever
m. to make up a lie
n. great number of people
o. concise, pithy
p. to use lively gestures
q. shade of difference
r. sly
s. coax, wheedle
t. to make greater

## IDIOMS

_____ 21. the sword of Damocles
_____ 22. Pyrrhic victory
_____ 23. a wet blanket
_____ 24. to beard the lion

u. an expensive conquest
v. spoilsport
w. defy an opponent in his home
x. any threatening danger

## WORDS FOR FURTHER STUDY      MEANINGS

Now check your answers on page 295. Make a record of those words you missed. You can learn them successfully by studying them and using them in your own original sentences. If you neglect them, then the effort you have expended in building up your vocabulary may be wasted.

1. _____  _____

2. _____  _____

3. _____  _____

4. _____  _____

5. _____  _____

❖ Using the clues listed below, fill in each blank in the following story with one of the new words you learned this week.

## *The Best Laid Plans*

Gloria Rogers overslept and then had to sprint to catch the same Greyhound Bus that she boarded on the last Thursday of every month. After a three-hour uneventful ride, she finally arrived at the bus terminal where a courtesy van was ready to transport bus passengers to Visitors Day at the State Penitentiary.

Although Gloria tried to act casual, she was more than a little nervous. Her boyfriend, Art, a convicted ①_____ , had managed to gain admittance to the prison's hospital on the ②_____ of having a gall bladder attack. Under her own slacks and bulky sweater, Gloria was wearing a set of clothes that she removed in the hospital bathroom and passed on to Art. He planned to use them after making his escape in the back of the prison ambulance that was parked outside his ward.

Art had spelled out his escape plan during Gloria's last visit, spending an hour trying to ③_____ her into being his accomplice. All that she had to do was appear to have a seizure. Then she would ④_____ a story about her epilepsy while Art, with the smuggled clothes concealed under his prison bathrobe, would slip out of the ward during the excitement. Unfortunately for the schemers, a ⑤_____ hospital guard spotted Art climbing into the rear of the ambulance and quickly foiled the escape attempt. The result was that Art had three years added to his sentence and Gloria was imprisoned for her role in the misadventure.

## Clues

① 2nd Day

② 3rd Day

③ 4th Day

④ 3rd Day

⑤ 3rd Day

## NEW WORDS

**loathe**
lōth

**reprimand**
rep´ rə mand

**lackluster**
lak´ lus´ tər

**caustic**
kô´ stik

**wrest**
rest

## THE PEP TALK

"If there's one thing I *loathe*," the coach said, "it's a quitter." He had good reason to *reprimand* us at half-time, because the scoreboard revealed that we were losing, 45–20. Our *lackluster* performance indicated to him that we had forgotten the rudimentary* aspects of basketball. His *caustic* remarks fired us up, however, and we dashed out, determined to *wrest* control of the game from our rivals.

**Sample Sentences** Use the new words in the following sentences.

1. With the help of his brothers he was able to _____ the leadership of the company from his partner.

2. Speaking in a monotone, the politician was booed for his _____ address.

3. In a _____ article, the drama critic slaughtered the hapless* actors.

4. I _____ spinach but I love other green vegetables.

5. When Ed arrived late, he knew that the grocer would _____ him.

**Definitions** Match the new words with their dictionary definitions.

6. loathe _____ **a.** dull

7. reprimand (v.) _____ **b.** to hate

8. lackluster _____ **c.** sarcastic, biting

9. caustic _____ **d.** take by force

10. wrest _____ **e.** to show sharp disapproval

---

**TODAY'S IDIOM**

*crocodile tears*—insincere tears
(crocodiles were said to cry while eating their prey)
When the football player broke his leg, his substitute wept *crocodile tears*.

---

ANSWERS ARE ON PAGE 296

# WEEK 3 ❖ DAY 2

**NEW WORDS**

**infamous**
in´ fə məs

**jostle**
jos´ əl

**dupe**
düp

**incipient**
in sip´ ē ənt

**inadvertent**
in əd vёrt´ nt

## THE HANDCUFF IS QUICKER THAN THE EYE

Slippery Eddie, the *infamous* pickpocket, was back at work, and every detective had to be especially vigilant.* Eddie's technique was to *jostle* a victim toward a confederate who would then slip the man's wallet out of his back pocket while Eddie was stammering an apology to the confused *dupe*. Within a week the *incipient* crimewave came to an end when Slippery Eddie *inadvertently* chose the chief of police for his victim. Although Eddie loathes* Sing Sing, it's his permanent address now.

**Sample Sentences** Can you put the new words in the right sentences?

1. By telling the truth, we stopped the _____ rumor from spreading.

2. The bombing of Pearl Harbor was referred to as an _____ deed.

3. The wealthy _____ consented to buy the often-sold Brooklyn Bridge.

4. When he attempted to _____ the old lady, she struck him with her umbrella.

5. Through an _____ error, the guided missile sped out of control.

**Definitions** Match the new words with their meanings.

6. infamous _____ a. having a bad reputation

7. jostle _____ b. just beginning to exist

8. dupe (n.) _____ c. to shove hard

9. incipient _____ d. a person easily tricked

10. inadvertent _____ e. heedless, not attentive

---
**TODAY'S IDIOM**

*to carry the day*—to win the approval of the majority

The secretary's motion that we adjourn for lunch *carried the day*, and we headed for the restaurant

---

## NEW WORDS

**ominous**
om´ ə nəs

**tremulous**
trem´ yə ləs

**repudiate**
ri pyü´ dē āt

**cessation**
se sā´ shən

**bristle**
bris´ əl

## COURTROOM DRAMA

There was an *ominous* silence when the jittery defendant rose in court. He explained in a *tremulous* voice what had led him to *repudiate* his confession made at the police station on the night of the crime. The audience began to buzz excitedly until the judge demanded a *cessation* of the noise. Although the district attorney *bristled* with anger, the defendant kept insisting that his rights had been violated because he had not been told that he could see a lawyer before confessing.

**Sample Sentences**  Fit the new words into the blanks.

1. After the weatherman had seen the _____ clouds, he prognosticated* rain.

2. The general attempted to _____ the testimony of the lieutenant, claiming that the young officer was not an authority on low level bombing.

3. Upon seeing the snake, the cat began to _____ with fear.

4. The widow's _____ hands revealed her nervousness.

5. The _____ of the bombing in Iraq was urged by the United Nations.

**Definitions**  Match the new words with their meanings.

6. ominous _____    a   a stopping

7. tremulous _____    **b.** to reject, decline

8. repudiate _____    **c.** stiffen with fear or anger

9. cessation _____    **d.** threatening

10. bristle (v.) _____    **e.** quivering

---

**TODAY'S IDIOM**

*Skid Row*—disreputable part of town, inhabited by derelicts and people "on the skid"

The presence of so many bars has turned our neighborhood into another *Skid Row*.

---

ANSWERS ARE ON PAGE 296

# WEEK 3 ❖ DAY 4

## NEW WORDS

**euphemism**
yü´ fə miz əm

**mundane**
mun´ dān

**incongruous**
in kong´ grü əs

**condolence**
kən dō´ ləns

**stipulate**
stip´ ū lāt

## CALL ME BY MY RIGHT NAME

My cousin refers to himself as a "sanitary engineer"—a *euphemism* for garbage collector. There are any number of people who try to find more respectable or glamorous titles for the *mundane* jobs they hold. It may seem *incongruous* to call an undertaker a "*condolence* counselor," or to refer to a taxi driver as a "transportation expediter," but some prefer those titles. As a matter of fact, our butcher has *stipulated* that from now on he wants to be known as a "meat coordinator." He became irate* when I inadvertently* called him "Butch."

**Sample Sentences** In which blanks do the new words belong?

1. We repudiated* the contract because it did not _____ a cost of living bonus.

2. The word "expired" is a _____ for "died."

3. When my neighbor's dog was run over, we sent a _____ card.

4. The philosopher dealt with spiritual things, ignoring the _____ ones.

5. The play was so _____ that it seemed to be the work of several authors.

**Definitions** Match the new words with their meanings.

6. euphemism _____    **a.** worldly

7. mundane _____    **b.** a less offensive term

8. incongruous _____    **c.** to specify a condition

9. condolence _____    **d.** inappropriate

10. stipulate _____    **e.** pity

---

### TODAY'S IDIOM

***to go up in smoke*—to come to no practical result**
**(kindling smokes but it will not light a fire)**

The mayor's plans to get the gubernatorial nomination
*went up in smoke* when he couldn't end the costly strike.

---

# REVIEW

WEEK **3** ❖ DAY **5**

The word "review" means "to view again" and that is the purpose of our weekly review. You will have noticed, of course, that many of the words that appear as new words are repeated in subsequent lessons. Sometimes they are in the paragraph, sometimes in the sample sentences, and occasionally in the idioms or directions. This continued emphasis on "viewing again" will help you to become familiar with the vocabulary.

In the following quiz, match the best possible definition with the word you have studied. Write the letter that stands for that definition in the appropriate answer space.

**REVIEW WORDS**

| | | **DEFINITIONS** |
|---|---|---|
| _____ | 1. bristle | **a.** despise |
| _____ | 2. caustic | **b.** menacing |
| _____ | 3. cessation | **c.** evil |
| _____ | 4. condolence | **d.** a pause |
| _____ | 5. dupe | **e.** just starting |
| _____ | 6. euphemism | **f.** trembling |
| _____ | 7. inadvertent | **g.** to have one's hair stand up |
| _____ | 8. incipient | **h.** stinging |
| _____ | 9. incongruous | **i.** earthly |
| _____ | 10. infamous | **j.** due to an oversight, negligent |
| _____ | 11. jostle | **k.** make a specific demand |
| _____ | 12. lackluster | **l.** to push, to elbow |
| _____ | 13. loathe | **m.** an easily fooled person |
| _____ | 14. mundane | **n.** expression of sympathy |
| _____ | 15. ominous | **o.** to scold severely |
| _____ | 16. reprimand | **p.** seize |
| _____ | 17. repudiate | **q.** having inconsistent elements |
| _____ | 18. stipulate | **r.** disown, refuse to accept |
| _____ | 19. tremulous | **s.** lacking brightness |
| _____ | 20. wrest | **t.** saying something in a less direct way |

## IDIOMS

| | | | |
|---|---|---|---|
| _____ | 21. crocodile tears | **u.** | run down district |
| _____ | 22. to carry the day | **v.** | hypocritical sympathy |
| _____ | 23. Skid Row | **w.** | to win the honors |
| _____ | 24. to go up in smoke | **x.** | end fruitlessly |

Now check your answers on page 296. Make a record of those words you missed. You can learn them successfully by studying them and using them regularly in speech and in your writing.

**WORDS FOR FURTHER STUDY**     **MEANINGS**

1. _____   _____

2. _____   _____

3. _____   _____

4. _____   _____

5. _____   _____

❖ Using the clues listed below, fill in each blank in the following story with one of the new words you learned this week.

## *Desert Storm Decision*

In the 1991 Persian Gulf War, where the United Nations forces, led by Americans, ousted the invading Iraqi army from Kuwait's soil, the ①_____ of combat took place in short order after the Allies were able to ②_____ control of the skies from the ③_____ Saddam Hussein's air force.

General H. Norman Schwarzkopf, the U.S. field commander, tended to ④_____ when asked by the media why he hadn't pursued the enemy all the way to Baghdad, saying:

"It would have been foolhardy for us to try to occupy that capital city and pile up American casualties from sniper attacks by Iraq's guerillas. That may be hard for you Monday morning quarterbacks to understand but I thoroughly agreed with the president who was convinced that such an action would have sent a bad message to the Arab world and would have splintered the Allied partnership."

Schwarzkopf reiterated that it was his mission to hurl back the invaders with a minimum of bloodshed but not, he added in a ⑤_____ tone, "to splatter Saddam over the desert sands. That dictator's days are numbered," the general concluded, "but I expect his end is likely to come at the hands of his own people."

## Clues

① 3rd Day

② 1st Day

③ 2nd Day

④ 3rd Day

⑤ 1st Day

## NEW WORDS

**alacrity**
ə lak´ rə tē

**disdain**
disdān´

**belligerent**
bə lij´ ər ənt

**intimidate**
in tim´ ə dāt

**feint**
fānt

## MULLINS A K.O. VICTIM

When the bell sounded, K.O. Mullins responded with *alacrity*. He sprang from his stool and charged across the ring, showing *disdain* for the champion's strength. Although this *belligerent* attitude impressed the referee, it failed to *intimidate* the champ. That intrepid* battler laid the hapless* Mullins low with an adroit* *feint* and an uppercut.

**Sample Sentences**  Use the new words in the following sentences.

1. Y2K concerns of the problems with computers failed to _____ our company.

2. The Germans were duped* by the Allies' _____ toward the south, leaving the way open for the Normandy invasion.

3. The waiter moved with _____ because he perceived* they were big tippers.

4. His _____ manner caused him to lose one friend after another.

5. When the curtain came down, the critic's face registered the _____ she felt for the lackluster* play.

**Definitions**  Match the new words with their meanings.

6. alacrity     _____     **a.** contempt

7. disdain (n.)     _____     **b.** a false attack

8. belligerent     _____     **c.** warlike

9. intimidate     _____     **d.** to overawe

10. feint     _____     **e.** briskness, lively action

---

### TODAY'S IDIOM

*to throw down the gauntlet*—to challenge someone
(when the gauntlet, or medieval glove, was thrown down,
the challenged one was required to pick it up)

The principal of our rival school *threw down the gauntlet*,
and we had no choice but to accept the challenge.

---

ANSWERS ARE ON PAGE 296

# WEEK 4 ❖ DAY 2

**NEW WORDS**

**pugnacious**
pug nā´ shəs

**promulgate**
prom´ əl gāt

**brash**
brash

**scoff**
skof

**belittle**
bi lit´ l

## MULLINS THROWS DOWN THE GAUNTLET*

The *pugnacious* K.O. Mullins demanded a rematch. He took a full-page newspaper advertisement to *promulgate* his challenge. When the champ's manager saw the *brash* announcement, he accosted* Mullins, who was surrounded by a throng* of newsmen. The manager openly *scoffed* at Mullins and *belittled* his fighting ability. Mullins then lost his temper and fearlessly punched the manager, knocking him off of his crutches.

**Sample Sentences** Use the new words in the following sentences.

1. We implored* the faculty advisor to _____ the requirements for the presidency of the club.

2. My mother liked the salesman's _____ personality, but he irritated most people.

3. I don't understand modern art, but I neither loathe* nor _____ at it.

4. Since everyone can outpunch my cousin, he cannot afford to be _____ .

5. Although Ralph can't play, he doesn't hesitate to _____ the efforts of our football team.

**Definitions** Match the new words with their meanings.

6. pugnacious _____    **a.** quarrelsome

7. promulgate _____    **b.** to make seem less important

8. brash _____    **c.** to sneer at

9. scoff _____    **d.** impudent

10. belittle _____    **e.** to make known officially

---
**TODAY'S IDIOM**

*feeling no pain*—drunk

Although the party had just begun,
after his first drink he was *feeling no pain*.

---

## NEW WORDS

**tangible**
tan´ jə bəl

**laceration**
las ə rā´ shən

**castigate**
kas´ tə gāt

**sordid**
sôr´ did

**octogenarian**
ok´ tə jə nār´ i ən

## MULLINS FORCED TO EAT HUMBLE PIE*

The irate* 80-year-old manager pressed charges against K.O. Mullins, suing him for assault. As *tangible* evidence of the attack, he pointed to a deep *laceration* over his eyebrow that had required ten stitches. When the case was brought before the court, the judge *castigated* Mullins for the *sordid* incident. In addition to a costly financial settlement, Mullins was required to make a public apology to the *octogenarian*.

**Sample Sentences** Use the new words in the following sentences.

1. The medic reached into his kit to find a bandage for the ugly _____ .

2. Mr. Dixon belittled* our request for _____ proof of his loyalty.

3. The kindly foreman was too reticent* to openly _____ the clumsy new worker.

4. When the teenager announced her engagement to the _____ , the public suspected it to be a publicity stunt.

5. Stories of their _____ youth poured forth from the unhappy felons.*

**Definitions** Match the new words with their meanings.

6. tangible _____ a. having actual form

7. laceration _____ b. to correct by punishing

8. castigate _____ c. jagged wound

9. sordid _____ d. dirty, base

10. octogenarian _____ e. person in his or her eighties

---

### TODAY'S IDIOM

*Hobson's choice*—to have no choice at all (Mr. Hobson owned a livery stable but he did not allow the customers to pick their own horses)

Despite all the talk about democracy in my family, my father usually gives the rest of us *Hobson's choice.*

---

ANSWERS ARE ON PAGE 296

# WEEK 4 ❖ DAY 4

NEW WORDS

solace
sol´ is

aspirant
əspī´ rənt

dregs
dregz

frenzy
fren´ zē

scurrilous
skėr´ ə ləs

## THE DECLINE OF MULLINS

Mullins sought *solace* in whiskey. Once a highly respected *aspirant* for the lightweight crown, he now found himself associating with the *dregs* of Skid Row.* He would work himself into an alcoholic *frenzy* in which he would trumpet *scurrilous* attacks on the champ, the old manager, and the judge. One avid* fight fan attributed Mullins' absence from the ring to sickness, saying that he was "recovering from a bad case of—SCOTCH."

**Sample Sentences** Use the new words in the following sentences.

1. Vigilant* censors protect the public from listening to _____ language on television.

2. The publisher scoffed* at the reports that he was an _____ for the job of Secretary of State.

3. In a _____ , the teenager overturned every drawer while searching for the car keys.

4. At the bottom of the beautiful wine bottle, only the _____ remained.

5. In trying to offer _____ to the deceased's wife, the reporter inadvertently* made the situation worse.

**Definitions** Match the new words with their meanings.

6. solace _____    **a.** most worthless part

7. aspirant _____    **b.** coarse

8. dregs _____    **c.** easing of grief

9. frenzy _____    **d.** wild fit

10. scurrilous _____    **e.** candidate for high position

---
### TODAY'S IDIOM

*to rule the roost*—to be in charge, to be master
(a roost is a perch where domestic birds can sleep)

Although he is a lowly private in the army, at home he *rules the roost*.

---

# REVIEW

WEEK **4** ❖ DAY **5**

Let's see how many of the new words studied during the course of this week you remember. Incidentally, try to keep a record of the many times you find your new words in magazines, newspapers, and books. Before you knew the meanings of those words you probably skipped right over them.

In the following quiz, match the best possible definition with the word you have studied. Write the correct letter in the appropriate answer space.

## REVIEW WORDS

_____ **1.** alacrity
_____ **2.** aspirant
_____ **3.** belligerent
_____ **4.** belittle
_____ **5.** brash
_____ **6.** castigate
_____ **7.** disdain
_____ **8.** dregs
_____ **9.** feint
_____ **10.** frenzy
_____ **11.** intimidate
_____ **12.** laceration
_____ **13.** octogenarian
_____ **14.** promulgate
_____ **15.** pugnacious
_____ **16.** scoff
_____ **17.** scurrilous
_____ **18.** solace
_____ **19.** sordid
_____ **20.** tangible

## DEFINITIONS

**a.** scorn
**b.** to make afraid
**c.** frantic outburst
**d.** person of eighty
**e.** to mock
**f.** make public, proclaim
**g.** pretense, sham
**h.** combative
**i.** candidate for better job
**j.** seeking war, hostile
**k.** speak of as unimportant
**l.** vulgar, using indecent language
**m.** insolent
**n.** punish, chastise
**o.** comfort
**p.** most worthless part
**q.** able to be touched
**r.** rough cut
**s.** filthy, ignoble
**t.** quick willingness

## IDIOMS

_____ **21.** to throw down the gauntlet
_____ **22.** feeling no pain
_____ **23.** Hobson's choice
_____ **24.** to rule the roost

**u.** be the boss, lay down the laws
**v.** under the influence of alcohol
**w.** to offer a challenge
**x.** to have no say in a matter

Check your answers on page 296. Make a record of those words you missed. You can master them with additional review.

**WORDS FOR FURTHER STUDY** — **MEANINGS**

1. _____ _____
2. _____ _____
3. _____ _____
4. _____ _____
5. _____ _____

# SENSIBLE SENTENCES?
## (From Week 4)

❖ Underline the word that makes sense in each of the sentences below.

1. We were impressed with the new maid because she cleaned the house with *(alacrity, solace)*.

2. All *(aspirants, lacerations)* for the basketball team must come to practice today.

3. Once he was a millionaire, but today he can be found among the *(dregs, octogenarians)* of society.

4. The newspaper specialized in printing the *(sordid, brash)* details of crime in the city.

5. After finding the *(pugnacious, tangible)* evidence in his drawer, Roger took it to the police.

6. The normally *(scurrilous, belligerent)* police dog was unusually quiet this morning.

7. Bobby, who was extremely modest, always *(belittled, castigated)* his own achievements.

8. Treated with *(frenzy, disdain)* by his stepfather, Artie grew closer to his natural father.

9. When the results of the bar exam were *(intimidated, promulgated)* Adele saw that she had passed handsomely.

10. I used to *(scoff, feint)* at Hank's stories of the fish he had caught, but he made a believer out of me.

ANSWERS ARE ON PAGE 296

# WORDSEARCH 4

❖ Using the clues listed below, fill in each blank in the following story with one of the new words you learned this week.

## *Want to Run for Office?*

In recent years, we have seen the phenomenon of incumbent politicians retiring in record numbers. When interviewed, many of them admitted that they had lost their taste for the job because of the abuse to which an ① _____ for office is subjected.

"My last campaign was a ② _____ affair in which my opponents did everything to ③ _____ my record and air ④ _____ charges about my private life," said one congressman. "I don't have to stand still for such treatment," he added, "which was terribly embarrassing to me and my entire family."

Citizen groups, appalled by the candidates' mudslinging, have sought to do something about the situation. Committees have been formed in a number of states to study ways to elevate the tone of the process, reduce the emotionalism, and eliminate the ⑤ _____ of name calling that is generated as election day draws near.

"Unless we clean up this mess," said the chairman of an Illinois caucus, "we will lose the best and the brightest from the political arena. After all, who but a masochist wants to be a punching bag, the subject of daily vilification in the media, and a target for every malcontent in town?"

## Clues

① 4th Day
② 3rd Day
③ 2nd Day
④ 4th Day
⑤ 4th Day

ANSWERS ARE ON PAGE 296

# WEEK 5 ❖ DAY 1

**NEW WORDS**

**rampant**
ram´ pənt

**inane**
in ān´

**ethics**
eth´ iks

**concur**
kən ker´

**clandestine**
klan des´ tən

## CHEATING

During my first weeks at the new school I observed that cheating was *rampant*. I had always considered it rather *inane* to cheat on a test because of my code of *ethics*, and because so much was at stake. Apparently the other students didn't *concur*. In fact, even the presence of a proctor did not intimidate* them. Far from being a *clandestine* activity, the cheating was open and obvious.

**Sample Sentences** Use the new words in the following sentences.

1. When the plague was _____ on the island, Dr. Arrowsmith's wife died.

2. The spies thought their meeting was a _____ one, but a throng* of F.B.I. agents gathered outside the building.

3. A special management committee was asked to investigate business _____ .

4. Orville Wright was criticized for his _____ desire to fly.

5. If I can get my parents to _____ , I'll join the Peace Corps.

**Definitions** Match the new words with their meanings.

6. rampant _____ **a.** secret, undercover

7. inane _____ **b.** code of principles

8. ethics _____ **c.** foolish

9. concur _____ **d.** agree

10. clandestine _____ **e.** going unchecked, widespread

---
**TODAY'S IDIOM**

*stock in trade*—the goods, tools, and other requisites of a profession

A quick wit and a warm smile were the salesman's *stock in trade*.

---

## NEW WORDS

**flagrant**
flā´ grənt

**admonish**
ad mon´ ish

**duress**
du̇ res´

**culprit**
kul´ prit

**inexorable**
in ek´ sər ə bəl

## CRACKING DOWN

Mr. Dorsey, our new principal, determined to do something about the *flagrant* cheating at our high school. He issued bulletins and began to *admonish* those teachers who did not proctor alertly. Under *duress,* the faculty reported the names of the *culprits.* Several crib sheets were turned in as tangible* evidence of the cheating. Mr. Dorsey's *inexorable* campaign against the wrong-doers seemed to be paying off.

**Sample Sentences** Into which sentences do the new words fit best?

1. The _____ was caught with his fingers in the cookie jar.

2. Television sleuths are _____ in their pursuit of lawbreakers.

3. The confession was signed under _____ , the attorney claimed.

4. I suspect that my father will _____ me for coming home late.

5. Parking in front of a hydrant is a _____ violation of the city's law.

**Definitions** Match the new words with their meanings.

6. flagrant _____ a. inflexible, unrelenting

7. admonish _____ b. compulsion, force

8. duress _____ c. outrageous, glaringly bad

9. culprit _____ d. the guilty person

10. inexorable _____ e. to warn, to reprove

---
### TODAY'S IDIOM
---

*to take down a peg*—to take the conceit out of a braggart
(ship's colors used to be raised or lowered by pegs—
the higher the colors, the greater the honor)

The alumni thought they had a great basketball team,
but our varsity *took them down a peg.*

ANSWERS ARE ON PAGE 296

# WEEK 5 ❖ DAY 3

NEW WORDS

**egregious**
i grē´ jəs

**distraught**
dis trôt´

**duplicity**
dü plis´ ə tē

**acrimonious**
ak´ rə mō´ nē əs

**paucity**
pô´ sə tē

## STAR PLAYER IS CAUGHT

The cheating scandal came to a head when Art Krause, our football captain, made the *egregious* mistake of getting caught cheating on a midterm exam. If Art were suspended for his part in that sordid* affair, our chances for winning the city championship would go up in smoke.* The *distraught* coach asked the principal to overlook Art's *duplicity,* but Mr. Dorsey replied in an *acrimonious* fashion that the players had been given "a plethora"* of athletic instruction but a *paucity* of moral guidance."

**Sample Sentences** Use the new words in the following sentences.

1. The bank teller's _____ error was difficult to correct.

2. We tried to ignore her _____ comments, but that took considerable restraint.

3. _____ is the stock in trade of all adroit* counterspies.

4. Although it was a creative writing class, the teacher complained about the _____ of talent there.

5. The soldiers were _____ to learn that their furloughs had been canceled.

**Definitions** Match the new words with their meanings.

6. egregious _____ a. scarcity

7. distraught _____ b. cunning, trickery

8. duplicity _____ c. mentally confused, crazed

9. acrimonious _____ d. remarkably bad

10. paucity _____ e. bitter

---

**TODAY'S IDIOM**

*to pass the buck*—to evade responsibility
(the "buck" may have been a piece of buckshot passed from one
poker player to another to keep track of whose turn it was to deal)

He always gives me a straight answer and never tries *to pass the buck.*

---

## NEW WORDS

**elicit**
i lis´ it

**pernicious**
pər nish´ əs

**tolerate**
tol´ ər āt

**construe**
kən strü´

**impunity**
im pyū´ nə tē

## OUR PYRRHIC VICTORY*

Mr. Dorsey summoned a representative group of teachers and student leaders to his office in order to *elicit* their reactions to the suspension of the football captain. He told them that cheating was a *pernicious* disease that could not be *tolerated* at our school. He loathed* having to discipline Art Krause so severely, but unless strict measures were taken, the student body would *construe* the incident as an open invitation to cheat with *impunity*. "We may lose a football game," the principal said, "but we can salvage our self-respect."

**Sample Sentences** Use the new words in the following sentences.

1. The border guards allowed the doctor to cross the frontier with _____ .

2. It isn't easy to _____ answers from a sleepy class on Monday morning.

3. Dentists appreciate patients who can _____ pain.

4. She hoped that we would not _____ her decision to run for office as a thirst for power.

5. The dictator's _____ rules failed to intimidate* the leaders of the underground.

**Definitions** Place the letter of the correct definition in the blank next to the new vocabulary word.

6. elicit _____ a. freedom from punishment

7. pernicious _____ b. to make a deduction, to infer

8. tolerate _____ c. to put up with, to bear

9. construe _____ d. to draw forth

10. impunity _____ e. harmful, causing injury

---

**TODAY'S IDIOM**

*to lionize a person*—to make a big fuss over someone
**(the lions at the Tower of London were considered its main attraction)**

When the famous poet Dylan Thomas visited the United States,
he was *lionized* wherever he lectured.

---

ANSWERS ARE ON PAGE 296

Congratulations! You have covered the first one hundred words in the book. With the same diligence you should be able to tackle the remaining work and to master most of the challenging words.

Take the following quiz by matching the best possible definition with the word you have studied. Write the letter that stands for that definition in the appropriate answer space.

## REVIEW WORDS

| | | |
|---|---|---|
| _____ | **1.** acrimonious | |
| _____ | **2.** admonish | |
| _____ | **3.** clandestine | |
| _____ | **4.** concur | |
| _____ | **5.** construe | |
| _____ | **6.** culprit | |
| _____ | **7.** distraught | |
| _____ | **8.** duplicity | |
| _____ | **9.** duress | |
| _____ | **10.** egregious | |
| _____ | **11.** elicit | |
| _____ | **12.** ethics | |
| _____ | **13.** flagrant | |
| _____ | **14.** impunity | |
| _____ | **15.** inane | |
| _____ | **16.** inexorable | |
| _____ | **17.** paucity | |
| _____ | **18.** pernicious | |
| _____ | **19.** rampant | |
| _____ | **20.** tolerate | |

## DEFINITIONS

**a.** double-dealing
**b.** cannot be moved by persuasion, inflexible
**c.** silly
**d.** flourishing
**e.** to scold, warn
**f.** harassed
**g.** to permit, to put up with
**h.** extract
**i.** damaging, harmful
**j.** outstanding for undesirable quality
**k.** notorious
**l.** force, coercion
**m.** exemption
**n.** moral philosophy
**o.** agree
**p.** hidden, secret
**q.** to interpret
**r.** one who commits a crime
**s.** shortage
**t.** caustic, bitter

## IDIOMS

| | |
|---|---|
| _____ **21.** stock in trade | **u.** to idolize |
| _____ **22.** to take down a peg | **v.** to humiliate |
| _____ **23.** pass the buck | **w.** the necessary equipment |
| _____ **24.** to lionize a person | **x.** to refuse to take responsibility |

Now check your answers on page 296. Make a record of those words you missed. You can learn them successfully by studying them and by using them in original sentences. Use a word three times and it is yours forever, a wise man once said.

## WORDS FOR FURTHER STUDY     MEANINGS

1. _____   _____

2. _____   _____

3. _____   _____

4. _____   _____

5. _____   _____

# WORDSEARCH 5

❖ Using the clues listed below, fill in each blank in the following story with one of the new words you learned this week.

## *Driving While Drunk*

Throughout literature we find recurring tales of forthright people who are outspoken in condemning illegal practices only to be brought low themselves when they, or members of their families, commit such acts. Since literature reflects life, we can expect to find similar instances in which a person's ①_____ are compromised, and he falls prey to the ②_____ evil that he had publicly denounced.

Take the story of Barry Vernon (not his real name), an aggressive Ohio district attorney. Vernon could be counted upon to make ③_____ remarks about anyone who was driving while intoxicated. On numerous speaking engagements, he railed against drunkenness and swore that any such ④_____ who was found behind the wheel of a car would be prosecuted to the full extent of the law.

As fate would have it, Vernon's own son smashed into several cars, injuring four people seriously, and then failed a sobriety test.

Following that ⑤_____ violation of the law, Vernon resigned from office, saying that as a private citizen he would continue his crusade against those who drive under the influence of alcohol. Meanwhile, he wished to spend more time with his son to try to understand the young man's behavior.

## Clues

① 1st Day

② 4th Day

③ 3rd Day

④ 2nd Day

⑤ 2nd Day

ANSWERS ARE ON PAGE 296

NEW WORDS

affluent
af´ lü ənt

feasible
fē´ zə bəl

discern
də zėrn´ or də sėrn´

sally
sal´ ē

consternation
kon´ stər nā´ shən

# WEEK 6 ❖ DAY 1

## THE NEWSPAPER UMBRELLA

Our neighbor is an *affluent* inventor whose latest brainstorm, a *feasible* umbrella substitute, has been featured in many magazines. As simply as the eye can *discern*, it is a hard plastic strip, about the size of a ruler, which fits comfortably into a woman's handbag or a man's suit jacket. If a person is caught in a sudden rainstorm, he swings the plastic open in the shape of a cross. Attached to each arm is a clip-like device. Next, he takes the newspaper he is carrying and slides it under each of the four clips. Now, equipped with a rigid head covering he can *sally* forth to face the elements. To the *consternation* of the umbrella manufacturers, it has been enjoying a brisk sale, especially among commuters. If it continues to do well, it could have a pernicious* effect upon the umbrella industry.

**Sample Sentences**  Fit the new words into the proper blanks.

1. Some prisoners planned a disturbance while others would _____ toward the gate.

2. Under duress* from the tax officer, the beggar admitted that he was truly _____ .

3. To the _____ of the sergeant, there was a paucity* of volunteers for the dangerous mission.

4. It's _____ to build an electric auto, but wouldn't you need a terribly long extension cord?

5. When we could _____ the city lights, we knew we were safe at last.

**Definitions**  Match the new words with their meanings.

6. affluent _____ **a.** suddenly rush forth

7. feasible _____ **b.** possible

8. discern _____ **c.** dismay

9. sally (v.) _____ **d.** rich

10. consternation _____ **e.** perceive*

--- **TODAY'S IDIOM** ---

*I'm from Missouri*—a skeptic, one who is not easily convinced
*You* might swallow his promises, but *I'm from Missouri.*

## NEW WORDS

**precocious**
pri kō´ shəs

**perfunctory**
pər fungk´ tər ē

**chagrin**
shə grin´

**perverse**
pər vers´

**deride**
di rīd´

## PATENT PENDING

My buddy Verne, a *precocious* automotive wizard, and I were inspired to do some inventing on our own. We thought it might be feasible* to park a car parallel to a space on the street. Then, by pressing a button, we could raise the four tires off the ground slightly, while dropping two special wheels perpendicular to the curb. It would then be child's play to roll into the narrowest of parking spaces. We took the idea to Ed Greene who runs the Ford agency in order to elicit* his reaction. After a *perfunctory* glance at our plans, to our *chagrin* Ed snorted that our idea was inane,* but we decided that he was just jealous of our brilliance. Tomorrow we are going to start on a computer that will enable us to measure the intelligence of *perverse* automobile dealers who like to *deride* the efforts of junior geniuses.

**Sample Sentences** Use the clues above to help find the proper words.

1. The children in Shakespeare's plays are so _____ that they all sound like grandparents.

2. Edith gave only _____ attention to the new millennium, skipping our New Year's Eve party.

3. The Wright brothers didn't become distraught* when a skeptic would _____ their work.

4. When I correct my kid brother's math errors, he is _____ enough to insist that he is right.

5. To the _____ of many taxpayers, some citizens seem to cheat the government with impunity.*

**Definitions** Match the new words with their meanings.

6. precocious _____ a. done without care, superficial

7. perfunctory _____ b. reaching maturity early

8. chagrin _____ c. feeling of disappointment, humiliation

9. perverse _____ d. contrary, persisting in error

10. deride _____ e. to ridicule, scoff* at

---
### TODAY'S IDIOM
---

***red-letter day*—day of happiness, time for rejoicing**
**(holidays are red-letter days on our calendars)**

My *red-letter day* came when I was chosen as senior class president.

ANSWERS ARE ON PAGE 297

# WEEK 6 ❖ DAY 3

**NEW WORDS**

**disparage**
dis par´ ij

**laudable**
lôd´ ə bəl

**fiasco**
fē as´ kō

**masticate**
mas´ tə kāt

**eschew**
es chü´

## HOLD THAT NOBEL PRIZE!

Speaking of inventions and discoveries, I just learned that an eminent* scientist in Ohio has developed a pill that contains all the nutritive value of three complete meals. In addition to providing us with the vitamins and minerals we need daily, this pill also gives a feeling of fullness. According to its sponsors, the pill will nourish and satisfy. I hate to *disparage* such a *laudable* achievement, but to me it seems like a most objectionable discovery. Rather than a scientific triumph, I'd be inclined to label it as an egregious* blunder, a scientific disaster, a laboratory *fiasco*. Is there anyone in his right mind who thinks that a pill can replace the pleasures of devouring hot corn bread, *masticating* on a thick steak, biting into crisp french fries, or attacking a chocolate sundae? I'm afraid that this is one pill I'll have to *eschew* from chewing.

**Sample Sentences**  Insert the new words in the following sentences.

1. The paradox* is that Javert's inexorable* pursuit of Jean Valjean was both _____ and despicable.

2. The affluent* storeowner _____ the efforts of his small competitor, saying that he could always tolerate* that kind of rivalry.

3. To aid in digestion, you must _____ each piece of meat one dozen times.

4. In an acrimonious* letter, her father described the project as a complete _____ .

5. Once he sought the limelight, but now he _____ all interviews.

**Definitions**  Match the new words with their meanings.

6. disparage      _____  **a.** to discredit, belittle*

7. laudable       _____  **b.** avoid

8. fiasco         _____  **c.** to chew up

9. masticate      _____  **d.** praiseworthy

10. eschew        _____  **e.** complete failure

---
**TODAY'S IDIOM**

*to let sleeping dogs lie*—to let well enough alone,
to avoid stirring up old hostilities

The lawyer wanted to open up the old case,
but his partner advised him *to let sleeping dogs lie.*

---

## NEW WORDS

**quell**
kwel

**voluble**
vol´ ū bəl

**confidant(e)**
kon´ fə dant´

**obsolescence**
ob´ sə les´ ns

**dubious**
dü´ bē əs

# WEEK 6 ❖ DAY 4

## PERFECT PRODUCTS

I guess we'll never be able to *quell* those persistent rumors about the invention of auto tires that will never wear out, stockings that cannot tear, and pens that won't run dry. A *voluble* economist informed me that such products will never be marketed. "Can you imagine," he asked, "a manufacturer cutting his own throat? Why would he sell you an item that you will never have to replace? No," my *confidant* whispered, "it's part of their scheme of planned *obsolescence* to sell you merchandise with a limited life span in order to keep you coming back for more." I am *dubious* about the existence of those perfect products, but then I'm from Missouri.*

**Sample Sentences**  Use the new words in the proper blanks.

1. When the duplicity* was revealed, the jury became _____ about Ed's innocence.

2. In order to _____ the riot, the police sallied* forth with tear gas.

3. A teenage boy's father should be his true _____ .

4. The _____ built into many products could be regarded as a flagrant* insult toward the duped* consumer.

5. I could not doze in the chair because of the _____ barber.

**Definitions**  Play the familiar matching game.

6. quell          _____  **a.** one to whom you confide your secrets

7. voluble        _____  **b.** talkative

8. confidant(e)   _____  **c.** process of wearing out

9. obsolescence   _____  **d.** put an end to

10. dubious       _____  **e.** doubtful

---

### TODAY'S IDIOM

*thumb's down*—signal of rejection (Roman emperors could condemn a gladiator who fought poorly by turning their thumbs down)

My father turned *thumbs down* on our plan
to hitchhike to Florida during Easter.

---

36

ANSWERS ARE ON PAGE 297

# WEEK 6 ❖ DAY 5                    REVIEW

After reading about these new ideas, you should be inventive enough to handle this review. If there is a necessity for it, you may turn back to the original lesson to check on the meaning of a word. As someone once remarked, "Necessity is the mother of invention."

Match the twenty words with their meanings. Write the letter that stands for the definition in the appropriate answer space.

**REVIEW WORDS**        **DEFINITIONS**

_____ 1. affluent       a. careless
_____ 2. chagrin        b. dread, dismay
_____ 3. confidant(e)   c. to chew
_____ 4. consternation  d. complete failure
_____ 5. deride         e. reaching maturity early
_____ 6. discern        f. talkative
_____ 7. disparage      g. practicable
_____ 8. dubious        h. to make fun of
_____ 9. eschew         i. contrary
_____ 10. feasible      j. wealthy
_____ 11. fiasco        k. keep away from
_____ 12. laudable      l. recognize
_____ 13. masticate     m. crush, stop
_____ 14. obsolescence  n. to discredit
_____ 15. perfunctory   o. person you tell your secrets to
_____ 16. perverse      p. disappointment
_____ 17. precocious    q. uncertain
_____ 18. quell         r. commendable
_____ 19. sally         s. sudden rushing forth
_____ 20. voluble       t. process of wearing out

**IDIOMS**

_____ 21. I'm from Missouri      u. occasion for rejoicing
_____ 22. red-letter day         v. I have to be convinced
_____ 23. let sleeping dogs lie  w. don't rake up old grievances
_____ 24. thumbs down            x. to signal rejection

Now check your answers on page 297. Make a record of those words you missed. Study them, work on them, use them in original sentences. Amaze your friends at parties!

**WORDS FOR FURTHER STUDY**          **MEANINGS**

1. _____  _____
2. _____  _____
3. _____  _____
4. _____  _____
5. _____  _____

# WORDSEARCH 6

❖ Using the clues listed below, fill in each blank in the following story with one of the new words you learned this week.

## *Trouble at Truman High*

It was a quiet morning at Harry S Truman High School. "Too quiet," Principal Edna Suarez remarked to her secretary. "It's just when things are this serene that I start to get an uneasy feeling."

Mrs. Suarez's sensitivity to life among 3,000 teenagers quickly proved to be accurate. The first evidence of trouble came with a phone call from the teacher in charge of the cafeteria who needed help to ①_____ a disturbance. When Mrs. Suarez arrived on the scene, much to her ②_____ , students were pounding on their tables, throwing food on the lunchroom floor, and making a complete ③_____ of school regulations. It took the principal only a moment to ④_____ who the two ringleaders were and to summon them to her office.

Vincent, 16, and Elena, 15, admitted to having stirred up the protest. They gave as their reasons the poor quality of food served and the dirty environment. "It's like a pigsty down there," Elena declared, "and the food is fit only for animals!"

What they had done, Mrs. Suarez told them, was inexcusable, and she ticked off a list of reasons that made their conduct dangerous and subject to school discipline. "What you were trying to do," Mrs. Suarez explained, "might be considered ⑤_____ by some but you could have come to me, alone or with a committee, to register your complaints. I would have investigated and, if there was merit to your charges, would have taken the necessary action. Now I'll have to ask you to bring your parents to see me on Monday and to stay home until then."

Vincent and Elena seemed to be chastened by Mrs. Suarez's lecture. However, on leaving her office, Elena told an assistant principal that in a similar incident on a television show she learned that direct, dramatic action usually gets quicker results than lengthy debate. He advised her to bring that question up in her social studies class when she returned from suspension.

## Clues

① 4th Day

② 1st Day

③ 3rd Day

④ 1st Day

⑤ 3rd Day

38

# WEEK 7 ❖ DAY 1

**NEW WORDS**

**implacable**
im plā´ ke bəl

**paroxysm**
par´ ək siz əm

**reprehensible**
rep´ ri hen´ sə bəl

**jurisdiction**
jür´ is dik´ shən

**skirmish**
sker´ mish

## MUCH ADO ABOUT A HAIRCUT

Perhaps you read about our school in the newspapers? We were one of the first to have a showdown on the topic of long hair for boys. Two honor students, Ron Harris and Len Chester, were sent to the principal by their French teacher, an *implacable* foe of nonconformists, who went into a *paroxysm* of anger when she spied the boys in the hall. At first it seemed like a simple case. The school would reprimand* the boys for their *reprehensible* appearance and order them to cut their hair or be suspended. But the boys' parents decided that the school had overstepped its *jurisdiction;* they took their case to the newspapers. What had started as a local *skirmish* now began to take on the appearance of a full-scale war.

**Sample Sentences**  Use the new words in the following sentences.

1. The detective was _____ in his search for the murder weapon.

2. Saying that it was beyond his _____ , Judge Klein refused to rule on the case.

3. In a _____ of rage, the tenant stormed out of the landlord's office.

4. The precocious* boy enjoyed an intellectual _____ with his elders.

5. The brash* student was forced to apologize for her _____ conduct.

**Definitions**  Match the new words with their meanings.

6. implacable     ____     **a.**  a fit, sudden outburst

7. paroxysm     ____     **b.**  cannot be pacified, inexorable*

8. reprehensible  ____     **c.**  small fight, brief encounter

9. jurisdiction    ____     **d.**  worthy of blame

10. skirmish      ____     **e.**  power, range of authority

---

### TODAY'S IDIOM

*cause célèbre*—a famous law case or controversy

It was a minor dispute, but the ambitious lawyer
sought to turn it into a *cause célèbre.*

---

## NEW WORDS

**harass**
har´ əs or hə rəs´

**monolithic**
mon´ l ith´ ik

**arbitrary**
är´ bə trer´ ē

**indigent**
in´ də jənt

**fray**
frā

## THE TEMPEST SPILLS OUT OF THE TEAPOT

Once the newspapers got the story, the case of the longhairs became a cause célèbre.* Ron and Len were interviewed, seen on TV, and regarded by their fellow students as heroes. "These are not delinquents or hoods," one reporter wrote, "but clean-cut American boys who are being *harassed* by a *monolithic* school system." A caustic* editorial referred to the school's decision as *arbitrary* and inane.* A false story even circulated about the boys being rock-'n-roll performers whose *indigent* families needed their salaries. Finally, the Civil Liberties Union jumped into the *fray* with a court order stipulating* that the principal be required to show cause why the boys should not be allowed to return to class.

**Sample Sentences** Use the new words in the following sentences.

1. After the _____ , the feuding families agreed to patch up their differences.

2. The _____ client was surprised when she was accosted* by her social worker in the elegant restaurant.

3. To my mind the decision was unreasonable and _____ .

4. George Orwell's *1984* depicts a frightening, _____ government.

5. If anonymous telephone callers _____ you, the phone company will give you an unlisted number.

**Definitions** Match the new words with their meanings.

6. harass _____ **a.** based on whim, dictatorial

7. monolithic _____ **b.** poor, needy

8. indigent _____ **c.** massively solid

9. arbitrary _____ **d.** a fight

10. fray _____ **e.** to trouble, torment

---
### TODAY'S IDIOM

*one swallow does not make a summer—*
**don't jump to conclusions based on incomplete evidence**

"Sure, the Yankees won their opening game,
but *one swallow does not make a summer*."

---

ANSWERS ARE ON PAGE 297

# WEEK 7 ❖ DAY 3

## NEW WORDS

**stymie**
stī´ mē

**effigy**
ef´ ə jē

**flout**
flout

**cognizant**
kog´ nə zənt

**turbulent**
tėr´ byə lənt

## HAIRCUT DILEMMA

The school authorities were *stymied*. Public opinion had been marshaled against them. No longer was it a simple case of disciplining two wayward lads. Suddenly it had taken on the appearance of a nightmare in which the principal was either hanged in *effigy* or pictured in cartoons making a villainous swipe at the two innocent Samsons. But the officials could not allow Ron and Len to *flout* their authority with impunity.* Members of the school board concurred* with the principal's action but they were *cognizant* of the popular support for the boys. Clearly a compromise was called for to resolve the *turbulent* situation.

**Sample Sentences**  In which of the following newspaper headlines do the new words belong?

1. "COACH OF LOSING TEAM HANGED IN _____"

2. "CAUSE OF CANCER CONTINUES TO _____ DOCTORS"

3. "F.B.I. _____ OF CLANDESTINE* GANGLAND MEETING"

4. "MANY MOTORISTS _____ TRAFFIC LAWS, STUDY REVEALS"

5. "_____ ATMOSPHERE IN ANGRY SENATE CHAMBER"

**Definitions**  Match the new words with their meanings.

6. stymie     _____    **a.** unruly, agitated

7. effigy     _____    **b.** to hinder, impede

8. flout     _____    **c.** show contempt, scoff*

9. cognizant     _____    **d.** aware

10. turbulent     _____    **e.** a likeness (usually of a hated person)

---
**TODAY'S IDIOM**

*a bitter pill to swallow*—a humiliating defeat

It was *a bitter pill to swallow* for the famous billiard player
to be overwhelmed by the 12-year-old girl.

---

## NEW WORDS

**terminate**
ter´ mə nāt

**forthwith**
fôrth´ with´

**exacerbate**
eg zas´ ər bāt

**revert**
ri vert´

**oust**
oust

## HAPPY ENDING?

Following an executive session, the school board ordered the principal to *terminate* the suspension and to send the boys back to class *forthwith*. Unless it could be shown that their presence disrupted the learning process, there was no reason to bar the boys. It was a bitter pill to swallow* for the principal whose irritation was *exacerbated* by the ruling. But some of the sting was taken out of the victory when the boys appeared in school the next day with their hair clipped to a respectable length. Everyone breathed a sigh of relief. Just as things were about to *revert* to normalcy, however, the same French teacher then demanded that a girl be *ousted* from school for wearing a mini skirt.

**Sample Sentences** Use the new words in the following sentences.

1. It seemed incongruous* to _____ his employment just when he was so successful.

2. Upon seeing the show, he called the TV studio _____ to protest.

3. The ushers moved with alacrity* to _____ the disorderly patrons.

4. After taking the drug, she began to _____ to the days of her childhood.

5. The arrest of the spy did much to _____ relations between the two countries.

**Definitions** Match the new words with their meanings.

6. terminate _____ **a.** to drive out, eject

7. forthwith _____ **b.** return

8. exacerbate _____ **c.** to end

9. revert _____ **d.** immediately

10. oust _____ **e.** to irritate, make worse

---

### TODAY'S IDIOM

*an ax to grind*—having a selfish motive in the background

I am always dubious* about the motives of a man
who tells me that he has no *ax to grind*.

---

ANSWERS ARE ON PAGE 297

Pupils want to be individuals these days, and many of them refuse to conform to regulations unless there are good reasons for such rules. In the area of vocabulary study, however, the only rule that makes sense to all is that true mastery derives from continuous practice.

Match the twenty words with their meanings. Write the letter that stands for the definition in the appropriate answer spaces. (Which two review words are almost synonymous?)

## REVIEW WORDS                    ## DEFINITIONS

| | REVIEW WORDS | | DEFINITIONS |
|---|---|---|---|
| _____ 1. | arbitrary | a. | having a massive structure |
| _____ 2. | cognizant | b. | to hinder |
| _____ 3. | effigy | c. | a conflict, fight |
| _____ 4. | exacerbate | d. | relentless, unappeasable |
| _____ 5. | flout | e. | immediately |
| _____ 6. | forthwith | f. | blameworthy |
| _____ 7. | fray | g. | range of authority |
| _____ 8. | harass | h. | to show contempt |
| _____ 9. | implacable | i. | poverty-stricken |
| _____ 10. | indigent | j. | to irritate |
| _____ 11. | jurisdiction | k. | violent outburst |
| _____ 12. | monolithic | l. | to end |
| _____ 13. | oust | m. | a likeness |
| _____ 14. | paroxysm | n. | go back |
| _____ 15. | reprehensible | o. | to torment |
| _____ 16. | revert | p. | riotous |
| _____ 17. | skirmish | q. | eject |
| _____ 18. | stymie | r. | small battle |
| _____ 19. | terminate | s. | aware |
| _____ 20. | turbulent | t. | based on whim |

## IDIOMS

| | IDIOMS | | |
|---|---|---|---|
| _____ 21. | cause célèbre | u. | having a selfish motive |
| _____ 22. | one swallow doesn't make a summer | v. | a humiliating defeat |
| _____ 23. | bitter pill to swallow | w. | don't jump to conclusions |
| _____ 24. | an ax to grind | x. | famous law case |

Now check your answers on page 297. Make a record of those words you missed.

Note: *fray* and *skirmish* are almost synonymous.

## WORDS FOR FURTHER STUDY          MEANINGS

1. _____   _____

2. _____   _____

3. _____   _____

4. _____   _____

5. _____   _____

# WORDSEARCH 7

❖ Using the clues listed below, fill in each blank in the following story with one of the new words you learned this week.

## The Reading of the Will

One full week after the funeral, the immediate family of millionaire Charles Hudson was gathered in a law office to hear the reading of the deceased's will. Mr. Hudson's wife, thirty years his junior, was prepared for a bitter ①_____ with his former wife and her son. The lawyer, Don Rollins, anticipated a ②_____ session because he was the only one who was ③_____ of the contents of the revised will that Hudson had ordered drawn up six months prior to his death.

The current Mrs. Hudson, attired in her smart widow's weeds, expected that she would receive the lion's share of the estate. The former Mrs. Hudson felt that she was entitled to most of the estate since she was practically ④_____ at the present time, despite her substantial alimony payments.

Lawyer Rollins cleared his throat and began to read:

"To my present spouse I leave my town house where she can continue to store the jewels, shoes, dresses, and furs she accumulated in two years of shopping and marriage.

"To my son, who has put off finding a career until my estate would enrich him, I leave the sum of ten dollars for cab fare to the unemployment office.

"To my former wife whose ⑤_____ behavior I tolerated for three decades, I leave my beach house where she can continue to work on her tan, something that she prized above our happiness.

"To the Society For the Prevention of Cruelty to Animals I leave the remainder of my entire estate, knowing they will put it to better use than anyone in this room."

The lawyer was wrong. No outcries. Silence, supreme silence, reigned among the shocked audience.

## Clues

① 1st Day

② 3rd Day

③ 3rd Day

④ 2nd Day

⑤ 1st Day

ANSWERS ARE ON PAGE 297

# WEEK 8 ❖ DAY 1

**NEW WORDS**

**emaciated**
i mā´ shē ā tid

**surge**
sėrj

**tranquil**
trang´ kwəl

**sanctuary**
sangk´ chü er´ i

**ascend**
ə send´

## ENTER DR. THOMAS A. DOOLEY

In 1956, *Look Magazine* named Thomas Dooley as one of the year's ten most outstanding men. Just under thirty years of age at the time, Dr. Dooley had already distinguished himself by caring for a half-million sick and *emaciated* Vietnamese refugees. When fighting broke out in the divided country of Viet Nam, the northern Communist Viet Minh forces *surged* southward, scattering thousands of refugees before them. At the time, Dr. Dooley was a lieutenant, assigned to a *tranquil* naval hospital in Yokosuka, Japan. Forthwith* he volunteered for duty on a navy ship that had been chosen to transport the refugees to *sanctuary* in Saigon. The curtain was beginning to *ascend* on Dooley's real career.

**Sample Sentences**  Use the new words in the following sentences.

1. The _____ residents of the Warsaw Ghetto managed to win several skirmishes* from the Nazis.

2. A firecracker terminated* the _____ climate of the neighborhood.

3. When Richard III violated the _____ of the church to seize the princes, he exceeded his jurisdiction.*

4. Chicago put its heaviest players up front, but they were helpless as the Giants' line _____ toward them.

5. Inexorably* the determined climber began to _____ the Himalayan peak.

**Definitions**  Match the new words with their meanings.

6. emaciated _____ **a.** to rush suddenly

7. surge _____ **b.** shelter

8. tranquil _____ **c.** quiet

9. sanctuary _____ **d.** abnormally thin, wasted away

10. ascend _____ **e.** to rise

---

### ── TODAY'S IDIOM ──

*sour grapes*—to disparage* something that you cannot have (from Aesop's fable about the fox who called the grapes sour because he could not reach them)

Marcia said that she didn't want to be on the Principal's Honor Roll anyway, but we knew that it was just *sour grapes* on her part.

---

malnutrition
mal´ nü trish´ ən

afflict
ə flikt´

besiege
bi sēj´

privation
prī vā´ shən

sinister
sin´ ə stər

## DOOLEY'S MISSION

Aboard the refugee ship, Dooley's destiny took shape. He became painfully cognizant* of the *malnutrition*, disease, ignorance, and fear that *afflicted* the natives. In addition, he discerned* how active the Communists had been in spreading their anti-American propaganda. Tom Dooley pitched in to build shelters in Haiphong, and to comfort the poor Vietnamese there before that *besieged* city fell to the powerful Viet Minh forces. He was seemingly unconcerned by the many *privations* he had to endure. For his services, Dooley received the U.S. Navy's Legion of Merit. He told the story of this exciting experience in *Deliver Us from Evil*, a best seller that alerted America to the plight of the Vietnamese as well as to the *sinister* menace of communism.

**Sample Sentences**  Use the new words in the following sentences.

1. The stool pigeon, the detective's confidant,* told him about the _____ plot.

2. By running up a white flag, the _____ troops indicated their desire to withdraw from the fray.*

3. Citizens of several Kentucky mountain communities are _____ by the worst poverty in the nation.

4. The emaciated* prisoners were obviously suffering from advanced _____ .

5. Albert Schweitzer endured considerable _____ as a jungle doctor.

**Definitions**  Match the new words with their meanings.

6. malnutrition _____  a. lack of necessities

7. afflict _____  b. faulty or inadequate diet

8. besiege _____  c. evil, ominous

9. privation _____  d. to surround, hem in

10. sinister _____  e. to trouble greatly, to distress

---
**TODAY'S IDIOM**
---

*to swap horses in midstream*—to vote against a candidate
running for reelection, to change one's mind

The mayor asked for our support, pointing out how foolish
it would be *to swap horses in midstream.*

ANSWERS ARE ON PAGE 297

# WEEK 8 ❖ DAY 3

**NEW WORDS**

**ubiquitous**
yü bik´ wə təs

**remote**
ri mōt´

**thwart**
thwôrt

**harbinger**
här´ bən jər

**malignant**
mə lig´ nənt

## STYMIED* BY PERSONAL SICKNESS

After an extensive lecture tour in 1956, Dr. Dooley returned to Laos to set up a mobile medical unit. Because the Geneva Agreement barred the entrance of military personnel to the country, he resigned from the Navy and went to work as a civilian. That story is told in *The Edge of Tomorrow*. Next year, despite a growing illness, the *ubiquitous* Dooley turned up in the *remote* village of Muong Sing, attempting to *thwart* his traditional enemies—disease, dirt, ignorance, starvation—and hoping to quell* the spread of communism. But his trained medical eye soon told him that the pain in his chest and back was a *harbinger* of a *malignant* cancer.

**Sample Sentences**  Use the new words in the following sentences.

1. Sprinting all over the court, the _____ referee called one foul after another.

2. Ben's reprehensible* table manners led his fraternity brothers to seat him in a _____ corner of the dining room.

3. The excellent soup was a _____ of the delicious meal to follow.

4. In an attempt to _____ the voracious* ants, he surrounded his house with a moat of burning oil.

5. The surgeon finally located the _____ tumor that had afflicted* his patient for many months.

**Definitions**  Match the new words with their meanings.

6. ubiquitous _____ **a.** distant, hidden away

7. remote _____ **b.** being everywhere at the same time

8. thwart _____ **c.** likely to cause death

9. harbinger _____ **d.** to hinder, defeat

10. malignant _____ **e.** a forerunner, advance notice

---

**TODAY'S IDIOM**

*to cool one's heels*—to be kept waiting

The shrewd mayor made the angry delegates *cool their heels* in his outer office.

---

WEEK 8 ❖ DAY 4

**excruciating**
ek skrü´ shē ā ting

**respite**
res´ pit

**reverberating**
ri vėr´ bə rāt´ ing

**fretful**
fret´ fəl

**succumb**
sə kum´

## "PROMISES TO KEEP"

From August, 1959 until his death in January, 1961, Dooley suffered almost continuous, *excruciating* pain. His normal weight of 180 was cut in half, and even the pain-killing drugs could no longer bring relief. Knowing that he did not have long to live, Dr. Dooley worked without *respite* on behalf of MEDICO, the organization he had founded to bring medical aid and hope to the world's sick and needy. The lines of Robert Frost kept *reverberating* in his mind during those *fretful* days: "The woods are lovely, dark and deep/ But I have promises to keep/ And miles to go before I sleep." When he finally *succumbed*, millions throughout the world were stunned and grief-stricken by the tragedy.

**Sample Sentences** Use the new words in the following sentences.

1. With _____ slowness, the minute hand inched its way around the clock.

2. The rescue team heard the miner's voice _____ through the caves.

3. Around income tax time _____ faces are ubiquitous.*

4. The voluble* insurance salesman gave my father no _____ .

5. Besieged* by debts, the corporation finally had to _____ to bankruptcy.

**Definitions** Match the new words with their meanings.

6. excruciating _____   **a.** an interval of relief, delay

7. respite _____   **b.** worrisome, irritable

8. reverberating _____   **c.** reechoing, resounding

9. fretful _____   **d.** agonizing, torturing

10. succumb _____   **e.** to give way, yield

---
**TODAY'S IDIOM**

*a red herring*—something that diverts attention from the main issue
(a red herring drawn across a fox's path destroys the scent)

We felt that the introduction of his war record was
a *red herring* to keep us from inquiring into his graft.

48                                                                 ANSWERS ARE ON PAGE 297

Shortly before his death, Dr. Dooley was selected by the U.S. Chamber of Commerce as one of America's ten most outstanding young men. There may be no connection between success of that type and an expanded vocabulary—but one never knows.

Match the twenty words with their meanings. Write the letter that stands for the definition in the appropriate answer space.

## REVIEW WORDS

_____ 1. afflict
_____ 2. ascend
_____ 3. besiege
_____ 4. emaciated
_____ 5. excruciating
_____ 6. fretful
_____ 7. harbinger
_____ 8. malignant
_____ 9. malnutrition
_____ 10. privation
_____ 11. remote
_____ 12. respite
_____ 13. reverberating
_____ 14. sanctuary
_____ 15. sinister
_____ 16. succumb
_____ 17. surge
_____ 18. thwart
_____ 19. tranquil
_____ 20. ubiquitous

## DEFINITIONS

a. lack of necessities
b. inadequate diet
c. being everywhere at once
d. to trouble greatly
e. agonizing
f. wasted away
g. distant
h. evil
i. to rush suddenly
j. place of protection
k. forerunner
l. to rise
m. to hinder
n. yield
o. postponement
p. to surround
q. becoming progressively worse
r. reechoing
s. worrisome
t. peaceful

## IDIOMS

_____ 21. sour grapes
_____ 22. swap horses in midstream
_____ 23. to cool one's heels
_____ 24. a red herring

u. a diversion
v. to be kept waiting
w. to change one's mind
x. claiming to despise what you cannot have

Now check your answers on page 297. Make a record of those words you missed.

## WORDS FOR FURTHER STUDY          MEANINGS

1. _____   _____

2. _____   _____

3. _____   _____

4. _____   _____

5. _____   _____

# SENSIBLE SENTENCES?
## (From Week 8)

❖ Underline the word that makes sense in each of the sentences below.

1. Eric was *(afflicted, besieged)* with an inoperable ailment.

2. The octogenarian refused to *(succumb, surge)* to pneumonia.

3. The *(remote, ubiquitous)* mayor was photographed in four different parts of the city yesterday.

4. We were worried lest the hostages be suffering from *(sanctuary, malnutrition)*.

5. The *(tranquil, sinister)* tone of the spring morning was suddenly broken by the loud explosion.

6. I heard his voice *(excruciating, reverberating)* through the corridors.

7. The senator's bid for a second term was *(thwarted, respited)* by the electorate.

8. After the king's death, his son *(ascended, succumbed)* to the throne in the normal order of succession.

9. The *(privations, harbingers)* that the poor people endured in their ghetto apartments were reprehensible.

10. The children were *(emaciated, fretful)* when awakened from their nap.

11. We were asked to *(swap horses in midstream, cool our heels)* while waiting for the bus.

ANSWERS ARE ON PAGE 297

# PARTS OF SPEECH
## (From Weeks 2–8)

❖ Choose the noun, verb, or adjective that answers each of the questions and write the corresponding letter in the appropriate answer space.

a. affluent
b. arbitrary
c. avid
d. cajole
e. elicit
f. euphemism
g. fray
h. harbinger
i. indigent
j. precocious
k. pugnacious
l. reprimand
m. skirmish
n. sour grapes
o. wrest

_____ 1. Which noun tells you that something is on the way?

_____ 2. Which verb means *to extract, to get something out of*?

_____ 3. Which adjective describes an action that is based on a whim?

_____ 4. Which adjective tells you about children who are very bright for their age?

_____ 5. If a wealthy family moved into your neighborhood, which adjective would be suitable for them?

_____ 6. Which adjective can be substituted for *enthusiastic*?

_____ 7. If you had to coax someone into doing something, which verb would be appropriate?

_____ 8. When we call a garbage collector a *sanitary engineer*, which noun comes to mind?

_____ 9. In seizing control, which verb is appropriate?

_____ 10. Which adjective describes a combative, quarrelsome person?

_____ 11. Which verb is a good synonym for *scold?*

_____ 12. What do you indulge in when you belittle that which you cannot possess?

_____ 13. Which adjective describes a poverty-stricken person?

_____ 14. Which two nouns are almost synonymous?

# WORDSEARCH 8

❖ Using the clues listed below, fill in each blank in the following story with one of the new words you learned this week.

## Aftermath of an Earthquake

The Egyptian earthquake in October 1992 killed 600 residents of Cairo and hospitalized thousands of others, many of whom were expected to ①_____ as a result of their injuries. Especially hard hit were the people who inhabited the city's slums, who had to seek ②_____ in those government buildings, schools, and factories that remained standing.

Muslim fundamentalists were active in providing relief to the survivors in the form of food, water, blankets, and tents to house the more than 300 families made homeless by the disaster. In the midst of a rubble-strewn street, a large tent was set up, bearing the banner, "Islam is the Solution." Believers took the opportunity to spread the message that the earthquake was a ③_____ of worse things to come, and that a wayward population must follow God's laws if they expected to ④_____ to heaven.

Throughout history, following volcanic eruptions, hurricanes, tidal waves, and other calamities that periodically ⑤_____ mankind, religious leaders have used such occurrences to bring the people back to their faith.

"Unless we return to Allah," said a priest, "we can expect more divine punishment."

Since many Egyptians had expressed unhappiness about their government prior to the earthquake, there was a good chance for Muslim fundamentalists to seize the opportunity to win new converts by showing that the answer to recovery was not through man's efforts but through God's.

## Clues

① 4th Day
② 1st Day
③ 3rd Day
④ 1st Day
⑤ 2nd Day

ANSWERS ARE ON PAGE 297

# WEEK 9 ❖ DAY 1

**NEW WORDS**

**impresario**
im´ prə sär´ ē ō

**extortion**
ek stôr´ shən

**adverse**
ad´ vers

**asset**
as´ et

**bigot**
big´ ət

## JUST SPELL THE NAME CORRECTLY

P. T. Barnum, the great circus *impresario*, was once accosted*
by a woman who showed him a scurrilous* manuscript about
himself, and said that unless he paid her, she would have the
book printed. Barnum rejected the *extortion* attempt. "Say
what you please," he replied, "but make sure that you
mention me in some way. Then come to me and I will estimate
the value of your services as a publicity agent." Barnum
obviously felt that *adverse* criticism was an *asset* for a public
figure. A man who seeks the limelight should not care what is
written about him but should be concerned only when they
stop writing about him. Barnum's philosophy suggests that
we might do well to review the plethora* of publicity given to
rabble-rousers and *bigots*.

**Sample Sentences**  Use the new words in the following sentences.

1. When the business manager was accused of _____ , his colleagues sought
to oust* him from the firm.

2. The eminent* _____ brought many cultural spectacles to our shores.

3. Attacked by the irate* crowd, the _____ asked the police for sanctuary.*

4. President Obama found that texting was an _____ to his communication
skills.

5. It was excruciatingly* painful for the actors to read the _____ reviews that
their performances had received.

**Definitions**  Match the new words with their meanings.

6. impresario _____  **a.** a narrow-minded, prejudiced person

7. extortion _____  **b.** unfavorable, harmful

8. adverse _____  **c.** one who presents cultural series, organizer

9. asset _____  **d.** a valuable thing to have

10. bigot _____  **e.** getting money by threats

---
**TODAY'S IDIOM**
---

*to spill the beans*—to give away a secret

Although he was naturally reticent,* when the felon* was intimidated*
by the members of the rival gang, *he spilled the beans.*

## NEW WORDS

**blatant**
blāt´ nt

**entourage**
än´ tü räzh

**virulent**
vir´ yə lent

**venom**
ven´ əm

**spew**
spyü

## BIGOTS* GET PUBLICITY

Today, the *blatant* bigot, the leader of a lunatic fringe, and the hate-monger, each with his tiny *entourage,* find it relatively easy to attract publicity. Newspapers give space to the *virulent* activities of those agitators on the grounds that they are newsworthy. TV producers and radio executives, seeking for sensationalism, often extend a welcome to such controversial characters. "Yes," said the host of one such program, "we invite bigots, but it is only for the purpose of making them look ridiculous by displaying their inane* policies to the public." Some civic-minded organizations have answered, however, that the hosts are not always equipped to demolish those guests, and even if they were, the audience would still be exposed to the *venom* they *spew* forth.

**Sample Sentences**  Use the new words in the following sentences.

1. The visiting dictator's ubiquitous* _____ of bodyguards disturbed our tranquil* city.

2. Europe's population was afflicted* by a _____ plague known as the Black Death.

3. From each candidate's headquarters acrimonious* charges would _____ forth daily.

4. Clym Yeobright's mother succumbed* to the _____ of a snake bite.

5. With _____ discourtesy the reporters continued to harass* the bereaved family.

**Definitions**  Match the new words with their meanings.

6. blatant       _____   **a.** group of attendants

7. entourage    _____   **b.** disagreeably loud, very showy

8. virulent      _____   **c.** poison, spite, malice

9. venom        _____   **d.** throw up, vomit, eject

10. spew         _____   **e.** full of hate, harmful

--- **TODAY'S IDIOM** ---

***to keep a stiff upper lip*—to be courageous in the face of trouble**

It was admirable to see how the British managed *to keep a stiff upper lip* in spite of the German bombing.

ANSWERS ARE ON PAGE 298

# Week 9 ❖ Day 3

NEW WORDS

**loath**
lōth

**solicit**
sə lis′ it

**astute**
ə stüt′ or ə styüt′

**advocate**
ad′ və kāt

**ineffectual**
in′ ə fek′ chü

## COPING WITH BIGOTS*

Suppose a bigot wished to organize a meeting in your neighborhood. Since we cherish freedom of speech, we are *loath* to deny the request, even if he preaches hatred. As a result, hate-mongers are given the opportunity to rent halls, conduct meetings, publish abusive literature, and *solicit* contributions. What can be done about them? One *astute* observer, Prof. S. Andhil Fineberg, *advocates* the "quarantine method." His plan is to give such groups no publicity and to ignore them completely. Without the warmth of the spotlight, he feels that the bigot will freeze and become *ineffectual*. Debating with such warped minds is not feasible* and only tends to exacerbate* the situation.

**Sample Sentences** Use the new words in the following sentences.

1. Since we felt that the ruling was arbitrary,* we were _____ to obey it.

2. Daily the volunteers went out to _____ funds for the indigent* families.

3. My neighbor was _____ enough to discern* the adverse* features of the mortgage.

4. The general was sure to _____ that we give the enemy no respite* from the bombings.

5. The play was so blatantly* bad that the impresario* fired its _____ director.

**Definitions** Match the new words with their definitions.

6. loath _____    **a.** keen, shrewd

7. solicit _____    **b.** to be in favor of, to support

8. astute _____    **c.** not effective

9. advocate (v.) _____    **d.** unwilling, reluctant

10. ineffectual _____    **e.** to beg, seek earnestly

---

**TODAY'S IDIOM**

*to have cold feet*—to hesitate because of fear or uncertainty

My cousin was all set to join the paratroops,
but at the last moment he got *cold feet*.

ANSWERS ARE ON PAGE 298

55

## NEW WORDS

**scrutinize**
skrüt´ n īz

**nefarious**
ni fer´ ē əs

**amicable**
am´ ə kə bəl

**vexatious**
vek sā´ shəs

**malady**
mal´ ə dē

## MORE THAN SILENCE

The quarantine method for handling bigots implies more than giving them the silent treatment. Prof. Fineberg urges community-relations organizations to *scrutinize* the *nefarious* activities of hate-mongers and to be prepared to furnish information about them to *amicable* inquirers. When a rabble-rouser is coming, those organizations should privately expose him to opinion-molders. In addition, constructive efforts should be taken to induce people to involve themselves in projects for improving intergroup relations. Bigger than the *vexatious* immediate problem is the need to find out the cause for such bigotry and to counteract this sinister* *malady* that afflicts* a segment of our society.

**Sample Sentences** Use the new words in the following sentences.

1. The _____ buzzing of the mosquitoes as they surged* about our heads nearly drove us insane.

2. Our _____ relations with Latin America are an asset* to hemispheric trade.

3. Once the virulent* _____ had run its course, my temperature dropped.

4. We were distraught* upon hearing the venom* spewed* forth by the _____ bigot.*

5. No sooner did the lawyer _____ the extortion* note than she called the police.

**Definitions** Match the new words with their definitions.

6. scrutinize _____     a. annoying

7. nefarious _____     b. villainous, vicious

8. amicable _____     c. examine closely

9. vexatious _____     d. disease

10. malady _____     e. friendly, peaceful

---
## TODAY'S IDIOM
---

***to look a gift horse in the mouth*—to be critical of a present**
**(from the practice of judging a horse's age by his teeth)**

Although I didn't have much use for Uncle Roy's present, I took it with a big smile since I have been taught never *to look a gift horse in the mouth.*

ANSWERS ARE ON PAGE 298

# WEEK 9 ❖ DAY 5      REVIEW

There is an excellent book entitled *How to Argue with a Conservative* that gives the reader the tools necessary for success in argumentation. At times you may have to engage in a verbal skirmish* with a bigot.* It would be to your advantage if you had the proper words at your fingertips.

Match the twenty words with their meanings. Write the letter that stands for the definition in the appropriate answer space.

## REVIEW WORDS

_____ 1. adverse
_____ 2. advocate
_____ 3. amicable
_____ 4. asset
_____ 5. astute
_____ 6. bigot
_____ 7. blatant
_____ 8. entourage
_____ 9. extortion
_____ 10. impresario
_____ 11. ineffectual
_____ 12. loath
_____ 13. malady
_____ 14. nefarious
_____ 15. scrutinize
_____ 16. solicit
_____ 17. spew
_____ 18. venom
_____ 19. vexatious
_____ 20. virulent

## DEFINITIONS

a. to support
b. keen, shrewd
c. something of value
d. villainous
e. seek earnestly
f. organizer
g. annoying
h. followers
i. disagreeably loud
j. examine closely
k. poison
l. harmful
m. not effective
n. prejudiced person
o. unfavorable
p. friendly
q. unwilling
r. vomit
s. disease
t. getting money by threats

## IDIOMS

_____ 21. to spill the beans
_____ 22. stiff upper lip
_____ 23. cold feet
_____ 24. look a gift horse in the mouth

u. to be critical of a present
v. hesitation because of fear
w. courage in the face of trouble
x. give away a secret

Now check your answers on page 298. Make a record of those words you missed. Once again, use those words in original sentences.

## WORDS FOR FURTHER STUDY      MEANINGS

1. _____    _____

2. _____    _____

3. _____    _____

4. _____    _____

5. _____    _____

# WORDSEARCH 9

❖ Using the clues listed below, fill in each blank in the following story with one of the new words you learned this week.

## This Century's Deadliest Disease

When the American public started to hear about the AIDS virus in the 1980s, there was a measure of concern but no real alarm. After all, some said, it was a problem solely for a small group of intravenous drug users who shared dirty needles, and for the homosexual community.

But as the numbers of afflicted people grew during the 1980s and 1990s, we began to ① _____ the tragic news stories more closely. The deaths of young people like Ryan White and Kimberly Bergalis, not members of the at-risk groups referred to above, convinced us that what was at first regarded merely as a ② _____ illness was actually a ③ _____ threat to the general community.

In the mid-1980s, ④ _____ medical researchers were optimistic that a vaccine for AIDS would be found in short order. Those predictions proved to be inaccurate. In October 1992, former Surgeon-General C. Everett Koop said that he doubted we would ever find a cure for the disease. With over 200,000 Americans already having succumbed to the ⑤ _____ killer, and another 300,000 who were HIV-positive and could contract a full-blown form of AIDS, Koop's statement sent chills throughout the country.

A prominent AIDS expert, however, took issue with Koop. "The fight will be difficult," said Dr. Harley Smith, "but we will find an answer very shortly." Now, in the twenty-first century, the answer is apparently at hand.

## Clues

① 4th Day
② 4th Day
③ 2nd Day
④ 3rd Day
⑤ 4th Day

ANSWERS ARE ON PAGE 298

# WEEK **10** ❖ DAY **1**

**NEW WORDS**

inclement
in klem´ ənt

peruse
pə rüz´

premonition
prē´ mə nish´ ən

desist
di zist´

recoil
ri koil´

## JERRY HART'S SIXTH SENSE

An uneasy feeling had made Jerry Hart miserable all day long. It was difficult to explain, but the similar sensations in the past had been accurate—trouble was on the way. Just as some people can predict the onset of *inclement* weather because of an aching in their bones, so could Jerry detect incipient* disaster. He sat at his desk, trying to *peruse* a company report but his efforts were ineffectual.* The gnawing at his insides, the tinge* of uneasiness, the *premonition* of calamity that besieged* him would not *desist*. When the phone rang, he *recoiled* with fear—it was his wife and she was hysterical. Their son had been bitten by a mad dog!

**Sample Sentences**  Use the new words in the following sentences.

1. After being admonished* by his father, he began to _____ the want ads daily.

2. When the black cat crossed her path, Ellen had a _____ of disaster.

3. The pickets promulgated* a warning that they would not _____ in their efforts to enhance* their standard of living.

4. As the snake prepared to strike, the girls _____ in horror.

5. She blamed her absence from the game on the _____ weather, but we knew that was sour grapes.*

**Definitions**  Match the new words with their meanings.

6. inclement  _____  a. unfavorable, stormy

7. peruse  _____  b. to read carefully

8. premonition  _____  c. cease

9. desist  _____  d. forewarning

10. recoil  _____  e. draw back

─── **TODAY'S IDIOM** ───

*to pay the piper*—to bear the consequences
(from the story of the **Pied Piper of Hamelin**)

The cruel leader was doing well at the present time, but
he knew that one day he might have *to pay the piper.*

## NEW WORDS

**pertinent**
pėrt´ n ənt

**mastiff**
mas´ tif

**obsess**
əb ses´

**doleful**
dōl´ fəl

**wan**
won

## CRISIS!

As soon as Jerry Hart could get the *pertinent* facts from his wife, he dashed out of the office on his way home. He jostled* people in the hallway, implored* the elevator operator to hurry, and with flagrant* disregard for an elderly gentleman jumped into the cab he had hailed. The twenty-minute taxi ride seemed interminable* and all the while horrible thoughts occurred to Jerry. Visions of an ugly *mastiff* with foaming jaws *obsessed* him. A crowd of people had gathered in front of his house so that Jerry had to force his way through them. Little Bobby was on his bed, surrounded by a doctor, a policeman, Jerry's *doleful* wife, his two daughters, and a half-dozen *wan* neighbors.

**Sample Sentences**  Use the new words in the following sentences.

1. The stockbroker was _____ with the idea of becoming a painter.

2. My nervous neighbor bought a pugnacious* _____ to frighten burglars.

3. _____ expressions abounded* throughout headquarters on the night of the election.

4. During the trial the astute* lawyer was able to elicit* the _____ information from the key witness.

5. After the tension, his normally ruddy face was _____ and tired.

**Definitions**  Match the new words with their meanings.

6. pertinent _____ a. sad, melancholy

7. mastiff _____ b. to the point

8. obsess _____ c. sickly pale

9. doleful _____ d. to haunt, preoccupy

10. wan _____ e. large dog

---

### TODAY'S IDIOM

*on the carpet*—being scolded

Because of her repeated lateness, Betty's boss called her *on the carpet*.

---

ANSWERS ARE ON PAGE 298

# WEEK 10 ❖ DAY 3

**NEW WORDS**

**histrionics**
his´ trē on´ iks

**elusive**
i lü´ siv

**frustrate**
frus´ trāt

**symptomatic**
simp´ tə mat´ ik

**interject**
in´ tər

## A TIME FOR DECISION

The doctor explained the situation calmly, avoiding *histrionics*. First of all, they didn't know whether the dog had rabies. Secondly, the *elusive* dog had *frustrated* all attempts to find him so far. Finally, the decision would have to be made whether Bobby was to undergo the painful vaccination administered daily for two weeks. Mrs. Hart said that a neighbor who had seen the dog claimed that it had been foaming at the mouth, barking, and growling constantly—all *symptomatic* of rabies. But the policeman *interjected* that there hadn't been a case of a mad dog in the county in over twenty years; he repudiated* the neighbor's report, advocating* that they do nothing for at least another day. Mr. and Mrs. Hart sat down to think about their next step.

**Sample Sentences**  Use the new words in the following sentences.

1. The warden _____ the prisoners' attempt to escape by adding more guards.

2. Most viewers hate it when a commercial is _____ into a suspense drama.

3. Saying that he would not tolerate* her _____ , the director fired the temperamental actress.

4. All his life he found happiness _____ , but wealth easy to come by.

5. The sordid* rioting was _____ of the problems facing the large cities.

**Definitions**  Match the new words with their meanings.

6. histrionics _____    **a.** having to do with signs or symptoms, indicative

7. elusive _____    **b.** hard to grasp

8. frustrate _____    **c.** insert, interrupt

9. symptomatic _____    **d.** display of emotions

10. interject _____    **e.** counteract, foil, thwart*

---

### TODAY'S IDIOM

*to show one's hand*—to reveal one's intentions

When someone joined in bidding for the antique,
the dealer was forced *to show his hand.*

---

## NEW WORDS

**inert**
in ėrt´

**salient**
sā´ lē ənt

**imminent**
im´ ə nənt

**squeamish**
skwē´ mish

**engrossed**
en grōst´

## THE PERTINENT* FACTS ABOUT RABIES

"Give me some of the rudimentary* information about the disease, Doc," said Jerry, glancing toward the *inert* figure of his son. "Well, as you know, the malady* used to be called 'hydrophobia' (fear of water) because one of the symptoms is an inability to swallow liquids. Actually, it is caused by a live virus from the saliva of an infected animal. If saliva gets into a bite wound, the victim may get rabies. The virus travels along the nerves to the spine and brain. Once the *salient* characteristics appear (ten days to six months) then death is *imminent*." "What are the symptoms?" asked Mrs. Hart. "Pain and numbness, difficulty in swallowing, headaches and nervousness. Also, muscle spasms and convulsions." The *squeamish* neighbors who were *engrossed* in the doctor's remarks gasped. "I think we should go ahead with the injections," the distraught* Mrs. Hart said. "I've heard enough."

**Sample Sentences** Use the new words in the following sentences.

1. The senator loathed* it when people said that an atomic war was _____ .

2. When his _____ partner complained about a lack of ethics,* the businessman laughed at his innocence.

3. _____ in his crossword puzzle, he failed to notice the paucity* of customers in the restaurant.

4. One of the _____ features of her poetry is a dependence upon euphemisms.*

5. Seeing the _____ player, the manager dashed out onto the field.

**Definitions** Match the new words with their meanings.

6. inert _____    **a.** outstanding, prominent

7. salient _____    **b.** without power to move

8. imminent _____    **c.** likely to happen, threatening

9. squeamish _____    **d.** absorbed

10. engrossed _____    **e.** easily shocked, over sensitive

---

### TODAY'S IDIOM

*to tilt at windmills*—to fight imaginary enemies (from *Don Quixote*)

The vice president told the committee, "We're really on your side, and if you fight us you'll be *tilting at windmills.*"

---

ANSWERS ARE ON PAGE 298

# WEEK 10 ❖ DAY 5                    REVIEW

At the end of this week's study, you will have covered 200 words and 40 idioms. In addition, you will have seen many of those words used several times in subsequent lessons. If you have been operating at only 75% efficiency, you have, nevertheless, added substantially to your arsenal of words.

Here's a thought: wouldn't it be wonderful if through genuine attention to the daily dosage you could move up to 80%—or even 90%? Start by matching the 20 words with their meanings. Write the letter that stands for the definition in the appropriate answer space. Did somebody say 100%?

## REVIEW WORDS

_____ 1. desist
_____ 2. doleful
_____ 3. elusive
_____ 4. engrossed
_____ 5. frustrate
_____ 6. histrionics
_____ 7. imminent
_____ 8. inclement
_____ 9. inert
_____ 10. interject
_____ 11. mastiff
_____ 12. obsess
_____ 13. pertinent
_____ 14. peruse
_____ 15. premonition
_____ 16. recoil
_____ 17. salient
_____ 18. squeamish
_____ 19. symptomatic
_____ 20. wan

## DEFINITIONS

a. sad
b. draw back
c. foil
d. cease
e. interrupt
f. stormy, harsh
g. indicative
h. appropriate
i. powerless to move
j. large dog
k. outstanding
l. read carefully
m. preoccupy
n. easily shocked
o. forewarning
p. about to happen
q. hard to grasp
r. pale
s. absorbed
t. display of emotions

## IDIOMS

_____ 21. to pay the piper
_____ 22. on the carpet
_____ 23. to show one's hand
_____ 24. to tilt at windmills

u. to reveal one's emotions
v. being scolded
w. fight imaginary enemies
x. to bear the consequences

Now check your answers on page 298. Make a record of those words you missed.

## WORDS FOR FURTHER STUDY          MEANINGS

1. _____ _____
2. _____ _____
3. _____ _____
4. _____ _____
5. _____ _____

63

# WORDSEARCH 10

❖ Using the clues listed below, fill in each blank in the following story with one of the new words you learned this week.

## *The Potato that Strangled Idaho*

People who are ①_____ about the sight of blood or ②_____ in horror from most forms of violence would do well to avoid some of the movies now being shown at their local cinemas. Producers have learned that films that scare the patrons out of their seats, ironically, put millions of fans into those seats, keeping them ③_____ in the goose pimple-inducing spectacles that flash across the screen.

Of course, each movie carries with it a rating that indicates its suitability for certain age groups, either because of its subject matter, language, presentation, or level of violence. Pictures with a "G" rating are approved for all audiences, while, at the other end of the scale, those that are given an "X" rating are for adults only with no children allowed under any circumstance. Getting an "R" rating indicates that the movie is restricted (no one under 18 admitted without an adult) but some Hollywood moguls consider the "R" to be the magnet that insures box office success. And we can be sure that as long as shock films ring up a merry tune on the cash registers, producers will not ④_____ from making them.

A director who specializes in making gory films involving monsters, vampires, and brutal serial killers boasted in a college lecture that his work was in good taste. One student who disagreed was provoked to ⑤_____ that in his opinion the diet of "shock-schlock" movies was in worse taste than those pictures that contained vulgar language and nudity. "At least they're honest," he declared.

### Clues

① 4th Day
② 1st Day
③ 4th Day
④ 1st Day
⑤ 3rd Day

ANSWERS ARE ON PAGE 298

**NEW WORDS**

**poignant**
poi´ nyənt

**inundate**
in´ un dāt

**fruitless**
früt´ lis

**garbled**
gär´ bəld

**sanguine**
sang´ gwən

## THE SEARCH FOR THE DOG (CONTINUED)

Meanwhile, the Harts had notified the local radio stations to broadcast a *poignant* appeal for the dog's owner to come forward. The station was *inundated* with phone calls but all leads were *fruitless*. From what Bobby had told them, a huge dog had leaped out from a red station wagon in the supermarket's parking lot. After biting Bobby it vanished. The six-year-old was too concerned with the bites he had received to see where the dog disappeared to. The boy's story was *garbled*, but he did remember that the animal was gray and had a collar. There was little tangible* evidence to go on, but the police remained *sanguine.*

**Sample Sentences**  Use the new words in the following sentences.

1. The sermon was _____ enough to bring tears to the brash* delinquent's eyes.

2. Although the message was _____ , its salient* points were clear enough.

3. After a _____ attempt to wrest* control of the government, the traitors were incarcerated.

4. Even though his boat was almost _____ , the skipper was loath* to radio for help.

5. Because the malignancy* had gone unchecked, the surgeons were not _____ about the patient's chances.

**Definitions**  Match the new words with their meanings.

6. inundate _____    **a.** useless

7. fruitless _____    **b.** confused, mixed up

8. poignant _____    **c.** optimistic

9. garbled _____    **d.** to flood

10. sanguine _____    **e.** moving, painful to the feelings

--- **TODAY'S IDIOM** ---

***to feather one's nest*—grow rich by taking advantage of circumstances**
While working as the tax collector, he adroitly* *feathered his own nest.*

**phlegmatic**
fleg mat´ ik

**corroborate**
kə rob´ ə rāt

**comprehensive**
kom´ pri hen´ siv

**zealous**
zel´ əs

**coerce**
kō érs´

## NO RELIEF

The normally *phlegmatic* Jerry Hart was deeply upset. Twenty-four hours had passed without result, and even if the rabies could not be *corroborated*, Jerry was determined to see that his son received the vaccine. At the suggestion of some friends, he organized a *comprehensive* search party, *zealously* fanning out in circles around the supermarket. They knocked on every door, inspected every dog, and came back empty-handed. Although the Harts were sick with worry (they had to be *coerced* into going to sleep), little Bobby seemed to be in great spirits. The excruciating* vigil continued.

**Sample Sentences** Use the new words in the following sentences.

1. Harriet's egregious* error disturbed even her _____ employer.

2. The fund raiser was so _____ that he solicited* money from a Salvation Army Santa Claus.

3. In order to get the job, you had to go through the drudgery* of filling out a ten-page _____ questionnaire.

4. The elusive* fugitive was _____ by his attorney into surrendering.

5. Even the swindler's nefarious* accomplice refused to _____ his alibi.

**Definitions** Match the new words with their meanings.

6. phlegmatic _____   **a.** enthusiastic

7. corroborate _____   **b.** calm, hard to rouse to action

8. comprehensive _____   **c.** confirm, support

9. zealous _____   **d.** thorough

10. coerce _____   **e.** to force

---

### TODAY'S IDIOM

*fair-weather friends*—unreliable, they fail one in time of distress

The general was chagrined* to learn that so many of his supposed supporters were actually *fair-weather friends*.

---

ANSWERS ARE ON PAGE 298

# WEEK 11 ❖ DAY 3

**NEW WORDS**

**elapse**
i laps´

**meticulous**
mə tik´ yə ləs

**domicile**
dom´ ə sīl

**lax**
laks

**sporadic**
spə rad´ ik

## THE POLICE FIND THE DOG

Forty hours had *elapsed* before the police work and the publicity paid off. By *meticulously* checking the registrations of every red station wagon in the neighborhood and then cross-checking dog licenses, the police narrowed the search to four owners. After a few telephone calls, the apologetic owner was located and directed to bring her muzzled German shepherd to the Hart *domicile*. Bobby identified the dog, and the animal was taken to a veterinary's clinic to have the necessary tests performed. The *lax* owner, Mrs. McGraw, admitted that the dog had a *sporadic* mean streak, but she scoffed* at the idea of rabies. Jerry Hart noticed for the first time in two days that his uneasy feeling had departed.

**Sample Sentences** Use the new words in the following sentences.

1. Inadvertently,* Emma had allowed two months to _____ before paying her rent.

2. The lackluster* battle was punctuated by _____ mortar fire.

3. A man's _____ is his castle.

4. Because the watchman was _____ , thievery was rampant* at the warehouse.

5. The _____ musician had nothing but disdain* for his disorganized friends.

**Definitions** Match the new words with their meanings.

6. elapse     _____    **a.** careless, negligent

7. meticulous     _____    **b.** to slip by

8. domicile     _____    **c.** occasional

9. lax     _____    **d.** home

10. sporadic     _____    **e.** careful

---

**TODAY'S IDIOM**

***to sow one's wild oats*—to lead a wild, carefree life**

During his teen years, the millionaire avidly* *sowed his wild oats.*

---

**NEW WORDS**

rash
rash

conjecture
kən jek´ chər

obviate
ob´ vē āt

lurid
lur´ id

quip
kwip

## ALL'S WELL THAT ENDS WELL

The Harts were greatly relieved to learn that the *rash conjecture* about the dog was not true. Because the German shepherd was not rabid, the necessity for the painful treatment was *obviated*. The police gave the dog's owner a summons for allowing the animal to go unmuzzled. Little Bobby was treated to an ice cream sundae and a Walt Disney double feature. The neighbors searched for other *lurid* happenings, and Jerry Hart went back to his office. "What kind of dog was that?" his secretary asked. "Oh, his bark was worse than his bite," *quipped* Jerry.

**Sample Sentences** Use the new words in the following sentences.

1. It was sheer _____ on the detective's part but it led to the arrest of the vexatious* counterfeiters.

2. The newspaper switched from mundane* coverage to _____ reporting.

3. It was exceedingly _____ of the lightweight to insult the belligerent* longshoreman.

4. The necessity for preparing sandwiches was _____ when the picnic was postponed.

5. Hamlet remembered that Yorick was always ready with a lusty _____ .

**Definitions** Match the new words with their definitions.

6. rash (adj.) _____ **a.** do away with, eliminate

7. conjecture _____ **b.** joke

8. obviate _____ **c.** guess

9. lurid _____ **d.** sensational

10. quip _____ **e.** too hasty, reckless

---

### TODAY'S IDIOM

*windfall*—unexpected financial gain

When the bankrupt company struck oil,
the surprised investor received a *windfall* of $20,000.

---

ANSWERS ARE ON PAGE 298

# WEEK 11 ❖ DAY 5 REVIEW

Many teachers have jested about their students who confused *rabies* with *rabbis*, Jewish clergymen. We know that those who get the message of this book, true vocabulary mastery, will make few such errors.

Match the twenty words with their meanings. Write the letter that stands for the definition in the appropriate answer space.

## REVIEW WORDS

|  | | DEFINITIONS |
|---|---|---|
| ____ | 1. coerce | a. to flood, to swamp |
| ____ | 2. comprehensive | b. home |
| ____ | 3. conjecture | c. painful to the feelings, moving |
| ____ | 4. corroborate | d. useless |
| ____ | 5. domicile | e. reckless |
| ____ | 6. elapse | f. confirm |
| ____ | 7. fruitless | g. calm, sluggish |
| ____ | 8. garbled | h. sensational |
| ____ | 9. inundate | i. hopeful |
| ____ | 10. lax | j. do away with |
| ____ | 11. lurid | k. confused, mixed up |
| ____ | 12. meticulous | l. guess |
| ____ | 13. obviate | m. to pass by |
| ____ | 14. phlegmatic | n. careless |
| ____ | 15. poignant | o. occasional |
| ____ | 16. quip | p. thorough |
| ____ | 17. rash | q. careful |
| ____ | 18. sanguine | r. to force |
| ____ | 19. sporadic | s. enthusiastic |
| ____ | 20. zealous | t. to joke |

## IDIOMS

| | | |
|---|---|---|
| ____ | 21. to feather one's nest | u. to lead a wild life |
| ____ | 22. fair-weather friends | v. unexpected financial gain |
| ____ | 23. to sow wild oats | w. unreliable acquaintances |
| ____ | 24. windfall | x. provide for oneself at the expense of others |

Now check your answers on page 298. Make a record of those words you missed. If you were able to get them all right, use the five spaces to create antonyms for numbers 7, 8, 10, 17, and 19.

### WORDS FOR FURTHER STUDY        MEANINGS

1. _____   _____

2. _____   _____

3. _____   _____

4. _____   _____

5. _____   _____

# WORDSEARCH 11

❖ Using the clues listed below, fill in each blank in the following story with one of the new words you learned this week.

## Assuming Blunders

"I pledge allegiance to the flag of the United States of America and to the republic for Richard Sands."

"Deliver us from evil. Lead us not into Penn Station."

Teachers who train students to memorize and then do rote recitations sometimes find that the youngsters have a ① _____ interpretation of the actual words. Eliza Berman, an educator who is ② _____ about her own use of language, invited colleagues to send her examples of confusion in students' writings. Little did she realize that they would quickly ③ _____ her letterbox with their pet mistakes. As a result, Ms. Berman was able to compile a fairly ④ _____ list of howlers that include the following:

"The inhabitants of ancient Egypt were called Mummies. They lived in the Sarah Dessert and traveled by Camelot."

"Homer wrote *The Oddity* in which Penelope was the first hardship Ulysses endured on his journey."

"Socrates died from an overdose of wedlock."

"King Alfred conquered the Dames."

"Indian squabs carried porpoises on their backs."

"Under the Constitution, the people enjoy the right to keep bare arms."

"In the Olympic Games, the Greeks ran, jumped, hurled the bisquits and threw the java."

"Lincoln was America's greatest Precedent."

Ms. Berman is not too ⑤ _____ about eliminating such errors from pupils' compositions and test papers. Her advice: enjoy!

## Clues

① 1st Day

② 3rd Day

③ 1st Day

④ 2nd Day

⑤ 1st Day

ANSWERS ARE ON PAGE 298

# WEEK **12** ❖ DAY **1**

**NEW WORDS**

**diatribe**
dī´ ə trīb

**inhibition**
in´ ə bish´ ən or
in´ hi bish´ ən

**fortuitous**
fô tü´ ə təs

**incoherent**
in´ kō hir´ ənt

**ilk**
ilk

## OFF BROADWAY

When Monte Ziltch told his boss, Mr. Foy, that he was quitting as an accountant to become an actor, the man was convulsed with laughter. After Mr. Foy realized that Monte was obsessed* with the idea, he became quite serious, launching into a *diatribe* on the importance of responsibility in the younger generation. Monte confessed that he had been developing ulcers as an accountant, and when his psychiatrist suggested that the sickness was a result of *inhibitions,* Monte agreed. Now a *fortuitous* opportunity to get into show business required Monte to make an immediate decision. Mr. Foy stormed out of the office, muttering *incoherently* about hippies, beatniks, and others of that *ilk.*

**Sample Sentences** Use the new words in the following sentences.

1. When a large expenditure is imminent,* my father goes into a long _____ on the need for economy.

2. It is often fruitless* to argue with racists, bigots*, and others of that _____ .

3. Since the patient's speech was garbled* and _____ , we could only conjecture* as to his message.

4. The meeting was a _____ one, but the jealous husband construed* it as pre-arranged and clandestine.*

5. After two drinks the usually phlegmatic* dentist lost all his _____ .

**Definitions** Match the new words with their meanings.

6. diatribe _____ a. kind, sort

7. inhibition _____ b. disjointed

8. fortuitous _____ c. accidental

9. incoherent _____ d. bitter criticism

10. ilk _____ e. restraint

---
**TODAY'S IDIOM**

*to wear one's heart on one's sleeve*—to make one's feelings evident
People who *wear their hearts on their sleeves* frequently suffer emotional upsets.

---

## NEW WORDS

**prestigious**
pre stij´ əs

**placard**
plak´ ärd

**integral**
in´ tə grəl

**remuneration**
ri myü´ nə rā´ shən

**nominal**
nom´ ə nəl

## AN ALL-ROUND MAN

The need for a decision came about when Monte was invited to join a *prestigious* summer stock company, starting in mid-June. As a mature "apprentice," he would be required to take tickets, paint scenery, prepare *placards*, assist with lighting, costumes, and props, and carry an occasional spear in a walk-on role. Since the company would stage five major plays during the summer, as well as a half-dozen shows for children, there was a chance that Monte might actually get a part before too many weeks had elapsed.* In addition, he would be attending the drama classes that were an *integral* part of the summer theater. The *remuneration* would be *nominal* but at last Monte Ziltch would be fulfilling a life-long ambition.

**Sample Sentences**  Use the new words in the following sentences.

1. The police posted a _____ asking all citizens to desist* from looting.

2. A salient* feature of the _____ company's success was its fair treatment of employees.

3. Derek Jeter's _____ from the New York Yankees made him a millionaire many times over.

4. For allowing his ferocious mastiff* to appear on a commercial, the trainer was paid a _____ sum.

5. She seemed to be an unimportant member of the president's entourage* but actually she played an _____ role in White House affairs.

**Definitions**  Match the new words with their meanings.

6. prestigious _____    **a.** essential

7. placard _____    **b.** poster

8. integral _____    **c.** slight

9. remuneration _____    **d.** reward, pay

10. nominal _____    **e.** illustrious

---

### TODAY'S IDIOM

***to wash dirty linen in public*—to openly discuss private affairs**

"Let's talk about it privately," his uncle said,
"rather than *wash our dirty linen in public*."

ANSWERS ARE ON PAGE 299

**NEW WORDS**

**expunge**
ek spunj´

**flamboyant**
flam boi´ ənt

**anathema**
ə nath´ ə mə

**schism**
siz´ əm

**utopia**
yü tō´ pē ə

## FROM LEDGERS TO SCRIPTS

During the first weeks of the summer, Monte Ziltch didn't even have time to consider whether he had made an egregious* mistake. He was too engrossed* with his work, performing a thousand and one odd jobs around the theater. First there was the opening production of *A Chorus Line*, then two weeks of *The Fantasticks*, followed by a poignant* *Diary of Anne Frank*, which did excellent business. All through those weeks, Monte painted, carried, nailed, collected, ran, studied, and perspired. He had *expunged* all traces of debits and credits from his mind, burying himself in the more *flamboyant* world of the theater. Accounting became *anathema* to him as the *schism* between his present *utopia* and his former drudgery* widened.

**Sample Sentences** Use the new words in the following sentences.

1. In *Lost Horizon* a character recoiled* at the idea of living in a _____ .

2. A pernicious* _____ developed between the two sisters.

3. The traitor's name was _____ in his father's domicile.*

4. Our theatrical pages were inundated* with press releases from the _____ producer.

5. After having made the rash* statements, the senator wished that he could _____ them from the record.

**Definitions** Match the new words with their meanings.

6. expunge _____ a. split

7. flamboyant _____ b. something greatly detested

8. anathema _____ c. place of perfection

9. schism _____ d. erase

10. utopia _____ e. showy, colorful

---

**TODAY'S IDIOM**

*to save face—to avoid disgrace*

Instead of firing the corrupt executive, they allowed
him to retire in order that he might *save face*.

---

## NEW WORDS

**timorous**
tim´ ər əs

**truncated**
trung´ kā tid

**jaunty**
jôn´ tē

**fractious**
frak´ shəs

**ostentatious**
os´ ten tā´ shəs

## IRONY FOR MERRYWEATHER

At last, Monte's chance to perform came. He had played the *timorous* Lion in a *truncated* version of "The Wizard of Oz," which the apprentices had staged. But now there was an open audition to cast the final show of the season. It was to be a *jaunty* original comedy, given a summer tryout prior to a Broadway opening. Monte, who by now had adopted the stage name of Monte Merryweather, read for the producers, hoping to get the part of the hero's *fractious* landlord. Unfortunately, the competition was too rough—but the director assigned Monte to a less *ostentatious* part. And so for the first two weeks in September the stage-struck accountant had a two-minute, two-line part. What was his role? The hero's accountant!

**Sample Sentences**  Use the new words in the following sentences.

1. It is frustrating* to have one's lengthy remarks printed in _____ form.

2. With his cap set at a _____ angle, the amicable* sailor strutted down the street.

3. In an _____ display of histrionics* the star refused to perform.

4. Under duress* the normally _____ husband was coerced* into demanding a raise.

5. Roger's _____ behavior compounded* the bad relationship he had already had with his partner.

**Definitions**  Match the new words with their meanings.

6. timorous _____ **a.** fearful

7. truncated _____ **b.** cut short

8. jaunty _____ **c.** sprightly, gay

9. fractious _____ **d.** showy

10. ostentatious _____ **e.** quarrelsome

---

### TODAY'S IDIOM

***Indian summer*—warm autumn weather**

Parts of the country were deep in snow,
but the East was enjoying an *Indian summer*.

---

ANSWERS ARE ON PAGE 299

How many of the new words have now become a part of your "working vocabulary"? At first, their use may be conscious, even studied. However, the squeaks will soon disappear. Try a few this weekend.

Match the twenty words with their meanings. Write the letter that stands for the definition in the appropriate answer space. (Note the resemblance between *flamboyant* and *ostentatious*).

## REVIEW WORDS

| | | | DEFINITIONS |
|---|---|---|---|
| _____ | 1. | anathema | a. well-known |
| _____ | 2. | diatribe | b. quarrelsome |
| _____ | 3. | expunge | c. kind, sort |
| _____ | 4. | flamboyant | d. poster |
| _____ | 5. | fortuitous | e. disjointed |
| _____ | 6. | fractious | f. sprightly |
| _____ | 7. | ilk | g. accidental |
| _____ | 8. | incoherent | h. in name only, slight |
| _____ | 9. | inhibition | i. restraint |
| _____ | 10. | integral | j. reward |
| _____ | 11. | jaunty | k. a curse |
| _____ | 12. | nominal | l. bitter criticism |
| _____ | 13. | ostentatious | m. erase |
| _____ | 14. | placard | n. colorful |
| _____ | 15. | prestigious | o. cut short |
| _____ | 16. | remuneration | p. essential |
| _____ | 17. | schism | q. fearful |
| _____ | 18. | timorous | r. showy |
| _____ | 19. | truncated | s. split |
| _____ | 20. | utopia | t. place of perfection |

## IDIOMS

| | | | |
|---|---|---|---|
| _____ 21. wear one's heart on one's sleeve | u. make one's feelings evident |
| _____ 22. wash dirty linen in public | v. warm autumn weather |
| _____ 23. save face | w. to avoid disgrace |
| _____ 24. Indian summer | x. openly discuss private affairs |

Now check your answers on page 299. Make a record of those words you missed.

## WORDS FOR FURTHER STUDY      MEANINGS

1. _____     _____

2. _____     _____

3. _____     _____

4. _____     _____

5. _____     _____

# SENSIBLE SENTENCES?
## (From Week 12)

❖ Underline the word that makes sense in each of the sentences below.

1. The senator went into a lengthy *(diatribe, remuneration)* about government waste in the military budget.

2. Most reformers are seeking to create a *(schism, utopia)*.

3. Lorraine was criticized sharply for the *(ostentatious, nominal)* way in which she furnished her apartment.

4. Anyone so *(ilk, timorous)* should not have been selected to guard the castle.

5. My brother was promoted to a *(prestigious, flamboyant)* job in his company.

6. Although his speech was *(anathema, jaunty)* we were able to sense its underlying seriousness.

7. The failing grade was *(expunged, truncated)* from her record when she submitted the excellent term paper.

8. I got my job as a result of a *(fractious, fortuitous)* meeting with the director of personnel.

9. The bookkeeper is such an *(integral, incoherent)* part of our organization that we pay her a very high salary.

10. We marched in front of the embassy with *(placards, inhibitions)* held high.

11. Don't *(save face, wash your dirty linen in public)* if you plan to run for office.

ANSWERS ARE ON PAGE 299

❖ Using the clues listed below, fill in each blank in the following story with one of the new words you learned this week.

## *Regis, Oprah, Ellen, et al.*

The television talk shows of our era, featuring such ①_____ public figures as Regis Philbin, Oprah Winfrey, and Ellen De Generes, attract millions of daytime viewers and constitute a powerful influence on the American scene. When the media can hold the attention of so sizable a chunk of couch potatoes, it pays to scrutinize it closely.

A student at Stanford University, doing her doctoral thesis on the unusual popularity of the afternoon talk shows, noted the fierce competition among those programs for guests who are off the beaten track. According to her:

"Almost every irregular, ②_____ life-style you can think of has already been featured on one of the shows and probably on all of them, when you add Montel Williams, Jerry Springer, and others of that ③_____ who serve as network hosts. They have shown teenagers who marry people in their sixties, daughters and mothers who date the same man, men who have gone through a marriage ceremony with other men, women with prominent tattoos, and other people who are totally free of ④_____ ."

"⑤_____ for our guests is so small," said a producer, "that these shows are inexpensive to put on. And say what you want about good taste, millions watch us every day, and as long as the ratings are that healthy, sponsors will pay good money to be identified with us."

## Clues

① 2nd Day
② 3rd Day
③ 1st Day
④ 1st Day
⑤ 2nd Day

## NEW WORDS

**importune**
im´ pôr tün´

**incontrovertible**
in´ kon trə vėr´ tə bəl

**surreptitious**
sȧr´ əp tish´ əs

**haven**
hā´ vən

**subjugate**
sub´ jə gāt

## A VISIT TO THE PRESIDENT

In the winter of 1941, Enrico Fermi and a number of other distinguished scientists *importuned* President Franklin Roosevelt for authorization to begin an all-out effort in atomic energy research. The scientists were alarmed by *incontrovertible* evidence of *surreptitious* German experiments, and they asked for speedy approval. Italian-born Enrico Fermi was the ideal man to lead the atomic research. Already in 1938 he had won the Nobel Prize for work with radioactive elements and neutron bombardment. Fermi had found a *haven* from the Fascists (his wife was Jewish) and he knew that if the Germans were the first to develop an atomic bomb it would mean that Hitler could *subjugate* the entire world. The international race for atomic supremacy was on.

**Sample Sentences**  Use the new words in the following sentences.

1. Although Eddie was not sanguine* about his chances, he continued to _____ his boss for a winter vacation.

2. In inclement* weather our barn is a _____ for many animals.

3. The dictator used duplicity* in order to _____ his rivals.

4. With a _____ movement, the meticulous* bookkeeper emptied the ash tray.

5. The expert's _____ testimony corroborated* the police report.

**Definitions**  Match the new words with their meanings.

6. importune      _____    **a.** undeniable

7. incontrovertible_____    **b.** ask urgently

8. surreptitious   _____    **c.** conquer

9. haven          _____    **d.** place of safety

10. subjugate      _____    **e.** stealthy, accomplished by secret

---
### TODAY'S IDIOM
---

*to take the bull by the horns*—to face a problem directly

After several days of delay, the minister decided *to take the bull by the horns*, and so he sent for the vandals.

ANSWERS ARE ON PAGE 299

# WEEK 13 ❖ DAY 2

**NEW WORDS**

**ultimate**
ul´ tə mit

**eventuate**
i ven´ chü āt

**emit**
i mit´

**subterranean**
sub´ tə rā´ nē ən

**viable**
vī´ ə bəl

## THE ULTIMATE WEAPON TAKES SHAPE

Enrico Fermi designed a device that could *eventuate* in a chain reaction. It consisted of layers of graphite, alternated with chunks of uranium. The uranium *emitted* neutrons, and the graphite slowed them down. Holes were left for long cadmium safety rods. By withdrawing those control rods Fermi could speed up the production of neutrons, thus increasing the number of uranium atoms that would be split (fission). When the rods were withdrawn to a critical point, then the neutrons would be produced so fast that the graphite and cadmium could not absorb them. In that manner a chain reaction would result. Slowly, Fermi's first atomic pile began to grow in a *subterranean* room at Columbia University. The big question remained—was it *viable*?

**Sample Sentences**  Use the new words in the following sentences.

1. A thorough investigation _____ in a comprehensive* report.
2. After two years of confinement in a _____ dungeon, the prisoner was thin and wan.*
3. The mayor issued a diatribe* against companies whose smokestacks _____ poisonous fumes.
4. Gaining better housing for all was the _____ goal of the zealous* reformer.
5. When the schism* in the company was healed, a _____ arrangement was worked out.

**Definitions**  Match the new words with their meanings.

6. ultimate        _____  **a.** underground
7. eventuate       _____  **b.** final
8. emit            _____  **c.** practicable, workable
9. subterranean    _____  **d.** to give off
10. viable         _____  **e.** to result finally

---

### TODAY'S IDIOM

*the lion's share*—the major portion

Because the salesman was essential to the business,
he demanded *the lion's share* of the profits.

---

**NEW WORDS**

**premise**
prem´ is

**jeopardize**
jep´ ər dīz

**incredulous**
in krej´ ə ləs

**permeate**
per´ mē āt

**propitious**
prə pish´

## THE SQUASH COURT EXPERIMENT

As the pile grew, so did the entire project. Fermi moved his materials to an abandoned squash court under a football stadium at the University of Chicago. His pace accelerated because they were proceeding on the *premise* that the Germans were close to atomic success. Six weeks after the pile had been started, its critical size was reached. Three brave young men *jeopardized* their lives by ascending* the pile, ready to cover it with liquid cadmium if anything went wrong. Almost fifty scientists and several *incredulous* observers mounted a balcony to watch. One physicist remained on the floor; it was his job to extract the final cadmium control rod. Unbearable tension *permeated* the atmosphere. Fermi completed his calculations, waited for a *propitious* moment, and then gave the signal.

**Sample Sentences**  Use the new words in the following sentences.

1. Acting on the _____ that there were no burglars around, the police became quite lax.*

2. After I had perused* the Yankee lineup, I was _____ about their chances of winning.

3. The trapeze artist was squeamish* about having to _____ his life.

4. A terrible odor that was impossible to expunge* _____ the skunk handler's clothing.

5. At a _____ moment the flamboyant* movie star made her grand entrance.

**Definitions**  Match the new words with their meanings.

6. premise _____  **a.** favorable

7. jeopardize _____  **b.** endanger

8. incredulous _____  **c.** to spread through

9. permeate _____  **d.** skeptical

10. propitious _____  **e.** grounds for a conclusion

---
### TODAY'S IDIOM
---

*out of the frying pan into the fire—*
**to go from a difficult situation to a worse one**

I thought I had escaped, but actually I went *out of the frying pan into the fire.*

ANSWERS ARE ON PAGE 299

# WEEK 13 ❖ DAY 4

**NEW WORDS**

**surmise**
sər mīz´

**curtail**
kėr tāl´

**repress**
ri pres´

**cryptic**
krip´ tik

**inchoate**
in kō´ it

## THE ITALIAN NAVIGATOR LANDS

The chain reaction took place precisely as Enrico Fermi had *surmised*. After twenty-eight minutes he *curtailed* the experiment, giving the signal to replace the control rod. The normally reserved scientists, unable to *repress* their excitement, let out a tremendous cheer and gathered around Fermi to shake his hand. Although it was time to celebrate, some of the men remarked soberly that "the world would never be the same again." On December 2, 1942, the news of Fermi's achievement was relayed in a *cryptic* telephone message:

"The Italian Navigator has reached the New World."
"And how did he find the natives?"
"Very friendly."
The Atomic Age was *inchoate*—but truly here!

**Sample Sentences**  Use the new words in the following sentences.

1. Publication of the lurid* magazine was _____ by the district attorney.

2. Although his remarks appeared _____ at first, we began to see how really pertinent* they were.

3. I had to _____ my desire to interject* my criticism during the debate.

4. Edna had _____ that she would be charged a nominal* sum and so she was outraged when she got the bill.

5. The young couple was disappointed to see the _____ state of their new house.

**Definitions**  Match the new words with their meanings.

6. surmise      _____    a. puzzling

7. curtail      _____    b. guess

8. repress      _____    c. to put down

9. cryptic      _____    d. to cut short

10. inchoate    _____    e. in an early stage

---
### TODAY'S IDIOM
---

*to keep the pot boiling*—to see that interest doesn't die down

Dickens *kept the pot boiling* by ending each chapter on
a note of uncertainty and suspense.

---

No matter what the theme, no matter what the source, we can expect that important concepts will require a mature vocabulary. This week's topic, scientific and biographical in nature, serves as a vehicle for teaching you twenty worthwhile words. You now have the chance to see whether you remember their definitions. Write the letter that stands for the definition in the appropriate answer space.

## REVIEW WORDS

| | | DEFINITIONS | |
|---|---|---|---|
| _____ | 1. cryptic | a. | ask urgently |
| _____ | 2. curtail | b. | undeniable |
| _____ | 3. emit | c. | guess |
| _____ | 4. eventuate | d. | accomplished by secret |
| _____ | 5. haven | e. | to put down |
| _____ | 6. importune | f. | favorable |
| _____ | 7. inchoate | g. | cut short |
| _____ | 8. incontrovertible | h. | workable |
| _____ | 9. incredulous | i. | underground |
| _____ | 10. jeopardize | j. | final |
| _____ | 11. permeate | k. | to result finally |
| _____ | 12. premise | l. | to spread through |
| _____ | 13. propitious | m. | conquer |
| _____ | 14. repress | n. | place of safety |
| _____ | 15. subjugate | o. | endanger |
| _____ | 16. subterranean | p. | a proposition for argument |
| _____ | 17. surmise | q. | skeptical |
| _____ | 18. surreptitious | r. | in an early stage |
| _____ | 19. ultimate | s. | puzzling |
| _____ | 20. viable | t. | to give off |

## IDIOMS

| | | | |
|---|---|---|---|
| _____ | 21. take the bull by the horns | u. | to maintain interest |
| _____ | 22. the lion's share | v. | from bad to worse |
| _____ | 23. out of the frying pan into the fire | w. | the major portion |
| _____ | 24. keep the pot boiling | x. | to face a problem directly |

Now check your answers on page 299. Make a record of those words you missed.

## WORDS FOR FURTHER STUDY     MEANINGS

1. _____  _____

2. _____  _____

3. _____  _____

4. _____  _____

5. _____  _____

❖ Using the clues listed below, fill in each blank in the following story with one of the new words you learned this week.

## *Drug Smugglers Beware*

The ①_____ message came to Officer Matt Jagusak: "Drug search tomorrow—bring pig."

Jagusak, with the Union County New Jersey Sheriff's Department Search and Rescue Unit, had to ②_____ his superiors to put Ferris E. Lucas, a super sniffer, to work. Lucas is a Vietnamese pot-bellied pig with a fantastic olfactory sense that is one million times greater than a human's and could be our ③_____ weapon in breaking up the drug trade.

A canine trainer offered the pig to Union City, suggesting that its intelligence and unique skill will make Lucas a ④_____ fighter against illegal narcotics. Jagusak has already taught his 55-pound porker-detective how to find cocaine, hashish, and marijuana. While some law enforcement officials were ⑤_____ at first, they quickly became believers when they saw the Sherlock Holmes of the sty locate underground drug scents that had eluded trained dogs.

"I don't care if it's a dog, a pig, or an elephant," Jagusak's boss said. "If it benefits the department and our community, we'll try it."

## Clues

① 4th Day

② 1st Day

③ 2nd Day

④ 2nd Day

⑤ 3rd Day

## NEW WORDS

**aspire**
ə spīr´

**inveigh**
in vā´

**nettle**
net´ l

**overt**
ō´ vėrt

**relegate**
rel´ ə gāt

# WEEK 14 ❖ DAY 1

## SUNDAY MORNING AT PEARL HARBOR

At breakfast time on Sunday morning, December 7, 1941, Dorie Miller was serving coffee aboard the battleship *West Virginia*. Dorie was black, and the highest job to which he could then *aspire* in the U.S. Navy was that of messman. While Dorie was technically a member of a great fighting fleet, he was not expected to fight. Most Army and Navy officers *inveighed* against blacks as fighting men. Although blacks were *nettled* by such *overt* prejudice, Dorie Miller apparently accepted being *relegated* to the role of a messhall servant. Now, as he poured the coffee, Dorie was wondering why the airplanes above were making so much noise on a peaceful Sunday morning.

**Sample Sentences**  Use the new words in the proper blanks.

1. Although the comic's quips* seemed to be mild, they began to _____ the nightclub's owner.

2. I had a premonition* that Eli would _____ to the position of captain.

3. The pickets agreed to _____ against the law that curtailed* their freedom.

4. _____ acts of violence by the prisoner jeopardized* his parole.

5. When they tried to _____ the star to a minor role she was furious.

**Definitions**  Match the new words with their meanings.

6. aspire     _____    **a.** irritate

7. inveigh     _____    **b.** open

8. nettle     _____    **c.** assign to an inferior position

9. overt     _____    **d.** to strive for

10. relegate     _____    **e.** attack verbally

---

### TODAY'S IDIOM

*to bury the hatchet*—to make peace

After not speaking to each other for a year, they decided *to bury the hatchet.*

---

ANSWERS ARE ON PAGE 299

# WEEK 14 ❖ DAY 2

NEW WORDS

**supine**
sü pīn´

**mammoth**
mam´ əth

**repulse**
ri puls´

**havoc**
hav´ ək

**raze**
rāz

## THE INFAMOUS* ATTACK

The coffee cups suddenly went spinning as an explosion knocked Dorie Miller flat on his back. Jumping up from his *supine* position, the powerfully built messman from Waco, Texas, headed for the deck. Everywhere that Dorie looked he saw smoke and *mammoth* warships lying on their sides. Overhead, dozens of Japanese dive bombers controlled the skies without a U.S. plane to *repulse* their attack. The *havoc* was enormous. Without hesitating, Dorie joined a team that was feeding ammunition to a machine gunner who was making an ineffectual* attempt to protect their battleship from being *razed* by the torpedo planes.

**Sample Sentences** Use the new words in the proper blanks.

1. From a _____ position, the hunter emitted* the animal's mating call.

2. Following the revolution, the people _____ the subterranean* dungeons of the dictator.

3. Management is sure to _____ any request for increased remuneration.*

4. _____ placards* announced the opening of the new movie.

5. The virulent* plague caused _____ among the populace.

**Definitions** Match the new words with their meaning.

6. supine _____ **a.** ruin

7. mammoth _____ **b.** drive back

8. repulse _____ **c.** huge

9. havoc _____ **d.** lying on the back

10. raze _____ **e.** destroy

---
**TODAY'S IDIOM**

*Philadelphia lawyer*—a lawyer of outstanding ability

His case is so hopeless that it would take a *Philadelphia lawyer* to set him free.

---

**NEW WORDS**

**lethal**
lē´ thəl

**scurry**
skėr´ ē

**incisive**
in sī´ siv

**precipitate**
pri sip´ ə tāt

**stereotype**
ster´ e ə tīp´

## THE HEROISM OF DORIE MILLER

Men all around Miller were succumbing* to the *lethal* spray of Japanese bullets. He dragged his captain to safety and turned back to see that the machine-gunner had been killed. Dorie took the big gun and trained it on the incoming bombers. Within the space of ten minutes he was credited with destroying four bombers while dodging the bullets of their fighter escorts. The enemy *scurried* away, having struck the *incisive* blow that *precipitated* U.S. entrance into World War II. Amidst the dead bodies and the ruined fleet were the heroes such as Dorie Miller. The Navy had told him that he did not have to fight but he hadn't listened. The Navy had attempted to *stereotype* him, but Dorie changed all that.

**Sample Sentences** Use the new words in the proper blanks.

1. Our editor castigated* the proposal with his _____ commentary.

2. Poe's hero watched the rats _____ across his inert* body.

3. The jockey received a _____ kick from the fractious* horse.

4. A quarrel was _____ among the relatives after they heard the terms of the reprehensible* will.

5. The laconic* Clint Eastwood was a _____ of the strong, silent Western hero.

**Definitions** Match the new words with their meanings.

6. lethal      _____    **a.** acute

7. scurry      _____    **b.** run hastily

8. incisive      _____    **c.** unvarying pattern

9. precipitate      _____    **d.** deadly

10. stereotype      _____    **e.** hasten

--- **TODAY'S IDIOM** ---

***to gild the lily*—to praise extravagantly**

There was no need for the announcer *to gild the lily* because we could see how beautiful the model was.

       ANSWERS ARE ON PAGE 299

# WEEK 14 ❖ DAY 4

**NEW WORDS**

**stentorian**
sten tôr´ē ən

**singular**
sing´ gye lər

**valor**
val´ ər

**bias**
bī´ əs

**sinecure**
sī´ nə kyür

## "FOR DISTINGUISHED DEVOTION TO DUTY"

Some months later Dorie Miller was serving on an aircraft carrier when Admiral Chester Nimitz, the Commander of the Pacific Fleet, came aboard to preside over a special awards ceremony. In *stentorian* tones the Admiral presented Miller with the prestigious* Navy Cross, commending him for a *singular* act of *valor* and "disregard for his own personal safety." Miller's heroism helped to shatter the *bias* against African-Americans in the armed forces. Although he could have accepted a *sinecure* at a U.S. naval base, Dorie chose to remain in the combat zone where he was killed in action in December, 1943.

**Sample Sentences** Use the new words in the proper blanks.

1. The director was ousted* from his _____ when he angered the mayor.

2. In his customary _____ tones, the sergeant reprimanded* those who thought the army was a haven* for incompetents.

3. The word "surrender" is anathema* to people of _____ .

4. A viable* peace was brought about as a result of the diplomat's _____ contribution.

5. The bigot's* _____ precipitated* a fistfight.

**Definitions** Match the new words with their meanings.

6. stentorian    _____    **a.** prejudice

7. singular    _____    **b.** soft job

8. valor    _____    **c.** courage

9. bias    _____    **d.** extraordinary

10. sinecure    _____    **e.** loud

---

### TODAY'S IDIOM

*to steal one's thunder*—to weaken one's position by stating the argument before that person does

I had planned to be the first to resign from the club, but my cousin *stole my thunder*.

---

ANSWERS ARE ON PAGE 299

Many people agree that a lawyer should be skillful with words. A Philadelphia lawyer,* it goes without saying, must have an extensive vocabulary in order to help him or her present a case.

Match the twenty words with their meanings. Write the letter that stands for the definition in the appropriate answer space.

## REVIEW WORDS

_____ 1. aspire
_____ 2. bias
_____ 3. havoc
_____ 4. incisive
_____ 5. inveigh
_____ 6. lethal
_____ 7. mammoth
_____ 8. nettle
_____ 9. overt
_____ 10. precipitate
_____ 11. raze
_____ 12. relegate
_____ 13. repulse
_____ 14. scurry
_____ 15. sinecure
_____ 16. singular
_____ 17. stentorian
_____ 18. stereotype
_____ 19. supine
_____ 20. valor

## DEFINITIONS

a. huge
b. evident, open
c. courage
d. to strive for
e. banish, assign to inferior position
f. deadly
g. soft job
h. prejudice
i. keen, acute
j. run quickly
k. hasten
l. remarkable, uncommon
m. attack verbally
n. drive back
o. lying on the back
p. destroy
q. conventional custom
r. irritate
s. ruin
t. loud

## IDIOMS

_____ 21. bury the hatchet
_____ 22. Philadelphia lawyer
_____ 23. gild the lily
_____ 24. steal one's thunder

u. to praise extravagantly
v. outstandingly able
w. to beat someone to the punch
x. make peace

Now check your answers on page 299. Make a record of those words you missed.

## WORDS FOR FURTHER STUDY   MEANINGS

1. _____   _____

2. _____   _____

3. _____   _____

4. _____   _____

5. _____   _____

❖ Using the clues listed below, fill in each blank in the following story with one of the new words you learned this week.

## Sugar and Spice and Everything Nice

Teen Talk Barbie, the best-selling $50 model, has gone a step too far in the opinion of the American Association of University Women. Representatives of that group were ① _____ to hear that one of the four phrases that the doll is programmed to utter is, "Math class is tough."

For years the university professors, as well as members of feminist organizations, have ② _____ against the ③ _____ that portrays girls as weak math and science students. "Because that brainwashing message is conveyed to girls at an early age, they come to accept what we consider to be a blatant ④ _____ ," said Dr. Ellen Kaner, a Dallas chemist. "We are just beginning to make progress in our campaign to recruit women for challenging, well-paying careers in math and science," she added, "and were shocked to learn that Barbie is spreading such harmful nonsense."

Executives of the company that manufactures Teen Talk Barbie had to ⑤ _____ to set matters right. They admitted that the phrase in question, one of 270 selected by computer chips, was a mistake. In a press release, their president said, "We didn't fully consider the potentially negative implications of this phrase. Not only will we remove it immediately but will swap with anyone who bought the offending doll."

We wonder how Ken feels about the matter.

## Clues

① 1st Day

② 1st Day

③ 3rd Day

④ 4th Day

⑤ 3rd Day

## NEW WORDS

**complicity**
kəm plis´ ə tē

**liquidation**
lik´ wə dā´ shən

**accomplice**
ə kom´ plis

**recant**
ri kant´

**culpable**
kul´ pə bəl

## DANNY ESCOBEDO GOES TO JAIL

In 1960, a young Chicagoan, Danny Escobedo, was given a 20-year jail sentence for first-degree murder. Danny had confessed to *complicity* in the killing of his brother-in-law after the police had refused to allow him to see his lawyer. Actually, Danny was tricked into blaming a friend for the *liquidation* of his sister's husband, thereby establishing himself as an *accomplice*. Despite the fact that Danny later *recanted* his confession, he was found *culpable* and jailed. Danny had been stereotyped* as a hoodlum and nobody raised an eyebrow over the hapless* felon's* troubles.

**Sample Sentences** Use the new words in the following sentences.

1. Proceeding on the premise* that the broker was guilty of _____ in the swindle, the detective followed him surreptitiously.*

2. After the _____ of the gang leader, a mammoth* conflict arose among his ambitious lieutenants who aspired* to be boss.

3. Once the incontrovertible* evidence was offered, the servant was held _____ in the theft of the jewels.

4. When the clergyman refused to _____ , his superiors were so nettled* that they relegated* him to an isolated parish in Alaska.

5. Although he was judged as a minor _____ , the driver had actually played an integral* part in planning the crime.

**Definitions** Match the new words with their meanings. Two of the words are very close in meaning.

6. complicity _____    **a.** deserving blame

7. liquidation _____    **b.** partnership in wrongdoing

8. accomplice _____    **c.** an associate in crime

9. recant _____    **d.** disposal of, killing

10. culpable _____    **e.** withdraw previous statements

## TODAY'S IDIOM

*woolgathering*—absentmindedness or daydreaming

When the young genius should have been doing his homework, he was frequently engaged in *woolgathering*.

ANSWERS ARE ON PAGE 300

# WEEK 15 ❖ DAY 2

NEW WORDS

**abrogate**
ab´ rə gāt

**alleged**
ə lejd´

**access**
ak´ ses

**invalidate**
in val´ ə dāt

**preclude**
pri klüd´

## ESCOBEDO'S LAWYER APPEALS

Barry Kroll, a Chicago lawyer, took an interest in Danny Escobedo's case. Kroll felt that his client's rights under the Constitution had been *abrogated*. Since the *alleged* accomplice,* Escobedo, had been denied *access* to an attorney, Kroll asked the courts to *invalidate* the conviction. He proposed that lawyers be entitled to sit in when the police question a suspect but the Illinois courts rejected that on the grounds that it would effectively *preclude* all questioning by legal authorities. If such a law were upheld, the police felt that it would play havoc* with all criminal investigations.

**Sample Sentences** Use the new words in the following sentences.

1. The manager was distraught* when he realized that the slugger's sickness would _____ a World Series victory.

2. It is symptomatic* of some newspapers that an _____ criminal is regarded in print as guilty.

3. The wealthy uncle decided to _____ his inane* nephew's sinecure.*

4. The general was sure to _____ the court-martial's decision once he learned of the flagrant* bias* of the presiding officer.

5. Once the druggist had been duped* into opening the store, the addict gained _____ to the pep pills.

**Definitions** Match the new words with their meanings.

6. abrogate _____ a. admittance

7. alleged _____ b. reported, supposed

8. access _____ c. to deprive of legal force, to nullify

9. invalidate _____ d. prevent

10. preclude _____ e. abolish

---

*to whitewash*—to conceal defects,
**to give a falsely virtuous appearance to something**

Although a committee was appointed to investigate the corruption, many citizens felt that their report would be a *whitewash* of the culprits.*

---

## NEW WORDS

**persevere**
pėr´ sə vir´

**landmark**
land´ märk´

**extrinsic**
ek strin´ sik

**declaim**
di klām´

**fetter**
fet´ ər

## AN HISTORIC SUPREME COURT RULING

Lawyer Kroll *persevered* in his defense of Danny Escobedo. The case was argued before the Supreme Court, and in 1964, in a *landmark* decision, the Court reversed Danny's conviction. Legal aid, said the judges, must be instantly available to a suspect. "A system of law enforcement that comes to depend on the confession," one Justice declared, "will, in the long run, be less reliable than a system that depends on *extrinsic* evidence independently secured through skillful investigation." A Justice who *declaimed* against the decision said, however, "I think the rule is ill-conceived and that it seriously *fetters* perfectly legitimate methods of criminal enforcement."

**Sample Sentences** Use the new words in the following sentences.

1. Collectors avidly* sought the rare coin for its _____ value.

2. If we _____ , we can overcome many of our inhibitions.*

3. The Battle of Midway was a _____ victory in the U.S. campaign for ultimate* victory over the Japanese in World War II.

4. I knew that my father would _____ against Mother's choice of ostentatious* fabrics.

5. The senator inveighed* against the policy because he felt it would _____ our Air Force.

**Definitions** Match the new words with their meanings.

6. persevere _____ a. to hamper

7. landmark (adj.)_____ b. foreign, coming from outside

8. extrinsic _____ c. speak loudly

9. declaim _____ d. persist

10. fetter (v.) _____ e. historic, turning point of a period

---
### TODAY'S IDIOM
---

*to break the ice*—to make a start by overcoming initial difficulties

The auto salesman had a poor week, but he finally
*broke the ice* by selling a fully equipped Cadillac.

# WEEK 15 ❖ DAY 4

**NEW WORDS**

**paragon**
par´ ə gon

**nomadic**
nō mad´ ik

**asperity**
a sper´ ə tē

**epithet**
ep´ ə thet

**controversial**
kon´ trə ver´

## THE EFFECTS OF THE ESCOBEDO DECISION

After Danny Escobedo's release from prison, hundreds of inmates began suits for their freedom on the grounds that their rights had been violated, too. Each case was heard on its merits, and in numerous instances people who had been convicted of serious offenses were freed because of the new standards established in the Escobedo case. After getting out, Danny was not a *paragon* of virtue, according to the police. He led a *nomadic* existence, drifting from job to job, and was arrested frequently. With *asperity,* and a few choice *epithets,* Danny referred to police harassment.* Although the Escobedo case was a *controversial* one, most agree that it inspired better police training, better law enforcement procedures, and improved scientific crime detection.

**Sample Sentences**  Use the new words in the following sentences.

1. In the desert, _____ tribes wander back and forth, enduring much privation.*

2. The town planners looked upon their utopia* as a _____ for other communities.

3. Some school principals attempt to repress* the publication of _____ editorials.

4. We were amazed at the display of _____ from our normally phlegmatic* neighbor.

5. A bitter quarrel was precipitated* when both politicians hurled vile _____ at each other.

**Definitions**  Match the new words with their meanings.

6. paragon        _____   **a.** harshness of temper

7. nomadic        _____   **b.** model of excellence

8. asperity       _____   **c.** wandering

9. epithet        _____   **d.** debatable

10. controversial  _____   **e.** descriptive name

─────── **TODAY'S IDIOM** ───────

*the grapevine*—a secret means of spreading information

*The grapevine* has it that Ernie will be elected
president of the school's student council.

ANSWERS ARE ON PAGE 300                                        93

# REVIEW

Police who have resorted to wire-tapping have been able to get evidence that was useful in gaining convictions. In a sense, everyone who listens to you is wire-tapping your conversation. Are the "detectives" impressed with the extent of your vocabulary? By the end of this week you will have gained a greater familiarity with 300 words and 60 idioms—enough to educate a conscientious wire-tapper.

Match the twenty words with their meanings. Write the letter that stands for the definition in the appropriate answer space. (Numbers 1 and 13 are close in meaning.)

## REVIEW WORDS

____ **1.** abrogate
____ **2.** access
____ **3.** accomplice
____ **4.** alleged
____ **5.** asperity
____ **6.** complicity
____ **7.** controversial
____ **8.** culpable
____ **9.** declaim
____ **10.** epithet
____ **11.** extrinsic
____ **12.** fetter (v.)
____ **13.** invalidate
____ **14.** landmark (adj.)
____ **15.** liquidation
____ **16.** nomadic
____ **17.** paragon
____ **18.** persevere
____ **19.** preclude
____ **20.** recant

## DEFINITIONS

**a.** descriptive name
**b.** coming from outside, foreign
**c.** supposed, reported
**d.** deserving blame
**e.** destruction, disposal of
**f.** an associate in crime
**g.** model of excellence
**h.** bitterness of temper
**i.** persist
**j.** repeal by law
**k.** prevent
**l.** speak loudly
**m.** partnership in wrongdoing
**n.** to deprive of legal force, cancel
**o.** renounce previous statements
**p.** to hamper, to chain
**q.** admittance
**r.** wandering
**s.** historic
**t.** debatable

## IDIOMS

____ **21.** woolgathering
____ **22.** to whitewash
____ **23.** break the ice
____ **24.** the grapevine

**u.** a means of spreading information
**v.** absentmindedness
**w.** to conceal defects
**x.** make a start

Now check your answers on page 300. Make a record of those words you missed.

## WORDS FOR FURTHER STUDY     MEANINGS

**1.** _____  _____

**2.** _____  _____

**3.** _____  _____

**4.** _____  _____

**5.** _____  _____

❖ Using the clues listed below, fill in each blank in the following story
with one of the new words you learned this week.

## *Questionable Advertisements*

The Nostalgia Factory, a Boston art gallery, staged an exhibit of
advertisements that had outraged various segments of the community. For
example, one of the fast food chains ran a TV commercial that showed
unattractive school cafeteria workers in hairnets, making that experience less
tasty than a visit to Roy Rogers. Another ad that drew criticism from
psychiatrists and groups such as the Alliance for the Mentally Ill suggested to
readers that, if they had paid $100 for a dress shirt, they were fit candidates
for a straitjacket. Similar sensitivity had restricted ad writers from using terms
such as "nuts" or "crazy."

Why such protests and where do they come from? Who is asking companies
to ① _____ contracts with those agencies that are ② _____ in creating
racist types of commercial messages? Parents who took exception to the
Burger King spot that announced, "Sometimes You Gotta Break the Rules,"
said no to it because it gave the wrong message to their children. And when
a potato chip maker's ad featured a "bandito," angry Mexican-Americans
used some choice ③ _____ in denouncing such a stereotype.

The conclusion to be reached is that segments of the population have become increasingly vocal about "insensitive" ads, demanding that
corporations ④ _____ and never again commission advertisements that
are clearly ⑤ _____ , provocative, and harmful to good human
relationships.

## Clues

① 2nd Day

② 1st Day

③ 4th Day

④ 1st Day

⑤ 4th Day

**NEW WORDS**

**indigenous**
in dij´ ən əs

**gregarious**
grə ger´ ē es

**habitat**
hab´ ə tat

**cursory**
kėr´ sər ē

**interloper**
in´ tər lō´ per

## MEET THE BEES

One of the most interesting inhabitants of our world is the bee, an insect that is *indigenous* to all parts of the globe except the polar regions. The honeybee is a *gregarious* insect whose *habitat* is a colony that he shares with as many as 80,000 bees. Although the individual bees live for only a few days, their colony can be operative for several years. A *cursory* study of the activities of these insects reveals an orderliness and a social structure that is truly amazing. For example, bees in a particular hive have a distinct odor; therefore, when an *interloper* seeks access* they can identify him quickly and repulse* his invasion.

**Sample Sentences** Use the new words in the following sentences.

1. Sherlock Holmes took a _____ glance at the cryptic* message and decoded it instantly.

2. The forest was replete* with the kind of wildlife that is _____ to Africa.

3. Electric eyes, watchdogs, and other nuances* were there to keep out an _____ .

4. The alcoholic was found supine* in his favorite _____—Ryan's Bar.

5. At the party, the _____ hostess scurried* from group to group, making friends and influencing people.

**Definitions** Match the new words with their meanings.

6. indigenous _____ **a.** hasty, not thorough

7. gregarious _____ **b.** native

8. habitat _____ **c.** natural environment

9. cursory _____ **d.** sociable

10. interloper _____ **e.** an unauthorized person

---

### TODAY'S IDIOM

*in a bee line*—taking the straightest, shortest route
**(that's the way a bee flies back to the hive after he has gathered food)**

When the couple left, the babysitter made a *bee line* for the refrigerator.

---

ANSWERS ARE ON PAGE 300

# WEEK 16 ❖ DAY 2

**NEW WORDS**

**prolific**
prə lif´ ik

**bulwark**
bu̇l´ wərk

**sedentary**
sed´ n ter´ ē

**frugal**
frü´ gəl

**antithesis**
an tith´ ə sis

## QUEENS, WORKERS, DRONES

Each colony of honeybees consists of three classes: a) the queen who is a *prolific* layer of eggs; b) the worker who is the *bulwark* of the colony; and c) the *sedentary* drone whose only function is to mate with a young queen. The queen lays the eggs that hatch into thousands of female workers; some queens live as long as five years and lay up to one million eggs. The *frugal* worker builds and maintains the nest, collects and stores the honey, and is the *antithesis* of the lazy drone, or male honeybee, who does not work and has no sting. When the drone is no longer needed, the workers, in effect, liquidate* him by letting him starve to death. It's a cruel, cruel world!

**Sample Sentences** Use the new words in the following sentences.

1. The usually _____ novelist was frustrated* by her failure to come up with a good plot.

2. Len, the gregarious* twin, was the _____ of Lon, the reticent one.

3. The typist shook off the fetters* of her _____ life and joined a mountain climbing expedition.

4. _____ shoppers occasionally badger* supermarket managers for bargains.

5. Some feel that the United States should be a _____ to the inchoate* democracies around the world.

**Definitions** Match the new words with their meanings.

6. prolific        _____   a. producing abundantly

7. bulwark        _____   b. thrifty

8. sedentary     _____   c. protection

9. frugal          _____   d. exact opposite

10. antithesis    _____   e. largely inactive, accustomed to sitting

---
**TODAY'S IDIOM**

*the world, the flesh, and the devil*—temptations that cause man to sin

By entering the monastery he sought to avoid *the world, the flesh, and the devil.*

---

ANSWERS ARE ON PAGE 300

**NEW WORDS**

altruistic
al´ trü is´ tik

embellish
em bel´ ish

cache
kash

coterie
kō´ tərē

cupidity
kyü pid´ ə tē

## SPOTLIGHT ON THE WORKER

Let us examine the activities of the *altruistic* workers in greater detail. After the workers have constructed a hive of waterproof honeycomb (made from beeswax), the queen begins to lay eggs in the first cells. While some workers *embellish* the hive, others fly out in search of nectar and pollen. With their long tongues they gather nectar and use their hind legs to carry the pollen from the flowers. They fly directly back to the hive and then dance around the honeycomb, their movements indicating the direction of the flowers. Meanwhile, other workers have been cleaning cells, caring for the young, and guarding the precious *cache* of nectar. Another special *coterie* is entrusted with heating or cooling the hive. Dedicated to the welfare of the queen and the entire insect community, all of these workers display a complete absence of *cupidity*.

**Sample Sentences**  Use the new words in the following sentences.

1. Through a fortuitous* remark, the _____ of the art thieves was discovered.

2. We warned him that his reprehensible* _____ would eventuate* in a loss of all his friends.

3. The good-hearted doctor went into the jungle purely for _____ reasons.

4. A _____ of bridge players made our clubroom their permanent habitat.*

5. Everytime the irate* motorist told about the accident he had a tendency to _____ the story.

**Definitions**  Match the new words with their meanings.

6. altruistic _____   **a.** secret hiding place

7. embellish _____   **b.** unselfish

8. cache _____   **c.** small group having something in common

9. coterie _____   **d.** adorn, touch up

10. cupidity _____   **e.** greed

---
**TODAY'S IDIOM**
---

*to make bricks without straw*—to attempt to do something without having the necessary materials (In the Bible we read that the Egyptians commanded the Israelites to do so)

My uncle's business schemes always fail because he tries *to make bricks without straw.*

ANSWERS ARE ON PAGE 300

# WEEK 16 ❖ DAY 4

NEW WORDS

**virtuosity**
ver´ chü os´ ə tē

**temerity**
tə mer´ ə tē

**amorous**
am´ ər əs

**progeny**
proj´ ə nē

**saturate**
sach´ ə

## THE SAGA OF THE QUEEN BEE

Although the *virtuosity* of the workers is remarkable, the queen bee is really the main story. Workers choose a few larvae to be queens, feeding them royal jelly, a substance rich in proteins and vitamins. While the queen is changing from a larva to a pupa, a team of workers builds a special cell for her. Soon the young queen hatches, eats the prepared honey, and grows strong. After she kills any rivals who have the *temerity* to challenge her, an *amorous* note is injected. She flies from the hive and mates with one or more drones on her first flight. Then the process of egg laying begins. When her *progeny* *saturate* the hive, scouts are dispatched to find a new location, and the bees swarm after their leader to begin the amazing cycle again.

**Sample Sentences** Use the new words in the following sentences; remember, past tenses may be required.

1. A landmark* in the history of _____ drama is *Romeo and Juliet*.

2. The eminent* artist, famous for his _____ , was admired by classicists and beatniks alike.

3. The Bantu chief and all his _____ were noted for their valor.*

4. For having the _____ to declaim* against the majority leader, the freshman senator was given the worst committee assignments.

5. Television in the new century was _____ with the rebirth of the old quiz shows.

**Definitions** Match the new words with their meanings.

6. virtuosity     _____    **a.** descendants

7. temerity     _____    **b.** full of love

8. amorous     _____    **c.** soak, fill up completely

9. progeny     _____    **d.** foolish boldness

10. saturate     _____    **e.** great technical skill

---
### TODAY'S IDIOM
---

***to have the upper hand*—to gain control**
I had him at my mercy, but now he has *the upper hand.*

# REVIEW

Even if you are as busy as the proverbial bee, you can always manage the fifteen to twenty minutes that are required for these daily vocabulary sessions.

Match the twenty words with their meanings. Write the letter that stands for the definition in the appropriate answer space.

## REVIEW WORDS

| | |
|---|---|
| ____ | **1.** altruistic |
| ____ | **2.** amorous |
| ____ | **3.** antithesis |
| ____ | **4.** bulwark |
| ____ | **5.** cache |
| ____ | **6.** coterie |
| ____ | **7.** cupidity |
| ____ | **8.** cursory |
| ____ | **9.** embellish |
| ____ | **10.** frugal |
| ____ | **11.** gregarious |
| ____ | **12.** habitat |
| ____ | **13.** indigenous |
| ____ | **14.** interloper |
| ____ | **15.** progeny |
| ____ | **16.** prolific |
| ____ | **17.** saturate |
| ____ | **18.** sedentary |
| ____ | **19.** temerity |
| ____ | **20.** virtuosity |

## DEFINITIONS

**a.** secret hiding place
**b.** thrifty
**c.** enjoying the company of others
**d.** exact opposite
**e.** adorn
**f.** unselfish
**g.** small exclusive group
**h.** greed
**i.** not thorough, hasty
**j.** descendants
**k.** an unauthorized person
**l.** native
**m.** largely inactive
**n.** natural environment
**o.** foolish boldness
**p.** fill up completely
**q.** protection
**r.** full of love
**s.** great technical skill
**t.** fertile

## IDIOMS

____ **21.** in a bee line
____ **22.** the world, the flesh, and the devil
____ **23.** make bricks without straw
____ **24.** have the upper hand

**u.** directly
**v.** gain control
**w.** attempt something without necessary materials
**x.** temptations

Now check your answers on page 300. Make a record of those words you missed.

## WORDS FOR FURTHER STUDY      MEANINGS

1. _____   _____
2. _____   _____
3. _____   _____
4. _____   _____
5. _____   _____

❖ Using the clues listed below, fill in each blank in the following story with one of the new words you learned this week.

## *Cheating a Cheater*

"Our neighborhood was so tough," the comedian joked, "that two guys held up a bank and were mugged as they ran to their getaway car."

Later that evening, as Roy and Timmy were discussing the comic's routine, Roy was reminded of a true (he said) story that went like this:

Mr. D., the gang kingpin in our community, loved money. Like Silas Marner, the ①_____ weaver of George Eliot's novel, he enjoyed counting his treasure each Friday night. Mr. D's ②_____ was concealed in a wall safe behind a painting in his office. The $50 and $100 bills made his hands dirty as he counted them but Mr. D didn't mind. The filth of the lucre did not disturb him at all.

One Friday evening, Roy continued, a brash ③_____ had the ④_____ to try to steal the ill-gotten gains. Having bought the combination from a relative who had installed Mr. D's safe, he stuffed his loot into a laundry bag and was halfway out the door when he spied a $10 bill on the floor. His ⑤_____ made him go back for that small change, and in that moment, Mr. D. arrived on the scene.

The quick-thinking thief blurted out, "I'll have the shirts back on Friday." Hoisting the laundry bag over his shoulder, he was out the door before the confused mobster could figure out what had happened.

Timmy, who had listened patiently, said, "I don't believe a word of that story because it would take a guy with a great deal of *starch* to pull it off!"

## Clues

① 2nd Day

② 3rd Day

③ 1st Day

④ 4th Day

⑤ 3rd Day

## NEW WORDS

**perpetrate**
pėr´ pə trāt

**consummate**
kən sum´ it

**subterfuge**
sub´ tər fyüj

**concoct**
kon kokt´

**fallacious**
fə lā´ shəs

## A PLAN TO FOOL THE NAZIS

One of the truly remarkable stories of World War II concerns a ruse* that was *perpetrated* with such *consummate* skill that it saved the lives of many Allied troops and helped to shorten the war. The simple, bold, and ingenious *subterfuge* which British officers *concocted* is the subject of Ewen Montagu's classic, *The Man Who Never Was*. In short, the idea was to plant *fallacious* documents concerning the Allied invasion of Europe upon a dead officer, have his body recovered by agents who would transmit the false information to Germany, and then observe the effects of the plan.

**Sample Sentences** Use the new words in the following sentences.

1. Because the inspector had given only cursory* attention to the reports, I surmised* that his conclusion would be _____ .

2. Johnny Cochrane, the famous and controversial* lawyer, gave _____ attention to the preparation of every case.

3. It was necessary for the interloper* to _____ a convincing story in order to gain access* to the exhibit.

4. In order to _____ the swindle, the jaunty* confidence man adopted an amorous* approach toward the wealthy widow.

5. The experienced teacher realized that Ricky's stomachache was merely a _____ to keep him from taking the French test.

**Definitions** Match the new words with their meanings.

6. perpetrate _____    **a.** devise

7. consummate _____    **b.** complete, of the highest degree

8. subterfuge _____    **c.** commit

9. concoct _____    **d.** ruse, trick

10. fallacious _____    **e.** misleading

---

## TODAY'S IDIOM

***to draw in one's horns*—to check one's anger, to restrain oneself**

The performer *drew in his horns* when he saw
that his critic was an eight-year-old boy.

---

ANSWERS ARE ON PAGE 300

**NEW WORDS**

**manifold**
man´ ə fōld

**assiduous**
ə sij´ ü əs

**impeccable**
im pek´ ə bəl

**fraught**
frôt

**resourceful**
ri sôrs´ fəl

## "MAJOR MARTIN" GOES TO WAR

After Commander Montagu and his colleagues had been given official approval for their dangerous escapade, they encountered *manifold* problems. First, they conducted an *assiduous* search for a body that looked as though it had recently been killed in an airplane disaster. Then, a detailed history of the man had to be invented that would be so *impeccable* that the enemy would accept its authenticity. This meant documents, love letters, personal effects, keys, photographs, etc. Each step was *fraught* with difficulty, but the schemers were unbelievably *resourceful*. As a result, in the late spring of 1942, "Major Martin" was prepared to do his part for his country.

**Sample Sentences** Use the new words in the following sentences.

1. Burdened by her _____ responsibilities, the young executive was precluded* from enjoying her new wealth.

2. Fear permeated* the crippled airplane as the passengers realized that their situation was _____ with danger.

3. Although basically frugal,* his taste in clothing is _____ .

4. The store owner was _____ enough to run a sale the day after his building had been razed* by the flames.

5. Florence Nightingale was a paragon* of mercy in her _____ care for the wounded soldiers.

**Definitions** Match the new words with their meanings.

6. manifold _____ a. able to meet any situation

7. assiduous _____ b. faultless

8. impeccable _____ c. complex, many

9. fraught _____ d. devoted, attentive

10. resourceful _____ e. filled

---

**TODAY'S IDIOM**

*to put the cart before the horse—*
**to reverse the proper order, do things backwards**

My assistant was so eager to get the job done
that he often *put the cart before the horse.*

---

ANSWERS ARE ON PAGE 300

## NEW WORDS

**murky**
mer kē

**component**
kəm poˊ nənt

**hoax**
hōks

**labyrinth**
labˊ ə rinth

**evaluate**
i valˊ yü

## THE PLOT THICKENS

A submarine took the body out to sea. Then, "Major Martin," the man who never was, was slid into the *murky* Atlantic waters off the coast of Huelva, Spain. Attached to this courier's coat was a briefcase that contained the *components* of the *hoax*. Shortly thereafter, the Spanish Embassy notified the British that the body had been recovered. But Commander Montagu learned that the important documents had already been scrutinized* and later resealed so that the British would not be suspicious. The secret information was transmitted to the German High Command, through a *labyrinth* of underground networks, to be *evaluated*. Now the true test of the months of assiduous* planning would come—the question remained, would the Germans swallow the bait?

**Sample Sentences** Use the new words in the following sentences.

1. The practical joker had the temerity* to perpetrate* a _____ upon the Dean of Boys.

2. A good motion picture producer should be skilled in all the manifold* _____ of film-making.

3. After wandering through the _____ , the young hero came face to face with the dragon who was indigenous* to the caves.

4. When I asked the English teacher to _____ my plan for the term paper, her incisive* comments were very helpful.

5. The _____ quality of the artist's latest painting is the antithesis* of her former style.

**Definitions** Match the new words with their meanings.

6. murky _____ a. dark, obscure

7. component _____ b. element

8. hoax _____ c. deception

9. labyrinth _____ d. arrangement of winding passages

10. evaluate _____ e. appraise, find the value of

───── **TODAY'S IDIOM** ─────

*to turn the tables*—to turn a situation to one's own advantage

The wrestler thought that he could pin me to the mat,
but I quickly *turned the tables* on him.

# WEEK 17 ❖ DAY 4

**NEW WORDS**

**exult**
eg zult´

**attest**
ə test´

**gullible**
gul´ ə bəl

**deploy**
di ploi´

**enigma**
i nig´ mə

## A PUZZLE FOR HIS MAJESTY

The conspirators had reason to *exult,* for all evidence *attested* to the fact that the German High Command was *gullible* about "Major Martin." Their defense troops were moved away from the true invasion sites and *deployed* to areas that were inconsequential. Subsequently, when the actual attack took place, Allied casualties were minimized. After the war, Commander Montagu received a medal from the king of England. At the presentation ceremony, the king politely inquired where the young officer had earned his citation. "At the Admiralty," Montagu replied, presenting the king with a genuine *enigma.*

**Sample Sentences** Use the new words in the following sentences.

1. Explaining that the bookkeeper was merely a _____ dupe,* the judge freed him from complicity* in the crime.

2. As the audience watched the master _____ his chess pieces, they applauded his virtuosity.*

3. An expert was summoned to _____ to the authenticity of the Rembrandts found in the Nazi cache* of stolen masterpieces.

4. When Osama Bin Laden was killed, our public had reason to _____ .

5. I could not solve the _____ of why an altruistic* person should exhibit such cupidity.*

**Definitions** Match the new words with their meanings.

6. exult      _____   **a.** to certify

7. attest      _____   **b.** easily cheated or fooled

8. gullible    _____   **c.** to position forces according to a plan

9. deploy      _____   **d.** riddle

10. enigma     _____   **e.** rejoice greatly

---
**TODAY'S IDIOM**
---

*a chip off the old block—*
**a son who is like his father (from the same block of wood)**

When we saw the alcoholic's son enter the liquor store,
we assumed that he was *a chip off the old block.*

---

ANSWERS ARE ON PAGE 300

**105**

Major Martin, if he had lived, would have used the word "bonnet" to refer to the hood of his auto, and he might have referred to a truck as a "lorry." As you can see, there are differences between American and British English. But Major Martin, undoubtedly, would have known all the words below—do you?

Match the twenty words with their meanings. Write the letter that stands for the definition in the appropriate answer space. (Note the similarity between numbers 13 and 20.)

## REVIEW WORDS

_____ **1.** assiduous
_____ **2.** attest
_____ **3.** component
_____ **4.** concoct
_____ **5.** consummate
_____ **6.** deploy
_____ **7.** enigma
_____ **8.** evaluate
_____ **9.** exult
_____ **10.** fallacious
_____ **11.** fraught
_____ **12.** gullible
_____ **13.** hoax
_____ **14.** impeccable
_____ **15.** labyrinth
_____ **16.** manifold
_____ **17.** murky
_____ **18.** perpetrate
_____ **19.** resourceful
_____ **20.** subterfuge

## DEFINITIONS

**a.** spread out in battle formation
**b.** a trick
**c.** busy, attentive
**d.** confirm as accurate, vouch for
**e.** devise
**f.** a riddle, puzzle
**g.** element, part
**h.** able to meet any situation
**i.** perfect, complete
**j.** filled
**k.** misleading, false
**l.** rejoice greatly
**m.** faultless
**n.** easily fooled
**o.** winding passages
**p.** find the value of, review
**q.** many
**r.** deception
**s.** commit
**t.** dark, obscure

## IDIOMS

_____ **21.** draw in one's horns
_____ **22.** put the cart before the horse
_____ **23.** turn the tables
_____ **24.** chip off the old block

**u.** restrain oneself
**v.** turn a situation to one's own advantage
**w.** do things backwards
**x.** son who is like his father

Now check your answers on page 300. Make a record of those words you missed.

## WORDS FOR FURTHER STUDY          MEANINGS

1. _____   _____

2. _____   _____

3. _____   _____

4. _____   _____

5. _____   _____

❖ Using the clues listed·below, fill in each blank in the following story with one of the new words you learned this week.

## *Brother, Can You Spare a Dime?*

The U.S. Department of Health and Human Services, in a ①_____ review of Social Security disability payments, focused on Jack Benson, a ②_____ Seattle panhandler. Mr. Benson had claimed that whatever money he collects on the street can be compared to the funds raised by legitimate charities, and, therefore, he is entitled to a federal deduction. Government officials regard his analogy as ③_____ and disagree. It is their contention that, since Benson's income is unearned, it should be subtracted from his disability payments.

Mr. Benson may not be highly regarded as a street beggar but that didn't stop him from going into the Federal District Court in Oregon to plead that his appeals for cash are an art form, thereby making him eligible for most of the $472 a month that he had been receiving. Not so, declared the government, quoting from a 1990 ruling that found that "money received through begging is better classified as 'gifts' rather than as 'wages' or 'net earnings from self-employment.'"

Mr. Benson's lawyer, plunging into the legal ④_____ , has not given up. She countered that, if Jack merely sat on a street corner with his hand out, the government had a good case. However, in her words, "Jack Benson is a ⑤_____ professional who has elevated begging to a respectable level because of his skill in actively seeking contributions."

It may take all of Benson's talent as a salesman to get the government to put some money in his collection basket.

## Clues

① 2nd Day

② 2nd Day

③ 1st Day

④ 3rd Day

⑤ 1st Day

## NEW WORDS

**abortive**
ə bôr´ tiv

**modify**
mod´ ə fī

**accommodate**
ə kom´ ə dāt

**spontaneous**
spon tā´ nē əs

**innate**
i nāt´ or in´ āt

## TEACHING CHIMPANZEES TO TALK

Two resourceful* psychologists at the University of Nevada have made splendid progress in vocabulary development in chimpanzees. Following a number of *abortive* attempts to teach French, German, or English to chimps, the researchers persevered* until they hit upon the American Sign Language system that is often used by deaf persons. They have had to *modify* the language somewhat in order to *accommodate* the animals' *spontaneous* gestures. With a mixture of *innate* movements and learned ones, some laboratory chimps now have an extensive vocabulary.

**Sample Sentences** Use the new words in the following sentences.

1. His _____ cunning allowed him to see through the spy's subterfuge.*

2. The divers made an _____ attempt to rescue the dog from the murky* waters.

3. Because Phil refused to _____ his philosophy, the directors were forced to invalidate* his appointment.

4. My English teacher admonished* me: "I realize that the speech was to be _____ , but it was not supposed to be incoherent* or fraught* with fallacious* statements."

5. A quarrel was precipitated* when the dietician refused to _____ the patient's special needs.

**Definitions** If vocabulary is getting to be your stock in trade,* you should have no trouble in matching the new words with their meanings.

6. abortive _____ a. fruitless,* useless, failing

7. modify _____ b. to make fit, adjust to

8. accommodate _____ c. natural

9. spontaneous _____ d. without preparation, unrehearsed

10. innate _____ e. to change

---

### TODAY'S IDIOM

***under the wire***—just in time

Hank hesitated about his term paper for two months and finally submitted it just *under the wire.*

---

ANSWERS ARE ON PAGE 301

NEW WORDS

**veneer**
və nir´

**myriad**
mir´ ē əd

**urbane**
er bān´

**crave**
krāv

**irrelevant**
i rel´ ə vənt

## CHIMPANZEES ARE SURPRISINGLY SMART

Washoe, the chimpanzee, has more than a *veneer* of intelligence; she can signal her desire to eat, go in or out, be covered, or brush her teeth. In addition, she can make signs for "I'm sorry," "I hurt," "Hurry," "Give me," and a *myriad* of other terms that are familiar to young children. This *urbane* animal can indicate that she *craves* more dessert by putting her fingers together ("more") and then placing her index and second fingers on top of her tongue ("sweet"). It is *irrelevant* that Washoe cannot actually talk. What is important, however, is the consummate* ease with which she has mastered her daily assignments.

**Sample Sentences** Use the new words in the following sentences.

1. Why did Silas Marner _____ wealth and practice cupidity*?

2. Once the hoax had been concocted*, a _____ of problems arose.

3. The defendant was alleged* to have been an army deserter, but the judge said that was _____ to the case.

4. By embellishing* her work with _____ humor, the sophisticated playwright succeeded on Broadway.

5. The lieutenant confessed to a _____ of ignorance in order to properly evaluate* his corporal's resourcefulness.*

**Definitions** Take the bull by the horns* and match the new words with their meanings.

6. veneer _____ **a.** to desire

7. myriad _____ **b.** countless number

8. urbane _____ **c.** polished, witty

9. crave _____ **d.** thin covering

10. irrelevant _____ **e.** not related to the subject

--- **TODAY'S IDIOM** ---

***to be at large***—not confined or in jail

Since the dangerous criminal was *at large,*
all the townspeople began to buy dogs for protection.

## NEW WORDS

**deem**
dēm

**inherent**
in hir´ ənt

**buff**
buf

**romp**
romp

**latent**
lāt´ nt

## EASY TO TRAIN

The chimpanzees are *deemed* by scientists to be the closest to man of all the living apes; consequently, they are fairly easy to train. Several years ago, two married researchers embarked on an interesting project: they reared and trained a chimp in almost the same manner as they would have raised a child. The animal did beautifully, convincing the couple of the *inherent* ability of the chimpanzee. Cinema *buffs* who have seen Tarzan's clever monkey *romp* through the jungle also recognize the *latent* intelligence of those animals.

**Sample Sentences**  Use the new words in the following sentences.

1. Whom do you _____ to be the bulwark* of the Republican party?

2. The firemen did not have to cajole* the enthusiastic _____ into helping them extinguish the blaze.

3. When the intercity competition began, our team was supposed to _____ over our hapless* rivals.

4. At the age of 42, the artist first became cognizant* of his _____ genius.

5. Certain mice have an _____ alertness that enables them to conquer the researchers' labyrinths.*

**Definitions**  Match the new words with their meanings.

6. deem        _____   **a.** lying hidden

7. inherent     _____   **b.** to move in a lively manner

8. buff (n.)    _____   **c.** inborn

9. romp        _____   **d.** a fan, follower

10. latent       _____   **e.** believe, to judge

--- **TODAY'S IDIOM** ---

*to go against the grain*—to irritate

My uncle is in favor of some protests, but
certain demonstrations *go against the grain.*

ANSWERS ARE ON PAGE 301

# WEEK 18 ❖ DAY 4

NEW WORDS

tortuous
tôr´ chü əs

itinerant
ī tin´ ər ənt

peregrination
per ə grə nā´ shən

conjugal
kon´ jə gəl

barometer
bə rom´ ə tər

## MORE FACTS ABOUT CHIMPS

Chimps in the laboratory have demonstrated their ability to find their way out of the most *tortuous* maze. They can press buttons, manipulate levers, avoid shocks, etc. When food is placed out of reach, the animals can prepare a ladder of boxes to reach it. In his natural habitat* the chimpanzee is something of an *itinerant*. He goes his nomadic* way through the jungle, living on fruit, insects, and vegetables. With the aid of his long, powerful hands he can swing rapidly from tree to tree and cover considerable ground in his *peregrinations*. Chimps are loyal in their *conjugal* relationships, taking only one mate at a time. That may be another *barometer* of these animals' superior intelligence.

**Sample Sentences** Use the new words in the following sentences.

1. The other drivers were nettled* about the ease with which our car ascended* the _____ road.

2. Arguments over money have often led to _____ havoc.*

3. The sedentary* twin was content to follow his brother's _____ on a map.

4. Signs were posted in the lobby to prevent _____ beggars and others of that ilk* from entering.

5. The warmth of Mr. Smythe's greeting each morning may be construed* as an excellent _____ of his health.

**Definitions** Match the new words with their meanings.

6. tortuous _____ a. wandering

7. itinerant _____ b. winding

8. peregrination _____ c. travel

9. conjugal _____ d. relating to marriage

10. barometer _____ e. instrument for measuring change

─────── **TODAY'S IDIOM** ───────

***to wink at*—to pretend not to see**

There was a plethora* of evidence to show that the border guards would *wink at* illegal shipments if they were paid in advance.

ANSWERS ARE ON PAGE 301

While it is true that scientists have had remarkable success in teaching chimpanzees to communicate, we can be certain that even super-monkeys would have difficulty with any of the words below. However, higher animals who apply themselves can master all of them.

Match the twenty words with their meanings. Write the letter that stands for the definition in the appropriate answer space. (Note the similarity between numbers 8 and 9.)

## REVIEW WORDS
_____ 1. abortive
_____ 2. accommodate
_____ 3. barometer
_____ 4. buff (n.)
_____ 5. conjugal
_____ 6. crave
_____ 7. deem
_____ 8. inherent
_____ 9. innate
_____ 10. irrelevant
_____ 11. itinerant
_____ 12. latent
_____ 13. modify
_____ 14. myriad
_____ 15. peregrination
_____ 16. romp
_____ 17. spontaneous
_____ 18. tortuous
_____ 19. urbane
_____ 20. veneer

## DEFINITIONS
a. not related to the subject
b. thin covering
c. fruitless, failing
d. natural
e. polished, civilized
f. to make fit, adjust to
g. on the spur of the moment
h. move in a lively manner
i. to desire
j. instrument for measuring change
k. winding
l. inborn
m. believe, to judge
n. going from place to place
o. a fan, follower, enthusiast
p. travel (n.)
q. relating to marriage, connubial*
r. countless number
s. to change
t. lying hidden

## IDIOMS
_____ 21. under the wire
_____ 22. to be at large
_____ 23. go against the grain
_____ 24. wink at

u. pretend not to see
v. just in time
w. to irritate
x. not confined or in jail

Now check your answers on page 301. Make a record of those words you missed.

## WORDS FOR FURTHER STUDY          MEANINGS
1. _____  _____
2. _____  _____
3. _____  _____
4. _____  _____
5. _____  _____

# WORDSEARCH 18

❖ Using the clues listed below, fill in each blank in the following story with one of the new words you learned this week.

## *A Shameful Situation*

The plight of the migrant farm worker continues to frustrate the U.S. Labor Department, court officials, legislators, religious groups, and community agencies. Men, women, and children toil six and seven days a week to earn as little as $50 to $60 a week after being overcharged for their food, medicine, and basic living needs. They are housed in ramshackle dormitories, often with non-functioning toilets—a ① _____ of their employers' contempt for them; they lack hot water and showers, and are given food that is barely fit for human consumption.

Unscrupulous contractors scour the countryside in search of homeless, ② _____, and unemployed men and women, offering to put them to work at good jobs picking fruits and vegetables. The U.S. Labor Department investigates the ③ _____ of complaints of abused workers, issues fines, and revokes the licenses of contractors. But many such shady employers pay the fines (which they ④ _____ to be operating expenses) and continue to run company stores that cheat the workers, subjugate them with drugs and alcohol, ⑤ _____ them with advances on their paltry wages at high interest, and use violence against those whom they regard as troublemakers.

Fred Jones, a typical migratory worker from South Carolina, claims to have worked for $6 cash out of his $158 check. His story is repeated by hundreds of others who have been treated shabbily by corrupt contractors. Until sufficient funds are allocated by state and federal agencies, and until there is the proper public response, these abuses will continue.

## Clues

① 4th Day

② 4th Day

③ 2nd Day

④ 3rd Day

⑤ 1st Day

## NEW WORDS

**megalomania**
meg´ ə lō mā´ nēə

**profligate**
prof´ lə git

**strife**
strīf

**legion**
lē´ jən

**coup**
kü

# WEEK 19 ❖ DAY 1

## TROUBLE IN RURITANIA

King Andre of Ruritania was afflicted* with *megalomania*, and the people of his country suffered, as a result. After ten years of his *profligate* rule, the treasury was bankrupt, unemployment was rampant*, domestic *strife* was mounting, and the number of the king's opponents who were incarcerated* were *legion*. Following a bloodless *coup*, his nephew, Prince Schubert, took command of the poor nation.

**Sample Sentences** Based upon your understanding of the new words, as discovered from the context, place them in the spaced provided.

1. With a singular* disregard for his family, the _____ husband spent his salary on alcohol.

2. Each spouse said that the other was culpable* for their conjugal* _____ .

3. "The number of my followers is _____ ," said the flamboyant* politician.

4. The necessity for executing the leaders of the abortive* _____ was obviated* when they committed suicide.

5. Hitler's _____ was a veneer* for his insecurity and feelings of inferiority.

**Definitions** Match the new words with their meanings.

6. megalomania _____  a. discord, disagreement

7. profligate _____  b. revolution

8. strife _____  c. wasteful

9. legion _____  d. a large number

10. coup _____  e. abnormal desire for wealth and power

---
**TODAY'S IDIOM**

*to play possum*—to try to fool someone;
to make believe one is asleep or dead

Sensing that his life was in jeopardy*, the hunter
*played possum* until the voracious* lion disappeared.

---

ANSWERS ARE ON PAGE 301

# WEEK 19 ❖ DAY 2

**NEW WORDS**

**amnesty**
am´ nə stē

**expatriate**
ek spā´ trē āt

**exonerate**
eg zon´ ə rāt´

**fiat**
fī´ ət

**mendacious**
men dā´ shəs

## PRINCE SCHUBERT IN ACTION

Prince Schubert's first move was to declare an *amnesty* for political prisoners and to invite home all Ruritanian *expatriates*. Those who had been jailed on false charges were *exonerated* by special tribunals. The young leader announced that he would abrogate* all of the oppressive *fiats* that his predecessor had promulgated.* Things began to look up temporarily for the citizens who perceived in Prince Schubert the sincerity, idealism, and honesty that had been lacking in the *mendacious* King Andre.

**Sample Sentences** Use the new words in the following sentences.

1. The publisher's _____ claims led to a myriad* of law suits.

2. When the jury began to deliberate, they were prepared to _____ the culprit.*

3. The itinerant* poet, living abroad for twenty years, was a voluntary _____ .

4. One cannot govern by _____ , the sedentary* mayor quickly learned; it is necessary to get out and meet the citizens if you want their cooperation.

5. We recognized the dictator's _____ as an obvious feint* that would be withdrawn after Christmas.

**Definitions** It will be a red letter day* for you if you can match the new words with their meanings.

| | | | |
|---|---|---|---|
| 6. amnesty | _____ | **a.** | an exile |
| 7. expatriate | _____ | **b.** | lying, untrue |
| 8. exonerate | _____ | **c.** | a general pardon |
| 9. fiat | _____ | **d.** | to free from guilt |
| 10. mendacious | _____ | **e.** | an official order, a decree |

---
**TODAY'S IDIOM**
---

*it's an ill wind that blows nobody good—*
**someone usually benefits from another person's misfortune**

When the star quarterback broke his leg, the coach gave the rookie his big chance and the youngster made good; the coach mumbled, *"It's an ill wind."*

ANSWERS ARE ON PAGE 301

**NEW WORDS**

**parsimonious**
pär´ sə mō´ nē əs

**pecuniary**
pi kyü´ nē er´ ē

**dismantle**
dis man´ tl

**sumptuous**
sump´ chü əs

**underwrite**
un´ dər rīt´

## REFORM MOVEMENT

In order to improve Ruritania's financial position, an astute* but *parsimonious* treasurer was installed and given wide *pecuniary* powers. He tried to get the little country back on its feet by slashing all waste from its budget, *dismantling* King Andre's *sumptuous* palaces, and firing all incompetents. In addition, Prince Schubert was able to get the United States to *underwrite* a substantial loan that would enable him to start a program of public works. Even so, Ruritania was still in desperate trouble.

**Sample Sentences** Prove that you are not a flash in the pan* by using the new words correctly in the following sentences.

1. I plan to _____ the stereo set and clean all the components.*

2. The _____ feast was prepared with impeccable* care.

3. Unless my boss modifies* his _____ attitude, a fractious* picket line is going to be erected.

4. Clarence Day deemed* that _____ matters are best handled by men.

5. When our rivals agreed to _____ the cost of our trip, a myriad* of suspicions began to form in my mind.

**Definitions** If you made mistakes above, you can now save face* by matching the new words correctly with their meanings.

6. parsimonious _____    **a.** agree to finance

7. pecuniary _____    **b.** financial

8. dismantle _____    **c.** to strip of covering, take apart

9. sumptuous _____    **d.** miserly

10. underwrite _____    **e.** lavish

---

**TODAY'S IDIOM**

***to know the ropes*—to be fully acquainted with the procedures**

The president of the senior class *knew the ropes* and quickly taught me my duties.

---

ANSWERS ARE ON PAGE 301

**NEW WORDS**

restrictive
ri strik´ tiv

balk
bôk

blunt
blunt

nostalgia
no stal´ jə

rife
rīf

## DISAPPOINTMENT AND DEDICATION

When Prince Schubert asked for additional *restrictive* measures, the people began to *balk*. Speaking on radio, the young reformer explained the reasons for higher taxes and food rationing; he was *blunt* when he stated the need for personal sacrifices. Nevertheless, the resistance to reform was great, and *nostalgia* for the "good old days" of King Andre began to grow. The people admitted that graft and corruption had been *rife* under Andre, but at least "everybody got his slice of the pie." Although Prince Schubert was tempted to quit, he determined that he would help the people in spite of themselves.

**Sample Sentences** Don't pass the buck*! Use the new words in the following sentences yourself.

1. The rebel's innate* hatred of _____ decrees led him to crave* freedom all the more.

2. A string of caustic* epithets* was directed at the recruit by his _____ sergeant.

3. Although the former farm girl pretended to be urbane*, a feeling of _____ always came over her when she heard country music.

4. Criticism of the author was _____ among the coterie* of intellectuals who used to praise him.

5. Jimmy was a lawbreaker, but he would _____ at the idea of carrying a lethal* weapon.

**Definitions** Match the new words with their meanings.

6. restrictive _____ a. widespread

7. balk (v.) _____ b. plain spoken

8. blunt _____ c. to refuse to move

9. nostalgia _____ d. yearning for the past

10. rife _____ e. harsh, confining

---
**TODAY'S IDIOM**

*behind the eight ball*—in trouble

Susan found herself *behind the eight ball* in chemistry when she failed to do the term project.
---

Ruritania is a mythical kingdom, impossible to find on a map and difficult to find in a dictionary. The words that you are about to review, however, are all legitimate, acceptable dictionary words.

Match the twenty words with their meanings. Write the letter that stands for the definition in the appropriate answer space.

## REVIEW WORDS

_____ 1. amnesty
_____ 2. balk
_____ 3. blunt
_____ 4. coup
_____ 5. dismantle
_____ 6. exonerate
_____ 7. expatriate
_____ 8. fiat
_____ 9. legion
_____ 10. mendacious
_____ 11. megalomania
_____ 12. nostalgia
_____ 13. parsimonious
_____ 14. pecuniary
_____ 15. profligate
_____ 16. restrictive
_____ 17. rife
_____ 18. strife
_____ 19. sumptuous
_____ 20. underwrite

## DEFINITIONS

a. revolution, overthrow
b. unrest, discord
c. take apart, disassemble
d. lavish
e. to free from guilt
f. agree to finance
g. false, lying
h. an exile
i. abnormal desire for power
j. plain spoken
k. harsh, confining
l. to refuse to move
m. wasteful
n. an official order, a decree
o. widespread
p. large number
q. financial
r. a general pardon
s. miserly
t. yearning for the past

## IDIOMS

_____ 21. to play possum
_____ 22. an ill wind
_____ 23. know the ropes
_____ 24. behind the eight ball

u. someone profits from another's misfortune
v. be fully acquainted with procedures
w. in trouble
x. try to fool someone

Now check your answers on page 301. Make a record of those words you missed.

## WORDS FOR FURTHER STUDY   MEANINGS

1. _____    _____

2. _____    _____

3. _____    _____

4. _____    _____

5. _____    _____

❖ Using the clues listed below, fill in each blank in the following story with one of the new words you learned this week.

## *Ogopogo*

Accounts of supersized creatures such as the Loch Ness Monster and the Abominable Snowman are ① _____ . Despite the lack of hard evidence, some people continue to believe that the depths of our lakes and isolated mountain caves remain the dwelling places of fantasy figures.

Now, a new star for the credulous has surfaced. Japanese television was asked to ② _____ a search for Ogopogo, a long-necked reptilian creature said to inhabit Lake Okanagan in the mountains of south-central British Columbia. Ogopogo stories are ③ _____ in that area as people produce photos of rippling water and shadows resembling an enormous serpent with flippers, gliding slowly in large circles.

Those who ④ _____ at what they regard as nonsense and pagan superstition are quite ⑤ _____ in belittling Ogopogo fans. Nevertheless, the legends, which have a life of their own, happily, have brought thousands of tourists and business to the Okanagan Valley.

Recognition of the creature now exists in British Columbia's environmental law which provides protection for Ogopogo. The official description reads, "An animal in Okanagan Lake, other than a sturgeon, that is more than three meters in length, and the mates or offspring of that animal."

Been wondering about the creature's name? Ogopogo comes from an English music hall song: "His mother was an earwig; his father was a whale; a little bit of head and hardly any tail—and Ogopogo was his name."

## Clues

① 1st Day

② 3rd Day

③ 4th Day

④ 4th Day

⑤ 4th Day

**NEW WORDS**

**reviled**
ri vīld´

**derogatory**
di rog´ ə tôr ē

**indict**
in dīt´

**nebulous**
neb´ yə ləs

**pesky**
pes´ kē

## LA CUCARACHA—THE COCKROACH

The poor cockroach has been called the "most *reviled* creature on the face of the earth." Nobody loves him—except, perhaps, another cockroach. Fiction, nonfiction, and poetry are replete* with *derogatory* references to these ubiquitous* bugs. Public health officials are quick to *indict* the insects as carriers of viruses that cause yellow fever and polio. Although past evidence has been somewhat *nebulous*, recent studies also show that an allergy to roaches may contribute significantly to asthma. Little wonder, therefore, that the *pesky* cockroach is under attack.

**Sample Sentences** Use the new words in the following sentences.

1. Because the contract offer was a _____ one, the union leaders balked* at it.

2. Ezra Pound, the expatriate* poet, was _____ for his pro-Fascist remarks.

3. When the grand jury refused to _____ him, the mobster was exonerated.*

4. Every time his accountant called with _____ pecuniary* problems, Ben was very blunt* with him.

5. The columnist was ordered to recant* her _____ statements.

**Definitions** Match the new words with their meanings.

6. reviled _____ **a.** annoying

7. derogatory _____ **b.** belittling*, disparaging*

8. indict _____ **c.** unclear, vague

9. nebulôus _____ **d.** scolded

10. pesky _____ **e.** accuse

---
### TODAY'S IDIOM
---

***left holding the bag*—to be left to suffer the blame**

The profligate* businessman left his distraught* partner *holding the bag*.

ANSWERS ARE ON PAGE 301

# WEEK 20 ❖ DAY 2

**NEW WORDS**

**redolent**
red´ l ənt

**repose**
ri pōz´

**omnivorous**
om niv´ ər əs

**disparate**
dis´ pər it

**abstemious**
ab ste´ mē əs

## WAITER, PLEASE TAKE THIS BOWL OF SOUP BACK TO THE KITCHEN

In addition to menacing our health, cockroaches are smelly, filthy, and ugly. Upon entering a cellar that is *redolent* with their aroma, you are not likely to forget the odor. And when you spy the foul culprits* creating havoc* in your sugar bowl or in *repose* atop your chocolate cake, your disposition may be exacerbated.* Roaches are *omnivorous* and will feast upon such *disparate* items as wallpaper, upholstery, nylon stockings, and beer. No one can accuse the hungry and thirsty bugs of being *abstemious.*

**Sample Sentences** The words above fit into the blanks below.

1. While the palace guards were in _____ , the rebels' coup* began in earnest.

2. Coach Fischer issued a fiat* that required that his players be _____ .

3. The _____ scent that came from the bakery created in Eloise a sense of nostalgia* for her grandmother's bread.

4. _____ eaters find the dietary laws in some hotels to be too restrictive.*

5. Regardless of how _____ their crimes were, all the prisoners were freed by the general amnesty.*

**Definitions** Match the new words with their meanings.

6. redolent       _____   **a.** different

7. repose (n.)    _____   **b.** fragrant

8. omnivorous     _____   **c.** moderate in eating or drinking

9. disparate      _____   **d.** eating any kind of food

10. abstemious    _____   **e.** state of rest

---

**TODAY'S IDIOM**

*a lick and a promise*—to do something in a hasty and superficial manner

The meticulous* housewife was in so much of a hurry that
she could only give the apartment *a lick and a promise.*

---

## NEW WORDS

**extant**
ek´ stənt or
ek stant´

**vicissitudes**
və sis´ ə tüdz

**edifice**
ed´ ə fis

**sultry**
sul´ trē

**trenchant**
tren´ chənt

## THE ROACH LIVES ON

Cockroaches are the oldest *extant* winged insects, having been traced back over 350 million years. They have endured the *vicissitudes* of weather, natural disasters, war, and planned liquidation.* They reside comfortably in caves in South America, in transcontinental airplanes, on mountain tops, in Park Avenue *edifices,* and in television sets. The climate may be *sultry* or frigid but roaches persevere.* In the words of one writer, "The miraculous survival of the roach is explained by its inherent* adaptability." In fact, a *trenchant* analysis made the point that any forthcoming nuclear war will be won by roaches, not Russians, Chinese, or Americans.

**Sample Sentences** Use the new words in the following sentences.

1. Hundreds of _____ copies of Shakespeare's signature came from the same prolific* forger.

2. The _____ of life in the Medical Corps are not for the squeamish.*

3. We originally planned on a skyscraper but had to settle for a truncated* _____ .

4. When he learned that the movie was to be replete* with _____ scenes, the cautious banker refused to underwrite* its cost.

5. General Fox submitted a _____ report on the enemy's latent* strength.

**Definitions** Match the new words with their meanings.

6. extant _____ a. keen, incisive*

7. vicissitudes _____ b. difficulties

8. edifice _____ c. extremely hot and moist, torrid

9. sultry _____ d. still existing

10. trenchant _____ e. a building

---
**TODAY'S IDIOM**

*tongue in cheek*—insincerely

Speaking with his *tongue in his cheek*, the parsimonious*
employer promised to double everyone's wages.

---

ANSWERS ARE ON PAGE 301

# WEEK 20 ❖ DAY 4

## NEW WORDS

**puissant**
pyü´ ə sent or
pyü is´ nt

**unabated**
un´ ə bāt´ id

**maudlin**
môd´ lən

**levity**
lev´ ə tē

**lugubrious**
lü gü´ brē əs

## TONGUE IN CHEEK*?

The U.S. Public Health Service admits to frustration* in its attempts to destroy the cockroach. As soon as the scientists devise a *puissant* chemical, some bugs succumb.* But the hardy ones survive and breed a resistant strain. Since the average female produces close to three hundred descendants, little hope is held out for a final solution to the roach problem. Nevertheless, extermination campaigns continue *unabated*. Surprisingly, some sentimental souls become *maudlin* as they consider the persecution of the insects. A writer noted for his *levity* made a *lugubrious* plea for a crash program of aid for the cockroach, calling him "a victim of his slum environment."

**Sample Sentences**  Use the new words in the following sentences.

1. She advocated* _____ music as appropriate background for the funeral scene.

2. Although the debater's rebuttal was _____ , it was totally irrelevant.*

3. The plague continued _____ , and the hapless* Friar John was unable to deliver the note to Romeo.

4. A good barometer* of the reunion's success was the number of _____ songs that the alumni sang.

5. Dean Flanigan admonished* us for our _____ at the graduation exercises.

**Definitions**  Match the new words with their meanings.

6. puissant _____ a. sentimental

7. unabated _____ b. very sad

8. maudlin _____ c. lightness of disposition

9. levity _____ d. without subsiding

10. lugubrious _____ e. powerful

---
**TODAY'S IDIOM**
---

*to take the wind out of one's sails*—to remove someone's advantage

Although Edna was bristling* with anger when she stormed in, I *took the wind out of her sails* by voicing my own displeasure at the way she had been treated.

There are many choice epithets* for cockroaches, and over the centuries man has been most resourceful* in concocting* adjectives to describe the insects. Whether you are going to get excited over a roach, write a poem, take a College Board examination, or compose a letter to a loved one, it helps to have a rich vocabulary.

Match the twenty words with their meanings. Write the letter that stands for the definition in the appropriate answer space.

| REVIEW WORDS | | DEFINITIONS | |
|---|---|---|---|
| ____ | **1.** abstemious | **a.** | different |
| ____ | **2.** derogatory | **b.** | sentimental |
| ____ | **3.** disparate | **c.** | building |
| ____ | **4.** edifice | **d.** | very sad |
| ____ | **5.** extant | **e.** | humor, lightness of disposition |
| ____ | **6.** indict | **f.** | vague, not clear |
| ____ | **7.** levity | **g.** | expressing a low opinion |
| ____ | **8.** lugubrious | **h.** | eating any kind of food |
| ____ | **9.** maudlin | **i.** | accuse |
| ____ | **10.** nebulous | **j.** | state of rest |
| ____ | **11.** omnivorous | **k.** | still existing |
| ____ | **12.** pesky | **l.** | powerful |
| ____ | **13.** puissant | **m.** | annoying |
| ____ | **14.** redolent | **n.** | fragrant |
| ____ | **15.** repose | **o.** | moderate in eating or drinking |
| ____ | **16.** reviled | **p.** | keen, sharp, biting |
| ____ | **17.** sultry | **q.** | torrid |
| ____ | **18.** trenchant | **r.** | difficulties |
| ____ | **19.** unabated | **s.** | without subsiding |
| ____ | **20.** vicissitudes | **t.** | scolded |

## IDIOMS

| | | | |
|---|---|---|---|
| ____ | **21.** left holding the bag | **u.** | insincerely |
| ____ | **22.** a lick and a promise | **v.** | left to suffer the blame |
| ____ | **23.** tongue in cheek | **w.** | do something in a cursory* manner |
| ____ | **24.** take the wind out of one's sails | **x.** | remove someone's advantage |

Now check your answers on page 301. Make a record of those words you missed.

**WORDS FOR FURTHER STUDY**      **MEANINGS**

1. _____    _____

2. _____    _____

3. _____    _____

4. _____    _____

5. _____    _____

# HAPLESS HEADLINES
## (From Week 20)

❖ Restore meaning to the headlines below by inserting the word that the careless typesetter omitted.

**a.** Pesky
**b.** Maudlin
**c.** Repose
**d.** Abstemious
**e.** Sultry
**f.** Vicissitudes
**g.** Redolent
**h.** Levity
**i.** Derogatory
**j.** Unabated
**k.** Reviled
**l.** Puissant
**m.** Nebulous
**n.** Trenchant
**o.** Lugubrious
**p.** Disparate
**q.** Indict
**r.** Extant
**s.** Omnivorous
**t.** Edifice

1. Rioting Continues _____ in Men's Correctional Facility

2. Torch Singer's _____ Songs Raise Temperature in Night Club

3. _____ Life-Style Results in Huge Weight Loss for Actor

4. Architect Celebrated for New All-Glass _____

5. Serious Judge Will Tolerate No _____ in His Courtroom

6. Grand Jury Set to _____ Bookkeeper in Million Dollar Fraud

7. Baseball Manager to Apologize for _____ Remarks about Umpire

8. Only Three Copies of Shakespeare's Handwriting _____ , Says Elizabethan Scholar

9. Handicapped Climbers Overcome Many _____ to Scale Mt. Everest

10. Dictator _____ by South American Patriots

# WORDSEARCH 20

❖ Using the clues listed below, fill in each blank in the following story with one of the new words you learned this week.

## *Chlorine Compounds on Trial*

The chances are that the water supply where you live is disinfected by chlorine, one of the elements on the periodic table. Yet, ①_____ complaints about chlorine continue ②_____ , identifying it as a health and environmental risk.

Greenpeace, the environmental activist group, stands ready to ③_____ chlorinated organic elements, alleging that they are toxic. The Federal Environmental Protection Agency is reexamining the health hazards that are prevalent when materials containing chlorine are processed at high temperatures. And, worldwide, nations are banning chlorine compounds that destroy the earth's protective ozone layer. Harsh treatment, it would seem, for one of nature's basic elements, a component of the table salt we use.

When we enter a pool that is ④_____ with the aroma of chlorine, we don't associate it with the ⑤_____ element now being blamed for tumors, reproductive problems, arrested development, destruction of wildlife, and sundry other ills that plague our planet.

A scientist with the Environmental Defense Fund thinks that chlorinated chemicals should be phased out. "We know they will be persistent if they get into the environment," she said. "They are soluble, so they will build up in the fat of fish, birds, and people."

## Clues

① 1st Day
② 4th Day
③ 1st Day
④ 2nd Day
⑤ 1st Day

ANSWERS ARE ON PAGE 301

# WEEK 21 ❖ DAY 1

**NEW WORDS**

scion
sī´ ən

indoctrinate
in dok´ trə nāt

opulence
op´ yə ləns

obsequious
əb sē´ kwē əs

fulsome
fül´ səm

## LOCKED IN AN IVORY EDIFICE*

Prince Siddhartha Gautama was the *scion* of a family of warrior-kings in northern India. He was being *indoctrinated* for the time when he would assume his father's throne. Growing up in an atmosphere of *opulence,* the young prince was constantly shielded from the cruel realities of the world. An army of *obsequious* servants and tutors catered to his every desire, providing Siddhartha with instruction in riding, fencing, dancing, and painting—while lavishing *fulsome* praise upon him. It wasn't until the prince was thirty that he took the first step that led to his becoming the Buddha, one of the world's greatest spiritual leaders.

**Sample Sentences** Use the new words in the following sentences. (Which two words are almost synonymous?)

1. It was not until the wreckers began to dismantle* the old edifice* that they discovered its real _____ .

2. As the _____ of a family of wealthy bankers, Rothschild never had to face the vicissitudes* of life.

3. Uriah Heep's _____ manner nettled* all but the most gullible.*

4. In order to _____ the captive, his jailers repeatedly reviled* capitalism while praising communism.

5. The actress received _____ compliments from her friends but trenchant* criticism from the reviewers.

**Definitions** Match the new words with their meanings.

6. scion _____ a. seeking favor, fawning

7. indoctrinate _____ b. child, descendant

8. opulence _____ c. wealth, riches

9. obsequious _____ d. excessive, insincere

10. fulsome _____ e. to teach certain principles

---
**TODAY'S IDIOM**

*two strings to one's bow*—two means of achieving one's aim

The salesman had *two strings to his bow*—if a phone call didn't get results, he would appear in person.

---

## NEW WORDS

**lush**
lush

**destitution**
des´ tə tü´ shən

**ponder**
pon´ dər

**supplication**
sup´ lə kā´ shən

**decadence**
dek´ ə dəns

## SIDDHARTHA'S EYES ARE OPENED

One day, Prince Siddhartha expressed the desire to leave his *lush* surroundings and ride out among his people. He was profoundly shaken by the misery, *destitution,* disease, and excruciating* pain with which his people were constantly afflicted.* Retiring to his room to *ponder* over what he had seen, he remained there for several days, deaf to the *supplication* of those who pleaded with him to come forth. It seemed to Siddhartha that his life had been redolent* with *decadence,* and he was determined to make amends.

**Sample Sentences** Use the new words in the following sentences.

1. The _____ stage setting drew applause from the theater buffs.*

2. In the hospital, the alcoholic had time to _____ over the need to be abstemious.*

3. As the traveler followed the tortuous* path up the Kentucky mountain, he was sickened by the _____ which he saw.

4. Through _____ , the fraternity head hoped to end the strife* among the members.

5. Rumors of Rome's _____ were rife* among the barbarian tribes.

**Definitions** Match the new words with their meanings.

6. lush _____ **a.** decay

7. destitution _____ **b.** extreme poverty

8. ponder _____ **c.** to consider carefully

9. supplication _____ **d.** earnest prayer

10. decadence _____ **e.** luxurious, elaborate

---
### TODAY'S IDIOM

*on tenter hooks*—in a state of anxiety
(cloth used to be stretched or "tentered" on hooks)

The indicted* clerk was kept *on tenter hooks* by the district attorney.

---

ANSWERS ARE ON PAGE 302

NEW WORDS

penance
pen´ əns

ascetic
ə set´ ik

desultory
des´ əl tôr´ ē

disciple
də sī´ pəl

metamorphosis
met´ ə mör´ fə sis

## THE ENLIGHTENED ONE

Siddhartha exchanged his sumptuous* garments for a monk's yellow robe and went out into the world to do *penance* for what he considered to be his previous life of sin. First he would cleanse himself by becoming an *ascetic;* then he would study Hindu wisdom in order to be prepared to help his suffering people. After six years of *desultory* wandering and attracting only a handful of *disciples,* Siddhartha came to a huge tree near the Indian city of Gaya. For seven weeks he sat beneath its branches, seeking an answer for his personal torment. Finally, it is said, he underwent a *metamorphosis,* becoming the Enlightened One—the Buddha.

**Sample Sentences**  Use the new words in the following sentences.

1. Billy the Vampire is the only extant* _____ of Count Dracula.

2. In a remarkable _____ , her lugubrious* mood changed to one of levity.*

3. Following a lengthy diatribe* against mendacity*, the priest imposed _____ upon the sinner.

4. The cave of the _____ lacked the opulence* and lush* decoration of his former mansion.

5. Larry's compositions proceed in a _____ manner despite the supplication* of his English teacher.

**Definitions**  Match the new words with their meanings.

6. penance          _____    **a.**  change

7. ascetic (n.)      _____    **b.**  atonement for sin

8. desultory         _____    **c.**  occurring by chance, disconnected

9. disciple          _____    **d.**  one who practices self-denial and devotion

10. metamorphosis _____    **e.**  follower

---
**TODAY'S IDIOM**

***the fat is in the fire*—the mischief is done**

We implored* him to desist* but he said that *the fat was already in the fire.*

---

## NEW WORDS

**bona fide**
bō´ nə fīd´

**salvation**
sal vā´ shən

**materialism**
mə tir´ ē ə liz´ əm

**nurture**
ner´ chər

**nirvana**
nir vä´ nə

## LOVE OVER HATRED, GOODNESS OVER EVIL

Buddha outlined the three paths that men might travel: worldly pleasure, self-torment, and the middle path. Only through the middle path could man achieve *bona fide* peace and *salvation*. One had to repudiate* *materialism*, keep his self-control, restrict speech, be open-minded, never lie or steal, reject selfish drives, *nurture* goodness, etc. Buddha continued to preach until the age of eighty, spreading the philosophy that man has the power to shape his own destiny. Through good deeds and pure thoughts man may reach *nirvana*. Interestingly enough, the man who objected to traditional religious worship was to become idolized by millions throughout the world.

**Sample Sentences** Use the new words in the following sentences.

1. In order to _____ good will, the management will do anything to accommodate* its guests' special needs.

2. When we saw the hundreds of _____ petitions, we realized that the number of people who supported the candidate was legion.*

3. The megalomaniac* believed that he alone had the answer to mankind's _____ .

4. Rosalie found solace* in the conviction that one day mankind would reach Shangri-la, Utopia,* _____ .

5. Disciples* of _____ may know the price of everything but the value of nothing.

**Definitions** Match the new words with their meanings.

6. bona fide _____ **a.** to nourish, support

7. salvation _____ **b.** attention to worldly things and neglect of spiritual needs

8. materialism _____ **c.** freedom from care and pain, Buddhist heaven

9. nurture _____ **d.** genuine

10. nirvana _____ **e.** deliverance from ruin

---
### TODAY'S IDIOM

*like Caesar's wife*—above suspicion

Mrs. Drake would have to be *like Caesar's wife* so that no tinge*
of scandal would embarrass her husband, our new mayor.

---

ANSWERS ARE ON PAGE 302

For the past twenty weeks, each of these review exercises has contained a bit of propaganda to point up the need for you to expand your vocabulary. This week is no exception.

Match the twenty words with their meanings. Write the letter that stands for the definition in the appropriate answer space.

## REVIEW WORDS

|  | DEFINITIONS |
|---|---|
| _____ 1. ascetic | **a.** one who practices self-denial |
| _____ 2. bona fide | **b.** wealth |
| _____ 3. decadence | **c.** concern with possessions |
| _____ 4. destitution | **d.** luxurious |
| _____ 5. desultory | **e.** decay |
| _____ 6. disciple | **f.** disconnected, random |
| _____ 7. fulsome | **g.** deliverance from ruin |
| _____ 8. indoctrinate | **h.** extreme poverty |
| _____ 9. lush | **i.** to teach certain principles |
| _____ 10. materialism | **j.** excessive |
| _____ 11. metamorphosis | **k.** nourish |
| _____ 12. nirvana | **l.** heavenly place |
| _____ 13. nurture | **m.** descendant |
| _____ 14. obsequious | **n.** earnest prayer |
| _____ 15. opulence | **o.** consider carefully |
| _____ 16. penance | **p.** follower |
| _____ 17. ponder | **q.** atonement for sin |
| _____ 18. salvation | **r.** seeking favor |
| _____ 19. scion | **s.** change |
| _____ 20. supplication | **t.** genuine |

## IDIOMS

| | |
|---|---|
| _____ 21. two strings to one's bow | **u.** in a state of anxiety |
| _____ 22. on tenter hooks | **v.** two means to achieve one's aim |
| _____ 23. fat is in the fire | **w.** above suspicion |
| _____ 24. like Caesar's wife | **x.** the mischief is done |

Now check your answers on page 302. Make a record of those words you missed.

## WORDS FOR FURTHER STUDY          MEANINGS

1. _____    _____

2. _____    _____

3. _____    _____

4. _____    _____

5. _____    _____

# WORDSEARCH 21

❖ Using the clues listed below, fill in each blank in the following story with one of the new words you learned this week.

## *History's Most Extraordinary Person?*

In a celebrated essay about Joan of Arc, Mark Twain wrote movingly of her brief moment in the spotlight—two short years in which she made an indelible mark on world history. At age 16 she was illiterate, had never strayed from her sleepy little village, knew nothing of military combat, or courts of law. But at age 17, in a complete ①_____ she was named Commander-in-Chief of the French army, vowing to restore her king to his throne. Joan attracted many fervent followers, and a ②_____ called her "France's ③_____ ."

After much gallantry in battle, this ④_____ heroine was brought low by treachery at the French court and captured by the enemy. Joan defended herself brilliantly at a court trial, although she could neither read nor write. She was able to forecast future events with remarkable accuracy, correctly predicting her own martyrdom.

Mark Twain understood how geniuses such as Napoleon, Edison, and Wagner could develop but one could ⑤_____ the facts for a lifetime without being able to explain how this humble peasant girl could display the qualities of a mature statesman, a learned jurist, and a military wizard. He concluded:

"Taking into account her origin, youth, sex, illiteracy, early environment, and the obstructing conditions under which she exploited her high gifts and made her conquests in the field and before the courts that tried her for her life— she is easily and by far the most extraordinary person the human race has ever produced."

## Clues

① 3rd Day

② 3rd Day

③ 4th Day

④ 4th Day

⑤ 2nd Day

ANSWERS ARE ON PAGE 302

# WEEK 22 ❖ DAY 1

**NEW WORDS**

**juxtapose**
juk stə pōz´

**plight**
plīt

**covert**
kō´ vərt

**cope**
kōp

**incompatibility**
in kəm pat´ ə bil´ ə tē

## FEMALE ALCOHOLICS

When we *juxtapose* the words "woman" and "alcoholic" many readers are surprised. However, the *plight* of America's several million female alcoholics is rapidly increasing in intensity. But the statistics are inexact because it is estimated that there are nine *covert* alcoholics for every one under treatment. Women drink to help themselves to *cope* with life's vicissitudes.* They drink because of financial pressures, *incompatibility,* frustration,* and related reasons.

**Sample Sentences**  Use the new words in the following sentences.

1. If we were to _____ our philosophies, your materialism* would conflict with my idealism.

2. Judge Felder commented with asperity* upon the wife's charge of _____ .

3. Just how our club's president is able to _____ with so many disparate* personalities is something I'll never understand.

4. The _____ of the refugees who wandered about in a desultory* fashion moved us to tears.

5. Woodrow Wilson stated that he found _____ agreements to be reprehensible.*

**Definitions**  Match the new words with their meanings.

6. juxtapose _____ a. quality of being mismated, lack of harmony

7. plight _____ b. to place side by side

8. covert _____ c. predicament, dangerous situation

9. cope _____ d. secret, hidden

10. incompatibility _____ e. to be a match for, to be able to handle

---

**TODAY'S IDIOM**

*plea bargain*—to agree to plead guilty to a lesser charge so as to avoid trial for a more serious offense.

The defendant finally took his lawyer's advice and agreed to a *plea bargain* of third-degree assault.

---

## NEW WORDS

**incapacitated**
in′ kə pas′ ə tāt id

**fabricate**
fab′ rə kāt

**connubial**
kə nü′ bē əl

**demur**
di mėr′

**appellation**
ap′ ə lā′ shən

## A PROFILE OF THE WOMAN WHO DRINKS TO EXCESS

The typical alcoholic woman is above average in intelligence, in her forties, married, with two children. She started drinking socially in high school or college. Although frequently *incapacitated,* she can *fabricate* a story skillfully and thus conceal her true physical condition. She often attributes her alcoholism to *connubial* stress, boredom, or depression. A large percentage of the women give family histories of alcoholism. Most female drinkers would *demur* at the *appellation* of "alcoholic"—and that makes their treatment all the more difficult.

IMPORTANT NOTE: How good a detective are you? Did you spot one of the *new* words that had been introduced earlier? (fabricate) It should be part of your vocabulary now. From time to time in the lessons that follow, your alertness will be tested as a previously learned word is reintroduced.

**Sample Sentences** Use the new words in the following sentences.

1. Dave's metamorphosis* from an honest person to one who could _____ an alibi so adroitly* was amazing.

2. The widow grew maudlin* as she reminisced about her former _____ bliss.

3. I will have to _____ even if I receive a bona fide* invitation to run for the G.O. council.

4. Because he was the scion* of the richest family on our block, Lenny was given the _____ of "Rockefeller."

5. He was ashamed to admit that a pesky* skin rash _____ him for weeks at a time.

**Definitions** Match the new words with their meanings.

6. incapacitated _____    **a.** to object
7. fabricate _____    **b.** a name
8. connubial _____    **c.** to lie, concoct*
9. demur _____    **d.** related to marriage
10. appellation _____    **e.** disabled, made unfit

## TODAY'S IDIOM

***in apple pie order*—in neat order, good condition**

The house was in dreadful condition when Mrs. Maslow arrived, but when she left it was *in apple pie order.*

ANSWERS ARE ON PAGE 302

# WEEK 22 ❖ DAY 3

## NEFARIOUS* EFFECTS OF ALCOHOL

Aside from the reasons offered earlier, doctors have other interesting reasons for the *escalation* in female drinking. They also indict* social acceptance and *indifference* to alcohol's *potential* danger as contributory factors. If women realized the harmful extent of the *cumulative* effect of alcohol, they might taper off in their public and *recondite* drinking. Forty-three percent of the female alcoholics in a survey showed evidence of liver damage, and a quarter of the whole group had a high white-blood-cell count. Almost five percent of the patients died shortly after their release from the hospital.

**NEW WORDS**

**escalation**
es´ kə lā´ shən

**indifference**
in dif´ ər əns

**potential**
pə ten´ shəl

**cumulative**
kyü´ myə lə tiv

**recondite**
rek´ ən dīt

**Sample Sentences** If you can still see clearly after all the references to liquor, use the new words in the following sentences.

1. Many derogatory* statements were heard from those who were opposed to further _____ of the conflict.

2. With complete _____ toward his personal safety, Lt. Regan openly challenged the puissant* forces of the enemy.

3. When destitution* grips an area, there is excellent _____ for trouble.

4. The _____ effect of the summer's sultry* weather was to shorten everyone's temper.

5. The poet's _____ language precluded* any understanding of her theme.

**Definitions** Match the new words with their meanings.

6. escalation _____    a. possible

7. indifference _____    b. accumulated

8. potential (adj.) _____    c. secret, hidden, obscure

9. cumulative _____    d. an increase, intensification

10. recondite _____    e. lack of concern

---

**TODAY'S IDIOM**

*apple polishing*—trying to gain favor by gifts or flattery

If the way to advancement in this company is through *apple polishing,* I quit!

## NEW WORDS

**palliate**
pal´ ē āt

**delude**
di lüd´

**prelude**
prel´ yüd

**chimerical**
kə mer´ ə kəl

**acknowledge**
ak nol´ ij

### DANGER SIGNALS

A potential* female alcoholic should be cognizant* of certain danger signals:

a. Using alcohol in an attempt to *palliate* her problems.
b. *Deluding* herself about the extent of her drinking habits.
c. Drinking at regular time periods, both day and night.
d. Reliance upon alcohol as a *prelude* to a major social obligation.
e. Making unrealistic promises about terminating* her drinking.
f. Using alcohol as a medication for real or *chimerical* illnesses.

If in evaluating* her drinking, a woman *acknowledged* that several of the danger signals applied to her, she should see a physician.

**Sample Sentences** Use the new words in the following sentences.

1. Monte refused to _____ the extrinsic* pressures that were causing him to do poorly in his sophomore year.

2. We must not allow fulsome* praise to _____ us about our actual abilities.

3. The drugs could only _____ the symptoms, not provide the cure.

4. As a _____ to his performance, the bullfighter vowed to do penance* for his sins.

5. The scheme sounded _____ , but we were indoctrinated* to believe that it could work.

**Definitions** Match the new words with their meanings.

6. palliate       _____   a. visionary, imaginary, fantastic

7. delude         _____   b. alleviate, relieve without curing

8. prelude        _____   c. introduction

9. chimerical     _____   d. to fool

10. acknowledge   _____   e. admit

--- **TODAY'S IDIOM** ---

*the Draconian Code*—a very severe set of rules (Draco, an Athenian lawmaker of the 7th century B.C., prescribed the death penalty for almost every violation.)

The head counselor ran our camp according to his own *Draconian Code.*

If you're driving, don't drink! Alcohol does not mix with gasoline! We have seen those slogans on many billboards. Here's a new one: "If you use words, use good ones!"

Match the twenty words with their meanings. Write the letter that stands for the definition in the appropriate answer space.

## REVIEW WORDS

| | | DEFINITIONS |
|---|---|---|
| _____ | 1. acknowledge | **a.** accumulated |
| _____ | 2. appellation | **b.** admit |
| _____ | 3. chimerical | **c.** relieve without curing |
| _____ | 4. connubial | **d.** to lie |
| _____ | 5. cope | **e.** to fool |
| _____ | 6. covert | **f.** a name |
| _____ | 7. cumulative | **g.** predicament |
| _____ | 8. delude | **h.** secret |
| _____ | 9. demur | **i.** intensification |
| _____ | 10. escalation | **j.** to be a match for |
| _____ | 11. fabricate | **k.** obscure, hidden |
| _____ | 12. incapacitated | **l.** imaginary, fantastic |
| _____ | 13. incompatibility | **m.** related to marriage |
| _____ | 14. indifference | **n.** possible |
| _____ | 15. juxtapose | **o.** to place side by side |
| _____ | 16. palliate | **p.** to object |
| _____ | 17. plight | **q.** introduction |
| _____ | 18. potential (adj.) | **r.** lack of concern |
| _____ | 19. prelude | **s.** lack of harmony |
| _____ | 20. recondite | **t.** disabled |

## IDIOMS

| | | |
|---|---|---|
| _____ | 21. plea bargain | **u.** trying to gain favor |
| _____ | 22. in apple pie order | **v.** severe set of rules |
| _____ | 23. apple polishing | **w.** admit guilt on a lesser charge |
| _____ | 24. Draconian Code | **x.** in good condition |

Now check your answers on page 302. Make a record of those words you missed.

**WORDS FOR FURTHER STUDY**     **MEANINGS**

1. _____  _____

2. _____  _____

3. _____  _____

4. _____  _____

5. _____  _____

# WORDSEARCH 22

❖ Using the clues listed below, fill in each blank in the following story with one of the new words you learned this week.

## *Hair Today, . . .*

The fact that a hair salon might charge $40 for a woman's shampoo and haircut but only $20 for the same services for a man is a matter of ①_____ to most citizens. Not so to New York City's Commission on Human Rights, which claimed that such a disparity is discriminatory. Commissioner Dennis De Leon has targeted "gender-based" pricing as a violation of city law.

Consider the ②_____ of the salon owners. They ③_____ the price difference, explaining that it takes much longer to cut a woman's hair and requires the use of additional products. But a spokesperson for the Department of Consumer Affairs said that beauty parlors will have to ④_____ with the situation honestly, just as dry cleaners and used-car dealers did when they were apprised of the law.

"I know that women are fighting for equality," said the owner of a chain of unisex hair salons, "but this is ridiculous. We cut a man's hair in no time but we have to get more money from our female customers because their styling and cutting takes so much longer."

The argument might be the ⑤_____ to an important court case. A city-proposed settlement, however, is to have those salons that are cited for violations of the law offer free haircuts to women for a period of three months before having to pay a stiff fine for repeated offenses.

"It's easier to comply," shrugged one owner (bald, himself).

**Clues**

① 3rd Day

② 1st Day

③ 4th Day

④ 1st Day

⑤ 4th Day

ANSWERS ARE ON PAGE 302

# WEEK 23 ❖ DAY 1

**NEW WORDS**

**heterogeneous**
het´ ər ə jē´ nē əs

**gamut**
gam´ ət

**perspicacious**
per´ spə kā´ shəs

**analogous**
ə nal´ ə gəs

**maladjusted**
mal´ ə jus´ tid

## FROM A TO Z

Ellis Sloane, a teacher of science at a large metropolitan high school, first paid little attention to the fact that his two biology classes were so disparate* in their performance. In most schools the classes are alphabetically *heterogeneous,* with youngsters' names running the *gamut* from Adams to Zilch. But Biology 121 had only A's and B's, whereas Biology 128 had T's, V's, W's, Y's, and Z's. Mr. Sloane, a *perspicacious* teacher, began to perceive* differences between the two groups: while their reading scores and I.Q.'s were roughly *analogous,* it was apparent that Biology 128 was replete* with *maladjusted* students, while Biology 121 had the normal ones.

**Sample Sentences**  Use the new words in the following sentences.

1. The Bureau of Child Guidance has been the salvation* for some _____ children.

2. Our algebra class is a _____ one in which bright students are juxtaposed* with slower ones.

3. Senator Thorpe was _____ enough to realize that the scurrilous* charge would have little effect upon the voters.

4. Although the lawyer acknowledged* that the two cases were hardly _____ , he still felt that he had a good precedent on his side.

5. The actress ran the _____ of emotions in a poignant* performance that thrilled the audience.

**Definitions**  Match the new words with their meanings.

6. heterogeneous _____   a. range

7. gamut _____   b. acutely perceptive, shrewd

8. perspicacious _____   c. poorly adjusted, disturbed

9. analogous _____   d. comparable, similar

10. maladjusted _____   e. dissimilar

---
**TODAY'S IDIOM**

*the distaff side*—women (distaff was a staff used in spinning)

The men had brandy on the porch, while *the distaff side* gathered to gossip in the kitchen.

---

ANSWERS ARE ON PAGE 302

**phenomenon**
fə nom′ ə non

**mortality**
môr tal′ ə tē

**decade**
dek′ ād

**susceptible**
sə sep′ tə bəl

**neurotic**
nù rot′ ik

## WHAT'S IN A NAME?

As Mr. Sloane pursued his investigation of the *phenomenon*, he discovered that a Dr. Trevor Weston of the British Medical Association had corroborated* his findings. Dr. Weston had studied British *mortality* rates over a *decade*, finding that people whose names began with letters ranging from "S" to "Z" had a life expectancy that averaged twelve years fewer than the rest of the population. Furthermore, those at the bottom of the alphabet tended to contract more ulcers, were more *susceptible* to heart attacks, and were more likely to be *neurotic* than those at the top of the alphabet.

**Sample Sentences** Use the new words in the following sentences.

1. Irritability is one of the salient* features of a _____ personality.

2. After a _____ of connubial* acrimony,* the couple decided to consult with a marriage counselor.

3. If a miner were to ponder* over the high _____ rate in his occupation, he might want to quit.

4. Ethan Frome soon learned that his querulous wife was _____ to a variety of ailments.

5. There was no paucity* of witnesses to describe the _____ of the flying saucer.

**Definitions** Match the new words with their meanings.

6. phenomenon _____ **a.** death

7. mortality _____ **b.** suffering from a nervous disorder

8. decade _____ **c.** ten years

9. susceptible _____ **d.** unusual occurrence

10. neurotic _____ **e.** easily affected, unusually liable

---

### TODAY'S IDIOM

*on the qui vive*—on the alert

My mother is always *on the qui vive* for bargains.

---

ANSWERS ARE ON PAGE 302

# WEEK 23 ❖ DAY 3

## NEW WORDS

**pedagogue**
ped´ ə gog

**enunciate**
i nun´ sē āt

**inordinate**
in ôrd´ n it

**irascible**
i ras´ ə bəl

**introspective**
in´ trə spek´ tiv

## THE PERILS OF THE ALPHABET

Dr. Weston is convinced that the *pedagogue* is the culprit.* Since teachers seat their pupils in alphabetical order, the "S" to "Z" child is usually the last to receive his test marks, the last to eat lunch, the last to be dismissed, and so on. As they are the last to recite, these youngsters feel frustrated* because what they had to say had usually been *enunciated* earlier. The *inordinate* amount of waiting that this group has to do causes them to become *irascible* and jittery. "S" to "Z" people also become quite *introspective,* convinced that they are inferior to those at the top of the alphabet.

**Sample Sentences** Use the new words in the following sentences.

1. Reporters were expecting the candidate to _____ his policy on the escalation* of the war.

2. His profligate* son made the parsimonious* old crank even more _____ .

3. Since Alice is so gregarious* it surprised me to learn that she is also an _____ girl.

4. Mr. Ford is proud to be called a teacher, but he demurs* at the title of _____ .

5. In an attempt to show how assiduous* he was, the executive spent an _____ amount of time on his report.

**Definitions** Match the new words with their meanings.

6. pedagogue _____ a. irritable

7. enunciate _____ b. excessive

8. inordinate _____ c. to utter, proclaim

9. irascible _____ d. looking into one's own feelings

10. introspective _____ e. teacher

---

## TODAY'S IDIOM

*to get one's back up*—to become angry

Every time his mother mentioned getting a haircut,
the young guitarist *got his back up.*

---

ANSWERS ARE ON PAGE 302

**perpetuate**
pər pech´ ü āt

**mandate**
man´ dāt

**compensatory**
kəm pen´ sə tô´ rē

**neutralize**
nü´ trə līz

**catastrophic**
kat´ ə strof´ ik

## IN THE NATURE OF EDUCATIONAL REFORM

Mr. Sloane did not want to *perpetuate* the disorders that stemmed from the alphabetical arrangement. Not only did he reverse the seating in his other classes, but he began to badger* the school's administration for a *mandate* to bring about such changes throughout the building. He called it a *compensatory* factor to *neutralize* the *catastrophic* effects of the traditional policy. Soon, Mr. Sloane earned the appellation* of "Mr. Backwards."

**Sample Sentences** Use the new words in the following sentences.

1. Don Ricardo hoped that his son would _____ the family business, but Manuel was too involved with chimerical* schemes to want to run a restaurant.

2. If the draconian* regulations are to continue unabated,* they will have _____ results.

3. Dr. Meyers prescribed medication to _____ the acid condition that had incapacitated* my uncle.

4. As a prelude* to his victory speech, the mayor announced that he considered the large vote to be a _____ from the people.

5. _____ education may help minority groups to cope* with their plight.*

**Definitions** Match the new words with their meanings.

6. perpetuate _____    **a.** serving to pay back

7. mandate _____    **b.** an authoritative order or command

8. compensatory _____    **c.** to counteract

9. neutralize _____    **d.** to cause to continue

10. catastrophic _____    **e.** disastrous

─── **TODAY'S IDIOM** ───

*to bring home the bacon*—to earn a living, to succeed

The man's inability *to bring home the bacon* was the
actual reason for the couple's incompatibility.*

ANSWERS ARE ON PAGE 302

You may not know the alphabet from *aardvark* to *zymurgy*, but you can certainly cope* with *analogous* to *susceptible*.

Match the twenty words with their meanings. Write the letter that stands for the definition in the appropriate answer space.

## REVIEW WORDS

_____ 1. analogous
_____ 2. catastrophic
_____ 3. compensatory
_____ 4. decade
_____ 5. enunciate
_____ 6. gamut
_____ 7. heterogeneous
_____ 8. inordinate
_____ 9. introspective
_____ 10. irascible
_____ 11. maladjusted
_____ 12. mandate
_____ 13. mortality
_____ 14. neurotic
_____ 15. neutralize
_____ 16. pedagogue
_____ 17. perpetuate
_____ 18. perspicacious
_____ 19. phenomenon
_____ 20. susceptible

## DEFINITIONS

a. disastrous
b. irritable
c. teacher
d. disturbed
e. to cause to continue
f. comparable, similar
g. shrewd
h. authoritative command
i. dissimilar
j. range
k. counteract
l. having a nervous disorder
m. excessive
n. looking into one's own feelings
o. unusual occurrence
p. death
q. easily affected
r. serving to pay back
s. ten years
t. to utter, proclaim

## IDIOMS

_____ 21. the distaff side
_____ 22. on the qui vive
_____ 23. to get one's back up
_____ 24. bring home the bacon

u. women
v. on the alert
w. become angry
x. earn a living

## WORDS FOR FURTHER STUDY                MEANINGS

Now check your answers on page 302. Make a record of those words you missed.

1. _____    _____

2. _____    _____

3. _____    _____

4. _____    _____

5. _____    _____

**YOU ARE NOW AT THE MID-POINT OF THE BOOK, AND YOU SHOULD PLAN TO DEVOTE SOME ADDITIONAL TIME TO A REVIEW OF THOSE WORDS THAT YOU MISSED DURING THE PAST TWENTY-THREE WEEKS.**

# WORDSEARCH 23

❖ Using the clues listed below, fill in each blank in the following story with one of the new words you learned this week.

## *Microsociety—An Antidote for School Boredom*

Money, taxes, employment, legislation—these are topics that we associate with the adult world. George Richmond, a Yale graduate who became a ①_____ in the New York City school system, felt that elementary school youngsters could also be interested, even excited, about such issues. He experimented in his own classes with the *Microsociety* in which basic instruction takes place and is reinforced as pupils operate their own businesses, pass laws, live within the parameters of a constitution that they drafted, seek redress within their own judicial system, buy and sell real estate, and so on.

Richmond's book on the *Microsociety* came to the attention of the school board in Lowell, Massachusetts, and their members decided to give it a try in 1981. In much less than a ②_____ the results were quite remarkable: students exceeded the norm in reading and math; 8th graders passed college level exams; school attendance went up to 96%; and the dropout rate took a nosedive in Lowell.

In *Microsociety*'s ③_____ classes, mornings are given over to the traditional curriculum. In the afternoon, the students apply what they learned in activities that run the ④_____ from keeping double entry books, doing financial audits, running a bank, and conducting court sessions to engaging in light manufacture that leads to retail and wholesale commerce.

Other ⑤_____ school systems have since adopted George Richmond's innovative ideas. "*Microsociety*," said a Yonkers, New York principal, "gets kids to role-play life!"

A *Time Magazine* reporter was much impressed with *Microsociety*'s results: "Such an approach would go a long way toward making U.S. public schools a cradle of national renewal."

## Clues

① 3rd Day

② 2nd Day

③ 1st Day

④ 1st Day

⑤ 1st Day

ANSWERS ARE ON PAGE 302

# WEEK 24 ❖ DAY 1

**NEW WORDS**

**anthropologist**
an´ thrə pol´ ə jist

**bizarre**
bə zär´

**inanimate**
in an´ ə mit

**fetish**
fet´ ish

**artifact**
är´ tə fakt

## PRIMITIVE MAGIC

In the course of their studies of other cultures, *anthropologists* have reported numerous customs and practices that seem *bizarre* to the average American. Many primitive people believe that certain *inanimate* objects have a will of their own and possess some magical powers. These *fetishes* may be simple things like a particular feather of a bird or a unique pebble. The *fetish* might have derived its power, according to members of some tribes, from a god who lives within the object and has changed it into a thing of magic. *Fetishes* need not only be natural objects, however. An *artifact* such as a sculpture or carving is also believed to possess supernatural powers.

**Sample Sentences**  Now use your new words in the following sentences.

1. Stones are _____ objects that have no life of their own.

2. It has been suggested that the man who builds a better mousetrap will find the world beating a path to his door to possess this _____ .

3. The explorers saw the golden statue and thought of how much money it would bring them. But their lives would be in danger if they moved it because it was a powerful _____ to the natives.

4. Margaret Mead, the famous _____ , fascinated thousands of readers with her studies of South Seas islanders.

5. It would be rather _____ for a young man to come to school wearing a dress.

**Definitions**  If you have studied the reading selection and the sample sentences, now try your hand at matching your new words with their definitions.

6. anthropologist _____    **a.** an object made by hand, rather than a thing as it occurs in nature

7. artifact _____    **b.** lifeless

8. bizarre _____    **c.** an object that is thought to have magic powers

9. fetish _____    **d.** an expert in the study of the races, beliefs, customs, etc. of mankind

10. inanimate _____    **e.** odd, peculiar, strange, weird

--- **TODAY'S IDIOM** ---

***to get down off a high horse**—to act like an ordinary person*

When Susan discovered that the young man who was trying to make conversation with her was the son of a millionaire, she immediately *got down off her high horse.*

## NEW WORDS

**taboo**
tə bü´

**imprudent**
im prüd´ nt

**prohibition**
prō´ ə bish´ ən

**imperative**
im per´ ə tiv

**taint**
tānt

## FORBIDDEN

An outgrowth of the idea of a fetish* is the closely related practice of *taboo*. Whereas the gods or supernatural powers merely inhabit an object that is a fetish and lend it magic, they will punish the *imprudent* native who violates their *prohibition* of an act or use of an object or word that has become *taboo*. If a *taboo* has been broken, it becomes *imperative* for the offender to be punished. In many cases, however, the *taint* on the community may be removed after the priests have performed a special ceremony. Often, the violator of the *taboo* will be punished or die merely through his own fears of the terrible thing he has done.

**Sample Sentences** Has the context in which your new words appear given you clues to their meaning? Try now to use them in these sample sentences.

1. Unsanitary conditions in the bottling factory caused hundreds of cases of soda to be _____ by dirt and foreign objects. The health department refused to allow the soda to be sold.

2. Although a New Jersey high school principal placed a _____ on boys wearing their hair long, one student fought in the courts and won his case.

3. It is considered _____ to give your computer code word to anyone not fully known to you.

4. It is _____ for certain South Seas islanders to eat some foods before they marry.

5. In the nuclear age it has become _____ for the nations of the world to learn to live in peace.

**Definitions** Now is your chance to test your knowledge of your new words by matching them with their definitions.

6. imperative   _____   **a.** contamination, undesirable substance that spoils something

7. imprudent   _____   **b.** the act of forbidding certain behavior

8. prohibition   _____   **c.** urgent, necessary, compulsory

9. taboo   _____   **d.** forbidden by custom or religious practice

10. taint (n.)   _____   **e.** unwise, not careful

---

### TODAY'S IDIOM

***the first water*—of the best quality, the greatest**

Lebron James is obviously a basketball player of *the first water* who would be of enormous value to any team.

---

146

ANSWERS ARE ON PAGE 303

# WEEK 24 ❖ DAY 3

**NEW WORDS**

**universal**
yü´ nə vėr´ səl

**contemptuous**
kən temp´ chü əs

**absurd**
ab sėrd´

**bigot**
big´ ət

**abhor**
ab hôr´

## AN ABSURDITY

Although it is probably *universal* human behavior to be *contemptuous* of the bizarre* superstitions practiced by inhabitants of unfamiliar cultures, it seems to be somewhat imprudent* to laugh at others before one takes a good, hard look at the *absurd* taboos* and fetishes* one accepts as part of one's everyday life. Isn't it somewhat *absurd* when the "dyed-in-the-wool" *bigot*, who illogically fears the taint* of close association with blacks (behavior that resembles fear of a taboo), spends most of the summer lying in the sun trying to acquire the color he claims to *abhor?* Since doctors tell us that excessive sun-tanning may be a cause of skin cancer, our strange yearning for sun-darkened skin has all the qualities of a fetish.*

**Sample Sentences** Did the starred review words seem familiar to you? Yet, how many were totally foreign several days ago? Keep up the good work now by using your new words in the following sentences.

1. Bob felt _____ of his best friend after he saw him cheating during an exam.

2. The teacher felt like laughing after he heard Sally's _____ excuse for not having done her homework.

3. One politician, a notorious _____ , hopes to get support as a presidential candidate on the basis of his prejudices and intolerance.

4. I _____ some one who is constantly changing channels with a remote while I'm trying to read in the same room.

5. Would relations between countries be simpler if a _____ language were spoken rather than hundreds of separate ones?

**Definitions** Match your new words with their definitions.

6. abhor _____  **a.** ridiculous

7. absurd _____  **b.** present everywhere

8. bigot _____  **c.** expressing a feeling that something is worthless

9. contemptuous _____  **d.** a person who is intolerant of other people or ideas

10. universal _____  **e.** to detest, to despise

---
### TODAY'S IDIOM

*dyed-in-the-wool*—set in one's ways

He was a *dyed-in-the-wool* Republican who would not consider voting for a Democrat.

---

ANSWERS ARE ON PAGE 303

## NEW WORDS

**vulnerable**
vul´ nər ə bəl

**entreaty**
en trē´ tē

**tradition**
trə dish´ ən

**originate**
ə rij´ ə nāt

**inviolable**
in vī´ ə lə bəl

## GESUNDHEIT!

During the Middle Ages most people believed that the devil could enter our bodies when we sneezed, because at that propitious* moment we left our bodies *vulnerable*. However, this catastrophic* event could be avoided if another person immediately made an *entreaty* to God. This was how the practice began of saying "God bless you" after someone sneezes. Although the *tradition* continues today, few people are aware of its history. A superstition *originates* in ignorance—when people are unsure of the causes of events. But it continues *inviolable* over the years because it usually represents our deepest fears.

**Sample Sentences** Use these new words in the following sentences.

1. Some bad habits _____ in adolescence and continue throughout a person's life.

2. The murderer made a(n) _____ to the governor for a pardon.

3. Despite the inexorable* torture, 007 kept the _____ secret of the labyrinth* leading to the underground headquarters.

4. It appears that many computers are _____ to "viruses" that can cause great damage.

5. Eskimos have a(n) _____ of rubbing noses to show affection.

## Definitions

6. vulnerable _____    **a.** begin, arise

7. entreaty _____    **b.** capable of being injured

8. tradition _____    **c.** custom that has been handed down

9. originate _____    **d.** appeal, plea

10. inviolable _____    **e.** safe (from destruction, etc.)

--- **TODAY'S IDIOM** ---

*blue chip*—a highly valuable asset, stock, or property
**In poker, the blue chips are those with the highest value.**

My father's broker recommended that for safety we invest in *blue chip* stocks only.

 ANSWERS ARE ON PAGE 303

And today it's time to strengthen your word knowledge again. You've noticed, of course, that the matching definitions are not always the definitions you may have been familiar with. This is the way language works. It is impossible to provide a one-word synonym or simple definition for a word that you will always be able to substitute for it. Therefore, in our weekly review we hope not only to check your learning, but also to teach you closely related meanings.

Match the best possible definition with the word you studied. Write the letter that stands for that definition in the appropriate answer space.

## REVIEW WORDS

| | | |
|---|---|---|
| _____ | 1. | abhor |
| _____ | 2. | absurd |
| _____ | 3. | anthropologist |
| _____ | 4. | artifact |
| _____ | 5. | bigot |
| _____ | 6. | bizarre |
| _____ | 7. | contemptuous |
| _____ | 8. | entreaty |
| _____ | 9. | fetish |
| _____ | 10. | imperative |
| _____ | 11. | imprudent |
| _____ | 12. | inanimate |
| _____ | 13. | inviolable |
| _____ | 14. | originate |
| _____ | 15. | prohibition |
| _____ | 16. | taboo |
| _____ | 17. | taint |
| _____ | 18. | tradition |
| _____ | 19. | universal |
| _____ | 20. | vulnerable |

## DEFINITIONS

a. a hand-made object
b. unwise
c. one who is not tolerant of others' ideas
d. completely protected
e. a magical object
f. widespread
g. begin, arise
h. person who studies mankind's customs
i. forbidden
j. long-standing practice
k. weird
l. able to be hurt
m. looking down on someone or something
n. to utterly hate
o. without life
p. forbidding of certain actions
q. necessary
r. ridiculous
s. plea, appeal
t. contaminate

## IDIOMS

| | | |
|---|---|---|
| _____ | 21. | to get off one's high horse |
| _____ | 22. | of the first water |
| _____ | 23. | dyed-in-the-wool |
| _____ | 24. | blue chip |

u. the greatest
v. a highly valued asset
w. to act like an ordinary person
x. set in one's ways

Check your answers on page 303. Record your errors and their correct meanings. These words must be studied independently if you want to master them. Use them in original sentences. Also, study the several different definitions a good dictionary provides for each of these problem words.

## WORDS FOR FURTHER STUDY      MEANINGS

1. _____     _____

2. _____     _____

3. _____     _____

# ADJECTIVE LEADERS AND NOUN FOLLOWERS
## (From Weeks 21–24)

a. fulsome
b. covert
c. bona fide
d. lush
e. bizarre
f. susceptible
g. inviolable
h. taboo
i. catastrophic
j. inanimate
k. imprudent
l. maladjusted
m. connubial
n. heterogeneous
o. inordinate

**Directions**  Write the letter corresponding to the vocabulary word (above) in the space provided opposite the noun (below) that it is most likely to precede.

_____ **1.** bliss

_____ **2.** diamond

_____ **3.** praise

_____ **4.** amount

_____ **5.** incident

_____ **6.** purchase

_____ **7.** meeting

_____ **8.** object

_____ **9.** earthquake

_____ **10.** law

❖ Using the clues listed below, fill in each blank in the following story with one of the new words you learned this week.

## Map Makers at Work

We are all caught up in the events that change history and the shape of the countries in Asia, Africa, and the Middle East. Each time a country changes its name or its borders, there are some people who have their work cut out for them. They are the map makers—the cartographers. These skilled artists know it is ① _____ to believe that this year's borders will remain fixed. Has there ever been an ② _____ border?

Looking through an atlas of just a few years back, we realize it is simply an ③ _____ of an ever-changing world. If there is one thing for map makers to do, it is to realize how ④ _____ it is for them to keep abreast of world events.

The study of world history is replete with exciting events that have shaken the economic and political past. Geography is the physical rendering of these events. As history moves and changes our lives, it is up to the cartographer to take the ⑤ _____ lines of a map and shape the picture of this world in motion. A quick search of Google Earth brings our ever-changing planet to our screen.

## Clues

① 2nd Day

② 4th Day

③ 1st Day

④ 2nd Day

⑤ 1st Day

## NEW WORDS

**awesome**
ô´ səm

**eruption**
i rup´ shən

**puny**
pyü´ nē

**debris**
də brē´

**dispersed**
dis pėrsd´

# WEEK 25 ❖ DAY 1

## THE EXPLOSION OF KRAKATOA

There are few sights that are more impressive and *awesome* than the *eruption* of an active volcano. There are few natural events that so singularly* dwarf man's *puny* attempts to control his environment. Perhaps the greatest volcanic *eruption* of modern times took place in 1883 when the island of Krakatoa in Indonesia blew up as the result of a volcanic explosion. An enormous tidal wave resulted that proved catastrophic* to the nearby coasts of Java and Sumatra. New islands were formed by the lava that poured out, and *debris* was scattered across the Indian Ocean for hundreds of miles. Volcanic material, *dispersed* seventeen miles into the atmosphere, created startlingly beautiful sunsets for years afterwards.

**Sample Sentences** Relying on the contextual clues in the paragraph above, use the new words in the following sentences.

1. Fred had been known for his gentle ways, so his friends were stunned by the _____ of angry words that issued from him.

2. We were surprised by the _____ resistance put up by the voracious* tiger to its capture.

3. After her house had burned to the ground, Mrs. Wiley searched through the _____ for her valuable jewelry.

4. Many of those who witnessed the first atomic explosion reported that it was an _____ sight.

5. The fluffy seeds of the milkweed are _____ by the wind.

**Definitions** Now take the final step in learning the new words.

6. awesome     _____    **a.** scattered, spread, broken up

7. debris      _____    **b.** weak, unimportant

8. dispersed   _____    **c.** inspiring terror, weird

9. eruption    _____    **d.** ruins, fragments

10. puny       _____    **e.** bursting out

─────────── **TODAY'S IDIOM** ───────────

*as broad as it is long*—it makes very little difference

Since both jobs pay $7.25 an hour and are equally boring,
it is about *as broad as it is long* whether I take one or the other.

ANSWERS ARE ON PAGE 303

# WEEK 25 ❖ DAY 2

**NEW WORDS**

**obliterate**
ə blit´ ə rāt

**deplorable**
di plôr´ ə bəl

**initiate**
i nish´ ē āt

**conflagration**
kon´ flə grā´ shən

**rue**
rü

## A UNIVERSAL* DANGER

Man's ability to *obliterate* life on this planet has increased at a rapid rate. We are now faced with the *deplorable* prospect of new weapons that can cause destruction of life and property on a scale far beyond our imagination. No matter who takes the first step to *initiate* a conflict, the possibility exists that the *conflagration* will spread and envelop the world. Much thought has been given to ways and means of preventing this catastrophe.* Some consider it mandatory* that the nuclear powers seek agreement on methods of limiting and controlling these weapons, for in the absence of such an agreement, we may *rue* the day atomic energy was made practical.

**Sample Sentences**  Complete the sentences by filling in the blanks.

1. Who could imagine a more bizarre* story than the one having to do with a cow causing the _____ in Chicago?

2. No matter how one tries to delete material from a computer, it is almost impossible to _____ it.

3. You will _____ that display of histrionics* when I asked you to help.

4. She could not imagine how she was going to get him to _____ a conversation about marriage.

5. The hometown fans thought the umpire's decision was _____ .

**Definitions**  Let's put the new words together with their meanings.

6. obliterate _____    a. regret

7. deplorable _____    b. sad, pitiable

8. initiate _____    c. erase, wipe out

9. conflagration _____    d. start, set going

10. rue _____    e. great fire

---
### TODAY'S IDIOM
---

***blow hot and cold*—swing for and against something**

I told Charlie to give up his summer job and come cross-country biking with us. He's *blowing hot and cold* on the deal at this point.

## NEW WORDS

**congenial**
kən jē´ nyəl

**hoard**
hôrd

**sage**
sāj

**aegis**
ē´ jis

**detriment**
det´ rə mənt

## TAKEN FOR GRANTED

The presence of an ever-flowing supply of fresh, clean water is taken for granted. Unfortunately, this *congenial* condition is fast disappearing. As our population increases, as industry consumes more water each year, the level of our underground water supply sinks measurably. There is no way to *hoard* water; there are many ways to conserve it. During a particularly dry spell, New York City found its reservoirs going dry. Only then did the residents begin to heed the *sage* advice to limit the wasteful uses of water. Under the *aegis* of the Water Commissioner, citizens were encouraged to develop habits that would save water. The continued imprudent* waste by each of us of this most basic resource will work to the *detriment* of all.

**Sample Sentences** Here's your opportunity to use your new words.

1. Isn't it a pity we can't _____ the ideal days of autumn?

2. A man may be a _____ everywhere, but at home he's called a "square" by his youngsters.

3. The tree in front of my house has the dubious* honor of being the spot voted the most _____ by the dogs of the neighborhood.

4. It was fortuitous* that at the last moment the mayor offered the _____ of his office in finding a solution to the problem.

5. A settlement that causes _____ to neither side is imperative.*

**Definitions** Remember, words may have many synonyms.

6. congenial _____ a. injury, damage, hurt

7. hoard (v.) _____ b. sympathetic, agreeable

8. sage _____ c. shield, protection, sponsorship

9. aegis _____ d. hide, store, accumulate

10. detriment _____ e. wise man, philosopher

─────────────── **TODAY'S IDIOM** ───────────────

*in the doldrums*—in a bored or depressed state

Mary has been *in the doldrums* since her best friend moved away.

ANSWERS ARE ON PAGE 303

# WEEK 25 ❖ DAY 4

**NEW WORDS**

**longevity**
lon jev´ ə tē

**imbibe**
im bīb´

**virile**
vir´ əl

**senile**
sē´ nīl

**doddering**
dod´ ər ing

## AN AGELESS STORY

Every so often we can read about a man or woman who has reached an age far beyond the limits we ordinarily expect. Reports of a man in Chile or a woman in Turkey who has celebrated the 105th or 110th birthday occur regularly. The natural question is, to what do these people owe their *longevity?* Frequently, the answer concerns the fact that the ancient one liked to *imbibe* regularly of some hard liquor. The photograph will show an apparently *virile* man or robust woman. Somehow, people who reach this advanced age seem to remain eternally sturdy. There are no signs that they have become *senile.* Smoking a pipe, or sewing on some garment, these rare specimens of hardy humanity are far from the *doddering* folk we expect to see.

**Sample Sentences** Use the new words in these sentences.

1. Far from being _____ , the old woman was considered the sage* of the neighborhood.

2. Scientists have placed the _____ of the planet earth unbelievably into the future.

3. It was deplorable* for us to see her _____ around the house with the aid of a cane.

4. If you _____ , don't drive!

5. The boys struck _____ poses to attract the girls on the beach.

**Definitions** Here's your chance to match the new words with their meaning.

6. longevity _____ a. long duration of life

7. imbibe _____ b. masterful, manly

8. virile _____ c. drink

9. senile _____ d. infirm, weak from old age

10. doddering _____ e. trembling, shaking

---
### TODAY'S IDIOM

***burn the midnight oil*—study or work late into the night**

If I'm going to pass the test tomorrow, I will have to *burn the midnight oil* tonight.

---

# REVIEW

WEEK **25** ❖ DAY **5**

Week by week your word-power is being built. It's like putting money in the bank. Remember, in our language there may be many synonyms and related meanings for each word. Knowing one synonym is good, but you will reap greater benefits from knowing several. Below is the matching review for this week.

## REVIEW WORDS

_____ **1.** aegis
_____ **2.** awesome
_____ **3.** conflagration
_____ **4.** congenial
_____ **5.** debris
_____ **6.** deplorable
_____ **7.** detriment
_____ **8.** dispersed
_____ **9.** doddering
_____ **10.** eruption
_____ **11.** hoard
_____ **12.** imbibe
_____ **13.** initiate
_____ **14.** longevity
_____ **15.** obliterate
_____ **16.** puny
_____ **17.** rue
_____ **18.** sage
_____ **19.** senile
_____ **20.** virile

## DEFINITIONS

**a.** trembling, shaking with old age
**b.** regret
**c.** bursting out
**d.** infirm, weak as a result of old age
**e.** wise man, philosopher
**f.** ruins, fragments
**g.** weak, unimportant
**h.** protection, sponsorship, shield
**i.** agreeable, sympathetic
**j.** broken up, scattered, spread
**k.** sad, pitiable
**l.** hurt, damage, injury
**m.** drink
**n.** great fire
**o.** manly, masterful
**p.** inspiring terror, weird
**q.** set going, start
**r.** accumulate, save, store up
**s.** long duration of life
**t.** wipe out, erase

## IDIOMS

_____ **21.** as broad as it is long
_____ **22.** blow hot and cold
_____ **23.** in the doldrums
_____ **24.** burn the midnight oil

**u.** in a bored or depressed state
**v.** makes very little difference
**w.** swing for and against something
**x.** work late into the night

Check your answers on page 303. Don't neglect words you fail to answer correctly. These problem words can be mastered quickly if you write them down, look up their meanings, and practice using them.

## WORDS FOR FURTHER STUDY          MEANINGS

**1.** _____    _____

**2.** _____    _____

**3.** _____    _____

❖ Using the clues listed below, fill in each blank in the following story with one of the new words you learned this week.

## *Save the Whales, at Least*

Have we all become tired of the much used word "environment"? How often we hear or read about the ①_____ state of the world's rivers, forests, air, and earth. When we lose sight of the fact that countless numbers of creatures have become extinct because their environment could no longer sustain them, then we ignore the possibility that these same changes could ②_____ many species that we take for granted.

Our life-style, and that of the billions of others on this earth, puts waste into the air and water. We may ③_____ this careless behavior. While there may still be enough clean water and air for us, the loss of animals and plants can only be a ④_____ to a good life for the generations that follow.

No one suggests that the solutions to our environmental problems are easy. The nations and people of the world are in competition for the limited riches of this planet. It will take the sagest and most dedicated leaders, under whose ⑤_____ educated and concerned citizens will live and work, to protect the environment.

## Clues
① 2nd Day
② 2nd Day
③ 2nd Day
④ 3rd Day
⑤ 3rd Day

## NEW WORDS

**lethargic**
lə thär´ jik

**prevalent**
prev´ ə lənt

**paramount**
par´ ə mount

**remiss**
ri mis´

**hostile**
hos´ tl

## INFORMING THE PUBLIC

Public opinion has an important place in a democracy. The public, often *lethargic*, is susceptible* to a wide variety of influences. The most *prevalent* of these is the mass media. These communications media—the press, radio, and television—have a *paramount* position in initiating,* influencing, and shaping public opinion. Bearing this responsibility, the mass media are often accused of being *remiss* in their duty to inform the public. There has been a great deal of *hostile* comment leveled against these opinion molders.

**Sample Sentences** Based upon your understanding of the new words as discovered from the context, place them in the spaces provided.

1. The audience became extremely _____ when the bigot* began to attack minority groups.

2. Long hair among boys is so _____ today, there is no longer a prohibition against it in most schools.

3. We are all susceptible* to a _____ feeling after a heavy meal.

4. A good politician seeks the _____ issue in his community.

5. We would be _____ if we overlooked the importance of the Internet to the interchange of ideas and information.

**Definitions** Matching words and definitions will prove you've learned them.

6. lethargic _____ **a.** prevailing, common, general

7. prevalent _____ **b.** lazy, indifferent

8. paramount _____ **c.** antagonistic, angry

9. remiss _____ **d.** supreme, foremost

10. hostile _____ **e.** careless, negligent

--- **TODAY'S IDIOM** ---

***to split hairs*—to make fine distinctions**

The mother and child spent a great deal of time arguing about the *hair-splitting* question of whether "going to bed" meant lights out or not.

ANSWERS ARE ON PAGE 303

# WEEK 26 ❖ DAY 2

**NEW WORDS**

rebuke
ri byük´

aversion
ə ver´ zhən

evince
i vins´

vogue
vōg

superficial
sü´ pər fish´ əl

## THE LACK OF FOREIGN NEWS

The critics *rebuke* the press for the fact that most newspapers devote somewhat less than 10 percent of their news space to foreign items. In many hundreds of papers this falls below two percent. Why is there this *aversion* to foreign news? Newsmen claim that readers *evince* no interest in foreign affairs. In order to increase reader interest in foreign news, the *vogue* among editors is to sensationalize it to the point of distortion. Many other papers do only the most *superficial* kind of reporting in this area.

**Sample Sentences** Insert the new words in these sentences.

1. The female _____ to mice is considered absurd* by boys.

2. After a _____ examination of the injured motorist, the doctor said that hospitalization was imperative.*

3. Many a husband has been given a _____ for having imbibed* too fully at an office party.

4. Youngsters often do not _____ any curiosity about the lives of their parents or grandparents.

5. Good manners are always in _____ .

**Definitions** Match the new words with their definitions.

6. rebuke (v.) _____ a. on the surface, slight

7. aversion _____ b. criticize, reproach, reprimand

8. evince _____ c. strong dislike, opposition

9. vogue _____ d. fashion

10. superficial _____ e. show plainly, exhibit

---

### TODAY'S IDIOM

***to strike while the iron is hot*—to take an action at the right moment**

As soon as John heard that his father had won in the lottery, he *struck while the iron was hot* and asked for an increase in his allowance.

---

## NEW WORDS

**jettison**
jet´ ə sən

**inevitable**
in ev´ ə tə bəl

**lucrative**
lü´ krə tiv

**tussle**
tus´ əl

**intrinsic**
in trin´ sik

## PLAYING IT SAFE

The average newspaper office receives many times the amount of foreign news than it has space to print. The editor must include or *jettison* items as he sees fit. It is *inevitable* that his ideas of what the reader want to know, or should know, are decisive. Because the newspaper owners do not want to endanger a *lucrative* business, there is the constant *tussle* between personal opinion and the desire not to offend too many readers or advertisers. It is *intrinsic* to the operation of all mass media that they avoid being extremist in their news coverage or editorials.

**Sample Sentences**  Insert the new words in these sentences.

1. Our conscience must always _____ against our yearning for what we know is taboo.*

2. Man sets the price of gold; it has no _____ value.

3. The pilot decided it would be imprudent* to _____ his fuel over the populated area.

4. It is _____ that children question what their elders accept as tradition.*

5. Each year the contracts offered to star sports figures become more _____ .

**Definitions**  Match the new words with their definitions.

6. jettison      _____   **a.**  sure, certain, unavoidable

7. inevitable    _____   **b.**  essential, natural, inborn

8. lucrative     _____   **c.**  a rough struggle

9. tussle (n.)   _____   **d.**  profitable

10. intrinsic    _____   **e.**  throw overboard, discard

---

### TODAY'S IDIOM

***once in a blue moon*—on a very rare occasion**

His wife complained that they go out to dinner and a show *once in a blue moon*

ANSWERS ARE ON PAGE 303

**NEW WORDS**

acute
ə kyüt´

gist
jist

transient
tran´ shənt

terse
térs

cogent
kō´ jənt

## A FAVORITE NEWS SOURCE

The electronic media—television and radio—have more *acute* problems than does the press when it comes to news reporting. A normal broadcast can cover only a small part of a news day. The object is to transmit the *gist* of a story without supplying its background. Another difficulty of electronic news broadcasting is its *transient* nature; the viewers or listeners may miss an important story if their attention wanders. On the other hand, because radio and television present news in a more *terse* and exciting way, they are accepted as the most *cogent* presentation of news and are preferred and believed above newspapers by most people.

**Sample Sentences** A slow and thorough study is needed today.

1. After the catastrophe,* there was an _____ need for emergency housing.

2. The young lover was susceptible* to _____ feelings of jealousy when he saw his sweetheart dancing with his best friend.

3. She tried to get the _____ of her message into a 25-word telegram.

4. The mayor made a _____ statement in which he rebuked* his election opponent for making a contemptuous* accusation.

5. The best debater makes the most _____ presentation.

**Definitions** This day's work requires careful study.

6. acute _____ **a.** forceful, convincing, persuasive

7. gist _____ **b.** concise, brief, compact

8. transient _____ **c.** essence, main point

9. terse _____ **d.** passing, short-lived, fleeting

10. cogent _____ **e.** sharp, keen, severe

--- **TODAY'S IDIOM** ---

*sleep on it*—postpone a decision while giving it some thought

He didn't want to show his hand* immediately, so he agreed to *sleep on it* for a few more days.

If you've ever watched or played baseball, you know how important a base hit is to each batter. Before the game players spend as much time as possible taking their batting practice. During the game the batter concentrates on every pitch. In the same way, each day you are getting in your "batting practice," and the weekly review is your chance to build up your "batting average." Collect new words with the same concentration that baseball players collect base hits.

## REVIEW WORDS

_____ 1. acute
_____ 2. aversion
_____ 3. cogent
_____ 4. evince
_____ 5. gist
_____ 6. hostile
_____ 7. inevitable
_____ 8. intrinsic
_____ 9. jettison
_____ 10. lucrative
_____ 11. paramount
_____ 12. prevalent
_____ 13. rebuke
_____ 14. remiss
_____ 15. superficial
_____ 16. lethargic
_____ 17. terse
_____ 18. transient
_____ 19. tussle
_____ 20. vogue

## DEFINITIONS

a. show plainly, exhibit
b. fleeting, passing, short-lived
c. throw overboard, discard
d. forceful, convincing, persuasive
e. on the surface, slight
f. a rough struggle
g. compact, brief, concise
h. reprimand, reproach, criticize
i. inborn, natural, essential
j. fashion
k. main point, essence
l. severe, keen, sharp
m. lazy, indifferent
n. negligent, careless
o. unavoidable, certain, sure
p. opposition, strong dislike
q. foremost, supreme
r. general, common, prevailing
s. angry, antagonistic
t. profitable

## IDIOMS

_____ 21. to strike while the iron is hot
_____ 22. to split hairs
_____ 23. sleep on it
_____ 24. once in a blue moon

u. on a very rare occasion
v. postpone a decision
w. take action at the right moment
x. to make a fine distinction

Check your answers on page 303. Take that extra moment now to review and study the words you got wrong.

## WORDS FOR FURTHER STUDY

## MEANINGS

1. _____  _____

2. _____  _____

3. _____  _____

❖ Using the clues listed below, fill in each blank in the following story with one of the new words you learned this week.

## *The Wild West*

History tells us that, in a showdown in 1881, a notorious outlaw, Billy the Kid, was killed. At least that is the ①_____ belief. The real Billy the Kid, William Bonney, is believed to have escaped and lived for many years in Texas. In fact, a man named Brushy Bill Roberts claimed to be the grown-up Billy the Kid.

When Roberts died in 1950, there was the ②_____ question about his true identity. As a result, a computer was brought in to test whether there was anything other than a ③_____ resemblance between the two men. A photo of the Kid and a photo of Roberts were compared on the computer.

In a ④_____ report from the computer technician, the identity of Roberts was proved to be different from that of the real Billy the Kid. Thus, computer analysis allows us to ⑤_____ the idea that Billy the Kid survived the famous gun duel.

## Clues

① 1st Day
② 3rd Day
③ 2nd Day
④ 4th Day
⑤ 3rd Day

## New Words

**pinnacle**
pin´ə kəl

**array**
ə rā´

**obscure**
əb skyur´

**ardent**
ärd´ nt

**culminate**
kul´ mə nāt

# WEEK 27 ❖ DAY 1

## A MUSICAL WORLD

Music reached its *pinnacle* in the nineteenth century. Every leading nation produced its share of great composers. There was a bewildering *array* of national schools and musical styles as the once *obscure* musician came into his own. Music became a widespread and democratic art. The *ardent* music lover turned to Vienna as the music center at the beginning of the nineteenth century. However, Paris was not far behind, especially in the field of operatic music. As the century progressed, the Germans became paramount* in orchestral and symphonic music. The growth of German music can be said to have *culminated* with Ludwig van Beethoven.

**Sample Sentences** Take command of the new words in these sentences.

1. The president faced an imposing _____ of reporters.
2. The party will _____ with the award for the most original costume.
3. The _____ of fame and success is often a transient* stage.
4. The _____ baseball fan went to every home game.
5. Space telescopes are making our _____ planets ever clearer.

**Definitions** Match-up time for new words and definitions.

6. pinnacle _____ a. passionate, eager
7. array _____ b. summit, peak, top, crown
8. obscure (adj.) _____ c. arrangement, system
9. ardent _____ d. unknown, lowly, unclear
10. culminate _____ e. reach the highest point

--- **Today's Idiom** ---

*to break the ice*—to make a beginning,
to overcome stiffness between strangers

All after-dinner speakers *break the ice* by telling
a story or joke at the start of their speeches.

164

ANSWERS ARE ON PAGE 304

# WEEK 27 ❖ DAY 2

**NEW WORDS**

constrict
kən strikt´

prodigy
prod´ ə jē

bereft
bi reft´

falter
fôl´ tər

exultation
eg´ zul tā´ shən

## A GIANT COMPOSER

Beethoven was able to free music from the traditions* that had tended to *constrict* it. He was a child *prodigy* who held an important musical post at the age of 14. He was a successful concert pianist, but when his health began to fail he turned to composing. Even though *bereft* of hearing at the age of 49, he did not *falter* in his work. Some of his later compositions reflect his sadness with his physical condition, but they also evince* an *exultation* about man and life.

**Sample Sentences** Place the new words in these sentences.

1. The catastrophe* left him _____ of all his possessions.

2. She was filled with _____ when she learned her SAT score was near the maximum.

3. It is imprudent* for a youngster to _____ her circle of friends so that there is no opportunity to meet new people.

4. There is universal* wonder when some _____ appears on the stage to perform at the age of 4 or 5.

5. Though he knew well the danger involved, the knight did not _____ as he entered the dragon's cave.

**Definitions** Your personal test follows through matching.

6. constrict _____    **a.** triumphant joy

7. prodigy _____    **b.** stumble, hesitate, waver

8. bereft _____    **c.** deprived of

9. falter _____    **d.** limit, bind, squeeze

10. exultation _____    **e.** marvel, phenomenon

---
### TODAY'S IDIOM

***loaded for bear*—to be well prepared**

When the enemy finally attacked the positions, the defenders were *loaded for bear*.

---

## NEW WORDS

**vitriolic**
vit´ rē ol´ ik

**invective**
in vek´ tiv

**besmirch**
bi smėrch´

**voluminous**
və lü mə nəs

**retrospect**
ret´ rə spekt

## A WORTHY SUCCESSOR

A successor to Beethoven was Johannes Brahms. Also a prodigy,* he was the object of *vitriolic* attacks by other composers because of the individuality of his work. They heaped *invective* upon him for the intensely emotional quality and Germanic style of his writings. However, it was impossible to *besmirch* his talents for long, and he was soon one of the most popular composers in Europe. He produced *voluminous* varieties of compositions. Today, in *retrospect*, his originality is appreciated, and he is placed among the top romantic composers.

**Sample Sentences** Complete the following sentences with the new words.

1. It is difficult to keep _____ out of our discussion about the enemy.

2. One has to be amazed at the _____ amount of information that can be stored on a computer chip.

3. The candidate tried to _____ his opponent's record.

4. In the future we will, in _____ , regard today's bizarre* behavior as quite ordinary.

5. The _____ language used by critics of the new play tended to obliterate* its good qualities.

**Definitions** Study the paragraph and sample sentences for the meanings.

6. vitriolic _____  **a.** insulting, abusive speech

7. invective _____  **b.** bulky, large

8. besmirch _____  **c.** soil, stain, dim the reputation

9. voluminous _____  **d.** biting, burning

10. retrospect _____  **e.** looking backward

───────── **TODAY'S IDIOM** ─────────

*to bring down the house*—to cause great enthusiasm

Popular entertainers can be counted on *to bring down the house* at every public performance.

ANSWERS ARE ON PAGE 304

**NEW WORDS**

**egotist**
ē´ gə tist

**humility**
hyü mil´ ə tē

**pungent**
pun´ jənt

**inveterate**
in vet´ ėr it

**adamant**
ad´ ə mant

## GRUFF BUT LIKEABLE

In his private life Brahms was considered by his friends as an *egotist*. He had an extremely lofty opinion of himself and his talents. He was not noted for his *humility*. Along with this quality, Brahms was known for his *pungent* sense of humor. While his closest friends could accept his biting jokes, others found him difficult to warm up to. Brahms was an *inveterate* stay-at-home. Cambridge University conferred an honorary degree upon him, but he was *adamant* about staying at home and did not go to receive the honor. Despite the ardent* and romantic nature of his music, Brahms never found the right girl and remained single throughout his life.

**Sample Sentences**  Use the new words in these sentences.

1. Doctors agree that it is imperative* that _____ smokers give up that imprudent* habit.

2. The _____ odor of burning leaves marks the autumn season.

3. The umpire was _____ about his decision to call the runner out.

4. We all expect _____ from the actors and actresses who win the Academy Awards.

5. However, we should not be surprised that an award winner is an _____ about his or her performance.

**Definitions**  Make the new words yours through the match-ups.

6. egotist _____  **a.** humbleness, modesty, meekness

7. humility _____  **b.** a vain, conceited person

8. pungent _____  **c.** unyielding, inflexible

9. inveterate _____  **d.** sharply stimulating, biting

10. adamant _____  **e.** habitual, firmly established

---

**TODAY'S IDIOM**

**to pull one's weight**—to do a fair share of the work

Everyone in a pioneer family had *to pull his or her own weight.*

---

Another week to build your vocabulary. Words stand for "things." The more "things" you can recognize, the better able you are to deal with the complicated and changing world. New and unusual situations are more easily handled by those who can utilize the largest number of "things" we call words.

## REVIEW WORDS

_____ **1.** adamant
_____ **2.** ardent
_____ **3.** array
_____ **4.** bereft
_____ **5.** besmirch
_____ **6.** constrict
_____ **7.** culminate
_____ **8.** egotist
_____ **9.** exultation
_____ **10.** falter
_____ **11.** humility
_____ **12.** invective
_____ **13.** inveterate
_____ **14.** obscure
_____ **15.** pinnacle
_____ **16.** prodigy
_____ **17.** pungent
_____ **18.** retrospect
_____ **19.** vitriolic
_____ **20.** voluminous

## DEFINITIONS

**a.** reach the highest point
**b.** inflexible, unyielding
**c.** triumphant joy
**d.** looking backward
**e.** peak, crown, summit
**f.** a conceited, vain person
**g.** bind, limit, squeeze
**h.** biting, burning
**i.** insulting, abusive speech
**j.** system, arrangement
**k.** modesty, meekness, humbleness
**l.** phenomenon, marvel
**m.** stain, soil, dim the reputation
**n.** sharply stimulating
**o.** deprived of
**p.** bulky, large
**q.** hesitate, waver, stumble
**r.** eager, passionate
**s.** firmly established, habitual
**t.** unclear, unknown, lowly

## IDIOMS

_____ **21.** to break the ice
_____ **22.** to pull one's own weight
_____ **23.** to bring down the house
_____ **24.** loaded for bear

**u.** to be well prepared
**v.** to cause great enthusiasm
**w.** to make a beginning
**x.** to do a fair share of the work

## WORDS FOR FURTHER STUDY

Check your answers on page 304. A word missed can now be made part of your vocabulary quite easily. Review the paragraph, sample sentence, definition, and then write your own sentence using the word.

**MEANINGS**

**1.** _____  _____

**2.** _____  _____

**3.** _____  _____

❖ Using the clues listed below, fill in each blank in the following story with one of the new words you learned this week.

## *Hot Enough For You?*

In ①_____ the year 1990 was a year of record high temperatures across the United States. The cause of this problem is complex. There are many proposed explanations, from an increase of population to the greenhouse effect. If, in fact, temperatures are continuing to rise as a result of human activity, there should be an ②_____ search for the causes and the cures.

Scientists are looking into even the most ③_____ aspects of modern society to determine what might be the long-range effects of our activities. They hope that investigations will ④_____ in a program to change the harmful ways we contribute to a dangerous trend.

A small increase in the earth's temperature will lead to major difficulties for everyone. We should not ⑤_____ in our efforts to avoid such disasters.

## Clues

① 3rd Day

② 1st Day

③ 1st Day

④ 1st Day

⑤ 2nd Day

## NEW WORDS

**vulnerable**
vul´ nər ə bəl

**bedlam**
bed´ ləm

**cacophony**
kə kof´ ə ni

**exploit**
eks´ ploit

**propinquity**
prō ping´ kwə ti

## A DANGEROUS SPORT

Racing car drivers are *vulnerable* to dangers that other sportsmen seldom face. Drivers agree that controlling a car at top speeds on a winding course is a singularly* awesome* experience. There is the *bedlam* caused by the roaring motors that move the car from a standing start to 100 miles an hour in eight seconds. One is shaken by the *cacophony* of the brakes, larger than the wheels and producing during the course of a 350-mile race enough heat to warm an eight-room house through a hard winter. The driver needs to be on the alert to *exploit* any mistake by an opponent, and he must be constantly aware of the *propinquity* of sudden death. All of this makes car racing one of the most demanding games of all.

*How was your recall today? Did you spot* vulnerable *as a reintroduced word?*

**Sample Sentences**  Insert the new words in the sentences.

1. Astronauts are alert to the _____ of sudden accidents.

2. The egotist* is _____ to slights and insults.

3. Electronic music is considered nothing more or less than _____ by many.

4. Advertisers spend large sums to _____ the lucrative* teenage market.

5. The winning team's dressing room was a scene of _____ .

**Definitions**  Match your new words to their definitions.

6. vulnerable _____   **a.** discord, harsh sound, dissonance

7. bedlam _____   **b.** open to attack, susceptible

8. cacophony _____   **c.** profit by, utilize

9. exploit (v.) _____   **d.** nearness in time or place

10. propinquity _____   **e.** confusion, uproar

---

### TODAY'S IDIOM

***a white elephant*—a costly and useless possession**

When he discovered the 30-volume encyclopedia, dated 1895,
in his attic, he knew he had *a white elephant* on his hands.

---

       ANSWERS ARE ON PAGE 304

# WEEK **28** ❖ DAY **2**

**disgruntled**
dis grun´ təld

**infallible**
in fal´ ə bəl

**panacea**
pan´ ə sē´ ə

**eradicate**
i rad´ i kāt

**impede**
im pēd´

## THE MYSTERY OF CREATIVITY

In order to create, it is said that a man must be *disgruntled*. The creative individual is usually one who is dissatisfied with things as they are; he wants to bring something new into the world—to make it a different place. There is no *infallible* way to identify a potentially creative person. The speed-up in the sciences has forced schools and industry to seek a *panacea* for the shortages that they face. The need to discover and develop the creative person has been the source of much study. The paramount* objectives of the studies are to *eradicate* anything that will *impede* the discovery of creative talent and to exploit* this talent to the limit.

**Sample Sentences** Place the new words in these sentences.

1. It is the prevalent* mood for youngsters to be _____ with the world situation.

2. Many people hoped that the United Nations would be the _____ for the problems of our time.

3. The criminal tried to _____ all of the witnesses to the bizarre* murder.

4. An _____ sign of spring is the blooming of the crocus.

5. Nothing could _____ the bigot* from his vitriolic* verbal attack.

**Definitions** Match the new words with their definitions.

6. disgruntled _____ **a.** exempt from error, right

7. infallible _____ **b.** unhappy, displeased

8. panacea _____ **c.** wipe out

9. eradicate _____ **d.** cure-all

10. impede _____ **e.** interfere, block, hinder

---
**TODAY'S IDIOM**

*lock, stock, and barrel*—entirely, completely

The company moved its operations to another state *lock, stock, and barrel.*

---

## NEW WORDS

**sedate**
si dāt´

**equanimity**
ē´ kwə nim´ ə tē

**compatible**
kəm pat´ ə bəl

**serenity**
sə ren´ ə tē

**revere**
ri vir´

## THE DUTCH

The first impression one gets of Holland is that it is a calm, *sedate,* and simple land. The slow rhythm of life is even seen in the barges on the canals and the bicycles on the roads. One gradually discovers this *equanimity* of daily existence is not in accord with the intrinsic* nature of the Dutch. These people are moved by strong feelings that are not *compatible* with the *serenity* of the world around them. There is a conflict between the rigid, traditional* social rules and the desire for liberty and independence, both of which the Dutch *revere.*

**Sample Sentences** Pay attention to the fine differences in meaning.

1. There is something absurd* about a well-dressed, _____ man throwing snowballs.

2. The _____ of the countryside was shattered by the explosion.

3. The speaker lost his _____ and began to use invective* when the audience started to laugh.

4. The boy and girl discovered they had many _____ interests.

5. There are not many people in this world whom one can _____ .

**Definitions** Match the new words with their definitions.

6. sedate       _____   a. peaceful repose

7. equanimity   _____   b. quiet, still, undisturbed, sober

8. compatible   _____   c. evenness of mind, composure

9. serenity     _____   d. honor, respect, admire

10. revere      _____   e. harmonious, well-matched

---
**TODAY'S IDIOM**
---

***a feather in one's cap*—something to be proud of**

If she could get the movie star's autograph, she knew it would be *a feather in her cap.*

---

# WEEK 28 ❖ DAY 4

**NEW WORDS**

**irrational**
i rash′ ən əl

**avarice**
av′ ər is

**insatiable**
in sā′ shə bəl

**nadir**
nā′ dər

**moribund**
môr′ ə bund

## TULIP FEVER

The tulip reached Holland in 1593 and was, at first, looked upon as a curiosity. There soon developed an *irrational* demand for new species. Specimens were sold at awesomely* high prices. In their *avarice*, speculators bought and sold the same tulip ten times in one day. The entire Dutch population suffered from the craze. There was an *insatiable* desire for each new color or shape. At one point a man purchased a house for three bulbs! Before long the inevitable* crash came and the demand for bulbs quickly reached its *nadir*. A $1,500 bulb could be bought for $1.50. With the *moribund* tulip market came financial disaster to thousands of people.

**Sample Sentences**  Fill in the blank spaces with the new words.

1. Who is not vulnerable* to some measure of _____ ?

2. The American consumer appears to have an _____ need for new products.

3. He looked upon the last-place finish of his team with equanimity;* from this _____ the only place to go was up.

4. We ought to expect some _____ behavior from a senile* person.

5. With the expansion of the supermarket, the small, local grocery store is in a _____ state.

**Definitions**  Match the new words with their definitions.

6. irrational _____ **a.** lowest point

7. avarice _____ **b.** dying, at the point of death

8. insatiable _____ **c.** unreasonable, absurd

9. nadir _____ **d.** greed, passion for riches

10. moribund _____ **e.** cannot be satisfied

---

**TODAY'S IDIOM**

*out on a limb*—in a dangerous or exposed position
He went *out on a limb* and predicted he would win the election by a wide margin.

---

ANSWERS ARE ON PAGE 304

# REVIEW

You have been learning how to use many new words by seeing them in a natural situation. Each day's story is the setting in which you meet the new words. The weekly review enables you to isolate the word and its many meanings. In this way you can reinforce your understanding and word power. At this point you have learned almost 600 words. Keep up the good work.

## REVIEW WORDS

| | DEFINITIONS |
|---|---|
| _____ **1.** avarice | **a.** susceptible, open to attack |
| _____ **2.** bedlam | **b.** exempt from error, right |
| _____ **3.** cacophony | **c.** well-matched, harmonious |
| _____ **4.** compatible | **d.** lowest point |
| _____ **5.** disgruntled | **e.** at the point of death, dying |
| _____ **6.** equanimity | **f.** peaceful repose |
| _____ **7.** eradicate | **g.** cure-all |
| _____ **8.** exploit | **h.** uproar, confusion |
| _____ **9.** impede | **i.** harsh sound, discord, dissonance |
| _____ **10.** infallible | **j.** wipe out |
| _____ **11.** insatiable | **k.** sober, still, quiet, undisturbed |
| _____ **12.** irrational | **l.** nearness in time and place |
| _____ **13.** moribund | **m.** displeased, unhappy |
| _____ **14.** nadir | **n.** absurd, unreasonable |
| _____ **15.** panacea | **o.** cannot be satisfied |
| _____ **16.** propinquity | **p.** utilize, profit by |
| _____ **17.** revere | **q.** composure, evenness of mind |
| _____ **18.** sedate | **r.** passion for riches, greed |
| _____ **19.** serenity | **s.** hinder, interfere, block |
| _____ **20.** vulnerable | **t.** admire, respect, honor |

## IDIOMS

| | |
|---|---|
| _____ **21.** lock, stock, and barrel | **u.** a costly and useless possession |
| _____ **22.** out on a limb | **v.** entirely, completely |
| _____ **23.** a feather in one's cap | **w.** in a dangerous or exposed position |
| _____ **24.** a white elephant | **x.** something to be proud of |

The answers can be found on page 304. Consistent study and use of difficult words will work quickly to bring them into your daily vocabulary.

## WORDS FOR FURTHER STUDY    MEANINGS

1. _____  _____

2. _____  _____

3. _____  _____

# DOING DOUBLE DUTY
## (From Weeks 25–28)

❖ Select seven of the twelve words below that can be used as more than one part of speech (for example: noun and verb, noun and adjective). Then compose sentences using each word both ways.

1. hoard
2. revere
3. transient
4. pungent
5. falter
6. sedate
7. sage
8. rebuke
9. paramount
10. obscure
11. exploit
12. senile

_____

_____

_____

_____

_____

_____

_____

_____

_____

_____

_____

_____

_____

_____

_____

ANSWERS ARE ON PAGE 304

# WORDSEARCH 28

❖ Using the clues listed below, fill in each blank in the following story with one of the new words you learned this week.

## Read My Lips

For many years it has been the goal of computer specialists to perfect a machine that would understand human speech. The problem is that the speaker has to be alone and in a quiet room. Noise will ① _____ the computer's ability. In the ② _____ of a special room, the computer works well.

Now, math wizards are trying to develop a computer that will read lips despite any surrounding ③ _____ . While some of us think it ④ _____ to believe that a computer can read lips, the experiments go on. And there has been some success.

Progress in all aspects of computer science has been so remarkable that we hesitate to rule out any possibility. There is one ⑤ _____ rule about the world of computers: the seemingly impossible gets done more quickly than we ever imagined.

### Clues
① 2nd Day
② 3rd Day
③ 1st Day
④ 4th Day
⑤ 2nd Day

NEW WORDS

**lithe**
līᵵH

**obese**
ō bēs´

**adherent**
ad hir´ ənt

**bliss**
blis

**pathetic**
pə thet´ ik

# WEEK 29 ❖ DAY 1

## A SPORT FOR EVERYONE

Of the many highly popular sports in the United States, football must be rated around the top. This sport allows the speedy and *lithe* athlete to join with the slower and *obese* one in a team effort. The skills and strengths of many men are welded together so that one team may work as a unit to gain mastery over its opponent. The knowledgeable *adherent* of a team can follow action covering many parts of the playing field at the same time. He is in a state of *bliss* when his team executes a movement to perfection. However, there is no one more *pathetic* than the same fan when the opposition functions to equal perfection.

**Sample Sentences** Use the new words in these sentences.

1. The disgruntled* _____ switched his loyalty to the opposition party.

2. It was a pleasure to watch the _____ body of the ballet dancer as she performed the most difficult steps.

3. There is something _____ about a great athlete who continues to compete long after he has been bereft* of his talents.

4. His insatiable* hunger for sweets soon made him _____ .

5. Oh, what _____ could be seen in the eyes of the ardent* couple as they announced their engagement!

**Definitions** Match the new words with their definitions.

6. lithe _____ **a.** backer, supporter

7. obese _____ **b.** very fat

8. adherent _____ **c.** sad, pitiful, distressing

9. bliss _____ **d.** graceful

10. pathetic _____ **e.** happiness, pleasure

---
**TODAY'S IDIOM**

***on the spur of the moment*—on impulse, without thinking**

*On the spur of the moment* he turned thumbs down* on the new job.

---

**NEW WORDS**

exhort
eg zôrt´

apathy
ap´ ə thē

fracas
frā´ kəs

inebriated
in ē´ brē ā tid

adversary
ad´ vər ser´ ē

## RAH! RAH! RAH!

The spectators at a football game play more than a superficial* role. A spirited cheer from the stands often gives the player on the field a reason to try even harder. Cheer leaders *exhort* the fans, who may be in a state of *apathy* because their team is losing, to spur on the team. In particularly close games between rivals of long standing, feelings begin to run high, and from time to time a *fracas* may break out in the stands. While the teams compete below, the fan who is a bit *inebriated* may seek out a personal *adversary*. On the whole the enthusiasm of the spectators is usually constricted* to cheering and shouting for their favorite teams.

**Sample Sentences** Complete the sentences with the new words.

1. The feeling of _____ was so prevalent* during the election campaign that the candidates hardly bothered to make speeches.

2. Doctors _____ obese* individuals to go on diets.

3. He was usually sedate,* but when _____ he became hostile.*

4. The _____ started when he besmirched* my good name.

5. My _____ became disgruntled* because my arguments were so cogent.*

**Definitions** Match the new words with their definitions.

6. exhort          _____     **a.** opponent, enemy, foe

7. apathy          _____     **b.** drunk, intoxicated

8. fracas          _____     **c.** lack of interest, unconcern

9. inebriated      _____     **d.** urge strongly, advise

10. adversary      _____     **e.** noisy fight, brawl

---

**TODAY'S IDIOM**

*a fly in the ointment*—some small thing that spoils or lessens the enjoyment

He was offered a lucrative* position with the firm, but *the fly in the ointment* was that he would have to work on Saturday and Sunday.

---

ANSWERS ARE ON PAGE 304

# WEEK 29 ❖ DAY 3

NEW WORDS

**indolent**
in´ dl ənt

**gusto**
gus´ tō

**garrulous**
gar´ ə ləs

**banal**
bā´ nl

**platitude**
plat´ ə tüd

## THE 23-INCH FOOTBALL FIELD

The football fan who cannot attend a contest in person may watch any number of games on television. This has the great advantage of permitting an *indolent* fan to sit in the comfort of his living room and watch two teams play in the most inclement* weather. However, some of the spirit, the *gusto,* is missing when one watches a game on a small screen away from the actual scene of the contest. Also, the viewer is constantly exposed to a *garrulous* group of announcers who continue to chatter in an endless way throughout the afternoon. Should the game be a dull one, the announcers discuss the most *banal* bits of information. Even in the poorest game there is constant chatter involving one *platitude* after another about the laudable* performances of each and every player.

**Sample Sentences**  Insert the new words in the sentences.

1. He began to eat the food served at the sumptuous* feast with _____ .

2. Men believe that women's conversation is filled with _____ comments concerning clothing or food.

3. During the most sultry* days of summer, one often hears the _____ , "Is it hot enough for you?"

4. The _____ person goes to great lengths to eschew* work.

5. She was usually so _____ , we considered anything under a five minute speech as a cryptic* remark.

**Definitions**  Match the new words with their definitions.

6. indolent _____ **a.** enthusiasm, enjoyment, zest

7. gusto _____ **b.** commonplace or trite saying

8. garrulous _____ **c.** lazy

9. banal _____ **d.** talkative, wordy

10. platitude _____ **e.** trivial, meaningless from overuse

── **TODAY'S IDIOM** ──

***to take French leave*—to go away without permission**
The star player was fined $100 when *he took French leave* from the training camp.

ANSWERS ARE ON PAGE 304

179

## NEW WORDS

**pique**
pēk

**dilettante**
dil ə tänt´

**atypical**
ā tip´ ə kəl

**nondescript**
non´ də skript

**wane**
wān

## WHAT'S ON?

One day each week is set aside for college football, and another for the professional brand. Most fans enjoy both varieties. Nothing can put an avid* viewer into a *pique* more quickly than missing an important contest. It is the *dilettante* who eschews* the amateur variety and watches only the professional games. The *atypical* fan will watch only his home team play; however, enthusiasts will continue to view the most *nondescript* contests involving teams that have no connection with their own town or school. Some intrepid* fans have been known to watch high school games when that was all that was offered. Public interest in football grows each year, while interest in other sports may be on the *wane*.

**Sample Sentences**   Complete these sentences with the new words.

1. The _____ will scoff* at those who admit that they know very little about modern art.

2. It is the _____ fisherman who does not embellish* the story about the fish that got away.

3. The detective had little to go on because of the _____ nature of the criminal.

4. Many virulent* diseases are now on the _____ .

5. He showed his _____ by slamming the door.

**Definitions**   Match the new words with their definitions.

6. pique _____   a. decrease, decline

7. dilettante _____   b. fit of resentment

8. atypical _____   c. one who has great interest, but little knowledge

9. nondescript _____   d. nonconforming

10. wane (n.) _____   e. undistinguished, difficult to describe

--- **TODAY'S IDIOM** ---

*in the arms of Morpheus*—asleep; Morpheus was the Roman god of dreams

The day's activities were so enervating, he was soon *in the arms of Morpheus*.

ANSWERS ARE ON PAGE 304

The regular, consistent study of these daily stories is the salient* clue to your success. Sporadic* study tends to disrupt the learning process. Don't give in to the temptation to put your work aside and then rush to "catch up."

## REVIEW WORDS

_____ 1. adherent
_____ 2. adversary
_____ 3. apathy
_____ 4. atypical
_____ 5. banal
_____ 6. bliss
_____ 7. dilettante
_____ 8. exhort
_____ 9. fracas
_____ 10. garrulous
_____ 11. gusto
_____ 12. indolent
_____ 13. inebriated
_____ 14. lithe
_____ 15. nondescript
_____ 16. obese
_____ 17. pathetic
_____ 18. pique
_____ 19. platitude
_____ 20. wane

## DEFINITIONS

a. urge strongly, advise
b. enemy, foe, opponent
c. graceful
d. pitiful, sad, distressing
e. lazy
f. meaningless from overuse, trivial
g. fit of resentment
h. difficult to describe, undistinguished
i. unconcern, lack of interest
j. intoxicated, drunk
k. very fat
l. pleasure, happiness
m. zest, enjoyment, enthusiasm
n. trite saying
o. one with little knowledge and great interest
p. nonconforming
q. brawl, noisy fight
r. supporter, backer
s. wordy, talkative
t. decline, decrease

## IDIOMS

_____ 21. on the spur of the moment
_____ 22. in the arms of Morpheus
_____ 23. to take French leave
_____ 24. a fly in the ointment

u. asleep
v. something that spoils or lessens the enjoyment
w. to go away without permission
x. without thinking, on impulse

Check your answers on page 304. Quick reinforcement of words you do not yet know will help you retain them. Right now . . . put down the words and meanings. Then, write a sentence using the word correctly.

## WORDS FOR FURTHER STUDY        MEANINGS

1. _____    _____

2. _____    _____

3. _____    _____

# WORDSEARCH 29

❖ Using the clues listed below, fill in each blank in the following story with one of the new words you learned this week.

## Each Citizen's Obligation

Of all the democracies in the world, the United States has the most lackluster record when it comes to citizen participation in elections. Every four years the experts try to analyze the reasons for voter ①_____ . Often the eligible voter turnout at election time falls below 50%. This, after months of political campaigning, including televised debates, is a ②_____ situation.

No matter how hard the candidates woo the voters, the end results are often disappointing. Are the voters so ③_____ that they would rather stay home watching television than cast a ballot? Does the voter feel that the candidates are stating one ④_____ after another and is therefore turned off?

The right to vote is so precious that revolutions have taken place where it has been denied. The civil rights struggles of the past were sparked by those who had been denied this right. The greatest ⑤_____ of democracy in this country is said to be the failure of citizen participation in the election process.

## Clues

① 2nd Day

② 1st Day

③ 3rd Day

④ 3rd Day

⑤ 2nd Day

ANSWERS ARE ON PAGE 304

# WEEK 30 ❖ DAY 1

**NEW WORDS**

**extinct**
ek stingkt´

**idyllic**
ī dil´ ik

**galvanize**
gal´ və nīz

**encumbrance**
en kum´ brəns

**gaudy**
gô´ dē

## IN DAYS GONE BY

The man who best described the now *extinct* life aboard a steamer on the Mississippi River is Mark Twain. Having actually worked aboard the river boats, his writing captures the tranquil* or turbulent* events of those days. In his book about life on the Mississippi, Twain recalls the *idyllic* times when man was not in such a great rush to get from one place to another. One chapter deals with the races conducted between the swiftest of the boats. When a race was set, the excitement would *galvanize* activity along the river. Politics and the weather were forgotten, and people talked with gusto* only of the coming race. The two steamers "stripped" and got ready; every *encumbrance* that might slow the passage was removed. Captains went to extremes to lighten their boats. Twain writes of one captain who scraped the paint from the *gaudy* figure that hung between the chimneys of his steamer.

**Sample Sentences**  Insert the new words in these sentences.

1.  Today, the trend* is to more and more _____ dress.

2.  It is amazing how lithe* football players can be, despite the _____ of the safety features of their uniforms.

3.  The dinosaur is an _____ species.

4.  City dwellers often yearn for the _____ life in the country.

5.  A dictator will use any pretext* to _____ his people into aggressive actions.

**Definitions**  Match the new words with their definitions.

6.  extinct        _____   a.  burden, handicap, load

7.  idyllic        _____   b.  showy, flashy

8.  galvanize      _____   c.  simple, peaceful

9.  encumbrance    _____   d.  excite or arouse to activity

10. gaudy          _____   e.  no longer existing

---

### TODAY'S IDIOM

*forty winks*—a short nap

During the night before the big test, he studied continuously,
catching *forty winks* now and then.

---

## NEW WORDS

**condescend**
kon´ di send´

**candor**
kan´ dər

**mortify**
môr´ tə fī

**jocose**
jō kōs´

**malign**
mə līn´

## THE JOHN J. ROE

Mark Twain's boat was so slow no other steamer would *condescend* to race with it. With the utmost *candor,* Twain comments that his boat moved at such a pathetic* pace, they used to forget in what year it was they left port. Nothing would *mortify* Twain more than the fact that ferryboats, waiting to cross the river, would lose valuable trips because their passengers grew senile* and died waiting for his boat, the *John J. Roe,* to pass. Mark Twain wrote in a *jocose* manner about the races his steamer had with islands and rafts. With quiet humor he continued to *malign* the riverboat, but his book is replete* with love for this sort of life.

**Sample Sentences** Insert the new words in these sentences.

1. He had such disdain* for us, he would not _____ to speak before our group.

2. It is most common to _____ the wealthy for their avarice.*

3. It is difficult to be _____ in the presence of so many doleful* people.

4. When we cannot speak with _____ , we utilize euphemisms.*

5. Good sportsmanship requires that one not _____ a defeated adversary.*

**Definitions** Match the new words with their definitions.

6. condescend _____ **a.** humorous, merry

7. candor _____ **b.** abuse, slander

8. mortify _____ **c.** stoop, lower oneself

9. jocose _____ **d.** frankness, honesty

10. malign _____ **e.** embarrass, humiliate

---

### TODAY'S IDIOM

*from pillar to post*—from one place to another

The company was so large and spread out, he was sent
*from pillar to post* before he found the proper official

---

ANSWERS ARE ON PAGE 305

# WEEK 30 ❖ DAY 3

**NEW WORDS**

**omnipotent**
om nip´ ə tənt

**zenith**
zē´ nith

**fledgling**
flej´ ling

**peremptory**
pə remp´ tər ē

**precedent**
pres´ ə dənt

## THE RIVERBOAT PILOT

The riverboat pilot was a man considered *omnipotent* by all. Mark Twain once held that high position. He writes that he felt at the *zenith* of his life at that time. Starting out as a *fledgling* pilot's apprentice, he could not abjure dreams of the time he would become, "the only unfettered and entirely independent human being that lived in the earth." Kings, parliaments, and newspaper editors, Twain comments, are hampered and restricted. The river pilot issued *peremptory* commands as absolute monarch. The captain was powerless to interfere. Even though the pilot was much younger than the captain, and the steamer seemed to be in imminent* danger, the older man was helpless. The captain had to behave impeccably,* for any criticism of the pilot would establish a pernicious* *precedent* that would have undermined the pilot's limitless authority.

**Sample Sentences**  Insert the new words in these sentences.

1. Under the aegis* of an adroit* master, he reached the _____ of his career.

2. We would scoff* at anyone calling himself _____ .

3. There is no _____ for voting when there is no quorum.*

4. The _____ poet lived a frugal* life.

5. No one had the temerity* to disobey the officer's _____ order.

**Definitions**  Match the new words with their definitions.

6. omnipotent _____ **a.** summit, top, prime

7. zenith _____ **b.** little known, newly developed

8. fledgling _____ **c.** absolute, compulsory, binding

9. peremptory _____ **d.** custom, model

10. precedent _____ **e.** almighty, unlimited in power or authority

---

### TODAY'S IDIOM

*in the lap of the gods*—out of one's own hands

I handed in my application for the job, and now it is *in the lap of the gods.*

---

## NEW WORDS

**wheedle**
hwē´ dl

**rustic**
rus´ tik

**jubilant**
jü´ bə lənt

**decorum**
di kôr´ əm

**charlatan**
shär´ lə tən

## THE DOUBLE CROSS

Many incidents that took place aboard his ship are re-told by Twain. One has to do with a wealthy cattle man who was approached by three gamblers. The cattle farmer had let it be known that he had a great deal of money, and the gamblers were trying to *wheedle* him into a card game. He protested that he knew nothing about cards. His *rustic* appearance confirmed that fact. On the last night before landing the three gamblers got him drunk. When the first hand was dealt, a *jubilant* expression came over his face. The betting became furious. All of the proper *decorum* was put aside, and ten thousand dollars soon lay on the table. With the last wager one of the gamblers showed a hand of four kings. His partner was to have dealt the sucker a hand of four queens. At this point the victim, the *charlatan,* removed the veneer* of respectability, and showed a hand of four aces! One of the three professional gamblers was a clandestine* confederate of the "rich cattle farmer." They had been planning this duplicity* for many weeks.

**Sample Sentences** Insert the new words in these sentences.

1. The child tried to _____ from her mother the place where the cookies had been cached.*

2. They could discern* that the faith healer was a _____ .

3. The _____ life is supposed to be a tranquil* one.

4. Repress* your uncouth manners and act with _____ at the party.

5. We were _____ when our indolent* cousin got a job.

**Definitions** Match the new words with their definitions.

6. wheedle  _____  a. coax, persuade, cajole*
7. rustic  _____  b. joyful, in high spirits
8. jubilant  _____  c. politeness, correct behavior
9. decorum  _____  d. pretender, fraud
10. charlatan  _____  e. countrified, unpolished

--- **TODAY'S IDIOM** ---

*Achilles heel*—**weak spot**

He wanted to lead an ascetic* life, but his obsession with liquor was his *Achilles heel.*

ANSWERS ARE ON PAGE 305

Because you are learning these new words in context, they will stay with you. It is the natural method for seeing new words. Your ability to master words as they appear in normal situations should carry over to your learning many other words as you read.

## REVIEW WORDS

| | DEFINITIONS |
|---|---|
| _____ 1. candor | **a.** arouse or excite to activity |
| _____ 2. charlatan | **b.** humiliate, embarrass |
| _____ 3. condescend | **c.** little known, newly developed |
| _____ 4. decorum | **d.** in high spirits, joyful |
| _____ 5. encumbrance | **e.** peaceful, simple |
| _____ 6. extinct | **f.** honesty, frankness |
| _____ 7. fledgling | **g.** unpolished, countrified |
| _____ 8. galvanize | **h.** top, prime, summit |
| _____ 9. gaudy | **i.** load, handicap, burden |
| _____ 10. idyllic | **j.** merry, humorous |
| _____ 11. jocose | **k.** correct behavior, politeness |
| _____ 12. jubilant | **l.** unlimited in power or authority, almighty |
| _____ 13. malign | **m.** no longer existing |
| _____ 14. mortify | **n.** lower oneself, stoop |
| _____ 15. omnipotent | **o.** persuade, coax, cajole* |
| _____ 16. peremptory | **p.** binding, compulsory, absolute |
| _____ 17. precedent | **q.** showy, flashy |
| _____ 18. rustic | **r.** slander, abuse |
| _____ 19. wheedle | **s.** fraud, pretender |
| _____ 20. zenith | **t.** custom, model |

## IDIOMS

| | |
|---|---|
| _____ 21. Achilles heel | **u.** a short nap |
| _____ 22. forty winks | **v.** weak spot |
| _____ 23. in the lap of the gods | **w.** from one place to another |
| _____ 24. from pillar to post | **x.** out of one's own hands |

Check your answers on page 305. Go right to it. Learn the words you have missed. Make them as much a part of your vocabulary as the other words you knew correctly.

## WORDS FOR FURTHER STUDY      MEANINGS

1. _____  _____

2. _____  _____

3. _____  _____

# WORDSEARCH 30

❖ Using the clues listed below, fill in each blank in the following story with one of the new words you learned this week.

## The Environmental Society

A great deal of controversy surrounds the efforts of environmentalists to protect rare species of animals and birds from becoming ①_____ . In order to save these creatures from destruction stemming from a loss of forests or water pollution, environmentalists try to ②_____ large numbers of people to pressure politicians into passing conservation legislation. Often, however, these proposed ③_____ laws are thought to be a burden placed upon business, resulting in a loss of employment.

In the 21st century, the energy and food requirements of an increasing population are at odds with those who would set aside land for birds or animals. There is a great temptation to ④_____ the motives of environmental advocates. It will take people of good will and ⑤_____ to resolve the many difficulties that lie ahead.

### Clues

① 1st Day
② 1st Day
③ 3rd Day
④ 2nd Day
⑤ 2nd Day

ANSWERS ARE ON PAGE 305

# WEEK 31 ❖ DAY 1

**NEW WORDS**

**heresy**
her´ ə sē

**prudent**
prüd´ nt

**ostensible**
o sten´ sə bəl

**fervid**
fėr´ vid

**spurious**
spyur´ ē əs

## CHOOSE SAGELY*

Today, the paramount* influence in the forming of public opinion is propaganda. It is not a *heresy* to our democratic beliefs to state that pressure groups play an important part in our lives. Propaganda makes one vulnerable* to the influences of others. The *prudent* person will choose between cogent* and specious propaganda efforts. While propaganda has the *ostensible* purpose of informing the public, the most *fervid* propagandists use methods that must be examined by the thoughtful citizen. The ability to distinguish the *spurious* from the true facts requires more than a perfunctory* examination of prevalent* propaganda efforts.

**Sample Sentences**  Use care. The words have many meanings.

1. His _____ appeal for action threw his adherents* into a frenzy*.

2. He accused the leader of the opposition of political _____ , and the mob was exhorted* to burn his effigy*.

3. In the bedlam* that followed it was not _____ to appear too apathetic*.

4. While the _____ enemy was the opposition leader, the main purpose of this rash* behavior was the eradication* of all opponents.

5. In the conflagration* that followed, no one questioned whether the original charge had been _____ .

**Definitions**  Study the fine differences. Be sure how to use them.

6. heresy _____ a. intense, enthusiastic, passionate

7. prudent _____ b. false, counterfeit, specious*

8. ostensible _____ c. unbelief, dissent, lack of faith

9. fervid _____ d. wise, cautious

10. spurious _____ e. outward, pretended, seeming

---

**TODAY'S IDIOM**

*cold shoulder*—to disregard or ignore

She was so piqued* at his uncouth behavior,
she gave him the *cold shoulder* for over a week.

---

ANSWERS ARE ON PAGE 305

**NEW WORDS**

**propagate**
prop´ ə gāt

**anomaly**
ə nom´ ə lē

**innocuous**
i nok´ yü əs

**surfeit**
sėr´ fit

**milieu**
mē lyu´

## A FREE SOCIETY

In a free society it is intrinsic* that individuals and groups have the inherent* right to *propagate* ideas and try to win converts. We do not look upon an idea different from ours as an *anomaly* that should be precluded*. Nor do we permit only *innocuous* or congenial* beliefs and forbid those that we believe are dubious* or spurious*. In a country of competing pressures we are accosted* by a *surfeit* of propaganda that tends to overwhelm us. Thus, we live in a *milieu* of ubiquitous* bombardment from countless, and often unrecognized, propagandists.

**Sample Sentences** Insert the new words in these sentences.

1. I must inveigh* against your attempt to _____ the belief that your political system will result in a panacea* for all problems.

2. It is incongruous* to find an abstemious* person in a _____ of avarice* and affluence*.

3. Siamese twins are considered a birth _____ .

4. There appears to be no such thing as an _____ heresy*.

5. When can we expect a respite* from the _____ of TV commercials?

**Definitions** Match the new words with their definitions.

6. propagate _____ a. excess, superabundance

7. anomaly _____ b. environment, setting

8. innocuous _____ c. irregularity, abnormality

9. surfeit _____ d. produce, multiply, spread

10. milieu _____ e. harmless, mild, innocent

---
### TODAY'S IDIOM

***without rhyme or reason*—making no sense**

*Without rhyme or reason* the pennant-winning baseball team decided to jettison* its manager.

---

ANSWERS ARE ON PAGE 305

# WEEK 31 ❖ DAY 3

## NEW WORDS

**strident**
strīd´ nt

**concomitant**
kon kom´ ə tənt

**lassitude**
las´ ə tüd

**deleterious**
del´ ə tir´ ē əs

**efficacy**
ef´ ə kə sē

## WHO LISTENS?

As the quantity of propaganda becomes greater, ideas are presented in more *strident* tones in order to overcome the increased competition. Those who are the targets of the propaganda find it more difficult to discern* between or analyze the new and expanded pressures. The *concomitant* situation that develops with the stepped-up propaganda is one in which the individual retreats into a state of *lassitude*. He has an aversion* to all attempts to influence him. So we can see the intrinsic* weakness inherent* in an increased level of propaganda. It has the *deleterious* result of reducing its *efficacy* upon the individuals or groups who were its objective.

**Sample Sentences**  Insert the new words in these sentences.

1. There are many _____ dangers to obesity.*

2. Her _____ voice added to the bedlam.*

3. After the frenzy* that accompanied the burning of the effigy,* they were all acutely* aware of a feeling of _____ .

4. The gist* of the report was that smoking will have a _____ effect on health.

5. The _____ of new drugs cannot be determined without a plethora* of evidence.

**Definitions**  Match the new words with their definitions.

6. strident _____ **a.** power to produce an effect

7. concomitant _____ **b.** bad, harmful

8. lassitude _____ **c.** accompanying, attending

9. deleterious _____ **d.** weariness, fatigue

10. efficacy _____ **e.** shrill, harsh, rough

---

### TODAY'S IDIOM

*swan song*—final or last (swans are said to sing before they die)

The ex-champion said that if he lost this fight it would be his *swan song*.

---

ANSWERS ARE ON PAGE 305

191

## NEW WORDS

**dissent**
di sent´

**ferment**
fər´ ment

**attenuated**
ə ten´ yü ā tid

**arbiter**
är´ bə tər

**incumbent**
in kum´ bənt

## THE PEOPLE DECIDE

The place of propaganda in a milieu* that is not free differs from its place in an open society. In a dictatorship there is no competing propaganda. Those who *dissent* from the official line may do so only in a clandestine* manner. Where there is no open *ferment* of ideas, the possibility of discerning* the true from the spurious* is *attenuated*. In a democracy, the inevitable* *arbiter* of what propaganda is to be permitted is the people. It is *incumbent* upon each citizen to choose between competing propagandas while remaining cognizant* of the value for a democracy in the existence of all points of view.

**Sample Sentences** Insert the new words in these sentences.

1. It is _____ on us to be zealous* in combatting the deleterious* effects of drugs.

2. With each generation it becomes the vogue* for the youth to be in a state of _____ .

3. The gist* of his ominous* suggestion was that we _____ from the majority opinion.

4. The strength of her appeal was _____ by the flamboyant* embellishments* for which many had a strong aversion.*

5. The Supreme Court is our ultimate* _____ of legality.

**Definitions** Always be cognizant* of the fact that words are used in the paragraphs and sentences with only one meaning. They often have many others. Look up the word *incumbent* for a good example.

6. dissent (v.) _____  **a.** morally required

7. ferment _____  **b.** weakened, thinned, decreased

8. attenuated _____  **c.** differ, disagree, protest

9. arbiter _____  **d.** uproar, agitation, turmoil

10. incumbent (adj.) _____  **e.** judge

---
### TODAY'S IDIOM
---

***to get the sack**—to be discharged or fired*

Despite the fact that he was so obsequious* toward the boss,
*he got the sack* because he was lethargic* about doing his job.

ANSWERS ARE ON PAGE 305

Once more it is time to review this week's words. Always keep in mind that the use of the word, its context, determines its meaning. Used as a noun, a word has a different meaning than when it is used as an adjective or a verb. First, master the words as they appear in the daily stories. Next, look up other meanings in your dictionary. Try writing sentences with the additional meanings.

## REVIEW WORDS

_____ 1. anomaly
_____ 2. arbiter
_____ 3. attenuated
_____ 4. concomitant
_____ 5. deleterious
_____ 6. dissent
_____ 7. efficacy
_____ 8. ferment
_____ 9. fervid
_____ 10. heresy
_____ 11. incumbent
_____ 12. innocuous
_____ 13. lassitude
_____ 14. milieu
_____ 15. ostensible
_____ 16. propagate
_____ 17. prudent
_____ 18. spurious
_____ 19. strident
_____ 20. surfeit

## DEFINITIONS

a. agitation, turmoil, uproar
b. attending, accompanying
c. abnormality, irregularity
d. cautious, wise
e. protest, differ, disagree
f. rough, harsh, shrill
g. multiply, spread, produce
h. lack of faith, dissent, unbelief
i. morally required
j. power to produce an effect
k. setting, environment
l. counterfeit, false, specious*
m. judge
n. harmful, bad
o. superabundance, excess
p. enthusiastic, passionate, intense
q. decreased, weakened, thinned
r. mild, innocent, harmless
s. fatigue, weariness
t. seeming, pretended, outward

## IDIOMS

_____ 21. cold shoulder
_____ 22. swan song
_____ 23. to get the sack
_____ 24. without rhyme or reason

u. to be discharged or fired
v. making no sense
w. final or last
x. to disregard or ignore

Check your answers on page 305. Get to work learning the words that gave you trouble.

## WORDS FOR FURTHER STUDY

MEANINGS

1. _____  _____

2. _____  _____

3. _____  _____

# WORDSEARCH 31

❖ Using the clues listed below, fill in each blank in the following story with one of the new words you learned this week.

## *Cross My Palm with Silver*

People are fascinated by those who say they can predict the future. Fortune tellers continue to attract gullible customers, and horoscopes are examined daily to see if there is something ① _____ to worry about in the day ahead. One specialist who seems to have found a way to predict something of our future is the palm reader. It is her belief that a long "life line" in the hand means the customer will enjoy longevity.

While this appears to be a ② _____ way to predict long life, a study done in England measured "life lines" of 100 corpses and came up with ③ _____ support for the claim: the length of life matched the length of line. The longer the line, the older the person lived to be.

However, there are scientists who ④ _____ with believers in this apparent connection. The "life line" of older people is longer only because the hand becomes more wrinkled with age. Length of line is a ⑤ _____ of length of life, not the reverse, say scientists.

## Clues

① 3rd Day

② 1st Day

③ 1st Day

④ 4th Day

⑤ 3rd Day

# WEEK 32 ❖ DAY 1

**NEW WORDS**

**profound**
prə found´

**alleviate**
ə lē´ vē āt

**prodigious**
prə dij´ əs

**expedite**
ek´ spə dīt

**celerity**
sə ler´ ə tē

## ANYONE FOR GOOGLE?

As automation permeates* many new areas of life, its effect upon us becomes concomitantly* more *profound.* Information processing, blogs, search engines of all types have found their ways into businesses, as well as our homes, schools, and libraries. Here they *alleviate* the burden of storing and providing us with an accumulation of information that is becoming more *prodigious* in this era of specialization and threatening to inundate* our society.

Youngsters in the primary grades now know how to manipulate their computers to extract information that would have taken their grandparents an eternity to produce. Machines whose *celerity* can scan thousands of words in nanoseconds help *expedite* the selection of pertinent* information for those schoolchildren.

**Sample Sentences** Insert your new words below.

1. We hoped that the arbiter* would _____ the solution to the fracas* that had been so elusive* for a long time.

2. He accepted the lucrative* position with _____ .

3. It is easy to construe* a superficial* remark to be a _____ one.

4. If we cannot _____ the harmful effects entirely, at least we can attenuate* them.

5. The enemy made a _____ effort to repress* the uprising.

**Definitions** Match the new words with their definitions.

6. profound _____ a. carry out promptly

7. alleviate _____ b. speed, rapidity

8. prodigious _____ c. make easier, lighten

9. expedite _____ d. deep, intense

10. celerity _____ e. extraordinary, enormous

--- **TODAY'S IDIOM** ---

*ivory tower*—isolated from life; not in touch with life's problems

Many artists have been said to be living in an *ivory tower.*

ANSWERS ARE ON PAGE 305

## NEW WORDS

**usurp**
yü zėrp´

**paltry**
pôl´ trē

**condone**
kən dōn´

**trivial**
triv´ ē əl

**bizarre**
bə zär´

## EVERYONE IS TALKING

Can anyone under the age of 20 remember a time when the dial telephone was the only method of voice communication over long distances? What a *bizarre* concept this must seem for today's youth. It has become an antiquated* cultural form of personal contact. The instrument for the modern communicator is the cell phone, which has *usurped* the wire-connected stationary model. With cell phone companies competing for customers, they eschew* offering a *paltry* number of minutes of talking time. The cell phone user can take advantage of a plethora* of special deals and carry on with significant or *trivial* conversations for seemingly endless time, and in almost any location. Often, these personal talks are held in the most public places, and those within hearing find it difficult to *condone* the inconvenience caused by the indiscriminate* use of this ubiquitous* instrument.

*Don't look back at the "new words." Did you spot* bizarre *as a reintroduced word?*

**Sample Sentences** (note the similarity of *trivial* and *paltry*)

1. Most of us scoff* at and belittle* _____ behavior.

2. They exacerbated* a _____ difference of opinion into a prodigious* conflict.

3. It is during a period of ferment* that a dictator can _____ power.

4. Do you expect me to _____ that reprehensible* act with such celerity?*

5. The most _____ defects may have a deleterious* effect upon the efficacy* of that new process.

**Definitions** Match the new words with their definitions.

6. usurp _____ **a.** petty, worthless

7. paltry _____ **b.** excuse, pardon

8. condone _____ **c.** seize, annex, grab

9. trivial _____ **d.** of little importance, insignificant

10. bizarre _____ **e.** fantastic, odd

───── **TODAY'S IDIOM** ─────

**to feather one's nest**—to enrich oneself on the sly or at every opportunity

He played up to his senile* aunt in the hope of
*feathering his nest* when she made out her will.

ANSWERS ARE ON PAGE 305

# WEEK 32 ❖ DAY 3

**NEW WORDS**

menial
mē´ nē el

venerable
ven´ ər ə bəl

extraneous
ek strā´ nē əs

ambiguous
am big´ yü əs

succinct
sək singkt´

## THE FUTURE IS HERE

We have ardently* taken to the cell phone as a replacement for the *venerable* dial-up model. The most striking feature of the cell phone is the variety of uses to which it can be put. The dial-up phone is restricted to the *menial* task of mere conversation. For the garrulous* person who isn't restricted to one place, the mobile cell phone has a myriad* of uses. Should one be in an area that requires silence, there is an ability to utilize the *succinct* text messaging feature. Should one come upon an *ambiguous* event that one wishes to keep, one may photograph it or make it into a film for further study. Do not preclude* from the list of uses the access to your computer, music, and weather reports. One can hardly imagine an *extraneous* technical marvel that will not embellish* the cell phone in the future.

**Sample Sentences**  Complete the sentences with the new words.

1. The prodigy* revered* the _____ master.

2. To those who could understand every nuance* of the cryptic* message, there was nothing _____ about it.

3. He could say the most vitriolic* things in a _____ way.

4. Although she did not find it congenial,* we cajoled* our daughter into doing some of the _____ tasks around the house.

5. The astute* voter is not susceptible* to the many _____ shibboleths that saturate* a politician's speech.

**Definitions**  Match the new words with their definitions.

6. menial       _____   **a.** vague, undefined, not specific

7. venerable    _____   **b.** humble, degrading

8. extraneous   _____   **c.** respected, worshiped

9. ambiguous    _____   **d.** foreign, not belonging

10. succinct    _____   **e.** brief, concise

---
### TODAY'S IDIOM ─

***the writing on the wall*—an incident or event that
shows what will happen in the future**

In retrospect* he should have seen *the writing on the wall* when his
girlfriend gave him only a cursory* greeting on his birthday.

---

## NEW WORDS

**archaic**
är kā´ ik

**emulate**
em´ yə lāt

**facetious**
fə sē´ shəs

**rabid**
rab´ id

**salubrious**
sə lü´ brē əs

## IT'S HAPPENING NOW

The flood of new technology makes each modern marvel appear *archaic* within the briefest time period. An assiduous* examination of today's communication methods will make clear how quickly a *rabid* purchaser of the newest product will want to *emulate* friends and buy the next one. The cell phone that can track down the location of a user, or the music-downloading pod that has a potential* to record almost countless songs are being replaced with more powerful and exciting products. It would not be *facetious* to claim that scientists will persevere* in devising ways for us to contact each other by voice, photographs, and print messages that give us access* to a more *salubrious* social network.

**Sample Sentences** Use the new words in these sentences.

1. Some maintain that the ascetic* leads a _____ life.

2. With all candor,* I cannot wish for a return to the _____ times when a moribund* society provided an opulent* existence for some, but a loathsome* life for the majority.

3. There is something _____ about an egotist* who has the temerity* to begin a speech with, "In all humility* . . . ."

4. It is not prudent* to malign* or castigate,* or be derogatory* in any way toward a _____ political adherent.*

5. The wish to _____ a great person is laudable.*

**Definitions** Match the new words with their definitions.

6. archaic          _____   **a.** healthful, wholesome

7. emulate          _____   **b.** out of date

8. facetious        _____   **c.** rival, strive to equal

9. rabid            _____   **d.** comical, humorous, witty

10. salubrious      _____   **e.** fanatical, furious, mad

─────── **TODAY'S IDIOM** ───────

*on the bandwagon*—joining with the majority; going along with the trend

Most advertisements showing many people using a product hope to convince the viewer to get *on the bandwagon* and buy the item.

ANSWERS ARE ON PAGE 305

When you can analyze a sentence and determine from the context the meaning of a previously unknown word, you are functioning at the best level. These words will become a permanent part of your ever-growing vocabulary.

**REVIEW WORDS**

_____ 1. alleviate
_____ 2. ambiguous
_____ 3. archaic
_____ 4. bizarre
_____ 5. celerity
_____ 6. condone
_____ 7. emulate
_____ 8. expedite
_____ 9. extraneous
_____ 10. facetious
_____ 11. menial
_____ 12. paltry
_____ 13. prodigious
_____ 14. profound
_____ 15. rabid
_____ 16. salubrious
_____ 17. succinct
_____ 18. trivial
_____ 19. usurp
_____ 20. venerable

**DEFINITIONS**

a. out of date
b. concise, brief
c. intense, deep
d. annex, grab, seize
e. wholesome, healthful
f. degrading, humble
g. rapidity, speed
h. fantastic, odd
i. humorous, comical, witty
j. not belonging, foreign
k. enormous, extraordinary
l. pardon, excuse
m. furious, mad, fanatical
n. undefined, vague, not specific
o. carry out promptly
p. lighten, make easier
q. respected, worshiped
r. strive to equal, rival
s. insignificant
t. petty, worthless

**IDIOMS**

_____ 21. to feather one's nest
_____ 22. ivory tower
_____ 23. the writing on the wall
_____ 24. on the bandwagon

u. joining with the majority
v. an event that predicts the future
w. out of touch with life
x. to enrich oneself at every opportunity

**WORDS FOR FURTHER STUDY**          **MEANINGS**

1. _____    _____

2. _____    _____

3. _____    _____

Check your answers on page 305. Take that extra moment now to review and study the words you got wrong.

# SELECTING ANTONYMS
## (From Weeks 29–32)

❖ Here are fifteen words taken from the last four weeks of study. Select and underline the correct antonym for each.

1. adversary (partner, foe)
2. dilettante (amateur, professional)
3. indolent (lazy, active)
4. inebriated (drunk, sober)
5. candor (falsehood, honesty)
6. gaudy (conservative, showy)
7. zenith (acme, nadir)
8. prodigious (huge, tiny)
9. condone (condemn, approve)
10. ambiguous (clear, confusing)
11. spurious (authentic, false)
12. innocuous (harmful, harmless)
13. deleterious (harmful, helpful)
14. succinct (concise, wordy)
15. rustic (rural, urbane)

ANSWERS ARE ON PAGE 305

❖ Using the clues listed below, fill in each blank in the following story with one of the new words you learned this week.

## *A Formidable Opponent*

One of the most interesting tests of a computer's ability to "think" occurred in 1992. The world's chess champion, a man of ①_____ mental ability in this sport, was challenged to compete against the most powerful computer programmed to play chess. The question was, could a machine ②_____ a human's place as the best chess player in the world?

The match took place before hundreds of chess enthusiasts and was recorded on film. While the computer lacked the champion's experience and emotional capacity, it worked with such ③_____ that it could search ahead for many thousands of choices, well beyond what any human could envision. In fact, the computer had already defeated many ④_____ chess masters in preparation for the contest.

The result of this test match was ⑤_____ as far as human self-esteem was concerned. The champion won fairly easily. However, there is almost total agreement that it is only a matter of time before we have an electronic chess champion, one incapable of making a blunder. At that point it will be checkmate for all of us.

### Clues

① 1st Day

② 2nd Day

③ 1st Day

④ 3rd Day

⑤ 4th Day

## NEW WORDS

**complacent**
kəm plā´ snt

**somber**
som´ bər

**debilitate**
di bil´ ə tāt

**impetuous**
im pech´ ü əs

**occult**
ə kult´

# WEEK 33 ❖ DAY 1

## AT A LOSS

With the trivial* sum of five dollars in his pockets, Robert Lacy was feeling far from *complacent* about the future. In fact, it was his *somber* estimate that no matter how frugal* he was, his money would run out before the next day. He owed $3.50 in debts to friends; with the remainder he would have to eat enough to maintain his strength. Hunger would *debilitate* him to the point where he could not continue his fervid* search for Evelyn. There was no hope of an *impetuous* stranger suddenly thrusting money upon him. There was still less solace* for him in the hope that, after all this time, he might develop the *occult* power that would give him a mental image of where Evelyn could be found.

**Sample Sentences** Use the new words in these sentences.

1. The guard was so _____ about the danger of escape that he gave the prisoner only a cursory* inspection.

2. We should be prudent* in our play or work during very hot weather, because the sun has the power to enervate* and _____ those that scoff* at its effects.

3. He looked for a propitious* moment to exhibit his _____ abilities.

4. The deleterious* results of his irate* outburst put the previously jocose* audience in a _____ mood.

5. They were so moved by the idyllic* setting, they exchanged surreptitious,* _____ kisses.

**Definitions** Match the new words with their definitions.

6. complacent   _____    a. secret, mysterious, supernatural

7. somber   _____    b. impulsive

8. debilitate   _____    c. self-satisfied

9. impetuous   _____    d. weaken

10. occult (adj.)   _____    e. gloomy, sad

---
#### TODAY'S IDIOM
---

***to hit the nail on the head*—to state or guess something correctly**

When Charlie said there were 3,627 beans in that jar, he *hit the nail on the head.*

ANSWERS ARE ON PAGE 306

**NEW WORDS**

**discreet**
dis krēt´

**foment**
fō ment

**glean**
glēn

**quarry**
kwôr´ ē

**slovenly**
sluv´ ən lē

## MAKING PLANS

Robert had arrived in New York a week earlier. He had begun by asking *discreet* questions of Evelyn's former landlord. There was no need to *foment* opposition at the very beginning. The landlord was recondite,* and all Robert had been able to *glean* from the cryptic* replies was that Evelyn had moved to a residence that catered to single women. Robert was in a hapless* situation; in this immense city his *quarry* could be hiding in one of dozens of such places. This would obviate* the possibility of his dashing from one place to another in an impetuous* manner. His search, while it had to be concluded with celerity,* could not be carried out in such *slovenly* fashion. He required a succinct* and meticulous* plan.

**Sample Sentences**  Use the new words in these sentences.

1. In order to _____ trouble, they fabricated* a deplorable* and blatant* untruth.

2. She loathed* doing menial* tasks, and she did them in a _____ manner.

3. Although it seemed inane,* they sought their _____ in the midst of rustic* surroundings that were not its natural habitat*.

4. Despite the plethora* of offers to write her life story, the recently divorced movie queen kept a _____ silence.

5. The reporters could not _____ anything from her servants.

**Definitions**  Match the new words with their definitions.

6. discreet _____   **a.** careful, cautious, prudent*

7. foment _____   **b.** gather, collect

8. glean _____   **c.** something hunted or pursued

9. quarry _____   **d.** disorderly, carelessly

10. slovenly _____   **e.** stir up, instigate

---

**TODAY'S IDIOM**

**on the dot—exactly on time**

Despite his having taken forty winks,* he got to his appointment *on the dot.*

---

ANSWERS ARE ON PAGE 306

## NEW WORDS

**abjure**
ab ju̇r´

**reproach**
ri prōch´

**penitent**
pen̄´ ə tənt

**evanescent**
ev´ ə nes´ nt

**tantamount**
tan´ tə mount

## A NEWSPAPER AD

On the premise* that Evelyn knew she was being sought, Robert's first step was to *abjure* fruitless* searching and place an ad in the leading morning newspaper. He would importune* in a most careful way for her return. The ad read, "Evelyn. Come out of hiding. I do not *reproach* you for your actions. I expect no *penitent* confession. There is nothing ambiguous* about my offer. Please contact. Robert." He added a box number for a reply. When Robert went to the paper the next morning, he felt sanguine* about the chances of locating her. His *evanescent* concerns disappeared; there was a letter for him, and with tremulous* fingers he tore it open. It contained one sentence, and it was *tantamount* to a challenge; "If you really care about me, you will find me by midnight, Friday, Evelyn."

**Sample Sentences**  Insert the new words in these sentences.

1. The inveterate* gambler became _____ and contrite when faced with the results of his reprehensible* behavior.

2. The optimist knows that the vicissitudes* of life are _____ , and she always looks on the sanguine* side of things.

3. You should not condone* his sordid* behavior; rather, _____ him for his fractious* manner.

4. At the zenith* of his career, he was _____ to a final arbiter* on matters of economic policy.

5. In vain, the entire family tried to importune* him to _____ gambling.

**Definitions**  Match the new words with their definitions.

6. abjure _____  **a.** equivalent, identical

7. reproach _____  **b.** rebuke*, reprimand*

8. penitent _____  **c.** renounce, abstain from

9. evanescent _____  **d.** regretful, confessing guilt

10. tantamount _____  **e.** fleeting, passing, momentary

---
**TODAY'S IDIOM**

***to take under one's wing***—to become responsible for

As the new term began, the senior took the freshman *under her wing*.

---

ANSWERS ARE ON PAGE 306

# WEEK 33 ❖ DAY 4

**NEW WORDS**

**propensity**
prǝ pen´ sǝ tē

**wary**
wer´ ē

**allay**
ǝ lā´

**deter**
di ter´

**connoisseur**
kon´ ǝ ser´

## AT THE BALLET

Evelyn was an anomaly*: she had a *propensity* for folk music and rock and roll dancing, and, at the same time, she was an avid* fan of classical ballet. At one time she had been a fledgling* ballet dancer. Robert headed for a theater where a venerable* ballet company was performing. He knew he had to be *wary* so that Evelyn might not see him first. It was Tuesday evening; two days gone with so little to show. Only three more remaining before the deadline set by Evelyn. He tried hard to *allay* the sudden fear that came over him that he might not locate her. Nothing would *deter* him from succeeding! And so, although he was far from a *connoisseur* of the dance, he was standing among the throng* in the lobby, hoping it would be a propitious* evening for him.

**Sample Sentences**  Insert the new words in these sentences.

1. The _____ scoffs* at the dilettante,* who has only a veneer* of knowledge.

2. It is difficult to _____ the concern of parents about how susceptible* their children are and how easily they succumb* to drugs.

3. Some girls have a _____ for swarthy men who wear gaudy* clothes.

4. Her father warned her to be _____ of adding the encumbrance* of a steady boyfriend as this would attenuate* her chances of finishing college.

5. This did not _____ her from getting into a deplorable* situation due to her rash* and perverse* actions.

**Definitions**  Match the new words with their definitions.

6. propensity _____ a. hinder, discourage

7. wary _____ b. expert

8. allay _____ c. disposition, inclination, bent

9. deter _____ d. calm, soothe

10. connoisseur _____ e. watchful, shrewd

---

### TODAY'S IDIOM

***out of one's depth***—in a situation that is too difficult to handle

We thought he knew the ropes,* but we found him behind the eight ball* because he was *out of his depth.*

---

ANSWERS ARE ON PAGE 306

While each day's story has five new words, there are many others that are repeated from previous weeks. These words are placed within the stories so that you might practice your grasp of their meanings. Repetition will help guarantee that these words will be firmly fixed as part of your ever-expanding vocabulary.

## REVIEW WORDS

| | | DEFINITIONS |
|---|---|---|
| _____ | 1. abjure | **a.** stir up, instigate |
| _____ | 2. allay | **b.** disorderly, carelessly |
| _____ | 3. complacent | **c.** regretful, confessing guilt |
| _____ | 4. connoisseur | **d.** abstain from, renounce |
| _____ | 5. debilitate | **e.** weaken |
| _____ | 6. deter | **f.** self-satisfied |
| _____ | 7. discreet | **g.** discourage, hinder |
| _____ | 8. evanescent | **h.** bent, inclination, disposition |
| _____ | 9. foment | **i.** sad, gloomy |
| _____ | 10. glean | **j.** identical, equivalent |
| _____ | 11. impetuous | **k.** something hunted or pursued |
| _____ | 12. occult | **l.** watchful, shrewd |
| _____ | 13. penitent | **m.** supernatural, mysterious, secret |
| _____ | 14. propensity | **n.** impulsive |
| _____ | 15. quarry | **o.** rebuke, reprimand* |
| _____ | 16. reproach | **p.** momentary, passing, fleeting |
| _____ | 17. slovenly | **q.** prudent,* careful, cautious |
| _____ | 18. somber | **r.** collect, gather |
| _____ | 19. tantamount | **s.** expert |
| _____ | 20. wary | **t.** soothe, calm |

## IDIOMS

| | | | |
|---|---|---|---|
| _____ | 21. out of one's depth | **u.** | exactly on time |
| _____ | 22. to hit the nail on the head | **v.** | in a situation that is too difficult to handle |
| _____ | 23. to take under one's wing | **w.** | to become responsible for |
| _____ | 24. on the dot | **x.** | to state or guess something correctly |

## WORDS FOR FURTHER STUDY — MEANINGS

Check your answers on page 306. The routine for checking and study should be well implanted by now. Some weeks you will have no words wrong. At other times, you may have several. Don't be discouraged by the differences from week to week

1. _____  _____

2. _____  _____

3. _____  _____

❖ Using the clues listed below, fill in each blank in the following story with one of the new words you learned this week.

## *Good Enough to Eat?*

There seems to be universal agreement that exposure to the ultraviolet light from the sun is deleterious to one's health. Also, except for tobacco industry spokesmen, there is no dispute about the damage done to us from cigarette smoke. What is shocking is the fact that almost everything we once regarded as either beneficial, or harmless, soon gets challenged by scientists. We are urged to ①_____ foods that have high fat content. There go butter and cheese. Even milk has now been added to the list of foods of which we must be ②_____ .

Whatever diet we are on, we cannot become ③_____ about its nutritional value. We are left, ultimately, with the ④_____ thought that, sooner or later, almost everything we eat or drink may be found to jeopardize our health.

Given that there are many obstacles to maintaining good health, would it be wise to embrace every new laboratory report in order to ⑤_____ information? Let's not discard old, proven, sensible food habits. Also, there is always the possibility that ice cream sundaes will be found to cure baldness, and that chocolate chip cookies will eliminate our cholesterol problems.

## Clues
① 3rd Day
② 4th Day
③ 1st Day
④ 1st Day
⑤ 2nd Day

**NEW WORDS**

**site**
sīt

**vigil**
vij´ əl

**cumbersome**
kum´ bər səm

**interrogate**
in ter´ ə gāt

**divulge**
də vulj´

## ANOTHER PLAN

Robert was far from tranquil* as he waited in the lobby for almost an hour after the performance had begun. Disgruntled,* he quit the *site* of his *vigil*. He had to face the fact that he was making no tangible* progress. Tomorrow he would telephone several women's residences. It was a *cumbersome* way of going about the hunt, but it was all that he could think of at the moment. He would *interrogate* the desk clerks, and perhaps he might uncover a pertinent* clue to Evelyn's whereabouts. If he could only get someone to *divulge* her hiding place! Perhaps tomorrow would culminate* in success.

**Sample Sentences** Insert the new words in these sentences.

1. With rancor he faced the _____ job of transporting the voluminous* records to his new office.

2. Before they began to _____ the criminal, they had to admonish* him that his testimony might be used to incarcerate* him.

3. The hunter maintained a discreet* and wary* _____ as he waited for the propitious* moment to bag his quarry*.

4. Even under duress,* he was adamant* and would not _____ the secret.

5. The newly married couple selected the _____ for their new home with meticulous* care.

**Definitions** Match the new words with their definitions.

6. site     _____     a. unwieldy, burdensome

7. vigil     _____     b. question

8. cumbersome     _____     c. wakeful watching

9. interrogate     _____     d. disclose, reveal

10. divulge     _____     e. location

---

**TODAY'S IDIOM**

***to take a leaf out of someone's book*—to imitate or follow the example**

The chip off the old block* *took a leaf from his father's book* and never sowed wild oats*.

---

ANSWERS ARE ON PAGE 306

# WEEK 34 ❖ DAY 2

## NEW WORDS

**fluctuate**
fluk´ chü āt

**unmitigated**
un mit´ ə gā´ tid

**commodious**
kə mō´ dē əs

**antiquated**
an´ tə kwā tid

**disheveled**
də shev´ əld

## A HOPE DASHED

The next day, Wednesday, saw Robert become more frustrated.* He would *fluctuate* between high hopes of finding Evelyn and *unmitigated* despair when he was almost ready to desist* in his search. The phone calls had elicited* almost nothing. Robert had rushed to one women's residence when the clerk described a girl who might just be Evelyn. The desk clerk phoned to her room on the pretext* that she had a special delivery letter. Robert waited in the *commodious* lobby, replete* with large, *antiquated* pieces of furniture. He watched from a discreet* distance as she came down the stairs. One look at her wan* face, slovenly* dress, and *disheveled* hair was enough to inform Robert that he needed no further scrutiny.* This could not be his impeccable* Evelyn.

**Sample Sentences** Insert the new words in these sentences.

1. He wasn't exactly an _____ liar; he merely embellished* the truth a little.

2. In his sumptuous* house he had a _____ den in which he kept an array* of trophies as incontrovertible* evidence of his skill.

3. Is it banal* to say that good manners are _____ in our milieu?*

4. The current trend* in the stock market is for stocks to _____ in a sporadic* fashion.

5. The nondescript,* indolent* beggar was in a _____ condition.

**Definitions** Match the new words with their definitions.

6. fluctuate _____    **a.** large, spacious

7. unmitigated _____    **b.** shift, alternate

8. commodious _____    **c.** disorderly clothing or hair

9. antiquated _____    **d.** unrelieved, as bad as can be

10. disheveled _____    **e.** out-of-date, obsolete

---
**TODAY'S IDIOM**

*brass tacks*—the real problem or situation

After some moments of congenial* levity,* they got down to *brass tacks*.

---

ANSWERS ARE ON PAGE 306

209

## NEW WORDS

**tenacious**
ti nā´ shəs

**façade**
fə säd´

**asinine**
as´ n īn

**grimace**
grə mās´

**calumny**
kal´ əm nē

## TO THE POLICE

Thursday was his next-to-last day. He had been *tenacious* in following up every lead. Now he was behind the eight ball.* He could hardly galvanize* himself to do anything else. The *façade* of hope he had worn for almost a week was crumbling; there was nothing left to be sanguine* about. In desperation he turned to the police and placed his problem within their jurisdiction.* They asked many questions, and they requested that he not expurgate anything. Some of the questions seemed *asinine*. When they inquired about his relationship to the missing girl, he replied, with a *grimace*, "Fiancee." When they suggested she might be hiding in that part of the city where the "punk" coterie* congregated, he was incredulous* and accused the police of *calumny* against her good name and reputation.

**Sample Sentences**  Insert the new words in these sentences.

1. He held on to his antiquated* beliefs with a _____ obsession.*

2. The woman was noted for her vituperative _____ against her innocuous,* although senile,* neighbor.

3. She could not abjure* a _____ when she saw the disheveled figure.

4. How _____ of the boy to fabricate* that bizarre* story!

5. His face wore the most doleful* _____ .

**Definitions**  Match the new words with their definitions.

6. tenacious _____ a. false accusation, slander

7. façade _____ b. silly, stupid

8. asinine _____ c. front, superficial appearance

9. grimace _____ d. tough, stubborn

10. calumny _____ e. facial expression of disgust

─── **TODAY'S IDIOM** ───

*hook, line, and sinker*—completely, all the way
The teacher fell for the practical joke *hook, line, and sinker.*

ANSWERS ARE ON PAGE 306

# WEEK 34 ❖ DAY 4

**pittance**
pit´ ns

**au courant**
ō´ kü raNt´

**fastidious**
fa stid´ ē əs

**noisome**
noi´ səm

**unkempt**
un kempt´

## EVELYN DISCOVERED

Failure was imminent,* and Robert was bereft* of hope. It was now Friday. Despite his abstemious* and parsimonious* way of living, his money had been reduced to a mere *pittance*. A perverse* impulse brought him to the section where young people in strange clothing and with uncouth* manners made him recoil* in unmitigated* disgust. He had never been *au courant* with the "hippies" and "punks." He was always *fastidious* about proper dress and behavior. A moment later he saw her! Evelyn! She was sitting at a table in a coffee shop, surrounded by a coterie* of the most *noisome* individuals he had ever seen. Evelyn was not incongruous,* for she herself was *unkempt*. So this was her new habitat*! At that instant Robert knew as an incontrovertible* fact that he had lost her. With a grimace,* he turned and walked, a doleful* and melancholy figure, toward the bus depot and home.

**Sample Sentences**  Insert the new words in these sentences.

1. Styles are such transient* things that what is _____ today, is archaic* tomorrow.

2. The tip he had been offered was a mere _____ , and the taxi driver threw it on the ground in disdain.*

3. Children think mothers are asinine* to get upset about _____ rooms.

4. It was inevitable* that they discover the hidden body by its _____ aroma.

5. He was so _____ about table manners that he lost his equanimity* when his son reached for the bread.

**Definitions**  Match the new words with their definitions.

6. pittance     _____  **a.** untidy, neglected
7. au courant   _____  **b.** foul, unwholesome
8. fastidious   _____  **c.** small amount
9. noisome      _____  **d.** particular, choosy
10. unkempt     _____  **e.** up-to-date

---
### TODAY'S IDIOM
---

*lily-livered*—cowardly

The *lily-livered* gangster got cold feet* and spilled the beans.*

As an "old hand" at vocabulary-building by the context method, you realize that this is the most natural and effective way. However, you also know that there is work and self-discipline too. You should carry these fine qualities right through life. The words you learn are valuable, the method is equally so.

## REVIEW WORDS

_____ 1. antiquated
_____ 2. asinine
_____ 3. au courant
_____ 4. calumny
_____ 5. commodious
_____ 6. cumbersome
_____ 7. disheveled
_____ 8. divulge
_____ 9. façade
_____ 10. fastidious
_____ 11. fluctuate
_____ 12. grimace
_____ 13. interrogate
_____ 14. noisome
_____ 15. pittance
_____ 16. site
_____ 17. tenacious
_____ 18. unkempt
_____ 19. unmitigated
_____ 20. vigil

## DEFINITIONS

a. stubborn, tough
b. slander, false accusation
c. small amount
d. neglected, untidy
e. location
f. reveal, disclose
g. alternate, shift
h. disorderly clothing or hair
i. superficial appearance, front
j. facial expression of disgust
k. up-to-date
l. unwholesome, foul
m. wakeful watching
n. question
o. as bad as can be, unrelieved
p. out-of-date, obsolete
q. stupid, silly
r. choosy, particular
s. burdensome, unwieldy
t. spacious, large

## IDIOMS

_____ 21. brass tacks
_____ 22. hook, line, and sinker
_____ 23. lily-livered
_____ 24. to take a leaf out of someone's book

u. cowardly
v. completely, all the way
w. to imitate or follow the example
x. the real problem or situation

## WORDS FOR FURTHER STUDY   MEANINGS

The answers can be found on page 306. The method of study and learning requires quick review and re-use of difficult words. Start now!

1. _____   _____
2. _____   _____
3. _____   _____

❖ Using the clues listed below, fill in each blank in the following story with one of the new words you learned this week.

## *Women in the Ring*

What sport requires the timing of tennis, the energy of aerobics, the stamina of cross-country running, and the physical contact of football? The answer is: boxing. And now that seemingly male spectacle is attracting women. What was once viewed as ① _____ brutality has been transformed in gymnasiums across the country into the latest form of workout, weight reduction, and energy stimulator.

To suggest that women should not expose themselves to the sharp jabs and powerful uppercuts of boxing because they are the "weaker" sex is ② _____ . Properly trained by experts, in good shape from punching bags and jumping rope, women can be as ③ _____ in the ring as men.

With women jockeys, race car drivers, hockey goalies, and basketball players, it would require a man with ④ _____ prejudice, if not sheer ignorance, to argue that boxing is solely a man's sport. Anyone who is ⑤ _____ with the status of liberated women need not be surprised by their entry into the ring.

## Clues

① 2nd Day

② 3rd Day

③ 3rd Day

④ 2nd Day

⑤ 4th Day

**parable**
par´ ə bəl

**whimsical**
hwim´ zə kəl

**lampoon**
lam pün´

**countenance**
koun´ tə nəns

**sanctimonious**
sangk´ tə mō´ nē əs

## A MODERN AESOP

The telling of a story in simple terms that has an inherently* important message is a venerable* art form. The *parable* may be found teaching a moral lesson in the Bible. Aesop is an incontrovertible* master of the fable. This story form is far from antiquated* as shown by the *whimsical* approach to life taken by the modern Aesop, James Thurber. His stories *lampoon* the strange behavior of his fellow men. Thurber seems unable to *countenance* the ideas that permeate* our society regarding the rules by which we should live. Least of all is he able to accept the *sanctimonious* notion that some people promulgate* that good always wins out against evil. Thurber's stories often take an exactly opposite point of view.

**Sample Sentences** Note that some words do not have a one word definition. Frequently, several words, or an entire sentence, is required.

1. Jonathan Swift was never reticent* to _____ the egotist* in order to bring him down with alacrity.*

2. What one person finds _____ , the other may find asinine.*

3. The expression, "Sour grapes,*" is the gist* of a famous _____ about a fox who couldn't get what he wanted.

4. We should eschew* our _____ façade;* away with pretext!*

5. If we want to live in a salubrious* milieu,* we can not _____ the noisome* fumes that are deleterious* to health.

**Definitions** Note the distinction between *countenance* as a noun and as a verb.

6. parable        _____   **a.** humorous, witty

7. whimsical      _____   **b.** hypocritically religious

8. lampoon (v.)   _____   **c.** tolerate,* approve

9. countenance (v.) _____ **d.** a moralistic story

10. sanctimonious  _____  **e.** ridicule

---
### TODAY'S IDIOM

***to pull up stakes*—to quit a place**

He could no longer rule the roost* or get the lion's share,*
so he *pulled up stakes* and moved on.

---

                                ANSWERS ARE ON PAGE 306

## MODERNIZING A PARABLE*

Thurber punctures in an incisive* way the platitudes* that come from stories handed down through the generations. These old saws are accepted by everyone. One such tale is about a tortoise who had read in an ancient book that a tortoise had beaten a hare in a race. The sage* old tortoise construed* this story to mean that he could outrun a hare. With *equanimity* he hunted for a hare and soon found one. "Do you have the *effrontery* to challenge me?" asked the incredulous* hare. "You are a *nonentity*," he scoffed* at the tortoise. A course of fifty feet was set out. The other animals gathered around the site*. At the sound of the gun they were off. When the hare crossed the finish line, the *flabbergasted* tortoise had gone approximately eight and three-quarter inches. The moral Thurber draws from this *debacle* for the tortoise: A new broom may sweep clean, but never trust an old saw.

*Which of the five "new words" have you seen before? Answer with equanimity.*

**Sample Sentences** Insert the new words in these sentences.

1. He was a precocious* youngster, but he soon reached the nadir* of his career, lost all of his prestige*, and became a _____ .

2. Do you have the _____ to take that supercilious and facetious* attitude toward something as sinister* as this?

3. These turbulent* times require a leader who does not go into a capricious* pique,* but rather one who faces acrimonious* criticism with _____ .

4. When the judge exonerated* the charlatan,* we were all _____ .

5. The fortuitous* appearance of a relief column permitted an adroit* escape from the imminent* _____ .

**Definitions** Match the new words with their definitions.

6. equanimity _____ **a.** calmness, self-control

7. effrontery _____ **b.** astounded

8. nonentity _____ **c.** boldness

9. flabbergasted _____ **d.** ruin, collapse

10. debacle _____ **e.** one of no importance

───── **TODAY'S IDIOM** ─────

***to raise Cain*—to cause trouble, make a fuss**

When he found he was left holding the bag,* he decided *to raise Cain.*

## NEW WORDS

**vivacious**
vī vā´ shəs

**gaunt**
gônt

**mien**
mēn

**hirsute**
hėr´ süt

**refute**
ri fyüt´

## THINGS HAVE CHANGED

Thurber modernizes an old story that everyone has read or heard. It has to do with a nefarious* wolf who kept a vigil* in an ominous* forest until a little girl came along carrying a basket of food for her grandmother. With alacrity,* this *vivacious* youngster told the wolf the address to which she was going. Hungry and *gaunt* the wolf rushed to the house. When the girl arrived and entered, she saw someone in bed wearing a nightcap and a nightgown. While the figure was dressed like her grandmother, the little girl surmised* with only a perfunctory* glance that it didn't have the old lady's *mien.* She approached and became cognizant* of the *hirsute* face of the wolf. She drew a revolver from her purse and shot the interloper* dead. Thurber arrives at a moral for this story that anyone would find difficult to *refute:* It is not so easy to fool little girls nowadays as it used to be.

**Sample Sentences** Insert the new words in these sentences.

1. She had a _____ of humility,* but it was only a façade.*

2. He did not waste time trying to _____ an irrelevant* and tortuous* argument.

3. You may have discerned* that it is no longer the latest vogue* among boys to permit their faces to become _____ .

4. They were struck by the anomaly* of one twin who was phlegmatic* while the other was _____ .

5. Women strive for the slender and au courant* _____ look.

**Definitions** Match the new words with their definition.

6. vivacious _____ **a.** thin, haggard

7. gaunt _____ **b.** lively, gay

8. mien _____ **c.** hairy

9. hirsute _____ **d.** appearance, bearing

10. refute _____ **e.** prove wrong or false

### TODAY'S IDIOM

*to leave no stone unturned*—to try one's best, to make every effort

Since you're from Missouri,* I'll *leave no stone unturned* to convince you.

ANSWERS ARE ON PAGE 306

# WEEK 35 ❖ DAY 4

**NEW WORDS**

**pensive**
pen´ siv

**whet**
hwet

**stupor**
stü´ pər

**wince**
wins

**cliché**
klē shā´

## ANOTHER SURPRISE

Thurber's stories are written in a jocose* manner, but they contain enough serious matter to make one *pensive*. He tells of some builders who left a pane of glass standing upright in a field near a house they were constructing. A goldfinch flew across the field, struck the glass and was knocked inert.* He rushed back and divulged* to his friends that the air had crystallized. The other birds derided* him, said he had become irrational,* and gave a number of reasons for the accident. The only bird who believed the goldfinch was the swallow. The goldfinch challenged the large birds to follow the same path he had flown. This challenge served to *whet* their interest, and they agreed with gusto.* Only the swallow abjured.* The large birds flew together and struck the glass; they were knocked into a *stupor*. This caused the astute* swallow to *wince* with pain. Thurber drew a moral that is the antithesis* of the *cliché* we all accept: He who hesitates is sometimes saved.

**Sample Sentences** Insert the new words in these sentences.

1. He was in such a _____ as a result of the accident that this precluded* his hearing my condolence.*

2. If you juxtapose* one _____ with another, you often get completely opposite lessons about life.

3. The hostile* rebuke* made the usually phlegmatic* boy _____ .

4. You cannot _____ his desire for the theater with dubious* histrionics.*

5. The fervid* marriage proposal made the shy girl _____ .

**Definitions** Match the new words with their definitions.

6. pensive _____ a. thoughtful, reflective

7. whet _____ b. stimulate, stir up

8. stupor _____ c. a commonplace phrase

9. wince _____ d. draw back, flinch

10. cliché _____ e. daze, insensible condition

---
**TODAY'S IDIOM**
---

*tongue in one's cheek*—not to be sincere

John's father surely had *his tongue in his cheek* when he told his son
to go sow wild oats* and to kick over the traces at his kindergarten party.

To strengthen your word power, keep adding words from all the sources you use during the day. The words learned while reading this book give you a firm basis. School texts, newspapers, magazines, etc., should all give you the opportunity to corroborate* the fact that your vocabulary is growing, and they should also be the source for new words.

## REVIEW WORDS

_____ 1. cliché
_____ 2. countenance
_____ 3. debacle
_____ 4. effrontery
_____ 5. equanimity
_____ 6. flabbergasted
_____ 7. gaunt
_____ 8. hirsute
_____ 9. lampoon
_____ 10. mien
_____ 11. nonentity
_____ 12. parable
_____ 13. pensive
_____ 14. refute
_____ 15. sanctimonious
_____ 16. stupor
_____ 17. vivacious
_____ 18. whet
_____ 19. whimsical
_____ 20. wince

## DEFINITIONS

a. astounded
b. one of no importance
c. witty, humorous
d. ridicule
e. hairy
f. prove wrong, disprove
g. flinch, draw back
h. self-control
i. collapse, ruin
j. hypocritically religious
k. a moralistic story
l. gay, lively
m. bearing, appearance
n. stir up, stimulate
o. boldness
p. approve, tolerate*
q. haggard, thin
r. reflective, thoughtful
s. a commonplace phrase
t. insensible condition, daze

## IDIOMS

_____ 21. tongue in one's cheek
_____ 22. to leave no stone unturned
_____ 23. to pull up stakes
_____ 24. to raise Cain

u. make a fuss, cause trouble
v. to make every effort, to try one's best
w. not to be sincere
x. to quit a place

Check your answers on page 306. Look back at the story to check the use of each word in its context. This will help fix it in your mind.

## WORDS FOR FURTHER STUDY    MEANINGS

1. _____    _____

2. _____    _____

3. _____    _____

❖ Using the clues listed below, fill in each blank in the following story with one of the new words you learned this week.

## *Beam Me Up, Scotty*

In 1966 a television program appeared that quickly established itself as the most successful science fiction series, moved on to become a series of popular films, and continues in reruns to be seen somewhere in this country every night of the year. This original series, *Star Trek,* became so popular that there are huge fan clubs across the country and the stars of the original series are mobbed when they make personal appearances.

What makes this form of science fiction so popular? Some may say that each story of the future is a ①_____ showing us our own world through a presentation of other worlds. There are those who would ②_____ this analysis and argue that it is the odd characters, the ③_____ aliens, who attract us. We watch with ④_____ as worlds battle, knowing it will turn out well in the end.

After many years and many TV episodes and movies, "Star Trek" and its successors continue to ⑤_____ our appetite and bring excitement to our screens. As long as space remains an almost total mystery, the unexplained will capture our imaginations.

## Clues

① 1st Day

② 3rd Day

③ 3rd Day

④ 2nd Day

⑤ 4th Day

## NEW WORDS

**genre**
zhän´ rə

**candid**
kan´ did

**unsavory**
un sā´ vər ē

**degrade**
di grād´

**venial**
vē´ nē əl

## A LADY NOVELIST

The nineteenth century saw the woman novelist attain the same prestige* as men. England was prolific* in producing women writers. One of the foremost in this *genre* was Charlotte Brontë. In *Jane Eyre* she presented a *candid* portrait of a woman caught up in a clandestine* affair with a married man. Miss Bronte's readers were engrossed* in this story. She took this *unsavory* subject and presented it in a way that did not *degrade* the relationship. She showed that true passion can be healthy. Miss Brontë did not disparage* Jane's feelings or besmirch* her character. The author was generous in her verdict. The affair was considered merely a *venial* sin because Jane was never false in her feelings or her actions.

**Sample Sentences**  Insert the new words in these sentences.

1. Harry held the fallacious* belief that the menial* job would _____ him in the eyes of his friends.

2. Betty's childish fabrications* were judged _____ sins, although they mortified* her mother.

3. Modern abstract painting is a highly lucrative* _____ .

4. It is reprehensible,* but it doesn't require much gossip to give a person a(n) _____ reputation.

5. In my _____ opinion he is a sanctimonious* fool.

**Definitions**  Match the new words with their definitions.

6. genre        _____   a. make contemptible, lower

7. candid       _____   b. disagreeable, offensive, morally bad

8. unsavory     _____   c. a certain form or style in painting or literature

9. degrade      _____   d. pardonable, forgivable

10. venial      _____   e. frank, open, honest

---
## TODAY'S IDIOM
---

*keep a stiff upper lip*—keep up courage, stand up to trouble

When he heard through the grapevine* that the fat was in the fire,* he knew he had *to keep a stiff upper lip* so as not to spill the beans.*

# WEEK 36 ❖ DAY 2

**epitome**
i pit´ ə mē

**dexterity**
dek ster´ ə tē

**grotesque**
grō tesk´

**compassion**
kəm pash´ ən

**repugnant**
ri pug´ nənt

## VICTOR HUGO

The *epitome* of French romantic writers in the nineteenth century was Victor Hugo. With the utmost *dexterity* he wrote poetry, novels, and drama. His highly popular novels, *Notre Dame de Paris* and *Les Miserables,* are replete* with melodramatic situations and *grotesque* characters. He had a profound* sense of social justice and a *compassion* for the poor, hapless,* and downtrodden. He could not work under the aegis* of Napoleon III and fled into exile. When the *repugnant* rule came to an end, the expatriate* returned. He was received with adulation* and acclaim as the idol of the Third Republic.

**Sample Sentences**  Insert the new words in these sentences.

1. He was made up in the most _____ way for his role as a man from outer space.

2. We all felt deep _____ for the innocent progeny,* who were bereft* of their parents who had succumbed* during the conflagration.*

3. The Taj Mahal in India is said to be the _____ of grace as an edifice.*

4. The sight of the corpse was _____ to the squeamish* onlookers.

5. With _____ he thwarted* the pugnacious* and belligerent* adversary.*

**Definitions**  Match the new words with their definitions.

6. epitome _____ a. strange, bizarre,* fantastic

7. dexterity _____ b. person or thing that embodies or represents the best

8. grotesque _____ c. distasteful, repulsive

9. compassion _____ d. sympathetic feeling, kindness

10. repugnant _____ e. mental or physical skill

---
### TODAY'S IDIOM

**to throw the book at someone—to give the maximum punishment**
The judge got his back up* and *threw the book* at the criminal.

---

## NEW WORDS

**acme**
ak´ mē

**copious**
ko´ pē əs

**vehemently**
vē´ ə ment lē

**depict**
di pikt´

**naive**
nä ēv´

## AN ENGLISH REALIST

The movement toward realism in the English novel of the nineteenth century reached its *acme* with the works of Charles Dickens and William Makepeace Thackeray. Charles Dickens was a prolific* writer. Among his *copious* works are *Oliver Twist*, a candid* exposure of the repugnant* poor laws; *Nicholas Nickleby*, in which the life of boys in a boarding school is *vehemently* attacked; *Hard Times*, in which the author wanted to *depict* the infamous* life in a factory during an early period of the industrial revolution; *The Pickwick Papers*, about a *naive* gentleman who has numerous misadventures. The novels, aimed at exposing the sordid* and pernicious* elements of English life, were said to have helped galvanize* people into action leading to improvement in these conditions.

**Sample Sentences** Insert the new words in these sentences.

1. At the _____ of his power, the dictator was obsessed* with the belief that those who dissented* were trying to usurp* his position.

2. As a perspicacious* newspaper reporter, he felt it incumbent* upon him to _____ the abortive* coup* as a reprehensible* act.

3. The urbane* gentleman was flabbergasted* by the fervid* interest in wrestling shown by the _____ young girl.

4. She lost her decorum* and wept _____ tears at the poignant* story.

5. He objected _____ to a vote taking place in the absence of a quorum.*

**Definitions** Match the new words with their definitions.

6. acme _____ **a.** unworldly, unsophisticated

7. copious _____ **b.** violently, eagerly, passionately

8. vehemently _____ **c.** peak, pinnacle,* zenith*

9. depict _____ **d.** ample, abundant, plentiful

10. naive _____ **e.** describe clearly, picture, portray

---
### TODAY'S IDIOM

*terra firma*—solid, firm land

The rough ocean crossing took the wind out of his sails*,
and he was happy to be on *terra firma* again.

---

ANSWERS ARE ON PAGE 307

# WEEK 36 ❖ DAY 4

**NEW WORDS**

**perfidious**
pər fid´ ē əs

**covet**
kuv´ it

**ingratiate**
in grā´ shē āt

**penury**
pen´ yer ē

**ignominious**
ig´ nə min´ ē əs

## A SCHEMING HEROINE

William Makepeace Thackeray was known for his moralistic study of upper and middle class English life. His best known work, *Vanity Fair*, has as its central character Becky Sharp. She is a *perfidious* woman who has an insatiable* desire to get ahead in the world. She *covets* the wealth of one man, but when marriage is not feasible* she succeeds in a plan to *ingratiate* herself into the heart of her employer's son. Their marriage is not a salubrious* one and Becky, who lives ostentatiously,* forms a surreptitious* liaison with another man. The affair culminates* in a debacle.* She is exposed, her husband leaves her, and she must live in *penury* in Europe. This is the *ignominious* end for a clever, but misguided woman.

**Sample Sentences** Insert the new words in these sentences.

1. Under the aegis* of a zealous* campaign manager, the candidate was able to _____ herself into the hearts of the public.

2. A favorite parable* has to do with teaching the lesson that one should not _____ that which belongs to someone else.

3. His fortune fluctuated* between _____ and wealth.

4. They made an effigy* of their _____ enemy.

5. There was bedlam* as the favored team went down to _____ defeat at the hands of the underdog.

**Definitions** Match the new words with their definitions.

6. perfidious _____ a. treacherous, false

7. covet _____ b. want, envy, wish

8. ingratiate _____ c. humiliating, disgraceful

9. penury _____ d. poverty

10. ignominious _____ e. win confidence, charm

---

**TODAY'S IDIOM**

***in seventh heaven*—the highest happiness or delight**

The oldest child was *in seventh heaven* when
her mother let her rule the roost* for a day.

---

ANSWERS ARE ON PAGE 307

# REVIEW

Whether you read a classic novel or a modern one, the one thing they have in common is their use of a rather extensive vocabulary. Don't be handicapped in your reading—increase your vocabulary by constant study and review.

## REVIEW WORDS

| | |
|---|---|
| ___ | 1. acme |
| ___ | 2. candid |
| ___ | 3. compassion |
| ___ | 4. copious |
| ___ | 5. covet |
| ___ | 6. degrade |
| ___ | 7. depict |
| ___ | 8. dexterity |
| ___ | 9. epitome |
| ___ | 10. genre |
| ___ | 11. grotesque |
| ___ | 12. ignominious |
| ___ | 13. ingratiate |
| ___ | 14. naïve |
| ___ | 15. penury |
| ___ | 16. perfidious |
| ___ | 17. repugnant |
| ___ | 18. unsavory |
| ___ | 19. vehemently |
| ___ | 20. venial |

## DEFINITIONS

a. open, honest, frank
b. kindness, sympathetic feeling
c. zenith,* pinnacle,* peak
d. wish, envy, want
e. false, treacherous
f. unsophisticated, unworldly
g. fantastic, strange, bizarre*
h. lower, make contemptible
i. a certain form or style in painting or literature
j. repulsive, distasteful
k. plentiful, abundant, ample
l. poverty
m. portray, picture, describe clearly
n. person or thing that represents the best
o. morally bad, disagreeable, offensive
p. physical or mental skill
q. passionately, violently, eagerly
r. charm, win confidence
s. forgivable, pardonable
t. disgraceful, humiliating

## IDIOMS

| | |
|---|---|
| ___ | 21. to throw the book at someone |
| ___ | 22. in seventh heaven |
| ___ | 23. terra firma |
| ___ | 24. keep a stiff upper lip |

u. keep up courage, stand up to trouble
v. to give maximum punishment
w. solid, firm land
x. the highest happiness or delight

Check your answers on page 307. Review incorrect words.

## WORDS FOR FURTHER STUDY          MEANINGS

1. _____    _____

2. _____    _____

3. _____    _____

# SENSIBLE SENTENCES?
## (From Weeks 33–36)

❖ Underline the word that makes sense in each of the sentences below.

1. We tried to *(deter, divulge)* him but he was determined to submit to open heart surgery.

2. The reporter lost his job when he labeled the senator's remarks as *(unmitigated, asinine)*.

3. Freddie had the *(effrontery, propensity)* to ask Robin for a date after having criticized her appearance.

4. Ordinarily, Jonathan was especially neat, but he looked quite *(disheveled, fastidious)* at the end of our camping trip.

5. After hearing the bad news, the students left the auditorium with *(venial, somber)* faces.

6. My Uncle Robert, who is really conservative about his investments, made money on Wall Street by not being *(impetuous, wary)*.

7. I knew I could confide in Caryl-Sue because she has a reputation for being *(discreet, sanctimonious)*.

8. The traitor's *(perfidious, pensive)* action resulted in the loss of many lives.

9. Our water commissioner was *(complacent, flabbergasted)* to learn that his own lawn sprinkler had been turned on during the water emergency.

10. Sophie was accepted by our wide circle of friends because of her *(vivacious, tenacious)* personality.

ANSWERS ARE ON PAGE 307

# WORDSEARCH 36

❖ Using the clues listed below, fill in each blank in the following story with one of the new words you learned this week.

## *1492–1992*

We are all aware that 1992 was the year during which there were ① _____ reminders that it marked the 500th anniversary of Columbus' arrival in this part of the hemisphere. Along with the celebrations and historical reenactments, there was controversy regarding the lives of those who had been here for many centuries before that fateful event.

Historical research shows that it would be extremely ② _____ to believe that "civilization" began on this continent with Columbus' arrival. The Native American tribes had formed nations and had come together in an organization known as the Five Nations. They had regulations for governance that were the ③ _____ of self-rule and that became the models on which our Constitution was partly based.

It was to remove the ④ _____ portrayal of the Native American as savage and wild that historians adopted 1992 as the year to ⑤ _____ them in their true light as members of civilizations worthy of study and respect.

### Clues

① 3rd Day
② 3rd Day
③ 2nd Day
④ 4th Day
⑤ 3rd Day

ANSWERS ARE ON PAGE 307

# WEEK 37 ❖ DAY 1

**NEW WORDS**

confront
kən frunt´

antipathy
an tip´ ə thē

servile
sėr´ vəl

volition
vō lish´ ən

sojourn
sō´ jėrn

## A MAN OF NATURE

Henry Thoreau attempted to *confront* the problem and solve the enigma* of how one might earn a living and yet not become an ignominious* slave to the task. He viewed the industrial revolution with *antipathy*. Man in a *servile* role to extraneous* possessions was a main target of his writings. He believed that one could attain genuine wealth not by accumulating objects or money, but through enjoyment and perusal* of nature. By his own *volition* he gave up friends and comforts for a two year *sojourn* by himself at Walden Pond. What others might judge as penury,* was seen by Thoreau as the epitome* of wealth.

**Sample Sentences**  Insert the new words in these sentences.

1. He found his _____ position a degrading* one and could not accept it with equanimity.*

2. The expatriate* decided to make his _____ in France a permanent one in order to give up his nomadic* way of life.

3. Why do we refuse to _____ the unsavory* problems of our times in a candid* and incisive* way?

4. He was a tenacious* competitor, and at his own _____ he placed his title in jeopardy* on many occasions.

5. Her _____ towards men was based on rather nebulous* events that she construed* to prove that they were all perfidious.*

**Definitions**  Match the new words with their definitions.

6. confront     _____     a.  temporary stay

7. antipathy    _____     b.  willpower, choice

8. servile      _____     c.  dislike, distaste, hate

9. volition     _____     d.  come face to face with

10. sojourn (n.) _____    e.  slavish, submissive

---
### TODAY'S IDIOM

**to tighten one's belt**—to get set for bad times or poverty

He knew he would have to draw in his horns* and
*tighten his belt* or he would wind up on skid row*.

---

## NEW WORDS

**austere**
ô stir´

**felicitous**
fə lis´ ə təs

**halcyon**
hal´ sē ən

**tenable**
ten´ ə bəl

**superfluous**
su̇ pér´ flü əs

## THE GOOD LIFE

Thoreau's book about the *austere* but happy life at Walden Pond propagated* his fame around the world. He built a small hut and began living an ascetic* existence. He found it to be a *felicitous* experience. In this idyllic* setting he was able to spend his time reading, studying nature, writing, and thinking. Far from being indolent,* he kept busy in many ways. At the end of the experiment he recalled the *halcyon* days with pleasure. He believed he had learned the secret of the truly happy life. The only *tenable* way of life is one in harmony with nature; material possessions are *superfluous*.

**Sample Sentences**   Insert the new words in these sentences.

1.  When he found his sinecure* was no longer _____ , he felt it a propitious* time to resign.

2.  Far from being ostentatious,* she was considered the acme* of fashion because of her _____ manner of dress.

3.  Because he was an itinerant* worker, he had to disdain* carrying _____ equipment.

4.  On that _____ occasion the amount of money he spent was irrelevant.*

5.  During the turbulent* days of the war, they wished for the _____ days of earlier times.

**Definitions**   Match the new words with their definitions.

6.  austere        _____   **a.**  supportable, defendable

7.  felicitous      _____   **b.**  simple, unadorned, hard

8.  halcyon        _____   **c.**  peaceful, calm

9.  tenable        _____   **d.**  happy

10.  superfluous    _____   **e.**  excessive, surplus

───── **TODAY'S IDIOM** ─────

*off the beaten track*—**not usual, out of the ordinary**

Because his ideas were always *off the beaten track,*
he lived under a sword of Damocles* on his job.

ANSWERS ARE ON PAGE 307

# WEEK 37 ❖ DAY 3

**NEW WORDS**

**motivate**
mō´ tə vāt

**rationalize**
rash´ ə nə līz

**therapy**
ther´ ə pē

**nascent**
nas´ nt

**iconoclast**
ī kon´ ə klast

## THE MIND'S SECRETS

The study of the human mind and behavior has had many prominent practitioners, but no one is more revered* than Sigmund Freud. An Austrian physician, he is said to be the father of psychoanalysis. He taught that man has a subconscious mind in which he keeps repugnant* memories that come to the surface surreptitiously* and *motivate* behavior. Man often tries to *rationalize* his actions, when, in reality, they are really the result of suppressed memories coming to the surface. Freud's approach to the disturbed person was to attempt *therapy* by examining the dreams that make cognizant* what the cause of the illness might be. Only with the airing of deleterious*, buried emotions can the person move from the *nascent* stage to that of full health. Freud was considered an *iconoclast* in the field of psychology when his ideas first appeared at the beginning of the twentieth century.

**Sample Sentences**  Insert the new words in these sentences.

1. The _____ was in favor of jettisoning* one of the traditions that had become an intrinsic* part of his life.

2. In order to complete the _____ , the doctor said a trip to a warm, dry climate was mandatory.*

3. Complacent* people are difficult to _____ to altruistic* actions.

4. It is pathetic* the way some citizens _____ their apathy* during election years.

5. His beard was in its _____ state; it would soon be a hirsute* masterpiece.

**Definitions**  Match the new words with their definitions.

6. motivate _____ a. beginning to exist or develop

7. rationalize _____ b. use or give a reason other than the real one

8. therapy _____ c. inspire, stimulate, provoke

9. nascent _____ d. image-breaker, attacker of beliefs

10. iconoclast _____ e. healing or curing process

---
**TODAY'S IDIOM**

*a square peg in a round hole*—an able man in the wrong job
It was a bitter pill to swallow* when they had to fire him
because he was *a square peg in a round hole*.

---

**NEW WORDS**

**erudite**
er´ u dīt

**phobia**
fō´ bē ə

**germane**
jər mān´

**vertigo**
ver´ tə gō

**conducive**
kən dü´ siv

## AMATEUR PSYCHOLOGISTS

The ideas of Freudian psychology have become part of our everyday life. Our language is replete* with clichés* that have their origin in Freud's writings. There is a surfeit* of amateur psychologists who, with celerity,* analyze an individual's problems from the slightest evidence. Despite their dubious* education and training in this field, they discuss symptoms and cures on a most *erudite* fashion. Should a person express a fear of heights, this *phobia* is examined; events from childhood are considered *germane* to the problem. Is it possible he or she was dropped as an infant? Perhaps something in a dream is pertinent* to explain the feelings of *vertigo* that accompany height. For some reason, non-trained people find the Freudian approach to the workings of the human mind most *conducive* to their practicing as amateur psychologists.

**Sample Sentences** Insert the new words in these sentences.

1. She could not countenance* the sight of a lethal* weapon; it was tantamount* to a _____ with her.

2. The _____ man was more than merely bilingual;* he spoke five languages.

3. I would never have the temerity* to walk across the steel girders high up on a new building; an onset of _____ would surely follow.

4. The bedlam* in the study hall was not _____ to good work habits.

5. Epithets* are not _____ when motivating* a child to a task.

**Definitions** Match the new words with their definitions.

6. erudite _____ a. very scholarly

7. phobia _____ b. dizziness

8. germane _____ c. persistent fear, strong dislike

9. vertigo _____ d. leading, helpful

10. conducive _____ e. appropriate, in close relationship to

---
### TODAY'S IDIOM
---

***to upset the apple cart*—to overturn or disturb a plan or intention**

It was a bitter pill to swallow* when *they upset the apple cart* and elected a dark horse.

ANSWERS ARE ON PAGE 307

The writings of Thoreau and Freud are replete* with ideas that require deep thought. In order to tackle their ideas, one must understand their vocabulary. Therefore, word mastery is the key to unlocking ideas of some of our greatest thinkers.

## REVIEW WORDS

|   | | DEFINITIONS | |
|---|---|---|---|
| _____ | **1.** antipathy | **a.** | choice, willpower |
| _____ | **2.** austere | **b.** | supportable, defendable |
| _____ | **3.** conducive | **c.** | provoke, stimulate, inspire |
| _____ | **4.** confront | **d.** | leading, helpful |
| _____ | **5.** erudite | **e.** | unadorned, simple, hard |
| _____ | **6.** felicitous | **f.** | hate, distaste, dislike |
| _____ | **7.** germane | **g.** | attacker of beliefs, image-breaker |
| _____ | **8.** halcyon | **h.** | in close relationship to, appropriate |
| _____ | **9.** iconoclast | **i.** | calm, peaceful |
| _____ | **10.** motivate | **j.** | come face to face with |
| _____ | **11.** nascent | **k.** | curing or healing process |
| _____ | **12.** phobia | **l.** | very scholarly |
| _____ | **13.** rationalize | **m.** | happy |
| _____ | **14.** servile | **n.** | submissive, slavish |
| _____ | **15.** sojourn | **o.** | beginning to develop or exist |
| _____ | **16.** superfluous | **p.** | dizziness |
| _____ | **17.** tenable | **q.** | surplus, excessive |
| _____ | **18.** therapy | **r.** | temporary stay |
| _____ | **19.** vertigo | **s.** | use or give a reason other than the real one |
| _____ | **20.** volition | **t.** | strong dislike, persistent fear |

## IDIOMS

| | | | |
|---|---|---|---|
| _____ **21.** to upset the apple cart | | **u.** | not usual, out of the ordinary |
| _____ **22.** to tighten one's belt | | **v.** | an able man in the wrong job |
| _____ **23.** off the beaten track | | **w.** | to get set for bad times or poverty |
| _____ **24.** a square peg in a round hole | | **x.** | to overturn or disturb a plan or intention |

## WORDS FOR FURTHER STUDY          MEANINGS

1. _____   _____

Check your answers on page 307.

2. _____   _____

3. _____   _____

# WORDSEARCH 37

❖ Using the clues listed below, fill in each blank in the following story with one of the new words you learned this week.

## *Make My Ostrich Burger Well Done*

Just about 100 years ago, there arose an industry in the state of Arizona that seems very odd to us today. We know of cattle ranches and sheep ranches, but would you believe . . . ostrich ranches? This ① _____ business became popular as women found ostrich feathers a ② _____ addition to their wardrobes.

Ostriches are easy to raise. They eat and drink less than cattle, and their eggs are large enough to feed ten people! During the ③ _____ days of ostrich ranching, feathers were sold for as much as $300 a pound, so it is easy to see why that business was so attractive.

However, women's fashions changed after World War I, and the market for ostrich plumes fell. Growers had to ④ _____ a shrinking market. The price tumbled to about $10 for a bird. As ostrich feathers became ⑤ _____ in the fashion world, ostrich ranching came to an end.

Interestingly enough, ostrich ranchers may be coming back into vogue because nutritionists tell us that ostrich meat is low in cholesterol. We may not go wild over the feathers, but pass the lean meat, please. Hold the mayo, too.

## Clues
① 3rd Day
② 2nd Day
③ 2nd Day
④ 1st Day
⑤ 2nd Day

# WEEK 38 ❖ DAY 1

**NEW WORDS**

glib
glib

homogenous
hō mə jē´ ne əs

malleable
mal´ ē ə bəl

legerdemain
lej ər də mān´

trend
trend

## THE ENIGMA* OF FASHION

Of all the pressures young people face, the most pernicious*
is that of fashion. By this is meant the current vogue* in
dress. The teenagers, who are so *glib* when they speak of
"individuality," are turned into a *homogeneous* mass by the
latest craze in fashion. How can youngsters who vehemently*
resist advice from the older generation become so *malleable* in
the hands of those who "make" fashion? Perhaps the sudden
shifts in fashion occur fortuitously*. Or is there some group
who, through *legerdemain*, switches styles and customs on
us right before our eyes? Today's teenagers seem to be quite
gullible* when it comes to embracing the latest *trend* in
fashions. But then, they have their elders as sage* examples
to follow.

**Sample Sentences**  Insert the new words in these sentences.

1. The charlatan* was able to wheedle* money out of the naïve* audience with a
   _____ talk on the medicine that would expunge* pain.

2. They could not follow the _____ of his ideas, but his verbal dexterity*
   galvanized* the gullible* listeners.

3. They were engrossed* as an ill man was "cured" before their eyes; some of the more
   urbane* said it was _____ .

4. He ingratiated* himself into their confidence, and the _____ crowd was
   shaped into a subjugated* mass.

5. While they started out as individuals, they became a _____ group whom
   he could motivate as he willed.

**Definitions**  Match the new words with their definitions.

6. glib          _____    **a.** capable of being shaped or formed
7. homogeneous   _____    **b.** sleight of hand, deceptive adroitness*
8. malleable     _____    **c.** smooth of speech
9. legerdemain   _____    **d.** same or uniform
10. trend        _____    **e.** general direction

---
**TODAY'S IDIOM**
---

***by hook or by crook***—any way at all, at any cost

He had bought the white elephant* without rhyme
or reason*; now he had to get rid of it *by hook or by crook.*

---

## NEW WORDS

**stagnant**
stag´ nənt

**fatal**
fā´ tl

**passé**
pa sā´

**procrastinate**
prō kras´ tə nāt

**facet**
fas´ it

# WEEK 38 ❖ DAY 2

## THE ECONOMICS OF FASHION

In dress, the fashion appears to be "set" by a few foreign designers and a handful of affluent* individuals who purchase these designs. The fashion industry is cognizant* of the fact that fashions must change rapidly and often or their economy would become *stagnant*. For this industry it would prove *fatal* if it were not vigilant* and prepared well in advance for a new fashion trend.* As the old fashion becomes *passé* and a new fashion seems to be in the making, the garment manufacturers cannot afford to *procrastinate*. They rush large sums of money into production for a mass market. Having invested heavily, the manufacturers do everything possible to influence and motivate* the purchasers. Through every *facet* of publicity and advertising the industry exploits* the natural desire for people to be au courant* with the latest fashions.

**Sample Sentences**  Insert the new words in these sentences.

1. To the consternation* of the distraught* parents they learned their son was accused of using the lethal* weapon on that _____ occasion.

2. We wish for halcyon* days when the warlike solutions will have become _____ .

3. Edna recalled with nostalgia* many _____ of her school days.

4. We all tend to _____ when faced with an unsavory* task.

5. The iconoclast* has the propensity* for reproaching* those who feel complacent* with leading a _____ existence.

**Definitions**  Match the new words with their definitions.

6. stagnant _____  **a.** delay, put off

7. fatal _____  **b.** motionless, dull, inactive

8. passé _____  **c.** deadly, disastrous

9. procrastinate _____  **d.** one side or view of person or situation

10. facet _____  **e.** outmoded, old-fashioned

--- **TODAY'S IDIOM** ---

*to get up on the wrong side of the bed*—to be in a bad mood

When his mother raised Cain* about his slovenly* room,
he accused her of *getting up on the wrong side of the bed.*

234

ANSWERS ARE ON PAGE 307

# WEEK 38 ❖ DAY 3

## NEW WORDS

**foist**
foist

**stigmatize**
stig´ mə tīz

**capitulate**
kə pich´ ə lāt

**audacity**
ô das´ ə tē

**tantalize**
tan´ tl īz

## WHAT NEXT?

Once the fashion industry has been able to *foist* a new style on the teenager, the older generation tends to *stigmatize* it as some form of rebellion. What is often ignored is that the young consumers *capitulate* to what is originated* by someone outside of their group. The feelings of individuality and *audacity* that the teenager gets from a new style of dress result from the propensity* of their elders to disparage* them. The actual situation is that the clothing fashions soon become accepted by all; there is nothing upsetting or revolutionary about them. While people are becoming complacent* about the "new," the clothing industry is busy planning how to *tantalize* the teenager with next year's "fashion." This arbitrary* decision is guaranteed to foment* consternation* among adults once again in the following year.

**Sample Sentences**  Insert the new words in these sentences.

1. Despite tenacious* resistance, they were ousted* from the strongpoint and had to _____ to the enemy.

2. It was an asinine* thing to do—to _____ his opponent as a bigot* and thus exacerbate* an already bitter campaign.

3. It is common to hear people disparage* those who paint in the modern genre*; they speak about the _____ of the artist who submits a high white canvas with a black border as a serious work.

4. They are dubious* of such an artist and accuse him of trying to _____ as a work of art a rudimentary* exercise.

5. It is reprehensible* to _____ a young child with the promise of a reward for being good when you have no intention of giving it.

**Definitions**  Match the new words with their definitions.

6. foist      _____    **a.** surrender, make terms

7. stigmatize      _____    **b.** to mark with a disgrace

8. capitulate      _____    **c.** boldness, daring

9. audacity      _____    **d.** pass off slyly, pass as genuine

10. tantalize      _____    **e.** tease or torment by offering something good, but not deliver

---
### TODAY'S IDIOM
---

***castles in the air*—a dream about some wonderful future**

People on Skid Row* often build *castles in the air.*

**retort**
ri tôrt´

**reticent**
ret´ ə sənt

**tacit**
tas´ it

**chicanery**
shi kā´ nə r ē

**docile**
dos´ əl

## SOMETHING FOR EVERYONE

To the derogatory* comments from the older generation the teenagers might *retort* that new fashions and styles are adopted by the elders with alacrity.* Though they complain, women emulate* their daughters by shortening or lengthening their hems. They may appear *reticent* about the bother and expense of altering their wardrobe, but they give *tacit* approval to the change by rushing to the department stores where they jostle* each other to buy copies of the more expensive dresses. The conclusion one might reach after observing how women countenance* the arbitrary* changes year after year is that they are naïve* or victims of some *chicanery* practiced by the clothing industry. Women may appear hapless* before the intimidation* of "style," but the real truth may lie in the fact that they are so *docile* because they secretly enjoy the yearly excitement around the latest fashions.

*There's another familiar word reintroduced today. Did you recognize* reticent?

**Sample Sentences** Insert the new words in these sentences.

1. The reporter divulged* the blatant* _____ involved in the awarding of the contract.

2. Even the most _____ person may become fractious* when he gets only a pittance* for his hard labor.

3. His egregious* behavior brought a _____ reproach* to his mother's eyes.

4. Most politicians are _____ when asked to divulge* their ambitions.

5. He refused to _____ to the rash* question about his propensity* for imbibing.*

**Definitions** Match the new words with their definitions.

6. retort (v.)      _____    **a.** understood, implied, not stated

7. reticent      _____    **b.** easy to manage

8. tacit      _____    **c.** to answer, reply

9. chicanery      _____    **d.** silent or reserved

10. docile      _____    **e.** trickery, underhandedness

—————— **TODAY'S IDIOM** ——————

***to maintain the status quo***—to keep things as they are

You hit the nail on the head* when you said we ought *to maintain the status quo* and not change horses in midstream.*

No matter what the fashion in dress, the fashion in education is an extensive vocabulary. Keep up with the fashion; build your vocabulary wardrobe.

## REVIEW WORDS

_____ 1. audacity
_____ 2. capitulate
_____ 3. chicanery
_____ 4. docile
_____ 5. facet
_____ 6. fatal
_____ 7. foist
_____ 8. glib
_____ 9. homogeneous
_____ 10. legerdemain
_____ 11. malleable
_____ 12. passé
_____ 13. procrastinate
_____ 14. reticent
_____ 15. retort
_____ 16. stagnant
_____ 17. stigmatize
_____ 18. tacit
_____ 19. tantalize
_____ 20. trend

## DEFINITIONS

a. reserved, silent
b. pass as genuine, pass off slyly
c. disastrous, deadly
d. smooth of speech
e. one side or view of person or situation
f. daring, boldness
g. reply, answer
h. uniform, same
i. capable of being formed or shaped
j. put off, delay
k. make terms, surrender
l. underhandedness, trickery
m. not stated, understood, implied
n. to mark with a disgrace
o. inactive, dull, motionless
p. general direction
q. old-fashioned, outmoded
r. easy to manage
s. deceptive adroitness,* sleight of hand
t. tease or torment by offering something good, but fail to deliver

## IDIOMS

_____ 21. castles in the air
_____ 22. to get up on the wrong side of the bed
_____ 23. by hook or by crook
_____ 24. to maintain the status quo

u. to be in a bad mood
v. a dream about a wonderful future
w. at any cost, any way at all
x. to keep things as they are

## WORDS FOR FURTHER STUDY        MEANINGS

1. _____   _____

2. _____   _____

3. _____   _____

Answers on page 307. Take that extra few minutes now to master the few words you made errors with.

# WORDSEARCH 38

❖ Using the clues listed below, fill in each blank in the following story with one of the new words you learned this week.

## TV—The Octopus

Is there anyone you know who can remember a time when there was *no* television? Perhaps a grandparent, but no one much younger is able to do so. At the beginning, only a handful of stations existed. Early programs imitated each other and tended to be ①_____ . Some time later, there was the cable TV expansion and greater variety was available. The developing ②_____ was for ever-larger numbers of programs dealing with information as well as entertainment.

The TV industry, never ③_____ when it comes to expanding viewer interests, brought even more channels to the air, broadcasting 24 hours every day of the week. The objective was to ④_____ special groups with programs directed to special tastes and interests. Soon channels devoted to games, to how to fix or make things, to romance dramas, to cartoons, etc., sprang into existence. It appears that every ⑤_____ of a viewer's interest is being addressed. As more and more channels come on the air, as the result of new technology, the variety is expanding beyond anything imagined by those who can recall the beginnings of this magical medium.

## Clues

① 1st Day

② 1st Day

③ 4th Day

④ 3rd Day

⑤ 2nd Day

ANSWERS ARE ON PAGE 307

# WEEK 39 ❖ DAY 1

**NEW WORDS**

**saga**
sä´ ga

**belated**
bi lāt´ tid

**decrepit**
di krep´ it

**imperturbable**
im pər tėr´ bə bəl

**vacillate**
vas´ ə lāt

## RULE, BRITANNIA

An unforgettable *saga* of World War II has to do with the small French coastal town of Dunkirk. There, in 1940, thousands of British troops made a *belated* escape from the awesome* power of the German army and air force. They were removed by an array* of private boats, from huge yachts to *decrepit* fishing boats. At their own volition,* the skippers came close to the shore, while German planes bombed implacably.* They remained *imperturbable* under heavy fire. When their vessels were loaded, they dashed back to England. Once unloaded, they did not *vacillate,* but returned with equanimity* to their vigil* in the danger zone. The British proved once again that they are paragons* of comradeship in times of jeopardy.*

**Sample Sentences** Insert the new words in these sentences.

1. The _____ of a lone man confronting* the turbulent* oceans in a small boat is an exploit* we find laudable.*

2. The speaker remained _____ while his audience shouted caustic* comments about his mendacious* activities.

3. The ingrate refused to accept Cindy's _____ gift.

4. When released from incarceration,* he was gaunt* and _____ .

5. We are all familiar with the cliché* that he who _____ is lost.

**Definitions** Match the new words with their definitions.

6. saga _____     **a.** hesitate, fluctuate

7. belated _____     **b.** heroic story

8. decrepit _____     **c.** broken down, worn out

9. imperturbable _____     **d.** late, delayed

10. vacillate _____     **e.** calm, steady, serene

---
### TODAY'S IDIOM
---

*a sacred cow*—**a person or thing that cannot be criticized**
**(From India, where cows may not be harmed because of religious rules)**

I decided to throw down the gauntlet* by exposing the boss's son who had been ruling the roost* as *the sacred cow* of the business.

## NEW WORDS

**staunch**
stônch

**opprobrium**
ə prō´ brē əm

**Machiavellian**
Mak´ ē ə vel ē ən

**unconscionable**
un kon´ shə ne bəl

**pandemonium**
pan´ də mō´ nē əm

## THE GOOD GUYS VS. THE BAD GUYS

The international adventure stories prevalent* on television follow meticulously* a plot that is inexorable* in its development. Those on the side of law and justice face perfidious* men and organizations. These are anathema* to those values the *staunch* heroes would defend. These infamous* men have no capacity for compassion,* and they treat the lovely women with *opprobrium.* The intrepid* heroes are placed in deleterious* situations as a result of the *Machiavellian* maneuvers of their opponents. One *unconscionable* act of duplicity* follows another until the total destruction of the "good guys" seems at hand. At the last moment, usually amidst the *pandemonium* of a battle, the cause for which the heroes strive triumphs. However, evil is ubiquitous,* and next week another fracas* will erupt.

**Sample Sentences**  Insert the new words in these sentences.

1. The coach heaped _____ upon the fledgling* ball player.

2. We are ready to rationalize* _____ activities on the part of our side if they are to the detriment* of our adversary.*

3. It was _____ to Abraham Lincoln to keep a book he had borrowed without making tenacious* efforts to return it.

4. There was _____ as the presidential nominee entered the convention site.*

5. She is such a _____ friend, my reprehensible* actions do not cause a schism* between us.

**Definitions**  Match the new words with their definitions.

6. staunch _____       **a.** scorn, insult

7. opprobrium _____    **b.** strong, trusty, firm

8. Machiavellian _____ **c.** without conscience, unreasonable

9. unconscionable_____ **d.** governed by opportunity, not principled

10. pandemonium _____  **e.** disorder, uproar

---
### TODAY'S IDIOM
---

***through thick and thin*—in spite of all sorts of difficulties**
He decided to stick with his fairweather friends* *through thick and thin.*

# WEEK 39 ❖ DAY 3

<br>

**NEW WORDS**

flay
flā

demeanor
di mē´ nər

delineation
di lin´ ē ā´ shən

vindicate
vin´ də kāt

heinous
hā´ nəs

## A FAMOUS MUTINY

One of the most repugnant* names in popular legend is that of
Captain William Bligh. He was the captain of the H.M.S. *Bounty*
in 1789, and the mutiny that erupted* aboard that ship was
the basis for a film in which Charles Laughton portrayed Bligh
as an awesome* bully and an unmitigated* villain. He would
*flay* both the body and the spirit of anyone who crossed him.
The crew developed such an aversion* to Bligh's mortifying
actions and *demeanor* that, led by Fletcher Christian, they set
the captain and 17 shipmates off in a lifeboat in the South
Pacific. The ship continued to the Pitcairn Islands where the
crew remained to live with the islanders. Laughton's *delineation*
of Bligh remains as the image we have of him. Only recently
has any attempt been made to *vindicate* Captain Bligh and to
remove the *heinous* reputation that permeates* history.

**Sample Sentences**  Insert the new words in these sentences.

1. The mayor tried to _____ his actions that had been called capricious* and irrational* by critics.

2. He castigated* his opponents and went to great lengths to _____ them with accusations of megalomania.*

3. His _____ was atypical*; usually phlegmatic*, he was belligerent* and garrulous* during the broadcast.

4. "The most _____ thing I have done," he said in a stentorian* voice, "is eradicate* the untruth that my party is not compatible* with progress."

5. Then he gave an incisive* _____ of his fulsome* opponents as an antiquated* group, complacent* about the noisome* conditions in a moribund* city.

**Definitions**  Match the new words with their definitions.

6. flay _____ a. hatefully evil

7. demeanor _____ b. absolve, justify

8. delineation _____ c. sketch, description in words

9. vindicate _____ d. conduct, bearing

10. heinous _____ e. strip off skin, scold harshly

---
**TODAY'S IDIOM**

*to take by storm*—to make a fast impression

The new opera star *took the critics by storm* and carried the day.*

---

## NEW WORDS

**turpitude**
tèr´ pə tü

**infraction**
in frak´ shən

**callous**
kal´ əs

**redress**
ri dres´

**vituperation**
vī tü´ pər ā´ shən

# WEEK 39 ❖ DAY 4

## FAIR PLAY!

Recently, there has been an attempt to improve Captain Bligh's tainted* image. Historians maintain that there was no *turpitude* in Bligh's actions aboard the H.M.S. *Bounty*. Perhaps he was imprudent* in failing to keep his temper under control. While an *infraction* aboard ship was quickly criticized, Bligh never carried out those *callous* actions the movie dramatized in order to depict* an evil man, say his defenders. After the mutiny, Captain Bligh astutely* navigated the lifeboat with the other 17 men for over 3,000 miles to safety. This prodigious* feat alone, say those who would restore Bligh's good name, should be enough to allow for a full *redress* of the wrongs that have been blamed on him for over 150 years. While the coterie* defending Captain Bligh do not ask the public to praise him, they do request a more benevolent* attitude toward this traditionally* reprehensible* figure, and an end to the *vituperation*\* heaped upon him for these many years.

**Sample Sentences** Insert the new words in these sentences.

1. We do not condone* or tolerate* an _____ of even the most trivial kind.

2. It takes a _____ person to watch with equanimity* as a gullible,* naive* girl falls for the line of a loathsome* boy.

3. How easy it is to heap _____ upon someone at the nadir* of his career.

4. There seems to be no way to _____ a grievance against at omnipotent* ruler.

5. From any facet* of his life, the acme* of moral _____ was reached by Adolf Hitler.

**Definitions** Match the new words with their definitions.

6. turpitude _____    **a.** unfeeling

7. infraction _____    **b.** vileness, evil wickedness

8. callous _____    **c.** to right a wrong, remedy

9. redress _____    **d.** violation

10. vituperation _____    **e.** blame, abuse

---

## TODAY'S IDIOM

***to be in fine fettle*—to be in high spirits, or feeling well**

He did a lot of woolgathering* and *was in fine fettle*
during the whole of the Indian summer.*

---

ANSWERS ARE ON PAGE 308

Our British cousins have a vocabulary that differs from ours in many ways. Isn't it fortunate that we have to be responsible for the American version of this language only?

## REVIEW WORDS

| | | DEFINITIONS |
|---|---|---|
| _____ | **1.** belated | **a.** description in words, sketch |
| _____ | **2.** callous | **b.** firm, trusty, strong |
| _____ | **3.** decrepit | **c.** fluctuate, hesitate |
| _____ | **4.** delineation | **d.** violation |
| _____ | **5.** demeanor | **e.** abuse, blame |
| _____ | **6.** flay | **f.** serene, steady, calm |
| _____ | **7.** heinous | **g.** uproar, disorder |
| _____ | **8.** imperturbable | **h.** hatefully evil |
| _____ | **9.** infraction | **i.** scold harshly, strip off the skin |
| _____ | **10.** Machiavellian | **j.** bearing, conduct |
| _____ | **11.** opprobrium | **k.** not principled, governed by opportunity |
| _____ | **12.** pandemonium | **l.** heroic story |
| _____ | **13.** redress | **m.** delayed, late |
| _____ | **14.** saga | **n.** unfeeling |
| _____ | **15.** staunch | **o.** evil, wickedness, vileness |
| _____ | **16.** turpitude | **p.** worn out, broken down |
| _____ | **17.** unconscionable | **q.** unreasonable, without conscience |
| _____ | **18.** vacillate | **r.** to right a wrong |
| _____ | **19.** vindicate | **s.** justify, absolve |
| _____ | **20.** vituperation | **t.** insult, scorn |

## IDIOMS

| | | | |
|---|---|---|---|
| _____ | **21.** through thick and thin | **u.** | to make a fast impression |
| _____ | **22.** to take by storm | **v.** | in spite of all sorts of difficulties |
| _____ | **23.** a sacred cow | **w.** | to be in high spirits, feeling well |
| _____ | **24.** to be in fine fettle | **x.** | a person who cannot be criticized |

## WORDS FOR FURTHER STUDY        MEANINGS

1. _____    _____

2. _____    _____

The answers can be found on page 308.

3. _____    _____

# WORDSEARCH 39

❖ Using the clues listed below, fill in each blank in the following story with one of the new words you learned this week.

## Psst . . . Need World Series Tickets?

Think about this for a moment. Is there anything wrong in buying something for one dollar and reselling it for two dollars? Naturally, you would be correct if you saw nothing amiss with this transaction; it's the way a capitalist economy works. But, if you bought a ticket to a rock concert or baseball game for ten dollars and sold it for twenty, you would be committing an ①_____ of the law. You might ask, "What's so ②_____ about this?" The answer is that you would be guilty of the practice known as "scalping." Does an individual who offers a scarce ticket at a price above the original price deserve the ③_____ connected with the word "scalping"?

These hard-working and risk-taking individuals see themselves as go-betweens in a world where people are willing to spend additional money for a popular event. However, law enforcement officials remain ④_____ in the face of all reason as they arrest and fine these enterprising salesmen. Those ⑤_____ believers in punishing law-breakers find nothing wrong with trying to halt the scalping of tickets. For others, it is a way of doing business that they claim hurts no one and is in keeping with a profit-driven economy.

## Clues

① 4th Day

② 3rd Day

③ 2nd Day

④ 1st Day

⑤ 2nd Day

ANSWERS ARE ON PAGE 308

# WEEK **40** ❖ DAY **1**

**NEW WORDS**

**rhetoric**
ret´ ər ik

**clique**
klēk

**extol**
ek stōl´

**mentor**
men´ tər

**facile**
fas´ əl

## A POLITICAL SHOW

The 2012 elections offered another example of politics as show business. Most politicians have prepared speeches dealing with the prevalent* topics of the day. They can maintain a fervid* flow of *rhetoric* for hours at a time. In each locality where he is to appear, the advance work is prepared by a *clique* of trustworthy aides. In preparation for the show, they have dispersed* leaflets, put up posters, and sent out cars and trucks with loudspeakers to *extol* the erudite* qualities of their candidate. Soon, the crowd gathers. Loyal party workers come forward to shake the hand of their *mentor*. Now, with the *facile* solutions to complex problems carefully memorized, the show is ready to begin. One moment facetious,* the next moment profound,* the candidate works to convince the incredulous* among the voters.

**Sample Sentences**  Insert the new words in these sentences.

1. It is not long before a young star has a _____ around him who sporadically* get their names into the newspapers.

2. At a time that requires tangible* proposals, all he offers is unconscionable*

   _____ .

3. The detective interrogated* the adamant* prisoner in such a _____ way that he confessed after giving incontrovertible* evidence.

4. Youngsters scoff* when their elders _____ the halcyon* days of long ago.

5. Amidst the adulation of the throng,* the film star, in all humility,* credited her _____ as the one most responsible.

**Definitions**  Match the new words with their definitions.

| | | | |
|---|---|---|---|
| 6. rhetoric | _____ | **a.** | counselor, coach, tutor |
| 7. clique | _____ | **b.** | use (sometimes exaggerated) of language |
| 8. extol | _____ | **c.** | easily accomplished or attained |
| 9. mentor | _____ | **d.** | praise highly |
| 10. facile | _____ | **e.** | small, exclusive group of people |

---
**TODAY'S IDIOM**

*to live in a fool's paradise*—to be happy without a real basis

He *lived in a fool's paradise* while he sowed wild
oats*, but he soon had to pay the piper.*

---

**NEW WORDS**

cant
kant

umbrage
um´ brij

magnanimous
mag nan´ ə məs

vilify
vil´ ə fī

elucidate
i lü´ sə dāt

## GETTING A GOOD LOOK

The television press interview is conducive* to close scrutiny* of a candidate. His public speeches may contain many *cant* phrases, but a sharp question by an astute* reporter can destroy a cliché*-filled statement. The politician now will procrastinate* in his answer; a new facet* of his personality may be revealed by his demeanor.* Perhaps he will take *umbrage* at a suggestion that he favors the affluent.* His record is searched for evidence that he has been equally *magnanimous* to the indigent.* He accuses the reporter of attempting to *vilify* him. Is he being accused of turpitude* in office? It is time to discreetly* go on to another topic. The candidate wishes to extol* the virtues of his program and record. The press wants to allude* to things that keep him in the midst of controversy. They insist that he *elucidate* positions that the politician would rather leave in a nebulous* state.

**Sample Sentences** Insert the new words in these sentences.

1. We feel so sanctimonious* when we _____ the character of a felon*.

2. The diplomat was astute* enough to see through the _____ of the Machiavellian* ambassador.

3. A somber* examination of those indigent* families, bereft* of hope, sunken in apathy,* should motivate* us to be more _____ in our attempts to improve their lot.

4. I was flabbergasted* when he took _____ at my whimsical* remarks.

5. The judge ordered the censor to _____ his reasons for removing passages from the book in such a capricious* manner.

**Definitions** Match the new words with their definitions.

6. cant _____    a. insincere or almost meaningless talk

7. umbrage _____    b. to make clear

8. magnanimous _____    c. resentment, offense

9. vilify _____    d. malign,* slander

10. elucidate _____    e. generous, noble

### TODAY'S IDIOM

***the sum and substance*—the heart or substantial part**

*The sum and substance* of our pyrrhic victory* was that our hopes for a stable future had gone up in smoke.*

ANSWERS ARE ON PAGE 308

# WEEK 40 ❖ DAY 3

**NEW WORDS**

vapid
vap´ id

unwieldy
un wēl´ dē´

proximity
prok sim´ ə tē

lassitude
las´ ə tüd

vitiate
vish´ ē āt

## SEEING IS LEARNING

While we are all cognizant* of the importance of words to create certain impressions, gesture is relegated* to a much lesser role. Gestures are an important concomitant* to even the most *vapid* speech, enhancing it and giving the hearer something to look at while he listens. The value of seeing at the same time as listening was shown when a class at a university, *unwieldy* because of its large size, was split up. One group was put into a room in *proximity* to good loudspeakers. Every nuance* of the lecturer's voice could be heard clearly. Because they had no person on whom to place their attention, they soon took on the appearance of extreme *lassitude;* most students became lethargic* and rested their heads on their desks. The separation of visual and aural communication tended to *vitiate* the learning process. The listening group received grades lower than those received by those who could look at as well as hear the instructor.

*Once more your keen eye and memory were being tested. Did you recognize* lassitude *as being from an earlier lesson?*

**Sample Sentences** Insert the new words in these sentences.

1. As the scion* of an affluent* family, he was often in _____ to opulence.*

2. After playing with his progeny* in the enervating sun, he staggered back to his room where he was overcome with _____ .

3. As a concomitant* to his belligerent* and vituperative* antipathy* toward his government, he became an expatriate,* but he found it a _____ life.

4. Kyra was so disgruntled* about having to move the _____ piano, she procrastinated* for days.

5. The irrelevant* evidence seemed to _____ the prosecutor's case and precluded* a conviction.

**Definitions** Match the new words with their definitions.

6. vapid        _____   **a.** bulky, difficult to handle
7. unwieldy     _____   **b.** destroy the use or value
8. proximity    _____   **c.** uninteresting, dull
9. lassitude    _____   **d.** nearness
10. vitiate     _____   **e.** weariness, weakness

---
### TODAY'S IDIOM

*on pins and needles*—to be on edge, jumpy

He was *on pins and needles* while he cooled his heels* in the principal's office.

---

## NEW WORDS

**augment**
ôg ment´

**fatuous**
fach´ ü əs

**contort**
kən tôrt´

**repertoire**
rep´ ər twär

**imperceptible**
im´ pər sep´ tə bəl

# WEEK 40 ❖ DAY 4

## THE HAMMY OLD DAYS

Actors depend upon their ability to gesticulate* almost as much as upon speech to obtain their desired histrionic* effects. With them, gesture serves much more than merely to *augment* speech. When their communication is by gesture alone, it is called pantomime. In the early silent motion picture period, gestures were flamboyant.* To show that he was distraught* about the danger in which the heroine had been placed, the hero would go through the most *fatuous* actions. He would stagger, beat his breast, tear his hair, and *contort* his face into the most doleful* appearance. There weren't many simple or restrained gestures in his *repertoire.* The heroine, to indicate her love, would fling her arms wide and ardently* jump into her sweetheart's arms. It was only much later that actors became skilled enough to communicate with the audience through discreet* gestures and almost *imperceptible* changes in facial expression that could transmit nuances* of emotion.

**Sample Sentences** Insert the new words in these sentences.

1. The new employee wanted to gain favor with his boss, and his obsequious* desires led to the most _____ behavior.

2. Her virtuosity* was demonstrated by the works she performed from her _____ .

3. He had always appeared virile,* so that the _____ decline toward senility* went unnoticed until he succumbed* and began to use a cane.

4. The paroxysm* of coughing served to _____ her body until she could gain a respite.*

5. The parsimonious* octogenarian* sought to _____ his wealth by removing it from its cache* and placing it in a bank.

**Definitions** Match the new words with their definitions.

6. augment _____    **a.** extremely slight or gradual

7. fatuous _____    **b.** enlarge, increase

8. contort _____    **c.** foolish, silly, inane*

9. repertoire _____    **d.** twist violently

10. imperceptible _____    **e.** works that an artist is ready to perform

## TODAY'S IDIOM

***to have at one's fingertips*—to have thorough knowledge, to have ready**
He *had at his fingertips* an extensive repertoire.*

ANSWERS ARE ON PAGE 308

If there's one thing a politician must know how to do, it is to use words effectively. He must weigh carefully each and every utterance. He must also select the proper word for the audience he is addressing. You may never run for office, but it would be comforting to know you were ready for it—vocabulary-wise!

## REVIEW WORDS

| | | DEFINITIONS |
|---|---|---|
| _____ | 1. augment | **a.** twist violently |
| _____ | 2. cant | **b.** increase, enlarge |
| _____ | 3. clique | **c.** nearness |
| _____ | 4. contort | **d.** destroy the use or value |
| _____ | 5. elucidate | **e.** praise highly |
| _____ | 6. extol | **f.** use (sometimes exaggerated) of language |
| _____ | 7. facile | **g.** to make clear |
| _____ | 8. fatuous | **h.** slander, malign* |
| _____ | 9. imperceptible | **i.** difficult to handle, bulky |
| _____ | 10. lassitude | **j.** works that an artist is ready to perform |
| _____ | 11. magnanimous | **k.** tutor, counselor, coach |
| _____ | 12. mentor | **l.** noble, generous |
| _____ | 13. proximity | **m.** insincere or almost meaningless talk |
| _____ | 14. repertoire | **n.** small, exclusive group of people |
| _____ | 15. rhetoric | **o.** extremely slight or gradual |
| _____ | 16. umbrage | **p.** dull, uninteresting |
| _____ | 17. unwieldy | **q.** weakness, weariness |
| _____ | 18. vapid | **r.** inane,* foolish, silly |
| _____ | 19. vilify | **s.** easily accomplished or attained |
| _____ | 20. vitiate | **t.** offense, resentment |

## IDIOMS

| | | | |
|---|---|---|---|
| _____ | 21. to live in a fool's paradise | **u.** | the heart or substantial part |
| _____ | 22. the sum and substance | **v.** | to be on edge, jumpy |
| _____ | 23. on pins and needles | **w.** | to have ready, to have a thorough knowledge |
| _____ | 24. to have at one's fingertips | **x.** | to be happy without a real basis |

Check your answers on page 308. Get to work learning the words that gave you trouble.

| WORDS FOR FURTHER STUDY | MEANINGS |
|---|---|
| 1. _____ | _____ |
| 2. _____ | _____ |
| 3. _____ | _____ |

# HAPLESS HEADLINES
## (From Weeks 36–40)

❖ From the list of vocabulary words below choose the best ones to complete each of the newspaper headlines.

a. Therapy
b. Facile
c. Fatal
d. Decrepit
e. Confront
f. Retort
g. Vehemently
h. Tacit
i. Legerdemain
j. Vapid
k. Phobia
l. Clique
m. Fatuous
n. Repertoire
o. Motivate
p. Capitulate
q. Glib
r. Lassitude
s. Mentor
t. Vertigo

1. U.S. Diplomats _____ Chinese over Alleged A-bomb Tests
2. Psychologist Claims Success in Treating Flying _____
3. Rebels _____, Throw Down Arms
4. Auto Accident Proves _____ to Family
5. _____ Salesman Arrested in Con Game
6. Witness _____ Denies Allegation
7. Pentagon Asks for Funds to Replace "_____" Aircraft
8. New Company Director Praises Former _____
9. *La Bohème* is Mainstay of Opera Star's _____
10. Speech _____ Urged After Stroke

ANSWERS ARE ON PAGE 308

❖ Using the clues listed below, fill in each blank in the following story with one of the new words you learned this week.

## *In Thailand, Mum's the Word*

In this country we take for granted our right to speak out about our elected officials in any way we wish, without fear of arrest or imprisonment. The most disrespectful language is allowed. While some may take ①_____ at an insult against the president, our Constitution protects that right.

Now, consider the country of Thailand. That land in southeastern Asia is ruled by a king. What happens to an individual who fails to ②_____ this monarch? There is a case of a person who joked that if he were king he could sleep late every day and drink wine in the afternoon. For this somewhat ③_____ remark, he was sent to prison for seven years. Or take the story of the woman who was hanging up the king's photograph. When the police asked her what she was doing, she replied, "I'm nailing it up there on my wall." She said "it" instead of "the king's photograph" and for this ④_____ alleged insult, she also was sent away for seven years.

While some U.S. citizens may ⑤_____ our leaders, in Thailand the less said the better.

## Clues

① 2nd Day

② 1st Day

③ 4th Day

④ 1st Day

⑤ 2nd Day

## NEW WORDS

**curry**
kėr´ē

**pall**
pôl

**succulent**
suk´ yə lənt

**satiety**
sə tī´ ə tē

**intrinsic**
in trin´ sik

## QUEEN OF THE SUPERMARKET

The American housewife is queen of all she surveys in the supermarket. She decides what items shall be purchased. Grocery manufacturers are well aware of her power to make one product a success and another a failure. They spend huge sums developing new products with which to *curry* her favor. Fearful that a successful product will soon begin to *pall*, the manufacturers, without cessation,* come out with "ncw and improved" versions to whet* her appetite. Sometimes it is only a box or package that has been changed—perhaps a colorful photo of a *succulent* meal on a TV dinner box. In the larger supermarkets the housewife is faced with a *satiety* of merchandise, particularly in the copiously* stocked laundry detergent section. While there may be almost no *intrinsic* difference among the many brands, advertising and packaging serves to importune* her to buy one rather than another.

*Did you spot it? The "new word" you've seen before? It's* intrinsic.

**Sample Sentences** Insert the new words in these sentences.

1. The connoisseur* of fine foods declared the restaurant the ultimate* in the preparation of _____ meat dishes.

2. She coveted* the antiquated* locket even though it had only an _____ value.

3. He discreetly* tried to _____ favor with his employer.

4. The host exhorted* his guests to eat to _____ .

5. Those conditions were not conducive* to a felicitous* evening as the dance would soon _____ for the lack of feminine companionship.

**Definitions** Match the new words with their definitions.

6. curry _____    **a.** excess, overly full, surfeit*

7. pall _____    **b.** within itself, inherent*

8. succulent _____    **c.** to seek favor by flattery

9. satiety _____    **d.** juicy

10. intrinsic _____    **e.** cease to please, become dull

---
### TODAY'S IDIOM
---

***a pretty kettle of fish*—a mess, troubles**

He thought it was an innocent white lie, but it got him into *a pretty kettle of fish.*

ANSWERS ARE ON PAGE 308

# WEEK 41 ❖ DAY 2

NEW WORDS

**potpourri**
pō´ pü rē´

**sanction**
sangk´ shən

**denote**
di nōt´

**allude**
ə lüd´

**insidious**
in sid´ ē əs

## IT'S WHAT'S OUTSIDE THAT COUNTS

Packaging of grocery items is a facet* of advertising that is too little appreciated by consumers. Walking up and down the aisles of a supermarket, one seldom stops to analyze the individual package in the *potpourri* of items on the shelves. The manufacturer had to glean* and test many different designs before he accepted the one you see in the array* before you. Before he will *sanction* the use of a particular can, box, or bottle, he must know many things about its efficacy.* He wants to know if the colors attract: a white box may *denote* cleanliness, a red one, strength. There may be a photo or a drawing that will *allude* to the product's use or special qualities. A lackluster* package may be fatal.* Next, the size and shape are important elements. The housewife may want a small package for easy storing, but a larger package may suggest economy. A round bottle may look attractive, but a square one is easier to stack. These are some of the *insidious* aspects of packaging, the main purpose of which is to attract your attention as you peruse* the crowded supermarket shelves.

**Sample Sentences**  Insert the new words in these sentences.

1. I cannot _____ your lax* attitude towards the imminent* threat of a conflagration.*

2. In some _____ way the glib* salesman played upon my repressed* desires and sold me a gaudy* sports car.

3. You can be sure the candidate will _____ to the moribund* state of our economy and offer his panacea.*

4. A _____ of today's musical hits sounds more like cacophony* than harmony.

5. His levity* at such a serious moment _____ a lack of feeling.

**Definitions**  Match the new words with their definitions.

6. potpourri _____  a. sly, seductive, treacherous

7. sanction _____  b. hint, suggest

8. denote _____  c. endorse, certify

9. allude _____  d. medley, mixture

10. insidious _____  e. indicate, show, mean

## ─── TODAY'S IDIOM ───

*the acid test*—a severe test

The new job was an *acid test* of his ability to bring home the bacon.*

ANSWERS ARE ON PAGE 308

## NEW WORDS

**propriety**
prə prī´ ə tē

**advent**
ad´ vent

**impious**
im´ pē əs

**proffer**
prof´ ər

**spate**
spāt

## "TRIED AND TRUE"

Few question the *propriety* of the current haste on the part of manufacturers to bring out "new and improved" products at the prevalent* rate. At one time, in the dim, distant past before the *advent* of television, it was the vogue* for products to be advertised on the merits of their "tried and true" qualities. Few advertisers were *impious* enough to jettison* any part of a product that had been accepted by the public. Year after year, the local grocery store owner would *proffer* the same box of cereal, the same house cleaner. The acceptance was of the time-tested product, and it appeared almost unconscionable* for the manufacturer to change his merchandise. Today's *spate* of transient* products would have been considered an anomaly* in those days.

**Sample Sentences** Insert the new words in these sentences.

1. A few years ago there was a _____ of science-fiction films about awesome* monsters causing pandemonium* on our planet, but after a surfeit* of that genre*, their popularity began to wane.*

2. With the _____ of text messaging, Roger was busy night and day.

3. We question the _____ of making fun of obese* people.

4. I'd like to _____ my belated* congratulations on your 25 years of married serenity.*

5. In the milieu* of city street life it is not atypical* to hear _____ comments about authority.

**Definitions** Match the new words with their definitions.

6. propriety _____ a. suitability, correctness
7. advent _____ b. offer for acceptance
8. impious _____ c. the coming of an important event
9. proffer _____ d. lacking respect, irreverent
10. spate _____ e. rush, flood

---

### TODAY'S IDIOM

***a blind alley*—a direction that leads nowhere**

The modus operandi was leading up *a blind alley*
and they were barking up the wrong tree.

---

ANSWERS ARE ON PAGE 308

# WEEK 41 ❖ DAY 4

**NEW WORDS**

**shibboleth**
shib´ ə lith

**bogus**
bō´ gəs

**substantiate**
səb stan´ shē āt

**nutritive**
nü´ trə tiv

**raucous**
rô´ kəs

## WHAT'S IN A NAME?

Supermarkets now carry their own products to compete with the national brands. These "house" brands are not in a felicitous* position because they cannot be advertised widely. Supermarkets overcome this encumbrance* by making these brands less expensive. Many people believe the *shibboleth*,* "You get what you pay for," and they purchase items on the premise* that quality varies as the price does. Are the claims made by nationally advertised brands *bogus*? How can one bread company *substantiate* its *nutritive* superiority over another? As there is no incontrovertible* evidence, the more expensive bread (or coffee, etc.) must compensate* by increased advertising. They make inordinate* claims, using those *raucous* techniques proven so successful in convincing the frugal* consumer to switch to a more costly brand.

**Sample Sentences** Insert the new words in these sentences.

1. Mothers should be vigilant* that their children's food has the proper _____ value.

2. There were _____ complaints about the inordinate* number of fatal* accidents caused by inebriated* drivers.

3. People often try to compensate* for their deplorable* lack of culture by repeating the _____ , "I know what I like."

4. He had the audacity* to try to foist* a _____ dollar on me.

5. The reporter wanted to elicit* the pertinent* facts from the reticent* witness so he could _____ the charge of moral turpitude* against the high city official.

**Definitions** Match the new words with their definitions.

6. shibboleth _____  **a.** pet phrase, slogan

7. bogus _____  **b.** harsh, shrill

8. substantiate _____  **c.** counterfeit, fake

9. nutritive _____  **d.** having nourishing properties

10. raucous _____  **e.** confirm, ratify

---
### TODAY'S IDIOM
---

***to twist around one's finger*—to control completely**

He winked at* the little girl's bad behavior; she had him *twisted around her finger*.

You can be sure of a balanced language if you are well acquainted with all the products (words) available in your supermarket (vocabulary).

| REVIEW WORDS | DEFINITIONS |
|---|---|
| _____ **1.** advent | **a.** suggest, hint |
| _____ **2.** allude | **b.** surfeit,* excess, fullness |
| _____ **3.** bogus | **c.** coming of an important event |
| _____ **4.** curry | **d.** having nourishing properties |
| _____ **5.** denote | **e.** slogan, pet phrase |
| _____ **6.** impious | **f.** correctness, suitability |
| _____ **7.** insidious | **g.** juicy |
| _____ **8.** intrinsic | **h.** mixture, medley |
| _____ **9.** nutritive | **i.** mean, show, indicate |
| _____ **10.** pall | **j.** to seek favor by flattery |
| _____ **11.** potpourri | **k.** irreverent, lacking respect |
| _____ **12.** proffer | **l.** fake, counterfeit |
| _____ **13.** propriety | **m.** ratify, confirm |
| _____ **14.** raucous | **n.** rush, flood |
| _____ **15.** sanction | **o.** become dull, cease to please |
| _____ **16.** satiety | **p.** treacherous, sly, seductive |
| _____ **17.** shibboleth | **q.** certify, endorse |
| _____ **18.** spate | **r.** inherent,* within itself |
| _____ **19.** substantiate | **s.** offer for acceptance |
| _____ **20.** succulent | **t.** shrill, harsh |

## IDIOMS

| | |
|---|---|
| _____ **21.** to twist around one's finger | **u.** a severe test |
| _____ **22.** the acid test | **v.** a direction that leads nowhere |
| _____ **23.** a pretty kettle of fish | **w.** a mess, trouble |
| _____ **24.** a blind alley | **x.** to control completely |

**WORDS FOR FURTHER STUDY**     **MEANINGS**

1. _____     _____

2. _____     _____

Check your answers on page 308.

3. _____     _____

❖ Using the clues listed below, fill in each blank in the following story with one of the new words you learned this week.

## *Age Discrimination*

One of the most ① _____ forms of discrimination is that based upon age. We have become aware through publicity and education that bias and discrimination based upon race, color, creed, and sex are not to be accepted. Through laws passed by the Congress of the United States and by individual states, we agree that using these criteria for hiring, promoting, or firing in the workplace is a ② _____ and undemocratic excuse. Many lawsuits have supported this most basic right to "life, liberty and the pursuit of happiness" protected by our Constitution.

Why is it, then, that so few question the ③ _____ of preventing those viewed as "too old" from getting positions, or, if already on the job, promotions? Advanced age also leads to the firing of such employees and their replacement with younger applicants. Is there something ④ _____ in youth that suggests that older workers cannot do the job as well? Until age discrimination goes the way of all of the other forms of prejudice, we may continue to ⑤ _____ the reasoning that "younger is better."

## Clues

① 2nd Day

② 4th Day

③ 3rd Day

④ 1st Day

⑤ 2nd Day

## NEW WORDS

**quandary**
kwon´ dər ē

**callous**
kal´ əs

**expedient**
ek spē´ dē ənt

**negligible**
neg´ lə jə bəl

**blasé**
blä zā´

## YOU CAN'T HELP BUT WATCH

The consumer is in a *quandary* about making a felicitous* selection among the array* of products. The advertisers must influence the malleable* consumer, and often they do it in the most *callous* ways. Television offers many tangible* advantages for reaching the consumer. As a result, the consumer is inundated* by commercials. The advertiser knows that a television commercial is the most *expedient* way to reach large numbers of people. The cost for each commercial film is prodigious,* but because the audience is so large, the cost per viewer is *negligible.* Each commercial is prepared in the most meticulous* way in order to catch the attention of even the most *blasé* viewer and hold it until the message is through.

*The reintroduced "new word" should have stood out immediately. Did it? It's* callous, *of course.*

**Sample Sentences** Insert the new words in these sentences.

1. It was fortuitous* that the accident occurred when there were _____ numbers of children in the buses.

2. He was in a _____ about which selection from his extensive repertoire* it would be feasible* to perform for the children.

3. Because she had committed only a venial* offense, he thought it _____ to abjure* a severe punishment.

4. Who can be _____ about the presence of many indigent* families in proximity* to affluence?*

5. People have become so _____ about the once thrilling, now mundane* flights into space.

**Definitions** Match the new words with their definitions.

6. quandary _____    **a.** indifferent, not responsive to excitement

7. callous _____    **b.** hardened, unfeeling

8. expedient (adj.) _____    **c.** doubt, dilemma

9. negligible _____    **d.** advisable, fit

10. blasé _____    **e.** trifling, inconsiderable

---
### TODAY'S IDIOM
---

***to do one's heart good**—to make one feel happy or better*

It *did my heart good* to see that inveterate* egotist* eat humble pie.*

---

ANSWERS ARE ON PAGE 309

### NEW WORDS

**ennui**
än´ wē

**comely**
kum´ lē

**frenetic**
frə net´ ik

**artifice**
är´ tə fis

**diversity**
də vėr´ sə tē

## TRICKS OF THE TRADE

Some television commercials, trying to break through the *ennui* built up in the viewer by the plethora* of competition, employ humor. Others feature a *comely* girl as a pretext* for getting the viewer to stay tuned in. At times raucous* music, accompanied by some *frenetic* activities, is designed to preclude* the viewer's loss of attention. The advertiser will employ every bit of *artifice* at the film maker's command to make a trenchant* commercial. The *diversity* of appeals made to the viewer is a concomitant* of the many ways people react to commercials. A great deal of time and money has gone into placing the consumer's psychological make-up under scrutiny.*

**Sample Sentences**  Insert the new words in these sentences.

1. The omnipotent* dictator employed all of his rhetoric* to vilify* those who would be brash* enough to suggest that a _____ of opinions should be expressed.

2. The fledgling* pianist knew that his mentor* would take umbrage* at his yawning during the lesson, but the feeling of _____ was overwhelming.

3. He was reticent* about revealing his clandestine* meetings with a _____ young girl counselor at this camp.

4. They furtively* employed every kind of _____ to be able to meet.

5. They were vigilant* in order that their surreptitious* meetings would not be discovered, and it often required _____ changes of plans to preclude* exposure.

**Definitions**  Match the new words with their definitions.

6. ennui        _____    **a.** frantic, frenzied

7. comely       _____    **b.** boredom

8. frenetic     _____    **c.** beautiful, handsome

9. artifice     _____    **d.** strategy, trickery

10. diversity   _____    **e.** variety, change

---

### TODAY'S IDIOM

***worth one's weight in gold*—extremely valuable, very useful**
The coach said the new star center was *worth his weight in gold.*

---

qualm
kwäm

expurgate
ek´ spər gāt

begrudge
bi gruj´

artless
art´ lis

gratuity
grə tü´ ə tē

# WEEK 42 ❖ DAY 3

## GOING TO THE SOURCE

The wide diversity* of reasons people have for buying one product rather than another are investigated by the advertising people in order to prepare efficacious* commercials. They do not have the slightest *qualm* about questioning the consumer about personal things in her own domicile.* The consumer is requested not to *expurgate** her answers. Generally, people are not reticent* and do not *begrudge* giving the time and effort. The questions delve rather deeply, and what the *artless* responses divulge* will help the advertiser decide what to put into his next commercial. After a large number of interviews, the copious* results make it feasible* to prognosticate* how well the commercial will do. The interviewer usually offers no *gratuity* to the person who has helped, but often a sample of the product is proffered* as thanks.

**Sample Sentences** Insert the new words in these sentences.

1. A successful television program can be built around the _____ comments of very young children.

2. At times, the producer must _____ some of the things said by these children because they are too candid.*

3. He had a serious _____ about hunting for the nearly extinct* quarry.*

4. He took umbrage* when I offered a _____ to augment* his small salary.

5. She did not _____ paying the pittance* extra for a better coat.

**Definitions** Match the new words with their definitions.

6. qualm _____ a. remove objectionable parts or passages

7. expurgate _____ b. to be resentful or reluctant

8. begrudge _____ c. innocent, naive*

9. artless _____ d. tip

10. gratuity _____ e. twinge of conscience

---

**TODAY'S IDIOM**

*to make the best of a bad bargain—*
**to change or go along with a poor situation**

After he bought the white elephant,* *he made the best of a bad bargain* and let sleeping dogs lie.*

---

ANSWERS ARE ON PAGE 309

# WEEK 42 ❖ DAY 4

## NEW WORDS

**manifest**
man´ ə fest

**delve**
delv

**capricious**
kə prish´ əs

**requisite**
rek´ wə zit

**replenish**
ri plen´ ish

## IT SEEMS TO WORK

Despite the antipathy* toward commercials expressed by the viewers, the remarkable success of television commercials in selling products makes it *manifest* that the advertiser has gleaned* what the viewer wants to see and hear from his research interview. This has helped the advertiser *delve* deeply into what motivates* people when they go into the supermarket to purchase products. The advertising agency is never *capricious* and can vindicate* spending large sums of money on research. Having uncovered what the public wants, the advertiser expedites* putting the *requisite* words, music, and photographs of the product on film. He will thus *replenish* the never-ending, ubiquitous* television commercial supply in the hope that the consumer will remember some facet* of the film and buy the product.

**Sample Sentences**  Insert the new words in these sentences.

1. If we _____ below and behind the rhetoric* and invective,* we may discover the profound* reasons for the ferment* in our land.

2. He was reticent* about emulating* those who, after eating almost to satiety,* rushed to _____ the food on their plates.

3. It was _____ that an arbiter* would be needed because neither side would capitulate* to a plan foisted* on them by the other side.

4. When the acrimonious* discussion about his _____ actions had attenuated,* he was able to vindicate* his conduct.

5. One mortifying* _____ for the position was that he would have to work for one year under the aegis* of a fatuous* egotist.*

**Definitions**  Match the new words with their definitions.

6. manifest _____ a. requirement

7. delve _____ b. evident, obvious

8. capricious _____ c. fanciful, whimsical*

9. requisite _____ d. to fill again, to restock

10. replenish _____ e. dig. do research

---

### TODAY'S IDIOM

***to make ends meet*—to manage on a given income**

He turned thumbs down* on a new car; he was
having enough trouble *making ends meet*, as it was.

---

As you watch your next television commercial try to imagine what questions were asked by the research people as they interviewed the possible consumers. Advertisers have to select their words carefully. You can select words only when you have large numbers at your command.

## REVIEW WORDS

| | | |
|---|---|---|
| _____ | **1.** | artifice |
| _____ | **2.** | artless |
| _____ | **3.** | begrudge |
| _____ | **4.** | blasé |
| _____ | **5.** | callous |
| _____ | **6.** | capricious |
| _____ | **7.** | comely |
| _____ | **8.** | delve |
| _____ | **9.** | diversity |
| _____ | **10.** | ennui |
| _____ | **11.** | expedient |
| _____ | **12.** | expurgate |
| _____ | **13.** | frenetic |
| _____ | **14.** | gratuity |
| _____ | **15.** | manifest |
| _____ | **16.** | negligible |
| _____ | **17.** | qualm |
| _____ | **18.** | quandary |
| _____ | **19.** | replenish |
| _____ | **20.** | requisite |

## DEFINITIONS

**a.** to remove objectionable parts or passages
**b.** twinge of conscience
**c.** handsome, beautiful
**d.** strategy, trickery
**e.** fit, advisable
**f.** indifferent, not responsive to excitement
**g.** fanciful, whimsical*
**h.** to do research, dig
**i.** to be resentful or reluctant
**j.** inconsiderable, trifling
**k.** boredom
**l.** obvious, evident
**m.** to restock, fill again
**n.** change, variety
**o.** dilemma, doubt
**p.** unfeeling, hardened
**q.** frenzied, frantic
**r.** requirement
**s.** tip
**t.** naive, innocent

## IDIOMS

| | | |
|---|---|---|
| _____ | **21.** | to make the best of a bad bargain |
| _____ | **22.** | to do one's heart good |
| _____ | **23.** | worth one's weight in gold |
| _____ | **24.** | to make ends meet |

**u.** extremely valuable, very useful
**v.** to make one feel happy or better
**w.** to manage on a given income
**x.** to change or go along with a poor situation

Check your answers on page 309. Learn those words you missed!

## WORDS FOR FURTHER STUDY          MEANINGS

**1.** _____    _____

**2.** _____    _____

**3.** _____    _____

❖ Using the clues listed below, fill in each blank in the following story with one of the new words you learned this week.

## An Historic Date

One event that takes place so rarely that almost no one alive when it happens can remember the previous occurrence is the changing of the century number. The passing of the ①_____ number of years brings about the end of the 20th century and the advent of the 21st. Is there anyone ②_____ enough to reach this historic date without experiencing the excitement of this once-in-a-lifetime moment?

While we may feel that events in our lifetime happen in a ③_____ way, the stroke of midnight on December 31, 2000, ushered in a new century. It served as a time to reflect upon the ④_____ of events in our lives, both positive and negative, that the 20th century encompassed. It is obvious to all that the past 100 years have altered the world in ways no one could anticipate at the end of the 19th century. There are many who ⑤_____ into the past and make predictions for the new century. December 31, 2000, was a time for reflection and promise.

## Clues

① 4th Day

② 1st Day

③ 4th Day

④ 2nd Day

⑤ 4th Day

## NEW WORDS

**roster**
ros´ tər

**stunted**
stunt´ id

**atrophy**
at´ rə fē

**maim**
mām

**ameliorate**
ə mē´ lyə rāt

## IT TAKES MORE THAN MEDICINE

If one were to look at the *roster* of physical handicaps, one would reach the somber* conclusion that the list is a long one. Included would be *stunted* development of an arm or leg due to a birth anomaly.* Others would be the result of a crippling disease that has caused muscles to *atrophy*. The list would go on with illnesses and injuries that *maim* and debilitate.* Modern medicine has done much to *ameliorate* the physical problems. However, there are an inordinate* number of problems of the handicapped that have still to be alleviated.* People are not naturally callous,* but in some perverse* way they have the propensity* to repress* any concern with the physically handicapped. The social problems seem to be inherent* in our own attitudes.

**Sample Sentences**  Insert the new words in these sentences.

1. If you heap opprobrium* on an impious* child, it probably will not _____ the conditions that led to the rebelliousness.

2. The coach knew he would have to add experienced players to the _____ to compensate* for the spate* of freshmen on the team.

3. There seems to be voluminous* evidence that the mother's smoking will _____ the baby's growth.

4. The prodigy* allowed his musical talent to _____ as he redirected his career.

5. When it seemed that Reggie would _____ his opponent, we broke up the fight.

**Definitions**  Match the new words with their definitions.

6. roster _____     **a.** checked in natural growth, held back in growth

7. stunted _____     **b.** waste away

8. atrophy _____     **c.** a list of names

9. maim _____     **d.** improve, relieve

10. ameliorate _____     **e.** disable, cripple

--- **TODAY'S IDIOM** ---

***to burn the midnight oil**—to study or work until very late*

The radio was such an enigma* that he had *to burn the midnight oil** for several nights in order to get it working.

ANSWERS ARE ON PAGE 309

# WEEK 43 ❖ DAY 2

**NEW WORDS**

**cynic**
sin´ ik

**unctuous**
ungk´ chủ əs

**benevolent**
bə nev´ ə lənt

**subservient**
səb sẻr´ vē ənt

**iniquity**
in ik´ wə tē

## DOING THE RIGHT THING

The obstacles that frustrate* the physically handicapped person who is seeking employment may turn him into a *cynic*. Too often a prospective employer, with a rather *unctuous* manner, actually tends to degrade* the handicapped by proffering* employment that is really beneath them and their abilities. The employer appears to be acting in a *benevolent* manner, but this attitude shows no compassion,* for he really expects the person seeking the job to remain *subservient*. This *iniquity* cannot but give the handicapped a feeling that they are being discriminated against. He does not expect a sinecure,* but he has an aversion* to the prevalent* belief that he should consider himself lucky to find any employment.

**Sample Sentences** Insert the new words in these sentences.

1. We had to wince* as we watched the newcomer try to wheedle* and ingratiate* himself into the teacher's favor in the most _____ manner.

2. It is easy to become a _____ when the same adults who inveigh* most vehemently* against the uncouth actions that they say permeate* our youth drink to satiety* and behave fatuously.*

3. We all have moments when we vacillate* between selfish and _____ desires.

4. While his demeanor* remained imperturbable,* there was latent* anger at the ignominious* and _____ role he had to play.

5. Those who are complacent* about any _____ in our society should be wary* of the unsavory* consequences for all.

**Definitions** Match the new words with their definitions.

6. cynic _____ a. servile, obsequious*

7. unctuous _____ b. pessimist, skeptic

8. benevolent _____ c. affectedly emotional

9. subservient _____ d. kindly, charitable

10. iniquity _____ e. injustice, wickedness

---
### TODAY'S IDIOM

***to lay one's cards on the table*—to talk frankly**

He knew he was out of his depth* so *he laid his cards on the table* and asked for assistance.

---

## NEW WORDS

**largess**
lär´ jis

**criterion**
krī tir´ ē ən

**repent**
ri pent´

**mollify**
mol´ ə fī

**mercenary**
mėr´ sə ner´ ē

## A BETTER WAY

Why is there any question about the propriety* of hiring the physically handicapped? No one who understands their needs can condone* this attitude. The offering of employment should not be considered a *largess*. There should be no need to vindicate* the hiring of a handicapped person. The only *criterion* should be what he is capable of doing. If this is the approach, the handicapped worker will not feel he is an encumbrance* to his boss. The employer, on the other hand, will find it conducive* to good work and will not *repent* his having tried something new just to *mollify* his conscience. Even for the most *mercenary* employer, there should be no reticence* in eliciting* the best that is possible from the handicapped worker.

**Sample Sentences** Insert the new words in these sentences.

1. He felt it would be ignominious* for him to accept any _____ from the charlatan* whose Machiavellian* schemes had made him affluent.*

2. Behind the façade* of ostensible* benevolence* there was a _____ streak.

3. The platitude, "I know what I like," is often used to rationalize* our lack of a _____ for things about which we are dubious.*

4. When Mother is in a pique* about some infraction* of a rule, it takes all of our dexterity* to _____ her.

5. After every election we _____ , in a belated* criticism, the apathy* and complacency* of so many people who failed to vote.

**Definitions** Match the new words with their definitions.

6. largess _____ a. gift, gratuity*, liberality

7. criterion _____ b. model, standard, test

8. repent _____ c. motivated* by desire for gain, greedy

9. mollify _____ d. pacify, appease

10. mercenary (adj.)_____ e. regret, desire to make amends

---
### TODAY'S IDIOM

*a bolt from the blue*—a great surprise
The windfall* from his distant cousin came like *a bolt from the blue.*

---

ANSWERS ARE ON PAGE 309

# WEEK 43 ❖ DAY 4

**pariah**
pə rī´ə

**aloof**
ə lüf´

**pragmatic**
prag mat´ ik

**vestige**
ves´ tij

**guise**
gīz

## JUST BE YOURSELF

Socially, the handicapped person is often treated as a *pariah*. Most people hold themselves *aloof* from normal contact with those who are "different." This social separation propagates* additional feelings of antipathy*. If "normal" individuals would socialize with the handicapped individual, they would learn in a *pragmatic* way that these are people who happen to have a physical handicap; the handicap does not make them any less human. The iniquity* of assuming that physical superiority equals moral superiority prevents all of us from direct human relationships. As long as there is a *vestige* of feeling that handicapped people are inferior, then we are all handicapped in one way or another. Under the *guise* of physical superiority we demonstrate a moral turpitude* that is harmful to all.

**Sample Sentences**  Insert the new words in these sentences.

1. After therapy*, there remained hardly a _____ of his phobia*.

2. He was stigmatized* as a _____ when he had the audacity* to boast of his nefarious* and sordid* career printing bogus* money.

3. Although many people say this is a propitious* time to invest in the stock market, there is a tenable* argument for remaining _____ .

4. In the _____ of maintaining national unity under military rule, there was a paucity* of even innocuous* dissent*.

5. "You can't argue with success," was his _____ reply to derogatory* remarks about a movie star who had only superficial* talent as an actor.

**Definitions**  Match the new words with their definitions.

| | | | |
|---|---|---|---|
| 6. | pariah | _____ | **a.** manner, appearance, mien* |
| 7. | aloof | _____ | **b.** social outcast |
| 8. | pragmatic | _____ | **c.** distant, apart, reserved |
| 9. | vestige | _____ | **d.** trace, evidence |
| 10. | guise | _____ | **e.** practical, based on experience |

---
### TODAY'S IDIOM
---

***to tell tales out of school*—to reveal harmful secrets**

The fat was in the fire* for the politician when his private secretary started *telling tales out of school* about his secret sources of income.

There are various kinds of handicaps. One that we can do something about, and *you* are now doing it, is the language handicap. Our fullest potential can be realized only when there is no barrier between what we want to say or write and our ability to express ourselves.

## REVIEW WORDS

_____ **1.** aloof
_____ **2.** ameliorate
_____ **3.** atrophy
_____ **4.** benevolent
_____ **5.** criterion
_____ **6.** cynic
_____ **7.** guise
_____ **8.** iniquity
_____ **9.** largess
_____ **10.** maim
_____ **11.** mercenary
_____ **12.** mollify
_____ **13.** pariah
_____ **14.** pragmatic
_____ **15.** repent
_____ **16.** roster
_____ **17.** stunted
_____ **18.** subservient
_____ **19.** unctuous
_____ **20.** vestige

## DEFINITIONS

**a.** based on experience, practical
**b.** mien,* appearance, manner
**c.** a list of names
**d.** skeptic, pessimist
**e.** test, model, standard
**f.** desire to make amends, regret
**g.** obsequious,* servile
**h.** held back or checked in natural growth
**i.** social outcast
**j.** evidence, trace
**k.** waste away
**l.** charitable, kindly
**m.** appease, pacify
**n.** wickedness, injustice
**o.** cripple, disable
**p.** reserved, apart, distant
**q.** greedy, motivated* by desire for gain
**r.** liberality, gift, gratuity*
**s.** affectedly emotional
**t.** relieve, improve

## IDIOMS

_____ **21.** to burn the midnight oil
_____ **22.** to lay one's cards on the table
_____ **23.** a bolt from the blue
_____ **24.** to tell tales out of school

**u.** to reveal harmful secrets
**v.** a great surprise
**w.** to talk frankly
**x.** to study or work until very late

## WORDS FOR FURTHER STUDY     MEANINGS

**1.** _____  _____

**2.** _____  _____

**3.** _____  _____

Check your answers on page 309.

❖ Using the clues listed below, fill in each blank in the following story with one of the new words you learned this week.

## *Whistle Blowing*

There appears to be a question of how much loyalty employees owe to their employers—whether private or governmental. Many companies go out of their way to encourage employees to make suggestions that will improve the way they operate. A ①_____ employer will not criticize or reprimand an employee who points out problems having to do with the way other employees are harming the business. In fact, it should be in the bosses' interest that the person who has become known as a "whistle blower" is encouraged to alert them to a problem.

However, many such whistle blowers face harsh punishment for calling attention to illegal or unethical actions. The whistle blower soon becomes a ②_____ in the workplace. Under the ③_____ of some minor error, or other excuse, the informer might be demoted, transferred, or fired. This ④_____ often goes unreported. As a result, the employees go back to "business as usual" without any change. They become used to whatever they may see around them and to the belief that they should not make waves. Thus, no attempt to ⑤_____ the situation actually takes place.

## Clues

① 2nd Day

② 4th Day

③ 4th Day

④ 2nd Day

⑤ 1st Day

**NEW WORDS**

**nullify**
nul´ ə fī

**deluge**
del´ yüj

**futility**
fyü til´ ə tē

**carnage**
kär´ nij

**technology**
tek nol´ ə jē

## HAVE WE MASTERED OUR ENVIRONMENT?

Natural disasters tend to *nullify* the best efforts of mankind. It is as though there are forces at work that are contemptuous* of our proud achievements. Who has not read of or seen the waters that *deluge* our towns and cities, jeopardizing* lives and culminating* in the destruction of the results of endless work in the space of a few moments? We are all vulncrablc* to feelings of *futility* as we view the *carnage* caused to cattle from the sudden inundation.* Despite the laudable* advances made in *technology,* it can be seen that we cannot yet say we have mastered our environment. Disasters of this type, leaving only pathetic* vestiges* of homes and shops, are accepted as inevitable,* and all we can do is to attempt to ameliorate* the conditions that result.

**Sample Sentences** Insert the new words in these sentences.

1. In spite of his efforts to cajole* the girl, she remained aloof,* and the _____ of his efforts made him lugubrious.*

2. To our consternation,* modern _____ has made feasible* a spate* of lethal* devices that could lead to the inadvertent* destruction of the world.

3. In order to _____ the height advantage of his adversary,* he abjured* smoking and did an inordinate amount of exercise until he was the acme* of litheness* and dexterity.*

4. We found it impossible to mollify* the irate* owner of three prize cats as he viewed the _____ caused by our large dog.

5. The office was _____ with requests for his autograph as the girls became cognizant* of his identity.

**Definitions** Match the new words with their definitions.

6. nullify _____ a. slaughter

7. deluge (v.) _____ b. to flood

8. futility _____ c. abolish, cancel

9. carnage _____ d. applied science

10. technology _____ e. uselessness

---
### TODAY'S IDIOM
---

***to build upon sand*—to have a poor base, or not sufficient preparation**

Because they were amateurs and without money, the political campaign was *built upon sand* and the candidate was a flash in the pan.*

ANSWERS ARE ON PAGE 309

# WEEK 44 ❖ DAY 2

**NEW WORDS**

**libel**
lī′ bəl

**defamatory**
di fam′ ə tôr ē

**plaintiff**
plān′ tif

**canard**
kə närd′

**deprecate**
dep′ rə kāt

## GOOD NEWS—AND BAD

One of the latent* dangers indigenous* to our constitutional guarantee of freedom of the press has to do with the protection of the individual against the detriment* that might come from news reports involving him. There are *libel* laws that protect against false charges. If an individual believes his character or livelihood have been damaged by a *defamatory* article, he can sue. As the *plaintiff* he must refute* the story and show how the defendant caused him harm by printing a *canard*. The defendant attempts to substantiate* the truth of the article. The printing of news may besmirch* an individual's character, but there is no way to alleviate* this problem without changes in the Constitution. This would be tantamount* to destroying the efficacy* of our coveted* right to learn the truth from the press. We all *deprecate* a situation in which someone suffers because of exposure in the newspapers. Only when the harm is caused by someone with a desire to malign* under the guise* of printing the news can the individual expect to win compensation* through the courts.

**Sample Sentences**  Insert the new words in these sentences.

1. The mayor vehemently* denied there was any antipathy* between the governor and himself and blamed this _____ on their political opponents.

2. I resent your _____ remark that depicts* me as a culprit.*

3. The egregious* calumny* of the defendant worked to the advantage of the _____ .

4. Publishers of newspapers and magazines augment* their staff with lawyers to represent them when they are sued for _____ .

5. The cynic* will _____ the motives of anyone who tries to ameliorate* the iniquities* in our society.

**Definitions**  Study these carefully for the fine differences in meaning.

6. libel (n.)    _____    a. express disapproval
7. defamatory    _____    b. the complaining party, in law
8. plaintiff    _____    c. degradation by writing or publishing
9. canard    _____    d. damaging character by false reports
10. deprecate    _____    e. a made-up sensational story

---
**TODAY'S IDIOM**
---

*a pretty kettle of fish*—a messy situation, a problem

He knew that when he attacked the sacred cow* he would be in *a pretty kettle of fish.* (Do you remember this idiom? It was used earlier in the book and should be familiar.)

## NEW WORDS

reputed
ri pyü´ tid

frail
frāl

potent
pōt´ nt

excoriate
ek skôr´ ē āt

devout
di vout´

## A PHILOSOPHER FOR OUR TIME

Soren Kierkegaard was a Danish philosopher who is *reputed* to be the forerunner of the current vogue* of existentialism. In appearance he was a *frail* and ungainly man. An extremely erudite* thinker and writer, he was a *potent* force in propagating* the new approach to life. His philosophy would *excoriate* those who believed that man could stand aside from life. In his philosophy it is a heresy* to take a detached point of view; it is incumbent* upon the individual to get involved. What is germane* is not that we exist, but that our existence is determined by our acts. He was a religiously *devout* man who fervidly* believed that the individual is always paramount.*

**Sample Sentences**  Insert the new words in these sentences.

1. Even though she was piqued* at his indolent* manner, it was pathetic* to listen to her _____ him in public.

2. His awesome* mental dexterity* compensated* for his _____ physical condition.

3. When Ben's muscles began to atrophy,* the doctor initiated* therapy* with a _____ new drug.

4. The drug is _____ to have a salubrious* effect on nascent* conditions of this type.

5. Although he was a _____ adherent* of the party, he remained aloof* during the vitriolic* primary campaign.

**Definitions**  Match the new words with their definitions.

6. reputed      _____    **a.** thought, supposed, believed

7. frail         _____    **b.** religious, sincere

8. potent        _____    **c.** delicate, weak

9. excoriate     _____    **d.** criticize severely

10. devout       _____    **e.** powerful, strong, intense

## TODAY'S IDIOM

*to toe the mark*—to obey or stick to a rule or policy

He wanted to kick over the traces,* but his parents made him *toe the mark*.

# WEEK 44 ❖ DAY 4

**NEW WORDS**

**diminutive**
də min´ yə tiv

**profuse**
prə fyüs´

**dulcet**
dul´ sit

**impromptu**
im promp´ tü

**malevolent**
mə lev´ ə lənt

## THE ISLAND OF WILD DOGS

The saga* of the introduction of that *diminutive* song bird, the canary, into the homes of the world as tame pets is an interesting one. In the sixteenth century a trading ship going to Italy stopped at an island named "Canis," from the Latin word for wild dog, which could be found there in *profuse* numbers, off the coast of Africa. The *dulcet* song of the wild birds whetted* the interest of the captain. In *impromptu* cages hundreds were taken aboard to be traded. The sailors called these gray-green birds, spotted with yellow, "canaries." As they approached the island of Elba, near Italy, a *malevolent* storm put the boat in jeopardy* of sinking. A member of the crew released the birds, and the intrepid* canaries instinctively flew towards land. The peasants on Elba took the wild canaries in as pets. Eventually, the birds found their way into homes throughout Europe where they were domesticated and bred for variety of song and shades of colors. The canaries prevalent* today differ greatly from the ones discovered over four hundred years ago.

**Sample Sentences**  Insert the new words in these sentences.

1. As the music reached a frenetic* tempo, the audience lost all decorum* and broke into _____ dancing.

2. He had no qualms* about opposing the clique* who insidiously* exerted a _____ influence on the president.

3. The connoisseur* was able to glean* a worthwhile painting from the _____ variety of poor ones at the exhibit.

4. Europeans drive _____ cars because their narrow roads and high prices for gasoline are not conducive* to or compatible* with our large ones.

5. The blasé devotee of the opera was awakened from his ennui* by the _____ tones of the new soprano.

**Definitions**  Match the new words with their definitions.

6. diminutive _____ **a.** ill-disposed, ill-intentioned

7. profuse _____ **b.** tiny, small

8. dulcet _____ **c.** spur of the moment, offhand

9. impromptu _____ **d.** sweet or melodious to the ear

10. malevolent _____ **e.** overflowing, abundant

— **TODAY'S IDIOM** —

*to be under a cloud*—to be in temporary disgrace or trouble

Until they discovered the real thief, he *was under a cloud.*

The history, or derivation, of words is called "etymology." This is a fascinating study and it gives insight to the background of words such as "canary," and thousands of others. Knowing the history of a word helps you remember it.

## REVIEW WORDS

|        |                    |
|--------|--------------------|
| _____  | 1. canard          |
| _____  | 2. carnage         |
| _____  | 3. defamatory      |
| _____  | 4. deluge          |
| _____  | 5. deprecate       |
| _____  | 6. devout          |
| _____  | 7. diminutive      |
| _____  | 8. dulcet          |
| _____  | 9. excoriate       |
| _____  | 10. frail          |
| _____  | 11. futility       |
| _____  | 12. impromptu      |
| _____  | 13. libel          |
| _____  | 14. malevolent     |
| _____  | 15. nullify        |
| _____  | 16. plaintiff      |
| _____  | 17. potent         |
| _____  | 18. profuse        |
| _____  | 19. reputed        |
| _____  | 20. technology     |

## DEFINITIONS

a. flood
b. express disapproval
c. intense, strong, powerful
d. sincere, religious
e. sweet or melodious to the ear
f. abundant, overflowing
g. slaughter
h. uselessness
i. criticize severely
j. damaging character by false reports
k. a made-up sensational story
l. small, tiny
m. cancel, abolish
n. ill-disposed, ill-intentioned
o. weak, delicate
p. the complaining party, in law
q. applied science
r. believed, thought, supposed
s. offhand, spur of the moment
t. degradation by writing or publishing

## IDIOMS

| | |
|---|---|
| _____ 21. a pretty kettle of fish | u. to be in temporary disgrace or trouble |
| _____ 22. to be under a cloud | v. to obey or stick to a rule or policy |
| _____ 23. to toe the mark | w. a messy situation, a problem |
| _____ 24. to build upon sand | x. to have a poor base, or not sufficient preparation |

Check your answers on page 309.

## WORDS FOR FURTHER STUDY          MEANINGS

1. _____   _____

2. _____   _____

3. _____   _____

# SENSIBLE SENTENCES?
## (From Weeks 41–44)

❖ Underline the word that makes sense in each of the sentences below.

1. The station's switchboard was *(deluged, deprecated)* by phone calls when the popular soap opera was cancelled.

2. The *(diminutive, frail)* ballplayer proved that size doesn't matter in some sports.

3. Peter was surprised when his normally nervous boss seemed so *(blasé, aloof)* about the bad financial news.

4. Our mouths began to water when the *(dulcet, succulent)* dish was set upon the table.

5. Coming from a small city in Costa Rica, Ligia was not used to the *(potent, frenetic)* pace of life in Boston.

6. With *(bogus, insidious)* identification papers, the terrorists attempted to board the waiting airplane.

7. When the time came for Lisa to select a subject to major in, she found herself in a *(quandary, potpourri)*.

8. The *(malevolent, benevolent)* dictator was generally beloved by his people even though he limited their freedoms.

9. Only a *(negligible, manifest)* amount of gas escaped from the laboratory during the experiment.

10. The president of the School Board intended to *(excoriate, nullify)* the parents at the opening meeting.

ANSWERS ARE ON PAGE 309

# WORDSEARCH 44

❖ Using the clues listed below, fill in each blank in the following story with one of the new words you learned this week.

## *Reprieve for Wolves*

One of the most difficult problems to resolve has to do with the conflicting interests of environmentalists and profit-making businesses. Examples of this dilemma appear frequently. While the dispute about cutting down a forest to preserve owls has been in the news, there appeared another conflict in the state of Alaska. Hoping to increase the number of tourists who seek to hunt deer and caribou, the State of Alaska ordered the killing of some of the ①_____ number of wolves that prey on those animals.

This resulted in a ②_____ of letters and articles condemning the ③_____ that would result from the anti-wolf policy. So, once again, the environmentalists, who maintain that the natural balance should not be interfered with, ran up against the Alaskan tourist industry, which wants to attract hunters who will increase the state's revenue. After much publicity about the wolf hunt and articles that tended to ④_____ this policy, Alaska decided to ⑤_____ the proposed action.

## Clues

① 4th Day

② 1st Day

③ 1st Day

④ 3rd Day

⑤ 1st Day

ANSWERS ARE ON PAGE 309

# WEEK 45 ❖ DAY 1

**NEW WORDS**

**wistful**
wist´ fəl

**raiment**
rā´ mənt

**brigand**
brig´ ənd

**corpulent**
kôr´ pyə lənt

**rail**
rāl

## IN DAYS OF YORE

Current novels are replete* with lurid* crimes, carnage* and death. Do you get *wistful* when you recall the romantic tales that begin with an innocent maiden travelling through the rustic* countryside? She is dressed in glittering *raiment*. The scene is idyllic.* Without warning, the group is set upon by a virile* *brigand*, who, in the most perfunctory* and callous* fashion, carries her off. Pandemonium* results! Her entourage* is in a state of bedlam.* Her *corpulent* escort is irate,* but unable to do anything to thwart* this debacle.* All he can do is *rail* against the catastrophe. What to do? What to do?

**Sample Sentences**  Insert the new words in these sentences.

1. The potpourri* of au courant* fashionable _____ includes the fatuous* and the discreet.*

2. While all disgruntled* men may _____ against malevolent* or Machiavellian* leaders, democracy offers a way to ameliorate* iniquities* through the ballot.

3. Is there any veracity in the platitude* that _____ men are jocose?*

4. To be candid,* there is little to be _____ about in the "good old days."

5. They captured the _____ , and he was incarcerated* for a mandatory* period.

**Definitions**  Match the new words with their definitions.

6. wistful       _____   **a.** dress, clothing

7. raiment       _____   **b.** scold, use abusive language

8. brigand       _____   **c.** longing, pensive,* wishful

9. corpulent     _____   **d.** robber, bandit

10. rail (v.)     _____   **e.** fleshy, obese,* excessively fat

---

### TODAY'S IDIOM

***to flog a dead horse*—to continue to make an issue of something that is over**

He thought he could keep the pot boiling* about his opponent's winking at* crime, but he *was flogging a dead horse.*

---

ANSWERS ARE ON PAGE 310

## NEW WORDS

**raconteur**
rak´ on tėr´

**sullen**
sul´ ən

**rift**
rift

**emissary**
em´ ə ser´ ē

**ruminate**
rü´ mə nāt

## WOE IS ME!

The *raconteur* of our story about idyllic* times gone by goes on to elucidate* how the comely* heroine is taken to the bandits' hideout. There, a *sullen* crew of cutthroats is gathered. They don't wish to procrastinate;* she must be taken immediately to a foreign land where much treasure will be paid for her. Their cupidity* knows no bounds. The leader wants to hold her for ransom from her wealthy parents. The gang demurs;* they are reticent.* There is a *rift* among the criminals. Their leader remains truculent, and they agree to wait for just two days for the ransom money. An *emissary* from the grief-stricken parents is expected at any moment. The wan* maiden, her spirits at their nadir,* has time to *ruminate* about her lugubrious* fate.

**Sample Sentences** Insert the new words in these sentences.

1. He alluded* to the _____ caused in the school by the plethora* of hirsute* boys who ignored the criterion* for appearance.

2. Well known as a(n) _____ , he was never chagrined* when asked to tell a story from his large repertoire.*

3. Despite all attempts to mollify* her, she remained _____ about the levity* caused by her slovenly* raiment.*

4. The obscure* country, an aspirant* for membership in the United Nations, sent a(n) _____ .

5. An anomaly* of our modern technology* is that the more we need to know, the less time we have to _____ .

**Definitions** Match the new words with their definitions.

6. raconteur _____ **a.** ill-humored, grim

7. sullen _____ **b.** ponder, reflect upon

8. rift _____ **c.** a skilled storyteller

9. emissary _____ **d.** a split, an opening

10. ruminate _____ **e.** an agent

---

### TODAY'S IDIOM

*the die is cast*—an unchangeable decision has been made

The fat was in the fire* and *the die was cast* when he decided to tell the white lie about how he had found the money.

---

ANSWERS ARE ON PAGE 310

# WEEK 45 ❖ DAY 3

**NEW WORDS**

**taut**
tôt

**livid**
liv´ id

**martinet**
märt´ n et´

**yen**
yen

**bagatelle**
bag´ ə tel´

## TO THE RESCUE

Back at the castle, the situation is *taut* with emotion. The fair maiden's mother is *livid* with fear and anxiety; she has attacks of vertigo.* She talks about her daughter's audacity* in riding out into the ominous* forests despite many similar kidnappings. The girl's father, a *martinet* who rules his family with an iron hand, staunchly* refuses to pay the ransom. Iniquity* shall not be rewarded! At this moment of crisis a heroic knight volunteers to rescue our heroine; he has had a secret *yen* for the young beauty. Avoiding rhetoric,* he pledges his all to castigate* those responsible for this ignominious* deed. He holds his life as a mere *bagatelle* against the duty he owes his beloved mistress. At the propitious* moment, he rides off to do or die for her.

**Sample Sentences**  Insert the new words in these sentences.

1. The rabid* baseball fan lost his equanimity* and became _____ when the star pitcher became pugnacious* and was removed from the game.

2. There was a _____ international situation caused by the proximity* of unidentified submarines to our coasts.

3. When one enlists in the army, one expects to be under the aegis* of a _____ .

4. His _____ for imbibing* and romping* with girls worked to his detriment*.

5. The little boy tried to wheedle* a larger allowance from his father by the caustic* observations that it was a mere _____ when compared to the allowances of his friends.

**Definitions**  Match the new words with their definitions.

6. taut _____    **a.** strict disciplinarian
7. livid _____    **b.** tense, keyed up, on edge
8. martinet _____    **c.** pale
9. yen _____    **d.** a trifle
10. bagatelle _____    **e.** strong desire, strong longing

---

### TODAY'S IDIOM

*a cat's paw*—a person used as a tool or dupe*

The spy used the innocent girl as *a cat's paw* to get military information from the grapevine.*

---

## NEW WORDS

**callow**
kal´ ō

**appalled**
ə pôld´

**penchant**
pen´ chənt

**decapitate**
di kap´ ə tāt

**termagant**
tėr´ mə gənt

## WELL DONE, SIR KNIGHT!

Seeking his adversaries,* the knight rides to their hideout. Despite his *callow* appearance, he is reputed* to disdain* danger and to be a prodigious* horseman. The kidnappers lose their equanimity* at his approach. They are *appalled* at the prospect, and they are in a quandary* as to which one will meet him on the field of combat. The leader, under duress,* rides out. "Do you have a *penchant* to die?" derides* the knight. More vituperative* remarks follow. They spur their horses toward each other. It takes but one blow for our hero to *decapitate* the villain. The others flee to avoid their imminent* destruction. The knight takes the maiden on his horse, and they ride back to the castle. Their wedding soon follows. Little does the knight realize that the fair maiden is a garrulous* *termagant* who will make his life miserable with caustic* remarks. Still, the cliché,* "And they lived happily ever after," must conclude our fabricated* tale.

**Sample Sentences** Insert the new words in these sentences.

1. We do not _____ criminals because of our aversion* to such repugnant* punishments.

2. I do not wish to deprecate* your _____ for cowboy music, but I find it banal.*

3. Why do you remain docile* while that _____ besmirches,* maligns,* and belittles* you?

4. Each long holiday weekend we are _____ at the carnage* on our highways.

5. It was deplorable* the way the capricious* girl led the _____ youth on a merry chase.

**Definitions** Match the new words with their definitions.

6. callow        _____    **a.** youthful, inexperienced

7. appalled      _____    **b.** behead

8. penchant      _____    **c.** a strong leaning in favor

9. decapitate    _____    **d.** a scolding woman, a shrew

10. termagant    _____    **e.** dismayed, shocked

---
### TODAY'S IDIOM

*coup de grâce*—the finishing stroke

When my girlfriend left me, it was a bitter pill to swallow,*
but the *coup de grâce* was that she kept my engagement ring.

---

ANSWERS ARE ON PAGE 310

Language grows and changes. In "days of yore" there were not nearly as many words in our language as we have today. Within the next 50 years hundreds of new words will be added. Educated and alert individuals make new words part of their vocabulary as quickly as they come into accepted use.

## REVIEW WORDS

|  | DEFINITIONS |
|---|---|
| ____ 1. appalled | a. behead |
| ____ 2. bagatelle | b. shocked, dismayed |
| ____ 3. brigand | c. pale |
| ____ 4. callow | d. a trifle |
| ____ 5. corpulent | e. bandit, robber |
| ____ 6. decapitate | f. an agent |
| ____ 7. emissary | g. grim, ill-humored |
| ____ 8. livid | h. clothing, dress |
| ____ 9. martinet | i. on edge, keyed up, tense |
| ____ 10. penchant | j. strict disciplinarian |
| ____ 11. raconteur | k. wishful, pensive,* longing |
| ____ 12. rail | l. a strong leaning in favor |
| ____ 13. raiment | m. an opening, a split |
| ____ 14. rift | n. a skilled storyteller |
| ____ 15. ruminate | o. inexperienced, youthful |
| ____ 16. sullen | p. excessively fat, fleshy, obese* |
| ____ 17. taut | q. reflect upon, ponder |
| ____ 18. termagant | r. a shrew, a scolding woman |
| ____ 19. wistful | s. use abusive language, scold |
| ____ 20. yen | t. strong desire, strong longing |

## IDIOMS

| | |
|---|---|
| ____ 21. a cat's paw | u. the finishing stroke |
| ____ 22. the die is cast | v. an unchangeable decision has been made |
| ____ 23. coup de grâce | w. to continue to make an issue of something that is over |
| ____ 24. to flog a dead horse | x. a person used as a tool or dupe |

Check your answers on page 310.

## WORDS FOR FURTHER STUDY     MEANINGS

1. _____  _____

2. _____  _____

3. _____  _____

# WORDSEARCH 45

❖ Using the clues listed below, fill in each blank in the following story with one of the new words you learned this week.

## Henry VIII and British History

Students in the United States should consider themselves lucky when it comes to studying the country's history. The United States has been a nation for approximately 225 years. We would be ①_____ if we had to learn as much history as students in Great Britain, for their history goes back some 1,000 years! In that time England has had many interesting and unusual rulers. One who has fascinated us is Henry VIII. Ruling some 450 years ago, he became well known because of his many marriages and his ②_____ for doing away with some wives who displeased him.

In physical appearance he was unattractive—he was large and ③_____ . When his first wife could not bear him a son who would be heir to the throne, he divorced her. This caused a break with the Pope who refused to recognize the divorce. Henry VIII sent an ④_____ to the Pope and renounced Catholicism. He then married Anne Boleyn but decided to ⑤_____ her after quickly tiring of her. His third wife died in childbirth, and he divorced his fourth. His fifth, Katherine Howard, was also beheaded. Only his sixth wife was able to live on after Henry's death in 1547. From this brief history of only one English ruler, it is easy to imagine how much an English history student must learn in order to prepare for an exam. In Henry VIII's case, one would have to get a "head start."

## Clues

① 4th Day
② 4th Day
③ 1st Day
④ 2nd Day
⑤ 4th Day

ANSWERS ARE ON PAGE 310

# WEEK 46 ❖ DAY 1

**NEW WORDS**

**ascertain**
as´ ər tān´

**dormant**
dôr´ mənt

**burgeoned**
bėr´ jənd

**potentate**
pōt´ n tāt

**disseminate**
di sem´ ə nāt

## A MIGHTY EMPIRE

One of the anomalies* of our approach to history is the propensity* to study the venerable* empires of Europe, but we do not feel it incumbent* upon us to *ascertain* anything about the civilizations in our own hemisphere. We deprecate* the history of this part of the world as though progress lay *dormant* and that other peoples were irrelevant* until the settlers of North America arrived at Plymouth Rock. In South America, from 2000 B.C. until their empire reached its acme* at the beginning of the 16th century, lived the Incas. The site* of the capital city of the Inca empire, Cusco, lay at a height of 11,000 feet. This civilization is reputed* to have *burgeoned* until it covered more than 2,500 miles of the western part of the continent. Its population fluctuated* between 4 and 7 million. This empire had a highly efficacious* political and social system. Its *potentate* ruled with absolute power. As the empire conquered new lands, it would *disseminate* its language, religion, and social customs.

**Sample Sentences**  Insert the new words in these sentences.

1. While some moribund* economies atrophied* after World War II, others _____ under the salubrious* effects of loans from the U.S.

2. In order to _____ the relationship between his girlfriend and his brother, he kept a wary* and discreet* vigil.*

3. We are quick to _____ calumny,* but reticent* about things that may be construed* as compliments.

4. He was appalled* at the apathy* concerning the important issue that had remained _____ for so long a time.

5. The callous* _____ kept an imperturbable* mien* when requested to alleviate* the unconscionable* conditions existing in his land.

**Definitions**  Match the new words with their definitions.

6. ascertain _____    **a.** spread, scatter
7. dormant _____    **b.** discover, find out about
8. burgeoned _____    **c.** resting, asleep
9. potentate _____    **d.** flourished, grew
10. disseminate _____    **e.** ruler

---
**TODAY'S IDIOM**

***straight from the shoulder*—in a direct, open way**

I took the wind out of his sails* by telling him *straight from the shoulder* that I was not going to wink at* his apple polishing.*

---

## NEW WORDS

**derived**
di rīvd´

**prerogative**
pri rog´ ə tiv

**nepotism**
nep´ ə tiz əm

**dearth**
dėrth

**internecine**
in´ tər nē´ sn

## A BATTLE FOR POWER

The Inca emperor *derived* his prodigious* power and authority from the gods. The paramount* god was the sun god. It was from him the ruler passed on his *prerogative* to rule to his most astute* son. This *nepotism* had worked with great efficacy* for centuries. The land holdings were immense;* there were rich farmlands and llamas and alpacas for wool. Precious metals were plentiful: silver, copper, bronze, and the most sacred of all, gold. This metal resembled the sun god whom they extolled.* There was no *dearth* of idols and ornaments hammered from this gleaming metal. There was always more gold coming from the mines to replenish* the supply. At the acme* of his power, the Inca ruler died without naming the requisite* successor. In 1528 two sons began an *internecine* struggle for control. For the next 4 years the empire sank into the lassitude* caused by civil war.

**Sample Sentences** Insert the new words in these sentences.

1. The emissary* from the president tried to allay* the fears that a deleterious* _____ feud was inevitable within the party.

2. A pragmatic* philosopher _____ the theory that we have noses in order to hold up our eyeglasses.

3. Your efforts to ingratiate* yourself into your boss's favor are nullified* by the unmitigated* _____ manifest* in this firm.

4. He gave his adversary* the dubious* _____ of choosing the weapon by which he was to meet his inevitable* end.

5. In the potpourri* of restaurants there is no _____ of succulent* dishes.

**Definitions** Match the new words with their definitions.

6. derived _____ **a.** scarcity, lack

7. prerogative _____ **b.** involving conflict within a group, mutually destructive

8. nepotism _____ **c.** an exclusive right or power

9. dearth _____ **d.** descended from, received from a source

10. internecine _____ **e.** favoritism toward relatives

---
## TODAY'S IDIOM
---

***to rub a person the wrong way*—to do something that irritates or annoys**

The quickest way *to rub a person the wrong way* is to give him the cold shoulder.*

ANSWERS ARE ON PAGE 310

# WEEK 46 ❖ DAY 3

**NEW WORDS**

**tyro**
tī rō

**sophistry**
sof´ ə strē

**factitious**
fak tish´ əs

**encomium**
en kō´ mē əm

**obloquy**
ob´ lə kwē

## A PERFIDIOUS* CONQUEROR

The feuding between the rival sons reached its pinnacle* in 1532; at that moment Francisco Pizarro came onto the scene. A native of Spain, he was sojourning* in Panama when he heard of the riches to be found in that far off land. Overwhelmed with cupidity,* but still a *tyro* when it came to wresting* power and wealth from hapless* people, he joined with an inveterate* adventurer. They gathered a small band of mercenaries.* The first two attempts failed, and Pizarro returned to Spain to request authority and money in order to conquer the West Coast of South America. Whether by *sophistry* or cajolery,* he was given the requisite* aid. With a force of 180 men, the dregs* of society, he invaded Inca territory. He reached the city where the current ruler, Atahualpa, was holding court. The Incas welcomed Pizarro who, in a *factitious* display of friendship, heaped *encomiums* upon Atahualpa. Unknown to the Incas, Pizarro had brought guns that were still beyond the technology* of these people. The *obloquy* of his next act, ambushing the Incas and taking Atahualpa prisoner, will live in the history books that are replete* with tales of conquest.

**Sample Sentences**  Insert the new words in these sentences.

1. Although he was erudite* about a copious* number of things, he was a naive,* callow* _____ when it came to relating to girls.
2. John Wilkes Booth's egregious* act remains an infamous* _____ .
3. Her _____ made use of every glib* artifice.*
4. In the office he played the _____ role of a martinet,* while at home he was filled with compassion*.
5. The modest prodigy* treated the fervid* _____ that followed his performance as though they were a mere bagatelle.*

**Definitions**  Match the new words with their definitions.

6. tyro         _____    a. high praise
7. sophistry    _____    b. beginner, novice
8. factitious   _____    c. false reasoning or argument
9. encomium     _____    d. sham, artificial
10. obloquy     _____    e. disgrace, shame, dishonor

---
### TODAY'S IDIOM
---

***to draw in one's horns*—to become cautious**

He knew he was out of his depth,* so he *drew in his horns* and quit the poker game.

## NEW WORDS

**hyperbole**
hī pė r´ bə lē

**munificent**
myü nif´ ə sənt

**prevarication**
pri var´ ə kā´ shen

**charisma**
kə riz´ mə

**genocide**
jen´ ə sīd

## THE END OF AN EMPIRE

The Machiavellian* Pizarro held the captured Atahualpa for ransom. He was adamant* about receiving a room filled with gold to the height of a man's shoulder. This was taken as a *hyperbole* at first, but Pizarro knew the gullible* Incas would be *munificent* when it came to rescuing their sacred ruler. They did not procrastinate,* and a frenetic* collection of gold took place. Pizarro, to whom *prevarication* was natural in dealing with the Incas, had no qualms* about executing their ruler as soon as he had the gold. The Inca empire was moribund,* but the *charisma* that surrounded Atahualpa was such that, after his death, the Incas fought on tenaciously* in his name for several years. Eventually, superior weapons quelled* all opposition. A policy of *genocide* was adopted by the Spanish conquerors, and almost two million of these proud people died in the carnage* that followed. The saga* of an ancient civilization thus came to an end.

**Sample Sentences**  Insert the new words in these sentences.

1. Even those who were not fans of the movie star candidly* admit the _____ that surrounded him.

2. The United Nations has outlawed _____ as the ultimate* crime, which must be eradicated.*

3. Her constant _____ made her a pariah* to her friends.

4. The rhetoric* soared into flagrant* _____ .

5. He was surprised by the _____ gratuity* given by the usually parsimonious* termagant.*

**Definitions**  Match the new words with their definitions.

6. hyperbole _____ a. quality of leadership inspiring enthusiasm

7. munificent _____ b. planned destruction of an entire people

8. prevarication _____ c. deviation from the truth, lying

9. charisma _____ d. generous

10. genocide _____ e. exaggerated figure of speech

---

## TODAY'S IDIOM

***to throw cold water*—to discourage a plan or idea**

I was going to pull up stakes* and move out lock, stock, and barrel,* but my wife *threw cold water* on the whole thing.

---

ANSWERS ARE ON PAGE 310

This is your *last* week. At this point you have worked with over 1100 of the most useful words and idioms in our language. The final review test will give you some idea of how well you have mastered them. From time to time you should re-read sections of this book to refresh your memory. Remember, keep learning new words at every opportunity!

## REVIEW WORDS

| | DEFINITIONS |
|---|---|
| _____ **1.** ascertain | **a.** lack, scarcity |
| _____ **2.** burgeoned | **b.** favoritism towards relatives |
| _____ **3.** charisma | **c.** novice, beginner |
| _____ **4.** dearth | **d.** artificial, sham |
| _____ **5.** derived | **e.** lying, deviation from the truth |
| _____ **6.** disseminate | **f.** ruler |
| _____ **7.** dormant | **g.** scatter, spread |
| _____ **8.** encomium | **h.** an exclusive power or right |
| _____ **9.** factitious | **i.** dishonor, disgrace, shame |
| _____ **10.** genocide | **j.** high praise |
| _____ **11.** hyperbole | **k.** quality of leadership inspiring enthusiasm |
| _____ **12.** internecine | **l.** asleep, resting |
| _____ **13.** munificent | **m.** grew, flourished |
| _____ **14.** nepotism | **n.** planned destruction of an entire people |
| _____ **15.** obloquy | **o.** false reasoning or argument |
| _____ **16.** potentate | **p.** mutually destructive, involving conflict in a group |
| _____ **17.** prerogative | **q.** received from a source, descended from |
| _____ **18.** prevarication | **r.** generous |
| _____ **19.** sophistry | **s.** exaggerated figure of speech |
| _____ **20.** tyro | **t.** find out about, discover |

## IDIOMS

| | |
|---|---|
| _____ **21.** to draw in one's horns | **u.** in a direct, open way |
| _____ **22.** straight from the shoulder | **v.** to discourage a plan or idea |
| _____ **23.** to throw cold water | **w.** to become cautious |
| _____ **24.** to rub a person the wrong way | **x.** to do something to irritate or annoy |

Check your answers on page 310.

**WORDS FOR FURTHER STUDY**          **MEANINGS**

1. _____     _____

2. _____     _____

3. _____     _____

# WHICH WORD COMES TO MIND?
## (From Weeks 45–46)

❖ Write the letter of the vocabulary word in the space adjacent to the sentence or phrase that brings it to mind.

    **a.** appalled
    **b.** brigand
    **c.** yen
    **d.** tyro
    **e.** corpulent
    **f.** prerogative
    **g.** genocide
    **h.** nepotism
    **i.** potentate
    **j.** dearth
    **k.** livid
    **l.** decapitate
    **m.** prevarication
    **n.** raconteur
    **o.** taut
    **p.** internecine

_____ **1.** "Hiring your nephew, eh?"

_____ **2.** "All hail the sultan!"

_____ **3.** "I just looked in the mirror; tomorrow we start our diet."

_____ **4.** The descent of the guillotine

_____ **5.** "I have a strong desire to own Japanese currency."

_____ **6.** George Washington to his father: "I cannot tell a lie."

_____ **7.** Now showing: *The Pirates of Penzance*

_____ **8.** Best storyteller in town

_____ **9.** The Civil War

_____ **10.** "He claims to have the right to change his mind."

ANSWERS ARE ON PAGE 310

❖ Using the clues listed below, fill in each blank in the following story with one of the new words you learned this week.

## *Words, Words, Words*

You have been strengthening and building a basic vocabulary as you have progressed through this book. The tests, quizzes, and exercises have helped you ① _____ how far you have advanced. We hope you have come to the end of *1100 Words You Need to Know* with a command of vocabulary that has ② _____ from week to week. Your interest and attention have paid off in many ways. You have ③ _____ pleasure and knowledge from reading passages on varied topics. You are better equipped to read, study, converse, and write with confidence.

The objectives that started you working on building your vocabulary should not now become ④ _____ . A permanent desire to master new words should be an added value obtained from this book. We hope that any ⑤ _____ you receive for your command of English vocabulary will spur you on to more and greater mastery of words you need to know.

## Clues

① 1st Day

② 1st Day

③ 2nd Day

④ 1st Day

⑤ 3rd Day

# BURIED WORDS                                    (From Week 1–46)

❖ Locate the word being defined from the review words of the week indicated. Then find the embedded word that fits the definition (e.g., the answer to the first example is *automaton,* which contains the "buried" word *tomato*).

| REVIEW WORD | BURIED WORD |
|---|---|
| **1st Week:** | |
| machine that behaves like a person | a common vegetable |
| unending | a fixed limit, definite period of time |
| **2nd Week:** | |
| to use lively gestures | a twitching of face muscles |
| basic, elementary | a small part of a dollar |
| **3rd Week:** | |
| expression of sympathy | a small portion, gratuity |
| lacking brightness | a strong passion |
| **4th Week:** | |
| able to be touched | a sharp taste |
| publish | a school dance |
| **5th Week:** | |
| exemption | a joke, play on words |
| shortage | a large community |
| **6th Week:** | |
| contrary | a part of a poem or song |
| dread, dismay | rear end of a boat |
| **7th Week:** | |
| to end | school semester |
| relentless, unappeasable | a heavy rope or chain |
| **8th Week:** | |
| forerunner | a drunken carousal, spree |
| distant | give expression to feelings |
| **9th Week:** | |
| harmful | a regulation |
| followers | anger |
| **10th Week:** | |
| read carefully | a trick |
| outstanding, prominent | foreign |
| **11th Week:** | |
| to pass by | part of a church |
| confirm | to enter and steal |

ANSWERS ARE ON PAGE 311

# BURIED WORDS

| REVIEW WORD | BURIED WORD |
|---|---|
| **12th Week:** | |
| bitter criticism | part of the body |
| perfection | mathematical term |
| **13th Week:** | |
| undeniable | open to view |
| in an early stage | unit of measurement |
| **14th Week:** | |
| soft job | a function in trigonometry |
| to strive for | a venomous serpent |
| **15th Week:** | |
| debatable | something found, a collection |
| an associate in crime | parasitic insects |
| **16th Week:** | |
| exact opposite | a tax |
| protection | military conflict |
| **17th Week:** | |
| perfect, complete | total |
| spread out in battle formation | a tactic to frustrate or embarrass an opponent |
| **18th Week:** | |
| polished, civilized | destructive or ruinous thing |
| going from place to place | prong of a fork |
| **19th Week:** | |
| lavish | a low place to collect water |
| agree to finance | formal or religious practice |
| **20th Week:** | |
| very sad | drag, move heavily |
| moderate in eating or drinking | stop, hold back |
| **21st Week:** | |
| descendant | an electrically charged part of an atom or molecule |
| decay | a vulgar person, a heel |
| **22nd Week:** | |
| relieve without curing | cease to please, a cloud |
| related to marriage | the core or point |
| **23rd Week:** | |
| serving to pay back | an outlaw, a political conservative |
| unusual occurrence | a prophetic sign |

ANSWERS ARE ON PAGE 311

# BURIED WORDS

| REVIEW WORD | BURIED WORD |
|---|---|
| **24th Week:** | |
| unwise | an overly modest person |
| looking down on someone or something | entice, attract, allure |
| | |
| **25th Week:** | |
| trembling, shaking with old age | strange |
| hurt, damage, injury | reduce by cutting, decorate |
| | |
| **26th Week:** | |
| prevailing, common, general | a valley (poetical) |
| angry, antagonistic | steps over a fence |
| | |
| **27th Week:** | |
| hesitate, waver, stumble | change, vary, transform |
| inflexible, unyielding | an obstruction |
| | |
| **28th Week:** | |
| hinder, interfere, block | mischievous child |
| discord, hard sound, dissonance | false, cheap imitation |
| | |
| **29th Week:** | |
| lack of interest | walkway |
| difficult to describe, undistinguished | style of writing |
| | |
| **30th Week:** | |
| slander, abuse | to arrange in line |
| persuade, coax, cajole | pay attention |
| | |
| **31st Week:** | |
| rough, harsh, shrill | three-pronged instrument |
| harmful, bad | take out, remove |
| | |
| **32nd Week:** | |
| out-of-date | a bowlike curve or structure |
| pardon, excuse | to put on as a garment |
| | |
| **33rd Week:** | |
| momentary, passing, fleeting | thin plate giving wind direction |
| self-satisfied | fine thread sewn in patterns |
| | |
| **34th Week:** | |
| facial expression of disgust | a spice, a club carried by an official |
| spacious, large | disgusting, distasteful |
| | |
| **35th Week:** | |
| a moralistic story | can be cultivated |
| haggard, thin | female relative |

ANSWERS ARE ON PAGE 311

# BURIED WORDS

| REVIEW WORD | BURIED WORD |
|---|---|
| **36th Week:** | |
| person or thing that embodies or represents the best | a large book or volume |
| wish, envy, want | a small bay |
| **37th Week:** | |
| temporary stay | a round vase |
| beginning, to develop or exist | the act of going up |
| **38th Week:** | |
| easy to manage | a shaded walk |
| underhandedness, trickery | stylish, elegant |
| **39th Week:** | |
| unreasonable, without conscience | child, or descendant |
| abuse, blame | to give out in measured amounts |
| **40th Week:** | |
| works that an artist is ready to perform | forward, free, saucy |
| weakness, weariness | a young woman |
| **41st Week:** | |
| slogan, pet phrase | trunk of a tree |
| rush, flood | the top of the head |
| **42nd Week:** | |
| requirement | locale, position |
| change, variety | plunge into |
| **43rd Week:** | |
| waste away | a memento of victory or success |
| desire to make amends, regret | closely confined |
| **44th Week:** | |
| ill-disposed, ill-intentioned | a brewed beverage |
| abundant, overflowing | to blend by melting |
| **45th Week:** | |
| a strong leaning in favor | to delight, fascinate, charm |
| inexperienced, youthful | to permit |
| **46th Week:** | |
| artificial, sham | perform, behave |
| mutually destructive, conflict within a group | to shut up, confine |

ANSWERS ARE ON PAGE 311

# WORDS IN CONTEXT

❖ Complete the passage by filling in the missing words. Select the correct word from the four given and insert the corresponding letter in the blank.

With the ____1.____ of the TV computerized games, many set owners have become ____2.____ in trying to outwit the electronic toys. The ____3.____ finds it almost impossible to react quickly enough. Before he or she can ____4.____ what is going on, the little lights have sped by. Those who have a ____5.____ for thinking and reacting quickly find these games a ____6.____ problem. While the experts' behavior appears ____7.____, they really are ____8.____ and ____9.____. If one is ____10.____ about trying again and again, then the ____11.____ of TV computer games can be mastered.

| | | | | |
|---|---|---|---|---|
| 1. | (a) rhetoric | (b) prelude | (c) advent | (d) retrospect |
| 2. | (a) reticent | (b) engrossed | (c) slovenly | (d) trivial |
| 3. | (a) wary | (b) tyro | (c) profuse | (d) deplorable |
| 4. | (a) ascertain | (b) obviate | (c) deem | (d) cajole |
| 5. | (a) lassitude | (b) pall | (c) legerdemain | (d) penchant |
| 6. | (a) perverse | (b) negligible | (c) lugubrious | (d) glib |
| 7. | (a) conjugal | (b) frenetic | (c) devout | (d) ambiguous |
| 8. | (a) connubial | (b) brash | (c) facile | (d) blunt |
| 9. | (a) aloof | (b) affluent | (c) overt | (d) imperturbable |
| 10. | (a) bogus | (b) elusive | (c) tenacious | (d) pecuniary |
| 11. | (a) effigy | (b) malady | (c) paroxysm | (d) repertoire |

It is ____12.____ that women have ____13.____ into fields of work that were, until recently, the ____14.____ of men. It did not happen because of the ____15.____ of the males, but it was largely due to the ____16.____ insistence by women that they occupy their rightful place in our society. While some men still ____17.____ women who seek to fill jobs previously closed to them, others take the ____18.____ view that the only ____19.____ for women should be their ability to do the work, and that ____20.____ obstacles have no place in a democracy.

| | | | | |
|---|---|---|---|---|
| 12. | (a) unctuous | (b) voluble | (c) manifest | (d) wistful |
| 13. | (a) perpetuated | (b) burgeoned | (c) advocated | (d) spewed |
| 14. | (a) acme | (b) taboo | (c) antipathy | (d) prerogative |
| 15. | (a) largess | (b) ultimate | (c) complicity | (d) avarice |
| 16. | (a) pernicious | (b) tenacious | (c) ostensible | (d) phlegmatic |
| 17. | (a) deprecate | (b) aspire | (c) permeate | (d) covet |
| 18. | (a) discreet | (b) pragmatic | (c) precocious | (d) rash |
| 19. | (a) remuneration | (b) reproach | (c) duplicity | (d) criterion |
| 20. | (a) puissant | (b) sporadic | (c) capricious | (d) zealous |

ANSWERS ARE ON PAGE 311

# ANSWERS

## ❖ WEEK 1

### Day 1

1. replete
2. eminent
3. steeped
4. voracious
5. indiscriminate

6. d
7. c
8. a
9. e
10. b

### Day 2

1. prognosticate
2. automatons
3. matron
4. abound
5. technology

6. d
7. b
8. e
9. c
10. a

### Day 3

1. compounded
2. annals
3. paradoxes
4. tinge
5. realm

6. b
7. e
8. d
9. c
10. a

### Day 4

1. drudgery
2. badgers *or* badgered
3. perceives *or* perceived
4. implored
5. interminable

6. e
7. c
8. a
9. b
10. d

### Day 5

#### REVIEW

1. n   7. i   13. p   19. k
2. o   8. h   14. b   20. m
3. r   9. e   15. c   21. v
4. d   10. t   16. q   22. u
5. g   11. j   17. a   23. w
6. l   12. s   18. f   24. x

#### SENSIBLE SENTENCES?

1. voracious
2. interminable
3. tinge
4. realm
5. eminent
6. abound
7. perceive
8. badgers
9. automatons
10. technology
11. yes
12. yes
13. yes
14. yes

#### WORDSEARCH 1

1. annals
2. replete
3. matron
4. implore
5. interminable

## ❖ WEEK 2

### Day 1

1. laconic
2. accost
3. reticent
4. throng
5. intrepid

6. a
7. d
8. b
9. c
10. e

### Day 2

1. hapless
2. irate
3. furtive
4. plethora
5. felon

6. e
7. b
8. d
9. c
10. a

### Day 3

1. vigilant
2. adroit
3. fabricate
4. pretext
5. gesticulate

6. c
7. a
8. b
9. e
10. d

### Day 4

1. rudimentary
2. cajoled
3. enhance
4. nuance
5. avid

6. a
7. c
8. e
9. d
10. b

### Day 5

#### REVIEW

1. f   7. k   13. o   19. n
2. l   8. r   14. q   20. c
3. b   9. p   15. d   21. x
4. s   10. h   16. g   22. u
5. t   11. e   17. a   23. v
6. m   12. i   18. k   24. w

#### WORDSEARCH 2

1. felon
2. pretext
3. cajole
4. fabricate
5. vigilant

# ANSWERS

## ❖ WEEK 3

### Day 1

| | | | |
|---|---|---|---|
| 1. wrest | | 6. b | |
| 2. lackluster | | 7. e | |
| 3. caustic | | 8. a | |
| 4. loathe | | 9. c | |
| 5. reprimand | | 10. d | |

### Day 2

| | | |
|---|---|---|
| 1. incipient | 6. a | |
| 2. infamous | 7. c | |
| 3. dupe | 8. d | |
| 4. jostle | 9. b | |
| 5. inadvertent | 10. e | |

### Day 3

| | | |
|---|---|---|
| 1. ominous | 6. d | |
| 2. repudiate | 7. e | |
| 3. bristle | 8. b | |
| 4. tremulous | 9. a | |
| 5. cessation | 10. c | |

### Day 4

| | | |
|---|---|---|
| 1. stipulate | 6. b | |
| 2. euphemism | 7. a | |
| 3. condolence | 8. d | |
| 4. mundane | 9. e | |
| 5. incongruous | 10. c | |

### Day 5

| REVIEW | | | | WORDSEARCH 3 |
|---|---|---|---|---|
| 1. g | 7. j | 13. a | 19. f | 1. cessation |
| 2. h | 8. e | 14. i | 20. p | 2. wrest |
| 3. d | 9. q | 15. b | 21. v | 3. infamous |
| 4. n | 10. c | 16. o | 22. w | 4. bristle |
| 5. m | 11. l | 17. r | 23. u | 5. caustic |
| 6. t | 12. s | 18. k | 24. x | |

## ❖ WEEK 4

### Day 1

| | | |
|---|---|---|
| 1. intimidate | 6. e | |
| 2. feint | 7. a | |
| 3. alacrity | 8. c | |
| 4. belligerent | 9. d | |
| 5. disdain | 10. b | |

### Day 2

| | | |
|---|---|---|
| 1. promulgate | 6. a | |
| 2. brash | 7. e | |
| 3. scoff | 8. d | |
| 4. pugnacious | 9. c | |
| 5. belittle | 10. b | |

### Day 3

| | | |
|---|---|---|
| 1. laceration | 6. a | |
| 2. tangible | 7. c | |
| 3. castigate | 8. b | |
| 4. octogenarian | 9. d | |
| 5. sordid | 10. e | |

### Day 4

| | | |
|---|---|---|
| 1. scurrilous | 6. c | |
| 2. aspirant | 7. e | |
| 3. frenzy | 8. a | |
| 4. dregs | 9. d | |
| 5. solace | 10. b | |

### Day 5

| REVIEW | | | | SENSIBLE SENTENCES? | | WORDSEARCH 4 |
|---|---|---|---|---|---|---|
| 1. t | 7. a | 13. d | 19. s | 1. alacrity | 6. belligerent | 1. aspirant |
| 2. i | 8. p | 14. f | 20. q | 2. aspirants | 7. belittled | 2. sordid |
| 3. j | 9. g | 15. h | 21. w | 3. dregs | 8. disdain | 3. belittle |
| 4. k | 10. c | 16. e | 22. v | 4. sordid | 9. promulgated | 4. scurrilous |
| 5. m | 11. b | 17. l | 23. x | 5. tangible | 10. scoff | 5. frenzy |
| 6. n | 12. r | 18. o | 24. u | | | |

## ❖ WEEK 5

### Day 1

| | | |
|---|---|---|
| 1. rampant | 6. e | |
| 2. clandestine | 7. c | |
| 3. ethics | 8. b | |
| 4. inane | 9. d | |
| 5. concur | 10. a | |

### Day 2

| | | |
|---|---|---|
| 1. culprit | 6. c | |
| 2. inexorable | 7. e | |
| 3. duress | 8. b | |
| 4. admonish | 9. d | |
| 5. flagrant | 10. a | |

### Day 3

| | | |
|---|---|---|
| 1. egregious | 6. d | |
| 2. acrimonious | 7. c | |
| 3. duplicity | 8. b | |
| 4. paucity | 9. e | |
| 5. distraught | 10. a | |

### Day 4

| | | |
|---|---|---|
| 1. impunity | 6. d | |
| 2. elicit | 7. e | |
| 3. tolerate | 8. c | |
| 4. construe | 9. b | |
| 5. pernicious | 10. a | |

### Day 5

| REVIEW | | | | WORDSEARCH 5 |
|---|---|---|---|---|
| 1. t | 7. f | 13. k | 19. d | 1. ethics |
| 2. e | 8. a | 14. m | 20. g | 2. pernicious |
| 3. p | 9. l | 15. c | 21. w | 3. acrimonious |
| 4. o | 10. j | 16. b | 22. v | 4. culprit |
| 5. q | 11. h | 17. s | 23. x | 5. flagrant |
| 6. r | 12. n | 18. i | 24. u | |

# ANSWERS

## ❖ WEEK 6

| Day 1 | | Day 2 | | Day 3 | | Day 4 | |
|---|---|---|---|---|---|---|---|
| 1. sally | 6. d | 1. precocious | 6. b | 1. laudable | 6. a | 1. dubious | 6. d |
| 2. affluent | 7. b | 2. perfunctory | 7. a | 2. disparaged | 7. d | 2. quell | 7. b |
| 3. consternation | 8. e | 3. deride | 8. c | 3. masticate | 8. e | 3. confidant | 8. a |
| 4. feasible | 9. a | 4. perverse | 9. d | 4. fiasco | 9. c | 4. obsolescence | 9. c |
| 5. discern | 10. c | 5. chagrin | 10. e | 5. eschews | 10. b | 5. voluble | 10. e |

### Day 5

| REVIEW | | | | WORDSEARCH 6 |
|---|---|---|---|---|
| 1. j | 7. n | 13. c | 19. s | 1. quell |
| 2. p | 8. q | 14. t | 20. f | 2. consternation |
| 3. o | 9. k | 15. a | 21. v | 3. fiasco |
| 4. b | 10. g | 16. i | 22. u | 4. discern |
| 5. h | 11. d | 17. e | 23. w | 5. laudable |
| 6. l | 12. r | 18. m | 24. x | |

## ❖ WEEK 7

| Day 1 | | Day 2 | | Day 3 | | Day 4 | |
|---|---|---|---|---|---|---|---|
| 1. implacable | 6. b | 1. fray | 6. e | 1. effigy | 6. b | 1. terminate | 6. c |
| 2. jurisdiction | 7. a | 2. indigent | 7. c | 2. stymie | 7. e | 2. forthwith | 7. d |
| 3. paroxysm | 8. d | 3. arbitrary | 8. b | 3. cognizant | 8. c | 3. oust | 8. e |
| 4. skirmish | 9. e | 4. monolithic | 9. a | 4. flout | 9. d | 4. revert | 9. b |
| 5. reprehensible | 10. c | 5. harass | 10. d | 5. turbulent | 10. a | 5. exacerbate | 10. a |

### Day 5

| REVIEW | | | | WORDSEARCH 7 |
|---|---|---|---|---|
| 1. t | 7. c | 13. q | 19. l | 1. skirmish |
| 2. s | 8. o | 14. k | 20. p | 2. turbulent |
| 3. m | 9. d | 15. f | 21. x | 3. cognizant |
| 4. j | 10. i | 16. n | 22. w | 4. indigent |
| 5. h | 11. g | 17. r | 23. v | 5. reprehensible |
| 6. e | 12. a | 18. b | 24. u | |

## ❖ WEEK 8

| Day 1 | | Day 2 | | Day 3 | | Day 4 | |
|---|---|---|---|---|---|---|---|
| 1. emaciated | 6. d | 1. sinister | 6. b | 1. ubiquitous | 6. b | 1. excruciating | 6. d |
| 2. tranquil | 7. a | 2. besieged | 7. e | 2. remote | 7. a | 2. reverberating | 7. a |
| 3. sanctuary | 8. c | 3. afflicted | 8. d | 3. harbinger | 8. d | 3. fretful | 8. c |
| 4. surged | 9. b | 4. malnutrition | 9. a | 4. thwart | 9. e | 4. respite | 9. b |
| 5. ascend | 10. e | 5. privation | 10. c | 5. malignant | 10. c | 5. succumb | 10. e |

### Day 5

| REVIEW | | | | SENSIBLE SENTENCES? | | PARTS OF SPEECH | | | WORDSEARCH 8 |
|---|---|---|---|---|---|---|---|---|---|
| 1. d | 7. k | 13. r | 19. t | 1. afflicted | 7. thwarted | 1. h | 7. d | 13. i | 1. succumb |
| 2. l | 8. q | 14. j | 20. c | 2. succumb | 8. ascended | 2. e | 8. f | 14. g, m | 2. sanctuary |
| 3. p | 9. b | 15. h | 21. x | 3. ubiquitous | 9. privations | 3. b | 9. o | | 3. harbinger |
| 4. f | 10. a | 16. n | 22. w | 4. malnutrition | 10. fretful | 4. j | 10. k | | 4. ascend |
| 5. e | 11. g | 17. i | 23. v | 5. tranquil | 11. cool our | 5. a | 11. l | | 5. afflict |
| 6. s | 12. o | 18. m | 24. u | 6. reverberating | heels | 6. c | 12. n | | |

297

# ANSWERS

## ❖ WEEK 9

### Day 1

1. extortion
2. impresario
3. bigot
4. asset
5. adverse

6. c
7. e
8. b
9. d
10. a

### Day 2

1. entourage
2. virulent
3. spew
4. venom
5. blatant

6. b
7. a
8. e
9. c
10. d

### Day 3

1. loath
2. solicit
3. astute
4. advocate
5. ineffectual

6. d
7. e
8. a
9. b
10. c

### Day 4

1. vexatious
2. amicable
3. malady
4. nefarious
5. scrutinize

6. c
7. b
8. e
9. a
10. d

### Day 5

| REVIEW | | | | WORDSEARCH 9 |
|---|---|---|---|---|
| 1. o | 7. i | 13. s | 19. g | 1. scrutinize |
| 2. a | 8. h | 14. d | 20. l | 2. vexatious |
| 3. p | 9. t | 15. j | 21. x | 3. virulent |
| 4. c | 10. f | 16. e | 22. w | 4. astute |
| 5. b | 11. m | 17. r | 23. v | 5. nefarious |
| 6. n | 12. q | 18. k | 24. u | |

## ❖ WEEK 10

### Day 1

1. peruse
2. premonition
3. desist
4. recoiled
5. inclement

6. a
7. b
8. d
9. c
10. e

### Day 2

1. obsessed
2. mastiff
3. doleful
4. pertinent
5. wan

6. b
7. e
8. d
9. a
10. c

### Day 3

1. frustrated
2. interjected
3. histrionics
4. elusive
5. symptomatic

6. d
7. b
8. e
9. a
10. c

### Day 4

1. imminent
2. squeamish
3. engrossed
4. salient
5. inert

6. b
7. a
8. c
9. e
10. d

### Day 5

| REVIEW | | | | WORDSEARCH 10 |
|---|---|---|---|---|
| 1. d | 7. p | 13. h | 19. g | 1. squeamish |
| 2. a | 8. f | 14. l | 20. r | 2. recoil |
| 3. q | 9. i | 15. o | 21. x | 3. engrossed |
| 4. s | 10. e | 16. b | 22. v | 4. desist |
| 5. c | 11. j | 17. k | 23. u | 5. interject |
| 6. t | 12. m | 18. n | 24. w | |

## ❖ WEEK 11

### Day 1

1. poignant
2. garbled
3. fruitless
4. inundated
5. sanguine

6. d
7. a
8. e
9. b
10. c

### Day 2

1. phlegmatic
2. zealous
3. comprehensive
4. coerced
5. corroborate

6. b
7. c
8. d
9. a
10. e

### Day 3

1. elapse
2. sporadic
3. domicile
4. lax
5. meticulous

6. b
7. e
8. d
9. a
10. c

### Day 4

1. conjecture
2. lurid
3. rash
4. obviated
5. quip

6. e
7. c
8. a
9. d
10. b

### Day 5

| REVIEW | | | | WORDSEARCH 11 |
|---|---|---|---|---|
| 1. r | 7. d | 13. j | 19. o | 1. garbled |
| 2. p | 8. k | 14. g | 20. s | 2. meticulous |
| 3. l | 9. a | 15. c | 21. x | 3. inundate |
| 4. f | 10. n | 16. t | 22. w | 4. comprehensive |
| 5. b | 11. h | 17. e | 23. u | 5. sanguine |
| 6. m | 12. q | 18. i | 24. v | |

# ANSWERS

## ❖ WEEK 12

### Day 1

| | |
|---|---|
| 1. diatribe | 6. d |
| 2. ilk | 7. e |
| 3. incoherent | 8. c |
| 4. fortuitous | 9. b |
| 5. inhibitions | 10. a |

### Day 2

| | |
|---|---|
| 1. placard | 6. e |
| 2. prestigious | 7. b |
| 3. remuneration | 8. a |
| 4. nominal | 9. d |
| 5. integral | 10. c |

### Day 3

| | |
|---|---|
| 1. utopia | 6. d |
| 2. schism | 7. e |
| 3. anathema | 8. b |
| 4. flamboyant | 9. a |
| 5. expunge | 10. c |

### Day 4

| | |
|---|---|
| 1. truncated | 6. a |
| 2. jaunty | 7. b |
| 3. ostentatious | 8. c |
| 4. timorous | 9. e |
| 5. fractious | 10. d |

### Day 5

| REVIEW | SENSIBLE SENTENCES? | WORDSEARCH 12 |
|---|---|---|
| 1. k  7. c  13. r  19. o | 1. diatribe      7. expunged | 1. prestigious |
| 2. l  8. e  14. d  20. t | 2. utopia        8. fortuitous | 2. flamboyant |
| 3. m  9. i  15. a  21. u | 3. ostentatious  9. integral | 3. ilk |
| 4. n  10. p  16. j  22. x | 4. timorous     10. placards | 4. inhibitions |
| 5. g  11. f  17. s  23. w | 5. prestigious  11. wash your dirty | 5. remuneration |
| 6. b  12. h  18. q  24. v | 6. jaunty            linen in public | |

## ❖ WEEK 13

### Day 1

| | |
|---|---|
| 1. importune | 6. b |
| 2. haven | 7. a |
| 3. subjugate | 8. e |
| 4. surreptitious | 9. d |
| 5. incontrovertible | 10. c |

### Day 2

| | |
|---|---|
| 1. eventuated | 6. b |
| 2. subterranean | 7. e |
| 3. emit | 8. d |
| 4. ultimate | 9. a |
| 5. viable | 10. c |

### Day 3

| | |
|---|---|
| 1. premise | 6. e |
| 2. incredulous | 7. b |
| 3. jeopardize | 8. d |
| 4. permeated | 9. c |
| 5. propitious | 10. a |

### Day 4

| | |
|---|---|
| 1. curtailed | 6. b |
| 2. cryptic | 7. d |
| 3. repress | 8. c |
| 4. surmised | 9. a |
| 5. inchoate | 10. e |

### Day 5

| REVIEW | WORDSEARCH 13 |
|---|---|
| 1. s  7. r  13. f  19. j | 1. cryptic |
| 2. g  8. b  14. e  20. h | 2. importune |
| 3. t  9. q  15. m  21. x | 3. ultimate |
| 4. k  10. o  16. i  22. w | 4. viable |
| 5. n  11. l  17. c  23. v | 5. incredulous |
| 6. a  12. p  18. d  24. u | |

## ❖ WEEK 14

### Day 1

| | |
|---|---|
| 1. nettle | 6. d |
| 2. aspire | 7. e |
| 3. inveigh | 8. a |
| 4. overt | 9. b |
| 5. relegate | 10. c |

### Day 2

| | |
|---|---|
| 1. supine | 6. d |
| 2. razed | 7. c |
| 3. repulse | 8. b |
| 4. mammoth | 9. a |
| 5. havoc | 10. e |

### Day 3

| | |
|---|---|
| 1. incisive | 6. d |
| 2. scurry | 7. b |
| 3. lethal | 8. a |
| 4. precipitated | 9. e |
| 5. stereotype | 10. c |

### Day 4

| | |
|---|---|
| 1. sinecure | 6. e |
| 2. stentorian | 7. d |
| 3. valor | 8. c |
| 4. singular | 9. a |
| 5. bias | 10. b |

### Day 5

| REVIEW | WORDSEARCH 14 |
|---|---|
| 1. d  7. a  13. n  19. o | 1. nettled |
| 2. h  8. r  14. j  20. c | 2. inveighed |
| 3. s  9. b  15. g  21. x | 3. stereotype |
| 4. i  10. k  16. l  22. v | 4. bias |
| 5. m  11. p  17. t  23. u | 5. scurry |
| 6. f  12. e  18. q  24. w | |

# ANSWERS

## ❖ WEEK 15

### Day 1

| | |
|---|---|
| 1. complicity | 6. b |
| 2. liquidation | 7. d |
| 3. culpable | 8. c |
| 4. recant | 9. e |
| 5. accomplice | 10. a |

### Day 2

| | |
|---|---|
| 1. preclude | 6. e |
| 2. alleged | 7. b |
| 3. abrogate | 8. a |
| 4. invalidate | 9. c |
| 5. access | 10. d |

### Day 3

| | |
|---|---|
| 1. extrinsic | 6. d |
| 2. persevere | 7. e |
| 3. landmark | 8. b |
| 4. declaim | 9. c |
| 5. fetter | 10. a |

### Day 4

| | |
|---|---|
| 1. nomadic | 6. b |
| 2. paragon | 7. c |
| 3. controversial | 8. a |
| 4. asperity | 9. e |
| 5. epithets | 10. d |

### Day 5

#### REVIEW

| | | | |
|---|---|---|---|
| 1. j | 7. t | 13. n | 19. k |
| 2. q | 8. d | 14. s | 20. o |
| 3. f | 9. l | 15. e | 21. v |
| 4. c | 10. a | 16. r | 22. w |
| 5. h | 11. b | 17. g | 23. x |
| 6. m | 12. p | 18. i | 24. u |

#### WORDSEARCH 15

1. abrogate
2. culpable
3. epithets
4. recant
5. controversial

## ❖ WEEK 16

### Day 1

| | |
|---|---|
| 1. cursory | 6. b |
| 2. indigenous | 7. d |
| 3. interloper | 8. c |
| 4. habitat | 9. a |
| 5. gregarious | 10. e |

### Day 2

| | |
|---|---|
| 1. prolific | 6. a |
| 2. antithesis | 7. c |
| 3. sedentary | 8. e |
| 4. frugal | 9. b |
| 5. bulwark | 10. d |

### Day 3

| | |
|---|---|
| 1. cache | 6. b |
| 2. cupidity | 7. d |
| 3. altruistic | 8. a |
| 4. coterie | 9. c |
| 5. embellish | 10. e |

### Day 4

| | |
|---|---|
| 1. amorous | 6. e |
| 2. virtuosity | 7. d |
| 3. progeny | 8. b |
| 4. temerity | 9. a |
| 5. saturated | 10. c |

### Day 5

#### REVIEW

| | | | |
|---|---|---|---|
| 1. f | 7. h | 13. l | 19. o |
| 2. r | 8. i | 14. k | 20. s |
| 3. d | 9. e | 15. j | 21. u |
| 4. q | 10. b | 16. t | 22. x |
| 5. a | 11. c | 17. p | 23. w |
| 6. g | 12. n | 18. m | 24. v |

#### WORDSEARCH 16

1. frugal
2. cache
3. interloper
4. temerity
5. cupidity

## ❖ WEEK 17

### Day 1

| | |
|---|---|
| 1. fallacious | 6. c |
| 2. consummate | 7. b |
| 3. concoct | 8. d |
| 4. perpetrate | 9. a |
| 5. subterfuge | 10. e |

### Day 2

| | |
|---|---|
| 1. manifold | 6. c |
| 2. fraught | 7. d |
| 3. impeccable | 8. b |
| 4. resourceful | 9. e |
| 5. assiduous | 10. a |

### Day 3

| | |
|---|---|
| 1. hoax | 6. a |
| 2. components | 7. b |
| 3. labyrinth | 8. c |
| 4. evaluate | 9. d |
| 5. murky | 10. e |

### Day 4

| | |
|---|---|
| 1. gullible | 6. e |
| 2. deploy | 7. a |
| 3. attest | 8. b |
| 4. exult | 9. c |
| 5. enigma | 10. d |

### Day 5

#### REVIEW

| | | | |
|---|---|---|---|
| 1. c | 7. f | 13. b | 19. h |
| 2. d | 8. p | 14. m | 20. b, r |
| 3. g | 9. l | 15. o | 21. u |
| 4. e | 10. k | 16. q | 22. w |
| 5. i | 11. j | 17. t | 23. v |
| 6. a | 12. n | 18. s | 24. x |

#### WORDSEARCH 17

1. assiduous
2. resourceful
3. fallacious
4. labyrinth
5. consummate

## ❖ WEEK 18

| Day 1 | | Day 2 | | Day 3 | | Day 4 | |
|---|---|---|---|---|---|---|---|
| 1. innate | 6. a | 1. crave | 6. d | 1. deem | 6. e | 1. tortuous | 6. b |
| 2. abortive | 7. e | 2. myriad | 7. b | 2. buff | 7. c | 2. conjugal | 7. a |
| 3. modify | 8. b | 3. irrelevant | 8. c | 3. romp | 8. d | 3. peregrination | 8. c |
| 4. spontaneous | 9. d | 4. urbane | 9. a | 4. latent | 9. b | 4. itinerant | 9. d |
| 5. accommodate | 10. c | 5. veneer | 10. e | 5. inherent | 10. a | 5. barometer | 10. e |

### Day 5

| REVIEW | | | | WORDSEARCH 18 |
|---|---|---|---|---|
| 1. c | 7. m | 13. s | 19. e | 1. barometer |
| 2. f | 8. l, d | 14. r | 20. b | 2. itinerant |
| 3. j | 9. d, l | 15. p | 21. v | 3. myriad |
| 4. o | 10. a | 16. h | 22. x | 4. deem |
| 5. q | 11. n | 17. g | 23. w | 5. accommodate |
| 6. i | 12. t | 18. k | 24. u | |

## ❖ WEEK 19

| Day 1 | | Day 2 | | Day 3 | | Day 4 | |
|---|---|---|---|---|---|---|---|
| 1. profligate | 6. e | 1. mendacious | 6. c | 1. dismantle | 6. d | 1. restrictive | 6. e |
| 2. strife | 7. c | 2. exonerate | 7. a | 2. sumptuous | 7. b | 2. blunt | 7. c |
| 3. legion | 8. a | 3. expatriate | 8. d | 3. parsimonious | 8. c | 3. nostalgia | 8. b |
| 4. coup | 9. d | 4. fiat | 9. e | 4. pecuniary | 9. e | 4. rife | 9. d |
| 5. megalomania | 10. b | 5. amnesty | 10. b | 5. underwrite | 10. a | 5. balk | 10. a |

### Day 5

| REVIEW | | | | WORDSEARCH 19 |
|---|---|---|---|---|
| 1. r | 7. h | 13. s | 19. d | 1. legion |
| 2. l | 8. n | 14. q | 20. f | 2. underwrite |
| 3. j | 9. p | 15. m | 21. x | 3. rife |
| 4. a | 10. g | 16. k | 22. u | 4. balk |
| 5. c | 11. i | 17. o | 23. v | 5. blunt |
| 6. e | 12. t | 18. b | 24. w | |

## ❖ WEEK 20

| Day 1 | | Day 2 | | Day 3 | | Day 4 | |
|---|---|---|---|---|---|---|---|
| 1. nebulous | 6. d | 1. repose | 6. b | 1. extant | 6. d | 1. lugubrious | 6. e |
| 2. reviled | 7. b | 2. abstemious | 7. e | 2. vicissitudes | 7. b | 2. puissant | 7. d |
| 3. indict | 8. e | 3. redolent | 8. d | 3. edifice | 8. e | 3. unabated | 8. a |
| 4. pesky | 9. c | 4. omnivorous | 9. a | 4. sultry | 9. c | 4. maudlin | 9. c |
| 5. derogatory | 10. a | 5. disparate | 10. c | 5. trenchant | 10. a | 5. levity | 10. b |

### Day 5

| REVIEW | | | | HAPLESS HEADLINES | | WORDSEARCH 20 |
|---|---|---|---|---|---|---|
| 1. o | 7. e | 13. l | 19. s | 1. j | 6. q | 1. pesky |
| 2. g | 8. d | 14. n | 20. r | 2. e | 7. i | 2. unabated |
| 3. a | 9. b | 15. j | 21. v | 3. d | 8. r | 3. indict |
| 4. c | 10. f | 16. t | 22. w | 4. t | 9. f | 4. redolent |
| 5. k | 11. h | 17. q | 23. u | 5. h | 10. k | 5. reviled |
| 6. i | 12. m | 18. p | 24. x | | | |

# ANSWERS

## ❖ WEEK 21

### Day 1
1. opulence
2. scion
3. obsequious
4. indoctrinate
5. fulsome
6. b
7. e
8. c
9. a
10. d

### Day 2
1. lush
2. ponder
3. destitution
4. supplication
5. decadence
6. e
7. b
8. c
9. d
10. a

### Day 3
1. disciple
2. metamorphosis
3. penance
4. ascetic
5. desultory
6. b
7. d
8. c
9. e
10. a

### Day 4
1. nurture
2. bona fide
3. salvation
4. nirvana
5. materialism
6. d
7. e
8. b
9. a
10. c

### Day 5

| REVIEW | | | | WORDSEARCH 21 |
|---|---|---|---|---|
| 1. a | 7. j | 13. k | 19. m | 1. metamorphosis |
| 2. t | 8. i | 14. r | 20. n | 2. disciple |
| 3. e | 9. d | 15. b | 21. v | 3. salvation |
| 4. h | 10. c | 16. q | 22. u | 4. bona fide |
| 5. f | 11. s | 17. o | 23. x | 5. ponder |
| 6. p | 12. l | 18. g | 24. w | |

## ❖ WEEK 22

### Day 1
1. juxtapose
2. incompatibility
3. cope
4. plight
5. covert
6. b
7. c
8. d
9. e
10. a

### Day 2
1. fabricate
2. connubial
3. demur
4. appellation
5. incapacitated
6. e
7. c
8. d
9. a
10. b

### Day 3
1. escalation
2. indifference
3. potential
4. cumulative
5. recondite
6. d
7. e
8. a
9. b
10. c

### Day 4
1. acknowledge
2. delude
3. palliate
4. prelude
5. chimerical
6. b
7. d
8. c
9. a
10. e

### Day 5

| REVIEW | | | | WORDSEARCH 22 |
|---|---|---|---|---|
| 1. b | 7. a | 13. s | 19. q | 1. indifference |
| 2. f | 8. e | 14. r | 20. k | 2. plight |
| 3. l | 9. p | 15. o | 21. w | 3. acknowledge |
| 4. m | 10. i | 16. c | 22. x | 4. cope |
| 5. j | 11. d | 17. g | 23. u | 5. prelude |
| 6. h | 12. t | 18. n | 24. v | |

## ❖ WEEK 23

### Day 1
1. maladjusted
2. heterogeneous
3. perspicacious
4. analogous
5. gamut
6. e
7. a
8. b
9. d
10. c

### Day 2
1. neurotic
2. decade
3. mortality
4. susceptible
5. phenomenon
6. d
7. a
8. c
9. e
10. b

### Day 3
1. enunciate
2. irascible
3. introspective
4. pedagogue
5. inordinate
6. e
7. c
8. b
9. a
10. d

### Day 4
1. perpetuate
2. catastrophic
3. neutralize
4. mandate
5. compensatory
6. d
7. b
8. a
9. c
10. e

### Day 5

| REVIEW | | | | WORDSEARCH 23 |
|---|---|---|---|---|
| 1. f | 7. i | 13. p | 19. o | 1. pedagogue |
| 2. a | 8. m | 14. l | 20. q | 2. decade |
| 3. r | 9. n | 15. k | 21. u | 3. heterogeneous |
| 4. s | 10. b | 16. c | 22. v | 4. gamut |
| 5. t | 11. d | 17. e | 23. w | 5. perspicacious |
| 6. j | 12. h | 18. g | 24. x | |

# ANSWERS

## ❖ WEEK 24

| Day 1 | | Day 2 | | Day 3 | | Day 4 | |
|---|---|---|---|---|---|---|---|
| 1. inanimate | 6. d | 1. tainted | 6. c | 1. contemptuous | 6. e | 1. originate | 6. b |
| 2. artifact | 7. a | 2. prohibition | 7. e | 2. absurd | 7. a | 2. entreaty | 7. d |
| 3. fetish | 8. e | 3. imprudent | 8. b | 3. bigot | 8. d | 3. inviolable | 8. c |
| 4. anthropologist | 9. c | 4. taboo | 9. d | 4. abhor | 9. c | 4. vulnerable | 9. a |
| 5. bizarre | 10. b | 5. imperative | 10. a | 5. universal | 10. b | 5. tradition | 10. e |

### Day 5

| REVIEW | | | | ADJ. LDRS./NOUN FOL. | | WORDSEARCH 24 |
|---|---|---|---|---|---|---|
| 1. n | 7. m | 13. d | 19. f | 1. m | 6. k | 1. imprudent |
| 2. r | 8. s | 14. g | 20. l | 2. c | 7. b | 2. inviolable |
| 3. h | 9. e | 15. p | 21. w | 3. a | 8. j | 3. artifact |
| 4. a | 10. q | 16. i | 22. u | 4. o | 9. i | 4. imperative |
| 5. c | 11. b | 17. t | 23. x | 5. e | 10. g | 5. inanimate |
| 6. k | 12. o | 18. j | 24. v | | | |

## ❖ WEEK 25

| Day 1 | | Day 2 | | Day 3 | | Day 4 | |
|---|---|---|---|---|---|---|---|
| 1. eruption | 6. c | 1. conflagration | 6. c | 1. hoard | 6. b | 1. senile | 6. a |
| 2. puny | 7. d | 2. obliterate | 7. b | 2. sage | 7. d | 2. longevity | 7. c |
| 3. debris | 8. a | 3. rue | 8. d | 3. congenial | 8. e | 3. doddering | 8. b |
| 4. awesome | 9. e | 4. initiate | 9. e | 4. aegis | 9. c | 4. imbibe | 9. d |
| 5. dispersed | 10. b | 5. deplorable | 10. a | 5. detriment | 10. a | 5. virile | 10. e |

### Day 5

| REVIEW | | | | WORDSEARCH 25 |
|---|---|---|---|---|
| 1. h | 7. l | 13. q | 19. d | 1. deplorable |
| 2. p | 8. j | 14. s | 20. o | 2. obliterate |
| 3. n | 9. a | 15. t | 21. v | 3. rue |
| 4. i | 10. c | 16. g | 22. w | 4. detriment |
| 5. f | 11. r | 17. b | 23. u | 5. aegis |
| 6. k | 12. m | 18. e | 24. x | |

## ❖ WEEK 26

| Day 1 | | Day 2 | | Day 3 | | Day 4 | |
|---|---|---|---|---|---|---|---|
| 1. hostile | 6. b | 1. aversion | 6. b | 1. tussle | 6. e | 1. acute | 6. e |
| 2. prevalent | 7. a | 2. superficial | 7. c | 2. intrinsic | 7. a | 2. transient | 7. c |
| 3. lethargic | 8. d | 3. rebuke | 8. e | 3. jettison | 8. d | 3. gist | 8. d |
| 4. paramount | 9. e | 4. evince | 9. d | 4. inevitable | 9. c | 4. terse | 9. b |
| 5. remiss | 10. c | 5. vogue | 10. a | 5. lucrative | 10. b | 5. cogent | 10. a |

### Day 5

| REVIEW | | | | WORDSEARCH 26 |
|---|---|---|---|---|
| 1. l | 7. o | 13. h | 19. f | 1. prevalent |
| 2. p | 8. i | 14. n | 20. j | 2. inevitable |
| 3. d | 9. c | 15. e | 21. w | 3. superficial |
| 4. a | 10. t | 16. m | 22. x | 4. cogent |
| 5. k | 11. q | 17. g | 23. v | 5. jettison |
| 6. s | 12. r | 18. b | 24. u | |

# ANSWERS

## ❖ WEEK 27

| Day 1 | | Day 2 | | Day 3 | | Day 4 | |
|---|---|---|---|---|---|---|---|
| 1. array | 6. b | 1. bereft | 6. d | 1. invective | 6. d | 1. inveterate | 6. b |
| 2. culminate | 7. c | 2. exultation | 7. e | 2. voluminous | 7. a | 2. pungent | 7. a |
| 3. pinnacle | 8. d | 3. constrict | 8. c | 3. besmirch | 8. c | 3. adamant | 8. d |
| 4. ardent | 9. a | 4. prodigy | 9. b | 4. retrospect | 9. b | 4. humility | 9. e |
| 5. obscure | 10. e | 5. falter | 10. a | 5. vitriolic | 10. e | 5. egotist | 10. c |

### Day 5

| REVIEW | | | | WORDSEARCH 27 |
|---|---|---|---|---|
| 1. b | 7. a | 13. s | 19. h | 1. retrospect |
| 2. r | 8. f | 14. t | 20. p | 2. ardent |
| 3. j | 9. c | 15. e | 21. w | 3. obscure |
| 4. o | 10. q | 16. l | 22. x | 4. culminate |
| 5. m | 11. k | 17. n | 23. v | 5. falter |
| 6. g | 12. i | 18. d | 24. u | |

## ❖ WEEK 28

| Day 1 | | Day 2 | | Day 3 | | Day 4 | |
|---|---|---|---|---|---|---|---|
| 1. propinquity | 6. b | 1. disgruntled | 6. b | 1. sedate | 6. b | 1. avarice | 6. c |
| 2. vulnerable | 7. e | 2. panacea | 7. a | 2. serenity | 7. c | 2. insatiable | 7. d |
| 3. cacophony | 8. a | 3. eradicate | 8. d | 3. equanimity | 8. e | 3. nadir | 8. e |
| 4. exploit | 9. c | 4. infallible | 9. c | 4. compatible | 9. a | 4. irrational | 9. a |
| 5. bedlam | 10. d | 5. impede | 10. e | 5. revere | 10. d | 5. moribund | 10. b |

### Day 5

| REVIEW | | | | DOING DOUBLE DUTY | | WORDSEARCH 28 |
|---|---|---|---|---|---|---|
| 1. r | 7. j | 13. e | 19. f | 1. hoard | 8. rebuke | 1. impede |
| 2. h | 8. p | 14. d | 20. a | 3. transient | 10. obscure | 2. serenity |
| 3. i | 9. s | 15. g | 21. v | 6. sedate | 11. exploit | 3. cacophony |
| 4. c | 10. b | 16. l | 22. w | 7. sage | | 4. irrational |
| 5. m | 11. o | 17. t | 23. x | | | 5. infallible |
| 6. q | 12. n | 18. k | 24. u | | | |

## ❖ WEEK 29

| Day 1 | | Day 2 | | Day 3 | | Day 4 | |
|---|---|---|---|---|---|---|---|
| 1. adherent | 6. d | 1. apathy | 6. d | 1. gusto | 6. c | 1. dilettante | 6. b |
| 2. lithe | 7. b | 2. exhort | 7. c | 2. banal | 7. a | 2. atypical | 7. c |
| 3. pathetic | 8. a | 3. inebriated | 8. e | 3. platitude | 8. d | 3. nondescript | 8. d |
| 4. obese | 9. e | 4. fracas | 9. b | 4. indolent | 9. e | 4. wane | 9. e |
| 5. bliss | 10. c | 5. adversary | 10. a | 5. garrulous | 10. b | 5. pique | 10. a |

### Day 5

| REVIEW | | | | WORDSEARCH 29 |
|---|---|---|---|---|
| 1. r | 7. o | 13. j | 19. n | 1. apathy |
| 2. b | 8. a | 14. c | 20. t | 2. pathetic |
| 3. i | 9. q | 15. h | 21. x | 3. indolent |
| 4. p | 10. s | 16. k | 22. u | 4. platitude |
| 5. f | 11. m | 17. d | 23. w | 5. adversary |
| 6. l | 12. e | 18. g | 24. v | |

# ANSWERS

## ❖ WEEK 30

### Day 1
| | |
|---|---|
| 1. gaudy | 6. e |
| 2. encumbrance | 7. c |
| 3. extinct | 8. d |
| 4. idyllic | 9. a |
| 5. galvanize | 10. b |

### Day 2
| | |
|---|---|
| 1. condescend | 6. c |
| 2. malign | 7. d |
| 3. jocose | 8. e |
| 4. candor | 9. a |
| 5. mortify | 10. b |

### Day 3
| | |
|---|---|
| 1. zenith | 6. e |
| 2. omnipotent | 7. a |
| 3. precedent | 8. b |
| 4. fledgling | 9. c |
| 5. peremptory | 10. d |

### Day 4
| | |
|---|---|
| 1. wheedle | 6. a |
| 2. charlatan | 7. e |
| 3. rustic | 8. b |
| 4. decorum | 9. c |
| 5. jubilant | 10. d |

### Day 5

#### REVIEW
| | | | | | | | |
|---|---|---|---|---|---|---|---|
| 1. f | 7. c | 13. r | 19. o |
| 2. s | 8. a | 14. b | 20. h |
| 3. n | 9. q | 15. l | 21. v |
| 4. k | 10. e | 16. p | 22. u |
| 5. i | 11. j | 17. t | 23. x |
| 6. m | 12. d | 18. g | 24. w |

#### WORDSEARCH 30
1. extinct
2. galvanize
3. peremptory
4. malign
5. candor

## ❖ WEEK 31

### Day 1
| | |
|---|---|
| 1. fervid | 6. c |
| 2. heresy | 7. d |
| 3. prudent | 8. e |
| 4. ostensible | 9. a |
| 5. spurious | 10. b |

### Day 2
| | |
|---|---|
| 1. propagate | 6. d |
| 2. milieu | 7. c |
| 3. anomaly | 8. e |
| 4. innocuous | 9. a |
| 5. surfeit | 10. b |

### Day 3
| | |
|---|---|
| 1. concomitant | 6. e |
| 2. strident | 7. c |
| 3. lassitude | 8. d |
| 4. deleterious | 9. b |
| 5. efficacy | 10. a |

### Day 4
| | |
|---|---|
| 1. incumbent | 6. c |
| 2. ferment | 7. d |
| 3. dissent | 8. b |
| 4. attenuated | 9. e |
| 5. arbiter | 10. a |

### Day 5

#### REVIEW
| | | | |
|---|---|---|---|
| 1. c | 7. j | 13. s | 19. f |
| 2. m | 8. a | 14. k | 20. o |
| 3. q | 9. p | 15. t | 21. x |
| 4. b | 10. h | 16. g | 22. w |
| 5. n | 11. i | 17. d | 23. u |
| 6. e | 12. r | 18. l | 24. v |

#### WORDSEARCH 31
1. deleterious
2. spurious
3. ostensible
4. dissent
5. concomitant

## ❖ WEEK 32

### Day 1
| | |
|---|---|
| 1. expedite | 6. d |
| 2. celerity | 7. c |
| 3. profound | 8. e |
| 4. alleviate | 9. a |
| 5. prodigious | 10. b |

### Day 2
| | |
|---|---|
| 1. bizarre | 6. c |
| 2. paltry | 7. d |
| 3. usurp | 8. b |
| 4. condone | 9. a |
| 5. trivial | 10. e |

### Day 3
| | |
|---|---|
| 1. venerable | 6. b |
| 2. ambiguous | 7. c |
| 3. succinct | 8. d |
| 4. menial | 9. a |
| 5. extraneous | 10. e |

### Day 4
| | |
|---|---|
| 1. salubrious | 6. b |
| 2. archaic | 7. c |
| 3. facetious | 8. d |
| 4. rabid | 9. e |
| 5. emulate | 10. a |

### Day 5

#### REVIEW
| | | | |
|---|---|---|---|
| 1. p | 7. r | 13. k | 19. d |
| 2. n | 8. o | 14. c | 20. q |
| 3. a | 9. j | 15. m | 21. x |
| 4. h | 10. i | 16. e | 22. w |
| 5. g | 11. f | 17. b | 23. v |
| 6. l | 12. t | 18. s | 24. u |

#### SELECTING ANTONYMS
| | | |
|---|---|---|
| 1. partner | 7. nadir | 13. helpful |
| 2. professional | 8. tiny | 14. wordy |
| 3. active | 9. condemn | 15. urbane |
| 4. sober | 10. clear | |
| 5. falsehood | 11. authentic | |
| 6. conservative | 12. harmful | |

#### WORDSEARCH 32
1. prodigious
2. usurp
3. celerity
4. venerable
5. salubrious

# ANSWERS

## ❖ WEEK 33

### Day 1

1. complacent
2. debilitate
3. occult
4. somber
5. impetuous
6. c
7. e
8. d
9. b
10. a

### Day 2

1. foment
2. slovenly
3. quarry
4. discreet
5. glean
6. a
7. e
8. b
9. c
10. d

### Day 3

1. penitent
2. evanescent
3. reproach
4. tantamount
5. abjure
6. c
7. b
8. d
9. e
10. a

### Day 4

1. connoisseur
2. allay
3. propensity
4. wary
5. deter
6. c
7. e
8. d
9. a
10. b

### Day 5

| REVIEW | | | | WORDSEARCH 33 |
|---|---|---|---|---|
| 1. d | 7. q | 13. c | 19. j | 1. abjure |
| 2. t | 8. p | 14. h | 20. l | 2. wary |
| 3. f | 9. a | 15. k | 21. v | 3. complacent |
| 4. s | 10. r | 16. o | 22. x | 4. somber |
| 5. e | 11. n | 17. b | 23. w | 5. glean |
| 6. g | 12. m | 18. i | 24. u | |

## ❖ WEEK 34

### Day 1

1. cumbersome
2. interrogate
3. vigil
4. divulge
5. site
6. e
7. c
8. a
9. b
10. d

### Day 2

1. unmitigated
2. commodious
3. antiquated
4. fluctuate
5. disheveled
6. b
7. d
8. a
9. e
10. c

### Day 3

1. tenacious
2. calumny
3. grimace
4. asinine
5. façade
6. d
7. c
8. b
9. e
10. a

### Day 4

1. au courant
2. pittance
3. unkempt
4. noisome
5. fastidious
6. c
7. e
8. d
9. b
10. a

### Day 5

| REVIEW | | | | WORDSEARCH 34 |
|---|---|---|---|---|
| 1. p | 7. h | 13. n | 19. o | 1. unmitigated |
| 2. q | 8. f | 14. l | 20. m | 2. asinine |
| 3. k | 9. i | 15. c | 21. x | 3. tenacious |
| 4. b | 10. r | 16. e | 22. v | 4. antiquated |
| 5. t | 11. g | 17. a | 23. u | 5. au courant |
| 6. s | 12. j | 18. d | 24. w | |

## ❖ WEEK 35

### Day 1

1. lampoon
2. whimsical
3. parable
4. sanctimonious
5. countenance
6. d
7. a
8. e
9. c
10. b

### Day 2

1. nonentity
2. effrontery
3. equanimity
4. flabbergasted
5. debacle
6. a
7. c
8. e
9. b
10. d

### Day 3

1. mien
2. refute
3. hirsute
4. vivacious
5. gaunt
6. b
7. a
8. d
9. c
10. e

### Day 4

1. stupor
2. cliché
3. wince
4. whet
5. pensive
6. a
7. b
8. e
9. d
10. c

### Day 5

| REVIEW | | | | WORDSEARCH 35 |
|---|---|---|---|---|
| 1. s | 7. q | 13. r | 19. c | 1. parable |
| 2. p | 8. e | 14. f | 20. g | 2. refute |
| 3. i | 9. d | 15. j | 21. w | 3. hirsute |
| 4. o | 10. m | 16. t | 22. v | 4. equanimity |
| 5. h | 11. b | 17. l | 23. x | 5. whet |
| 6. a | 12. k | 18. n | 24. u | |

# ANSWERS

## ❖ Week 36

### Day 1
1. degrade
2. venial
3. genre
4. unsavory
5. candid
6. c
7. e
8. b
9. a
10. d

### Day 2
1. grotesque
2. compassion
3. epitome
4. repugnant
5. dexterity
6. b
7. e
8. a
9. d
10. c

### Day 3
1. acme
2. depict
3. naive
4. copious
5. vehemently
6. c
7. d
8. b
9. e
10. a

### Day 4
1. ingratiate
2. covet
3. penury
4. perfidious
5. ignominious
6. a
7. b
8. e
9. d
10. c

### Day 5

| REVIEW | | | | SENSIBLE SENTENCES? | | WORDSEARCH 36 |
|---|---|---|---|---|---|---|
| 1. c | 7. m | 13. r | 19. q | 1. deter | 6. impetuous | 1. copious |
| 2. a | 8. p | 14. f | 20. s | 2. asinine | 7. discreet | 2. naive |
| 3. b | 9. n | 15. l | 21. v | 3. effrontery | 8. perfidious | 3. epitome |
| 4. k | 10. i | 16. e | 22. x | 4. disheveled | 9. flabbergasted | 4. ignominious |
| 5. d | 11. g | 17. j | 23. w | 5. somber | 10. vivacious | 5. depict |
| 6. h | 12. t | 18. o | 24. u | | | |

## ❖ Week 37

### Day 1
1. servile
2. sojourn
3. confront
4. volition
5. antipathy
6. d
7. c
8. e
9. b
10. a

### Day 2
1. tenable
2. austere
3. superfluous
4. felicitous
5. halcyon
6. b
7. d
8. c
9. a
10. e

### Day 3
1. iconoclast
2. therapy
3. motivate
4. rationalize
5. nascent
6. c
7. b
8. e
9. a
10. d

### Day 4
1. phobia
2. erudite
3. vertigo
4. conducive
5. germane
6. a
7. c
8. e
9. b
10. d

### Day 5

| REVIEW | | | | WORDSEARCH 37 |
|---|---|---|---|---|
| 1. f | 7. h | 13. s | 19. p | 1. nascent |
| 2. e | 8. i | 14. n | 20. a | 2. felicitous |
| 3. d | 9. g | 15. r | 21. x | 3. halcyon |
| 4. j | 10. c | 16. q | 22. w | 4. confront |
| 5. l | 11. o | 17. b | 23. u | 5. superfluous |
| 6. m | 12. t | 18. k | 24. v | |

## ❖ Week 38

### Day 1
1. glib
2. trend
3. legerdemain
4. malleable
5. homogeneous
6. c
7. d
8. a
9. b
10. e

### Day 2
1. fatal
2. passé
3. facets
4. procrastinate
5. stagnant
6. b
7. c
8. e
9. a
10. d

### Day 3
1. capitulate
2. stigmatize
3. audacity
4. foist
5. tantalize
6. d
7. b
8. a
9. c
10. e

### Day 4
1. chicanery
2. docile
3. tacit
4. reticent
5. retort
6. c
7. d
8. a
9. e
10. b

### Day 5

| REVIEW | | | | WORDSEARCH 38 |
|---|---|---|---|---|
| 1. f | 7. b | 13. j | 19. t | 1. homogeneous |
| 2. k | 8. d | 14. a | 20. p | 2. trend |
| 3. l | 9. h | 15. g | 21. v | 3. reticent |
| 4. r | 10. s | 16. o | 22. u | 4. tantalize |
| 5. e | 11. i | 17. n | 23. w | 5. facet |
| 6. c | 12. q | 18. m | 24. x | |

# ANSWERS

## ❖ Week 39

| Day 1 | | Day 2 | | Day 3 | | Day 4 | |
|---|---|---|---|---|---|---|---|
| 1. saga | 6. b | 1. opprobrium | 6. b | 1. vindicate | 6. e | 1. infraction | 6. b |
| 2. imperturbable | 7. d | 2. Machiavellian | 7. a | 2. flay | 7. d | 2. callous | 7. d |
| 3. belated | 8. c | 3. unconscionable | 8. d | 3. demeanor | 8. c | 3. vituperation | 8. a |
| 4. decrepit | 9. e | 4. pandemonium | 9. c | 4. heinous | 9. b | 4. redress | 9. c |
| 5. vacillates | 10. a | 5. staunch | 10. e | 5. delineation | 10. a | 5. turpitude | 10. e |

### Day 5

| REVIEW | | | | WORDSEARCH 39 |
|---|---|---|---|---|
| 1. m | 7. h | 13. r | 19. s | 1. infraction |
| 2. n | 8. f | 14. l | 20. e | 2. heinous |
| 3. p | 9. d | 15. b | 21. v | 3. opprobrium |
| 4. a | 10. k | 16. o | 22. u | 4. imperturbable |
| 5. j | 11. t | 17. q | 23. x | 5. staunch |
| 6. i | 12. g | 18. c | 24. w | |

## ❖ Week 40

| Day 1 | | Day 2 | | Day 3 | | Day 4 | |
|---|---|---|---|---|---|---|---|
| 1. clique | 6. b | 1. vilify | 6. a | 1. proximity | 6. c | 1. fatuous | 6. b |
| 2. rhetoric | 7. e | 2. cant | 7. c | 2. lassitude | 7. a | 2. repertoire | 7. c |
| 3. facile | 8. d | 3. magnanimous | 8. e | 3. vapid | 8. d | 3. imperceptible | 8. d |
| 4. extol | 9. a | 4. umbrage | 9. d | 4. unwieldy | 9. e | 4. contort | 9. e |
| 5. mentor | 10. c | 5. elucidate | 10. b | 5. vitiate | 10. b | 5. augment | 10. a |

### Day 5

| REVIEW | | | | HAPLESS HEADLINES | | WORDSEARCH 40 |
|---|---|---|---|---|---|---|
| 1. b | 7. s | 13. c | 19. h | 1. e | 6. g | 1. umbrage |
| 2. m | 8. r | 14. j | 20. d | 2. k | 7. d | 2. extol |
| 3. n | 9. o | 15. f | 21. x | 3. p | 8. s | 3. fatuous |
| 4. a | 10. q | 16. t | 22. u | 4. c | 9. n | 4. imperceptible |
| 5. g | 11. l | 17. i | 23. v | 5. q | 10. a | 5. vilify |
| 6. e | 12. k | 18. p | 24. w | | | |

## ❖ Week 41

| Day 1 | | Day 2 | | Day 3 | | Day 4 | |
|---|---|---|---|---|---|---|---|
| 1. succulent | 6. c | 1. sanction | 6. d | 1. spate | 6. a | 1. nutritive | 6. a |
| 2. intrinsic | 7. e | 2. insidious | 7. c | 2. advent | 7. c | 2. raucous | 7. c |
| 3. curry | 8. d | 3. allude | 8. e | 3. propriety | 8. d | 3. shibboleth | 8. e |
| 4. satiety | 9. a | 4. potpourri | 9. b | 4. proffer | 9. b | 4. bogus | 9. d |
| 5. pall | 10. b | 5. denotes | 10. a | 5. impious | 10. e | 5. substantiate | 10. b |

### Day 5

| REVIEW | | | | WORDSEARCH 41 |
|---|---|---|---|---|
| 1. c | 7. p | 13. f | 19. m | 1. insidious |
| 2. a | 8. r | 14. t | 20. g | 2. bogus |
| 3. l | 9. d | 15. q | 21. x | 3. propriety |
| 4. j | 10. o | 16. b | 22. u | 4. intrinsic |
| 5. i | 11. h | 17. e | 23. w | 5. sanction |
| 6. k | 12. s | 18. n | 24. v | |

# ANSWERS

## ❖ WEEK 42

### Day 1
1. negligible
2. quandary
3. expedient
4. callous
5. blasé
6. c
7. b
8. d
9. e
10. a

### Day 2
1. diversity
2. ennui
3. comely
4. artifice
5. frenetic
6. b
7. c
8. a
9. d
10. e

### Day 3
1. artless
2. expurgate
3. qualm
4. gratuity
5. begrudge
6. e
7. a
8. b
9. c
10. d

### Day 4
1. delve
2. replenish
3. manifest
4. capricious
5. requisite
6. b
7. e
8. c
9. a
10. d

### Day 5

#### REVIEW
1. d  7. c  13. q  19. m
2. t  8. h  14. s  20. r
3. i  9. n  15. l  21. x
4. f  10. k  16. j  22. v
5. p  11. e  17. b  23. u
6. g  12. a  18. o  24. w

#### WORDSEARCH 42
1. requisite
2. blasé
3. capricious
4. diversity
5. delve

## ❖ WEEK 43

### Day 1
1. ameliorate
2. roster
3. stunt
4. atrophy
5. maim
6. c
7. a
8. b
9. e
10. d

### Day 2
1. unctuous
2. cynic
3. benevolent
4. subservient
5. iniquity
6. b
7. c
8. d
9. a
10. e

### Day 3
1. largess
2. mercenary
3. criterion
4. mollify
5. repent
6. a
7. b
8. e
9. d
10. c

### Day 4
1. vestige
2. pariah
3. aloof
4. guise
5. pragmatic
6. b
7. c
8. e
9. d
10. a

### Day 5

#### REVIEW
1. p  7. b  13. i  19. s
2. t  8. n  14. a  20. j
3. k  9. r  15. f  21. x
4. l  10. o  16. c  22. w
5. e  11. q  17. h  23. v
6. d  12. m  18. g  24. u

#### WORDSEARCH 43
1. benevolent
2. pariah
3. guise
4. iniquity
5. ameliorate

## ❖ WEEK 44

### Day 1
1. futility
2. technology
3. nullify
4. carnage
5. deluged
6. c
7. b
8. e
9. a
10. d

### Day 2
1. canard
2. defamatory
3. plaintiff
4. libel
5. deprecate
6. c
7. d
8. b
9. e
10. a

### Day 3
1. excoriate
2. frail
3. potent
4. reputed
5. devout
6. a
7. c
8. e
9. d
10. b

### Day 4
1. impromptu
2. malevolent
3. profuse
4. diminutive
5. dulcet
6. b
7. e
8. d
9. c
10. a

### Day 5

#### REVIEW
1. k  7. l  13. t  19. r
2. g  8. e  14. n  20. q
3. j  9. i  15. m  21. w
4. a  10. o  16. p  22. u
5. b  11. h  17. c  23. v
6. d  12. s  18. f  24. x

#### SENSIBLE SENTENCES?
1. deluged
2. diminutive
3. blasé
4. succulent
5. frenetic
6. bogus
7. quandary
8. benevolent
9. negligible
10. excoriate

#### WORDSEARCH 44
1. profuse
2. deluge
3. carnage
4. excoriate
5. nullify

# ANSWERS

## ❖ WEEK 45

| Day 1 | | Day 2 | | Day 3 | | Day 4 | |
|---|---|---|---|---|---|---|---|
| 1. raiment | 6. c | 1. rift | 6. c | 1. livid | 6. b | 1. decapitate | 6. a |
| 2. rail | 7. a | 2. raconteur | 7. a | 2. taut | 7. c | 2. penchant | 7. e |
| 3. corpulent | 8. d | 3. sullen | 8. d | 3. martinet | 8. a | 3. termagant | 8. c |
| 4. wistful | 9. e | 4. emissary | 9. e | 4. yen | 9. e | 4. appalled | 9. b |
| 5. brigand | 10. b | 5. ruminate | 10. b | 5. bagatelle | 10. d | 5. callow | 10. d |

### Day 5

| REVIEW | | | | WORDSEARCH 45 |
|---|---|---|---|---|
| 1. b | 7. f | 13. h | 19. k | 1. appalled |
| 2. d | 8. c | 14. m | 20. t | 2. penchant |
| 3. e | 9. j | 15. q | 21. x | 3. corpulent |
| 4. o | 10. l | 16. g | 22. v | 4. emissary |
| 5. p | 11. n | 17. i | 23. u | 5. decapitate |
| 6. a | 12. s | 18. r | 24. w | |

## ❖ WEEK 46

| Day 1 | | Day 2 | | Day 3 | | Day 4 | |
|---|---|---|---|---|---|---|---|
| 1. burgeoned | 6. b | 1. internecine | 6. d | 1. tyro | 6. b | 1. charisma | 6. e |
| 2. ascertain | 7. c | 2. derived | 7. c | 2. obloquy | 7. c | 2. genocide | 7. d |
| 3. disseminate | 8. d | 3. nepotism | 8. e | 3. sophistry | 8. d | 3. prevarication | 8. c |
| 4. dormant | 9. e | 4. prerogative | 9. a | 4. factitious | 9. a | 4. hyperbole | 9. a |
| 5. potentate | 10. a | 5. dearth | 10. b | 5. encomiums | 10. e | 5. munificent | 10. b |

### Day 5

| REVIEW | | | | WHICH WORD? | | WORDSEARCH 46 |
|---|---|---|---|---|---|---|
| 1. t | 7. l | 13. r | 19. o | 1. h | 6. m | 1. ascertain |
| 2. m | 8. j | 14. b | 20. c | 2. i | 7. b | 2. burgeoned |
| 3. k | 9. d | 15. i | 21. w | 3. e | 8. n | 3. derived |
| 4. a | 10. n | 16. f | 22. u | 4. l | 9. p | 4. dormant |
| 5. q | 11. s | 17. h | 23. v | 5. c | 10. f | 5. encomium |
| 6. g | 12. p | 18. e | 24. x | | | |

# ANSWERS

## Buried Words

1st Week: au**tomato**n
in**term**inable

2nd Week: ges**tic**ulate
ru**dime**ntary

3rd Week: con**dole**nce
lack**lust**er

4th Week: **tang**ible
**prom**ulgate

5th Week: im**pun**ity
pau**city**

6th Week: per**verse**
con**stern**ation

7th Week: **term**inate
impla**cable**

8th Week: har**binge**r
re**mote**

9th Week: vi**rule**nt
entou**rage**

10th Week: per**use**
**salien**t

11th Week: e**lapse**
cor**rob**orate

12th Week: diat**ribe**
uto**pia**

13th Week: incont**rovert**ible
**inch**oate

14th Week: **sine**cure
**asp**ire

15th Week: con**trove**rsial
accomp**lice**

16th Week: an**tithe**sis
bul**wark**

17th Week: con**summ**ate
de**ploy**

18th Week: ur**bane**
it**ine**rant

19th Week: **sump**tuous
under**write**

20th Week: **lug**ubrious
ab**stem**ious

21st Week: sc**ion**
de**cad**ence

22nd Week: **pall**iate
con**nub**ial

23rd Week: compensa**tory**
phen**omen**on

24th Week: im**prud**ent
con**tempt**uous

25th Week: d**odd**ering
de**trim**ent

26th Week: pre**val**ent
ho**stile**

27th Week: f**alter**
a**dam**ant

28th Week: **imp**ede
caco**phony**

29th Week: a**path**y
nonde**script**

30th Week: ma**lign**
w**heed**le

31st Week: **strident**
**delete**rious

32nd Week: **arch**aic
con**done**

33rd Week: e**vane**scent
comp**lace**nt

34th Week: gri**mace**
comm**odious**

35th Week: p**arable**
g**aunt**

36th Week: epi**tome**
**cove**t

37th Week: sojo**urn**
n**ascent**

38th Week: **mall**eable
**chic**anery

39th Week: uncon**scion**able
vitupe**ration**

40th Week: re**pert**oire
**lass**itude

41st Week: shib**bole**th
s**pate**

42nd Week: requi**site**
**dive**rsity

43rd Week: a**trophy**
re**pent**

44th Week: m**ale**volent
pro**fuse**

45th Week: p**enchant**
c**allow**

46th Week: **fact**itious
**intern**ecine

## Words in Context

| | | | | | | | | | |
|---|---|---|---|---|---|---|---|---|---|
| 1. | c | 5. | d | 9. | d | 13. | b | 17. | a |
| 2. | b | 6. | b | 10. | c | 14. | d | 18. | b |
| 3. | b | 7. | b | 11. | d | 15. | a | 19. | d |
| 4. | a | 8. | c | 12. | c | 16. | b | 20. | c |

# ANSWER SHEET—FINAL REVIEW TEST

1. Ⓐ Ⓑ Ⓒ Ⓓ
2. Ⓐ Ⓑ Ⓒ Ⓓ
3. Ⓐ Ⓑ Ⓒ Ⓓ
4. Ⓐ Ⓑ Ⓒ Ⓓ
5. Ⓐ Ⓑ Ⓒ Ⓓ
6. Ⓐ Ⓑ Ⓒ Ⓓ
7. Ⓐ Ⓑ Ⓒ Ⓓ
8. Ⓐ Ⓑ Ⓒ Ⓓ
9. Ⓐ Ⓑ Ⓒ Ⓓ
10. Ⓐ Ⓑ Ⓒ Ⓓ
11. Ⓐ Ⓑ Ⓒ Ⓓ
12. Ⓐ Ⓑ Ⓒ Ⓓ
13. Ⓐ Ⓑ Ⓒ Ⓓ
14. Ⓐ Ⓑ Ⓒ Ⓓ
15. Ⓐ Ⓑ Ⓒ Ⓓ
16. Ⓐ Ⓑ Ⓒ Ⓓ
17. Ⓐ Ⓑ Ⓒ Ⓓ
18. Ⓐ Ⓑ Ⓒ Ⓓ
19. Ⓐ Ⓑ Ⓒ Ⓓ
20. Ⓐ Ⓑ Ⓒ Ⓓ
21. Ⓐ Ⓑ Ⓒ Ⓓ
22. Ⓐ Ⓑ Ⓒ Ⓓ
23. Ⓐ Ⓑ Ⓒ Ⓓ
24. Ⓐ Ⓑ Ⓒ Ⓓ
25. Ⓐ Ⓑ Ⓒ Ⓓ
26. Ⓐ Ⓑ Ⓒ Ⓓ
27. Ⓐ Ⓑ Ⓒ Ⓓ
28. Ⓐ Ⓑ Ⓒ Ⓓ
29. Ⓐ Ⓑ Ⓒ Ⓓ
30. Ⓐ Ⓑ Ⓒ Ⓓ
31. Ⓐ Ⓑ Ⓒ Ⓓ
32. Ⓐ Ⓑ Ⓒ Ⓓ
33. Ⓐ Ⓑ Ⓒ Ⓓ
34. Ⓐ Ⓑ Ⓒ Ⓓ
35. Ⓐ Ⓑ Ⓒ Ⓓ
36. Ⓐ Ⓑ Ⓒ Ⓓ
37. Ⓐ Ⓑ Ⓒ Ⓓ
38. Ⓐ Ⓑ Ⓒ Ⓓ

39. Ⓐ Ⓑ Ⓒ Ⓓ
40. Ⓐ Ⓑ Ⓒ Ⓓ
41. Ⓐ Ⓑ Ⓒ Ⓓ
42. Ⓐ Ⓑ Ⓒ Ⓓ
43. Ⓐ Ⓑ Ⓒ Ⓓ
44. Ⓐ Ⓑ Ⓒ Ⓓ
45. Ⓐ Ⓑ Ⓒ Ⓓ
46. Ⓐ Ⓑ Ⓒ Ⓓ
47. Ⓐ Ⓑ Ⓒ Ⓓ
48. Ⓐ Ⓑ Ⓒ Ⓓ
49. Ⓐ Ⓑ Ⓒ Ⓓ
50. Ⓐ Ⓑ Ⓒ Ⓓ
51. Ⓐ Ⓑ Ⓒ Ⓓ
52. Ⓐ Ⓑ Ⓒ Ⓓ
53. Ⓐ Ⓑ Ⓒ Ⓓ
54. Ⓐ Ⓑ Ⓒ Ⓓ
55. Ⓐ Ⓑ Ⓒ Ⓓ
56. Ⓐ Ⓑ Ⓒ Ⓓ
57. Ⓐ Ⓑ Ⓒ Ⓓ
58. Ⓐ Ⓑ Ⓒ Ⓓ
59. Ⓐ Ⓑ Ⓒ Ⓓ
60. Ⓐ Ⓑ Ⓒ Ⓓ
61. Ⓐ Ⓑ Ⓒ Ⓓ
62. Ⓐ Ⓑ Ⓒ Ⓓ
63. Ⓐ Ⓑ Ⓒ Ⓓ
64. Ⓐ Ⓑ Ⓒ Ⓓ
65. Ⓐ Ⓑ Ⓒ Ⓓ
66. Ⓐ Ⓑ Ⓒ Ⓓ
67. Ⓐ Ⓑ Ⓒ Ⓓ
68. Ⓐ Ⓑ Ⓒ Ⓓ
69. Ⓐ Ⓑ Ⓒ Ⓓ
70. Ⓐ Ⓑ Ⓒ Ⓓ
71. Ⓐ Ⓑ Ⓒ Ⓓ
72. Ⓐ Ⓑ Ⓒ Ⓓ
73. Ⓐ Ⓑ Ⓒ Ⓓ
74. Ⓐ Ⓑ Ⓒ Ⓓ
75. Ⓐ Ⓑ Ⓒ Ⓓ
76. Ⓐ Ⓑ Ⓒ Ⓓ

77. Ⓐ Ⓑ Ⓒ Ⓓ
78. Ⓐ Ⓑ Ⓒ Ⓓ
79. Ⓐ Ⓑ Ⓒ Ⓓ
80. Ⓐ Ⓑ Ⓒ Ⓓ
81. Ⓐ Ⓑ Ⓒ Ⓓ
82. Ⓐ Ⓑ Ⓒ Ⓓ
83. Ⓐ Ⓑ Ⓒ Ⓓ
84. Ⓐ Ⓑ Ⓒ Ⓓ
85. Ⓐ Ⓑ Ⓒ Ⓓ
86. Ⓐ Ⓑ Ⓒ Ⓓ
87. Ⓐ Ⓑ Ⓒ Ⓓ
88. Ⓐ Ⓑ Ⓒ Ⓓ
89. Ⓐ Ⓑ Ⓒ Ⓓ
90. Ⓐ Ⓑ Ⓒ Ⓓ
91. Ⓐ Ⓑ Ⓒ Ⓓ
92. Ⓐ Ⓑ Ⓒ Ⓓ
93. Ⓐ Ⓑ Ⓒ Ⓓ
94. Ⓐ Ⓑ Ⓒ Ⓓ
95. Ⓐ Ⓑ Ⓒ Ⓓ
96. Ⓐ Ⓑ Ⓒ Ⓓ
97. Ⓐ Ⓑ Ⓒ Ⓓ
98. Ⓐ Ⓑ Ⓒ Ⓓ
99. Ⓐ Ⓑ Ⓒ Ⓓ
100. Ⓐ Ⓑ Ⓒ Ⓓ
101. Ⓐ Ⓑ Ⓒ Ⓓ
102. Ⓐ Ⓑ Ⓒ Ⓓ
103. Ⓐ Ⓑ Ⓒ Ⓓ
104. Ⓐ Ⓑ Ⓒ Ⓓ
105. Ⓐ Ⓑ Ⓒ Ⓓ
106. Ⓐ Ⓑ Ⓒ Ⓓ
107. Ⓐ Ⓑ Ⓒ Ⓓ
108. Ⓐ Ⓑ Ⓒ Ⓓ
109. Ⓐ Ⓑ Ⓒ Ⓓ
110. Ⓐ Ⓑ Ⓒ Ⓓ
111. Ⓐ Ⓑ Ⓒ Ⓓ
112. Ⓐ Ⓑ Ⓒ Ⓓ
113. Ⓐ Ⓑ Ⓒ Ⓓ
114. Ⓐ Ⓑ Ⓒ Ⓓ

115. Ⓐ Ⓑ Ⓒ Ⓓ
116. Ⓐ Ⓑ Ⓒ Ⓓ
117. Ⓐ Ⓑ Ⓒ Ⓓ
118. Ⓐ Ⓑ Ⓒ Ⓓ
119. Ⓐ Ⓑ Ⓒ Ⓓ
120. Ⓐ Ⓑ Ⓒ Ⓓ
121. Ⓐ Ⓑ Ⓒ Ⓓ
122. Ⓐ Ⓑ Ⓒ Ⓓ
123. Ⓐ Ⓑ Ⓒ Ⓓ
124. Ⓐ Ⓑ Ⓒ Ⓓ
125. Ⓐ Ⓑ Ⓒ Ⓓ
126. Ⓐ Ⓑ Ⓒ Ⓓ
127. Ⓐ Ⓑ Ⓒ Ⓓ
128. Ⓐ Ⓑ Ⓒ Ⓓ
129. Ⓐ Ⓑ Ⓒ Ⓓ
130. Ⓐ Ⓑ Ⓒ Ⓓ
131. Ⓐ Ⓑ Ⓒ Ⓓ
132. Ⓐ Ⓑ Ⓒ Ⓓ
133. Ⓐ Ⓑ Ⓒ Ⓓ
134. Ⓐ Ⓑ Ⓒ Ⓓ
135. Ⓐ Ⓑ Ⓒ Ⓓ
136. Ⓐ Ⓑ Ⓒ Ⓓ
137. Ⓐ Ⓑ Ⓒ Ⓓ
138. Ⓐ Ⓑ Ⓒ Ⓓ
139. Ⓐ Ⓑ Ⓒ Ⓓ
140. Ⓐ Ⓑ Ⓒ Ⓓ
141. Ⓐ Ⓑ Ⓒ Ⓓ
142. Ⓐ Ⓑ Ⓒ Ⓓ
143. Ⓐ Ⓑ Ⓒ Ⓓ
145. Ⓐ Ⓑ Ⓒ Ⓓ
146. Ⓐ Ⓑ Ⓒ Ⓓ
147. Ⓐ Ⓑ Ⓒ Ⓓ
148. Ⓐ Ⓑ Ⓒ Ⓓ
149. Ⓐ Ⓑ Ⓒ Ⓓ
150. Ⓐ Ⓑ Ⓒ Ⓓ

# FINAL REVIEW TEST

❖ Below are 150 of the words that you have been studying, each followed by four possible definitions. Select the best answer from among the choices given and fill in the corresponding circle on the answer sheet.

To attain a mark of 60%, you would have to get 90 correct answers; 105 correct answers are worth a mark of 70%, 120 for 80%, 135 for 90%. After you have completed the test, check your answers on page 322.

1. implore
   (a) reject
   (b) beg for assistance
   (c) summon
   (d) scold

2. voracious
   (a) greedy
   (b) vicious
   (c) dull
   (d) careless

3. badger
   (a) to pester
   (b) to cheat
   (c) remind
   (d) to insult

4. laconic
   (a) tense
   (b) bashful
   (c) troublesome
   (d) brief in expression

5. plethora
   (a) overabundance
   (b) helpless fit
   (c) a weakness
   (d) angry reaction

6. cajole
   (a) force
   (b) demand
   (c) coax
   (d) promise

7. inadvertent
   (a) unappetizing
   (b) unintentional
   (c) unaware
   (d) unknown

8. mundane
   (a) forgetful
   (b) friendly
   (c) doubtful
   (d) worldly

9. jostle
   (a) joke with
   (b) interrupt
   (c) to push
   (d) leap quickly

10. brash
    (a) impudent
    (b) stubborn
    (c) angry
    (d) upset

11. sordid
    (a) varied
    (b) guilty
    (c) unable to speak
    (d) dirty

12. solace
    (a) pity
    (b) comfort
    (c) forgetfulness
    (d) great happiness

13. acrimonious
    (a) bitter
    (b) brilliant
    (c) tender
    (d) out of tune

14. egregious
    (a) important
    (b) infected
    (c) remarkably bad
    (d) swollen

15. paucity
    (a) overweight
    (b) deafness
    (c) shortage
    (d) doubt

16. eschew
    (a) keep away from
    (b) sneeze repeatedly
    (c) invite
    (d) deny

17. voluble
    (a) priceless
    (b) talkative
    (c) sinful
    (d) whining

18. perfunctory
    (a) careless
    (b) hopeful
    (c) without end
    (d) evil

19. chagrin
    (a) loneliness
    (b) dismay
    (c) opportunity
    (d) suspicion

20. exacerbate
    (a) present arguments
    (b) plead with
    (c) question closely
    (d) irritate

# FINAL REVIEW TEST

21. indigent
    (a) unreasonable
    (b) watchful
    (c) angry
    (d) poor

22. stymie
    (a) hinder
    (b) invent
    (c) confiscate
    (d) cancel

23. fretful
    (a) lacking ambition
    (b) dark
    (c) worrisome
    (d) mischievous

24. harbinger
    (a) smooth-talker
    (b) leader
    (c) forerunner
    (d) bit of advice

25. sanctuary
    (a) cemetery
    (b) agreement
    (c) place of protection
    (d) approval

26. astute
    (a) keen
    (b) reliable
    (c) cheap
    (d) able

27. blatant
    (a) boastful
    (b) disagreeably loud
    (c) blossoming
    (d) rigid

28. nefarious
    (a) hungry
    (b) watchful
    (c) footsore
    (d) villainous

29. virulent
    (a) harmful
    (b) sloppy
    (c) sickly
    (d) revolutionary

30. histrionics
    (a) unreasonable acts
    (b) nervousness
    (c) display of emotions
    (d) studies of the past

31. salient
    (a) traveling
    (b) resentful
    (c) sober
    (d) outstanding

32. wan
    (a) pale
    (b) sleepy
    (c) jealous
    (d) unlucky

33. corroborate
    (a) represent
    (b) confirm
    (c) search
    (d) produce

34. lurid
    (a) outraged
    (b) sensational
    (c) capable
    (d) guilty

35. sanguine
    (a) hopeful
    (b) objectionable
    (c) rugged
    (d) hard to discover

36. sporadic
    (a) occasional
    (b) special
    (c) to the point
    (d) blotchy

37. anathema
    (a) treatment
    (b) violence
    (c) apparatus
    (d) a curse

38. fortuitous
    (a) lucky
    (b) significant
    (c) accidental
    (d) huge

39. archaic
    (a) rival
    (b) out of date
    (c) healthful
    (d) comical

40. timorous
    (a) courageous
    (b) ambitious
    (c) fearful
    (d) tense

41. eventuate
    (a) to result finally
    (b) pay your respects
    (c) borrow
    (d) interrupt

42. inchoate
    (a) vague
    (b) in an early stage
    (c) uneasy
    (d) ingenious

43. propitious
    (a) suspicious
    (b) hasty
    (c) frank
    (d) favorable

44. viable
    (a) workable
    (b) sensitive
    (c) tasty
    (d) quiet

# FINAL REVIEW TEST

45. incisive
   (a) acute
   (b) sluggish
   (c) massive
   (d) jittery

46. inveigh
   (a) compose
   (b) react to
   (c) attack verbally
   (d) penetrate

47. sinecure
   (a) urgent message
   (b) silly response
   (c) big responsibility
   (d) soft job

48. nettle
   (a) mix
   (b) suggest
   (c) irritate
   (d) suspend

49. abrogate
   (a) publish
   (b) portray
   (c) permit
   (d) cancel

50. extrinsic
   (a) loaded
   (b) containing wisdom
   (c) coming from outside
   (d) uncertain

51. asperity
   (a) artful handling
   (b) bitterness of temper
   (c) foolishness
   (d) concern

52. altruistic
   (a) unselfish
   (b) troublesome
   (c) dangerous
   (d) dignified

53. sedentary
   (a) hypnotic
   (b) largely inactive
   (c) scornful
   (d) musical

54. progeny
   (a) vigor
   (b) descendants
   (c) minority opinion
   (d) disease

55. cupidity
   (a) affection
   (b) fate
   (c) greed
   (d) harmony

56. impeccable
   (a) faultless
   (b) bold
   (c) open to criticism
   (d) slow to respond

57. perpetrate
   (a) plant
   (b) consume in haste
   (c) slice
   (d) commit

58. assiduous
   (a) sly
   (b) thrifty
   (c) busy
   (d) educated

59. abortive
   (a) failing
   (b) outside the law
   (c) drowsy
   (d) unprepared

60. tortuous
   (a) spiteful
   (b) inflicting pain
   (c) frank
   (d) winding

61. peregrination
   (a) form of address
   (b) travel
   (c) insistence
   (d) hospitality

62. myriad
   (a) geometric figure
   (b) voter's choice
   (c) countless number
   (d) minority decision

63. fiat
   (a) police squad
   (b) official order
   (c) carriage
   (d) council

64. mendacious
   (a) lying
   (b) abusive
   (c) healing
   (d) merciful

65. profligate
   (a) soothing
   (b) obvious
   (c) distinct
   (d) wasteful

66. disparate
   (a) different
   (b) critical
   (c) religious
   (d) uneven

67. lugubrious
   (a) well-oiled
   (b) warlike
   (c) very sad
   (d) beyond dispute

68. puissant
   (a) ordinary
   (b) studious
   (c) powerful
   (d) dictatorial

# FINAL REVIEW TEST

69. desultory
    (a) disconnected
    (b) incomplete
    (c) polished
    (d) dry

70. fulsome
    (a) gratified
    (b) superior
    (c) sensitive
    (d) excessive

71. chimerical
    (a) accurate
    (b) imaginary
    (c) regional
    (d) rigid

72. recondite
    (a) observant
    (b) sincere
    (c) secret
    (d) willing to bargain

73. gamut
    (a) range
    (b) sleeve
    (c) intestine
    (d) bridge

74. irascible
    (a) conceited
    (b) patriotic
    (c) bumbling
    (d) irritable

75. perspicacious
    (a) vicious
    (b) shrewd
    (c) sweaty
    (d) light on one's feet

76. taint
    (a) weaken
    (b) widen
    (c) contaminate
    (d) cause

77. aegis
    (a) fear
    (b) hope
    (c) kinship
    (d) protection

78. evince
    (a) prove
    (b) throw away
    (c) exhibit
    (d) wonder

79. termagant
    (a) shrew
    (b) insect
    (c) ruler
    (d) coward

80. mien
    (a) appearance
    (b) hostile
    (c) cheerful
    (d) important

81. elucidate
    (a) hide
    (b) make clear
    (c) paint
    (d) sharpen

82. germane
    (a) sickly
    (b) foreign
    (c) charming
    (d) appropriate

83. mollify
    (a) turn against
    (b) appease
    (c) hope for
    (d) shorten

84. indolent
    (a) lazy
    (b) badly behaved
    (c) owing money
    (d) timely

85. impromptu
    (a) dangerous
    (b) not understood
    (c) wisely planned
    (d) spur of the moment

86. umbrage
    (a) dark color
    (b) offense
    (c) waste
    (d) generosity

87. artifice
    (a) trickery
    (b) historic finding
    (c) newness
    (d) gradual change

88. vacillate
    (a) follow closely
    (b) fluctuate
    (c) aggravate
    (d) dominate

89. vestige
    (a) trace
    (b) cloak
    (c) entrance
    (d) hope

90. adamant
    (a) ambitious
    (b) timely
    (c) wasteful
    (d) inflexible

91. nepotism
    (a) without religion
    (b) favoritism
    (c) patriotism
    (d) deception

92. reticent
    (a) reserved
    (b) in pain
    (c) cooperative
    (d) without example

93. tyro
(a) ruler
(b) beginner
(c) fire-setter
(d) warmer

94. staunch
(a) evil smelling
(b) tight fitting
(c) whiten
(d) strong

95. equanimity
(a) sharing
(b) self-control
(c) hostility
(d) lively

96. taut
(a) tense
(b) make fun of
(c) pale
(d) gradual

97. mortify
(a) calm down
(b) embarrass
(c) strengthen
(d) pretend

98. vapid
(a) wet
(b) quick
(c) remarkable
(d) foolish

99. covet
(a) disguise
(b) wish for
(c) bury
(d) change

100. condone
(a) repeat
(b) punish
(c) forbid
(d) pardon

101. fatuous
(a) heavy
(b) interesting
(c) silly
(d) important

102. imbibe
(a) drink
(b) enter
(c) clear away
(d) change

103. ennui
(a) fashionable
(b) boredom
(c) together
(d) hopeless

104. salubrious
(a) sad
(b) dangerous
(c) painful
(d) healthful

105. carnage
(a) slaughter
(b) carrying away
(c) marriage
(d) anger

106. aloof
(a) painful
(b) reserved
(c) interested
(d) dishonest

107. vertigo
(a) dizziness
(b) color blindness
(c) ambition
(d) extreme height

108. foment
(a) become alcoholic
(b) investigate
(c) stir up
(d) calm down

109. inveterate
(a) anxious
(b) unknown
(c) questionable
(d) habitual

110. refute
(a) fame
(b) waste
(c) disobey
(d) disprove

111. celerity
(a) stardom
(b) speed
(c) clearness
(d) sourness

112. heinous
(a) interference
(b) talkative
(c) evilly wicked
(d) powerful

113. quandary
(a) dilemma
(b) quiet place
(c) hopeful sign
(d) crowd

114. efficacy
(a) cheapness
(b) ease
(c) mystery
(d) effectiveness

115. austere
(a) wild
(b) feverish
(c) unadorned
(d) wishful

116. moribund
(a) marvelous
(b) ambitious
(c) gradual
(d) dying

# FINAL REVIEW TEST

117. noisome
(a) unwholesome
(b) challenging
(c) loud
(d) newly arrived

118. spate
(a) rush
(b) excess
(c) insult
(d) shortage

119. nadir
(a) climax
(b) secret place
(c) lowest point
(d) happiest moment

120. halcyon
(a) peaceful
(b) ancient
(c) innermost
(d) careful

121. pragmatic
(a) repeating
(b) fat
(c) practical
(d) imaginative

122. atrophy
(a) prize
(b) begin again
(c) change direction
(d) waste away

123. discreet
(a) patient
(b) colorful
(c) cautious
(d) generous

124. callow
(a) cowardly
(b) unfeeling
(c) inexperienced
(d) private

125. ruminate
(a) reflect upon
(b) move away
(c) reclassify
(d) start anew

126. congenial
(a) clever
(b) agreeable
(c) masterful
(d) selective

127. decorum
(a) behavior
(b) attractiveness
(c) liveliness
(d) meeting place

128. banal
(a) not allowed
(b) nearly finished
(c) trivial
(d) highly respected

129. encomium
(a) highest prize
(b) secret plan
(c) new idea
(d) high praise

130. avarice
(a) clear path
(b) wealth
(c) greed
(d) positive statement

131. malign
(a) slander
(b) exterminate
(c) join with
(d) dismiss

132. venial
(a) hopeless
(b) unseen
(c) pardonable
(d) deadly

133. dulcet
(a) hard to hear
(b) sweet to the ear
(c) soft to the touch
(d) easy to see

134. entreaty
(a) plea
(b) agreement
(c) capture
(d) sudden end

135. pensive
(a) limited
(b) thoughtful
(c) aged
(d) retired

136. bizarre
(a) busy
(b) in a hurry
(c) timely
(d) fantastic

137. requisite
(a) forgotten thought
(b) requirement
(c) added problem
(d) lovely object

138. livid
(a) disappointed
(b) enraged
(c) bored
(d) pale

139. pique
(a) resentment
(b) condition
(c) hidden from light
(d) wishful thinking

**140.** galvanize
  (a) prepare to eat
  (b) arouse to activity
  (c) store away
  (d) experiment

**141.** extol
  (a) explain
  (b) apologize for
  (c) praise highly
  (d) describe honestly

**142.** allude
  (a) avoid
  (b) cover up
  (c) yearn for
  (d) suggest

**143.** slovenly
  (a) slowly
  (b) wisely
  (c) dangerously
  (d) carelessly

**144.** prerogative
  (a) ask again
  (b) exclusive right
  (c) divided power
  (d) first born

**145.** raiment
  (a) clothing
  (b) arrest
  (c) left over
  (d) bright color

**146.** abhor
  (a) yearn for
  (b) hate
  (c) distrust
  (d) join together

**147.** jocose
  (a) dizzy
  (b) merry
  (c) sticky
  (d) talkative

**148.** mentor
  (a) coach
  (b) enemy
  (c) stranger
  (d) writer

**149.** hirsute
  (a) overly dressed
  (b) out-of-date
  (c) hairy
  (d) bald

**150.** excoriate
  (a) complete
  (b) win easily
  (c) criticize severely
  (d) clean thoroughly

# Answers to Final Review Test

| | | | | | | | | | |
|---|---|---|---|---|---|---|---|---|---|
| 1. | b | 31. | d | 61. | b | 91. | b | 121. | c |
| 2. | a | 32. | a | 62. | c | 92. | a | 122. | d |
| 3. | a | 33. | b | 63. | b | 93. | b | 123. | c |
| 4. | d | 34. | b | 64. | a | 94. | d | 124. | c |
| 5. | a | 35. | a | 65. | d | 95. | b | 125. | a |
| 6. | c | 36. | a | 66. | a | 96. | a | 126. | b |
| 7. | b | 37. | d | 67. | c | 97. | b | 127. | a |
| 8. | d | 38. | c | 68. | c | 98. | d | 128. | c |
| 9. | c | 39. | b | 69. | a | 99. | b | 129. | d |
| 10. | a | 40. | c | 70. | d | 100. | d | 130. | c |
| 11. | d | 41. | a | 71. | b | 101. | c | 131. | a |
| 12. | b | 42. | b | 72. | c | 102. | a | 132. | c |
| 13. | a | 43. | d | 73. | a | 103. | b | 133. | b |
| 14. | c | 44. | a | 74. | d | 104. | d | 134. | a |
| 15. | c | 45. | a | 75. | b | 105. | a | 135. | b |
| 16. | a | 46. | c | 76. | c | 106. | b | 136. | d |
| 17. | b | 47. | d | 77. | d | 107. | a | 137. | b |
| 18. | a | 48. | c | 78. | c | 108. | c | 138. | d |
| 19. | b | 49. | d | 79. | a | 109. | d | 139. | a |
| 20. | d | 50. | c | 80. | a | 110. | d | 140. | b |
| 21. | d | 51. | b | 81. | b | 111. | b | 141. | c |
| 22. | a | 52. | a | 82. | d | 112. | c | 142. | d |
| 23. | c | 53. | b | 83. | b | 113. | a | 143. | d |
| 24. | c | 54. | b | 84. | a | 114. | d | 144. | b |
| 25. | c | 55. | c | 85. | d | 115. | c | 145. | a |
| 26. | a | 56. | a | 86. | b | 116. | d | 146. | b |
| 27. | b | 57. | d | 87. | a | 117. | a | 147. | b |
| 28. | d | 58. | c | 88. | b | 118. | a | 148. | a |
| 29. | a | 59. | a | 89. | a | 119. | c | 149. | c |
| 30. | c | 60. | d | 90. | d | 120. | a | 150. | c |

# PANORAMA OF WORDS

❖ Originally introduced in the preceding edition, this section, in which you will find the 1100 words in sources as strikingly disparate as the *Toronto Globe & Mail*, Truman Capote, William Shakespeare, Agatha Christie, Thomas Mann, *TIME*, Machiavelli, and Tom Clancy, validates the contention that this selected group of vocabulary words has been widely used by educated writers.

Most issues of your local newspaper, for example, will contain at least a dozen of the words you have encountered in these pages. But they also appear in advertisements, obituary notices, weather forecasts, cartoons, and brochures of all sorts. Wherever else you come in contact with adult vocabulary—radio and TV shows, news broadcasts, college entrance exams, movie scripts, books—you are likely to find more than a few of the words in *1100 Words You Need to Know*.

Now, for a useful summary of what you have learned in the forty-six lessons, read through "The Panorama of Words," noting the varied sources of their usage. Be aware that some of the following quotations have been adapted or edited for brevity.

# PANORAMA OF WORDS

**abhor** "I *abhor* the process of hiring public servants." Senator Wayne Morse, speech, 4/17/61

**abjure** "Galileo was summoned before the inquisition where he was ordered to *abjure* his theory." S. F. Mason, *Science Digest*, 5/98

**abortive** "His company made an *abortive* attempt to circle the enemy position but they fell back under fire." Captain Ron Herbert, *Keep Your Medals*

**abounds** "A smart thriller that *abounds* with suspense and excitement!" Newspaper ad for film *The General's Daughter*

**abrogate** "I decided to *abrogate* the agreement since General Motors was not living up to its part of the bargain." Paul Sawyer, *Seeking Justice*

**abstemious** "Be more *abstemious* Or else, good night your vow." William Shakespeare, *The Tempest*

**absurd** "Many rules in the English language are *absurd* because they are based on Latin rules." Bill Bryson, *Mother Tongue*

**access** "Everything was simplified, and we were gaining *access* to infinity: soon the moon, SOON THE MOON!" Editorial, *Le Figaro* (Paris), 8/14/61

**accommodate** "The awards will be given out at a place that will *accommodate* C-Span." James Barron, "Public Lives," *New York Times*, 6/10/99

**accomplice** "His chief *accomplice* was Democratic boss John Dingell, who sold out his party in the dark of night." Maureen Dowd, "The God Squad," *New York Times*, 6/20/99

**accost** Sir Toby: "You mistake, knight: *accost* is front her, board her, woo her, assail her." William Shakespeare, *Twelfth Night*

**acknowledged** "They used the Swiss routes and camp sites—which they later *acknowledged*—and by the end of April were established in full strength at their fifth camp." James Ramsey Ullman, "Victory on Everest"

**acme** "He was the *acme* of a political figure." John Gunther, *Inside U.S.A.*

**acrimonious** "We quickly learn of the *acrimonious* relationship between the Montagues and the Capulets." *Playbill*, Summary of *Romeo & Juliet*

**acute** "The candidate presented an *acute* problem for his party because of his independent views." Jewell Bellush and Dick Netzer, *Urban Politics*

**adamant** "The candidate was *adamant* in his refusal to answer an embarrassing question about his early use of drugs." *TIME*, 8/12/99

**adherents** "The state employs a flag as a symbol for *adherents* to the government as presently organized." U.S. Supreme Court decision, 1943

**admonished** "A little drummer boy grinned in me face whin I had *admonished* him wid the buckle av my belt for riotin' all over the place." Rudyard Kipling, "The Courting of Dinah Shadd"

**adroit** "Amazingly *adroit* in building model airplanes while he was in junior high, Eric moved on to an aeronautic career in his twenties." Val Bakker, "Early Decision" [adapted]

**advent** "Industrial canning and the *advent* of freezing have reduced home canning to a curiosity." Molly O'Neill, *New York Times*, 7/18/99

**adversaries** "Both fighters had nothing but kind words to say about their *adversaries.*" Hal Butler, "The Battle in the Rain"

**adverse** "Illogical as it may seem, *adverse* criticism can be very rewarding." S. Andhil Fineberg, "Deflating the Professional Bigot"

**advocates** "*Advocates* of marriage classes contend that giving teens these tools could eventually curb the divorce rate." Jodie Morse, "Hitched in Home Room," *TIME*, 6/21/99

**aegis** "The Federal Reserve will remain under the *aegis* of the veteran head who was reappointed by the President yesterday." *New York Times*, 1/5/00

**afflicted** "It *afflicted* the neighborhood with the stench of slime that was now laid bare." Edmund Wilson, "The Man Who Shot Snapping Turtles"

**affluent** "You are *affluent* when you buy what you want, do what you wish and don't give a thought to what it costs." J. P. Morgan, quoted in *Crown Treasury of Relevant Quotations*

**alacrity** "When the price of A.T.&T. dropped significantly, fund managers moved with *alacrity* to accumulate more shares." Ted David, CNBC *Financial News*

**allay** "The President's message was an attempt to *allay* the fears of senior citizens." "The Future of Medicare," *Washington Post*, 3/16/98

**alleged** "I harvested the intelligence that Ricks was *alleged* to have laid off all that portion of the State of Florida that has been under water into town lots and sold them to innocent investors." O'Henry, "The Man Higher Up"

**alleviate** "The report of the transportation division pointed out that the overcrowded highways required immediate attention in order to *alleviate* the long delays." *The Queens Courier*, 1/11/00

**alludes** "Gertrude Stein's phrase, 'A rose, is a rose, is a rose' *alludes* to nothing more or less than what she writes." Alice B. Toklas, *Time Capsule*, 1933

**aloof** "Greta Garbo held herself so *aloof* from her co-stars, they felt they had not been introduced." Alistair Cooke, *The Great Movie Stars*

**altruism** "The conflict is between selfishness and *altruism.*" Former Senator Estes Kefauver, campaign speech

**ambiguous** "If you disagree with a friend, be firm, not *ambiguous.*" Samuel Ornage, *The Golden Book*

**ameliorate** "Our aim should be to *ameliorate* human affairs." John Stuart Mill

**amicable** "Their parting is effective Friday, and was described in their joint statement as '*amicable*'." Bill Carter, "Lou Dobbs Quits CNN," *New York Times*, 6/9/99

**amnesty** "No one is advocating wholesale *amnesty* for inmates solely because of advancing age." Tamerlin Drummond, "Cellblock Seniors," *TIME*, 6/21/99

**amorous** "A complete gentleman ought to dress well, dance well, have a genius for love letters, be very *amorous* but not overconstant." Sir George Etherege, *The Man of Mode*

**analogous** "Not with the brightness natural to cheerful youth, but with uncertain, eager, doubtful flashes, *analogous* to the changes on a blind face groping its way." Charles Dickens, *Hard Times*

**anathema** "The founding document of the American Reform movement depicted ritual

# PANORAMA OF WORDS

as anachronistic, even *anathema* in an enlightened age." Samuel G. Freedman, "The Un-Reformation," *New York*, 6/21/99

**annals** "He would begin these *annals* with Columbus, and he would keep on with them until his hand was too palsied to hold a pen." Catherine Drinker Bowen, *Yankee from Olympus*

**anomaly** "My mother was American, my ancestors were officers in Washington's army, and I am an *anomaly*." Winston Churchill, speech, 1953

**anthropologist** "Burning tobacco, *anthropologists* have found, was a religious practice over 2000 years ago in the Mayan culture." *Journal of Urban Health*, 9/99

**antipathy** "There is no need to anticipate any *antipathy* from your future in-laws when you plan a wedding." "Wedding Guide," *Courier-Life Publications*, 7/99

**antiquated** "The custom of throwing rice at a newly married couple is an *antiquated* one, originally meaning a wish for many children." "Wedding Guide," *Courier-Life Publications*, 7/99

**antithesis** "Drunkenness is the *antithesis* of dignity." Bergen Evans, "Now Everyone is Hip About Slang"

**apathy** "The younger generation exhibits *apathy* toward the issue of freedom of the press." Herbert Brucker, *Journalist*

**appalled** "A calm and steady temperament deserted him while he stared, *appalled*, at the contents." John Cheever, *The Wapshot Chronicle*

**appellation** "He went under the *appellation* of 'Pretty Boy' but to his victims he was anything but that." Dexter Holcomb, *Did the Roaring Twenties Really Roar?* [adapted]

**arbiter** "Sonja Henie became the supreme *arbiter* of skating fashions." Maribel Y. Vinson, "Ice Maiden"

**arbitrary** "My *arbitrary* decision not to run puts Massachusetts at a disadvantage and probably was a mistake." Representative Martin Meehan in *Newsday*, 6/1/99

**archaic** "Many procedures of the law have long seemed *archaic* to laymen." Supreme Court Justice William O. Douglas, quoted in *San Francisco Examiner*, 1/4/71

**ardent** "There is no more *ardent* performer than Judy Garland as she allows her emotions to shine through." Penelope Houston, *Sight and Sound*, 1954

**arrayed** "She *arrayed* herself in what seemed unbelievably beautiful clothes." Sherwood Anderson, *Winesburg, Ohio*

**artifact** "In caves in Chile, remains of horses have been found along with human *artifacts*." A. Hyatt Verrill, *The Strange Story of Our Earth*

**artifice** "The successful advertiser will use any *artifice* to get his message seen." E. S. Turner, *The Shocking History of Advertising*

**artless** "Behind the naive, *artless* manner, there was a woman scheming for success." John Simon, *Reverse Angle*

**ascended** "As he set himself to fan the fire again, his crouching shadow *ascended* the opposite wall." James Joyce, "Ivy Day in the Committee Room"

**ascertain** "Scientists have been trying to *ascertain* why dinosaurs became extinct so suddenly." A. Hyatt Verrill, *The Strange Story of Our Earth*

**ascetic** "You don't have to be an *ascetic* to wonder if there isn't something a bit manic about the pace of getting and spending in today's America." Paul Krugman, "Money Can't Buy Happiness. Er, Can It?," *New York Times*, 6/1/99

**asinine** "We have developed what I believe is an *asinine* rating system for motion pictures." Harold Owen, Jr., *The Motion Picture*

**asperity** "The path of beauty is not soft and smooth, but full of harshness and *asperity*." Havelock Ellis, *The Dance of Life*

**aspirants** "A number of playwrights, small *aspirants* to the big screen, must already be pricing beach houses in Malibu." Ross Wetzsteon, Introduction to *New Plays USA*

**aspire** "To humility indeed it does not even *aspire*." John Henry Newman, *The Idea of a University*

**assets** "Berkshire Hathaway is a diversified holding company with *assets* in manufacturing, insurance, aircraft safety training, etc." "Warren's Buffet's Fabulous Fund," *Mutual Funds Magazine*, 6/99

**assiduously** "Richard Greenberg is aiming here for big laughs at the expense of the generation he so *assiduously* chronicled in the past." Peter Marks, "Making Mincemeat of Boomer Values"

**astute** From an *astute* standpoint, that's exactly what the ballplayers should do instead of running out to mob the other guy." Tim McCarver, *Baseball for Brain Surgeons*

**atrophy** "Some people thought that too much reading would *atrophy* a girl's brain forever." Ann McGovern, *The Secret Soldier*

**attenuated** "The players' strike resulted in an *attenuated* and boring season." *Sports Illustrated*, 10/96

**attest** "Thousands of satisfied users can *attest* to the great features such as Voicemail and Caller ID that work the same way wherever you go on our network." Newspaper ad for Internet company, *New York Times*, 6/12/99

**atypical** "He is an *atypical* candidate, without glamour, fame or wealth." *New York Post*, 8/15/99

**au courant** "He seemed to be *au courant* with everything." Arnold Bennett, *Lord Raingo*

**audacity** "Boldness be my friend! Arm me, *audacity*, from head to foot!" William Shakespeare, *Cymbeline*

**augmented** "The Russian army was *augmented* by helicopters and rocket-launching tanks in its attack on the defenders." *Newsday*, 11/27/99

**austere** "New York City was founded by *austere* puritan colonists who could never imagine the city as it is today." Moses Riechin, *The Promised City*

**automaton** "She's an *automaton*; she has every quality in the world, and I've often wondered why it is with all that I'm so completely indifferent to her." W. Somerset Maugham, *The Treasure*

**avarice** "He could not disguise his *avarice* under a cloak of religion." Ambrose Bierce

**aversion** "During the last years of his administration the mayor showed an *aversion* to taking political risks." Jewell Bellush and Dick Netzer, *Urban Politics*

**avid** "CUNY will have no more *avid* and fierce supporter for its mission than himself." Karen Arenson, "New Vice-Chairman of CUNY," *New York Times*, 6/10/99

# PANORAMA OF WORDS

**awesome** "Africa has some of the most *awesome* jungles in the world." John Hersey, *Into the Valley*

**badger** "There are other do's and don'ts: don't threaten your children, don't *badger* them." Newspaper ad for *Partnership for a Drug-Free America*, *New York Times*, 11/4/99

**bagatelle** "He saw the benefits to his people as a mere *bagatelle*." Winston Churchill, *Great Contemporaries*

**balk** "She rested on the stair—a young woman of a beauty that should *balk* even the justice of a poet's imagination." O. Henry, "Roads of Destiny"

**banal** "*Mansfield Park* is a bore! What might have been attractive on a TV screen proved to be uninteresting and *banal* on the big screen." "Koch Goes To The Movies," *Queens Courier*, 1/12/00

**barometer** "We watched carefully to see the ties that Mr. Smythe would wear as they were a sure *barometer* of the mood he would be in." Loring Brewster, "Vermont's Mr. Chips"

**bedlam** "There was *bedlam* as the crowd awoke to the relief of victory." Dick Thatcher, *Against All Odds*

**begrudge** "Taxpayers never seem to *begrudge* the use of their money when spent on local projects important to them." *Newsday*, 8/22/99

**belated** "When he made his *belated* entrance into the political campaign, he was told he had no chance." Jewell Bellush and Dick Netzer, *Urban Politics*

**belittle** "To say this is not to *belittle* subject matter, which is clearly essential to any proper education." William H. Kilpatrick, "Progressive Education"

**belligerence** "North Korea's *belligerence* in planning to test a long-range missile has led to a dramatic change of course for Japan and South Korea." Howard French, "Two Wary Neighbors Unite," *New York Times*, 8/4/99

**benevolence** "My relationship to this land is purely spiritual: It's a place of absolute silence, absolute *benevolence*." Stephen Trimble, *Wilderness*

**bereft** "The pictures of the *bereft* survivors searching for their loved ones are painful to see." *Newsday*, 9/19/99

**besiege** "He felt unable to carry the Confederate lines and settled down to *besiege* their fortifications." David Herbert Donald, *Lincoln*

**besmirch** "A primary attack on any witness against your client is an attempt to *besmirch* his or her character." Quoted in *New York Times Magazine*, 9/20/70

**bias** "U.S. SUIT CHARGES *BIAS* IN NASSAU COUNTY PROPERTY TAXES" Headline, *New York Times*, 6/15/99

**bigot** "For only by claiming the limelight can the *bigot* draw followers and an income." S. Andhil Fineberg, "Deflating the Professional Bigot"

**bizarre** "The police claim they were responding to the *bizarre* behavior of the man when they were forced to shoot him." *New York Post*, 9/27/99

**blasé** "When he hit the home run that broke the record, he could no longer maintain his previously *blasé* attitude." *Newsday*, 9/8/98

**blatant** "It's a classic *blatant* pyramid scheme." Robert Hanley, "Gifting Club," *New York Times*, 6/23/99

**bliss** "Is there anything to match the *bliss* on a teenager's face the day she obtains her license to drive?" *Car and Driver*, 9/99

**bluntly** "Managers will put it *bluntly*: 'You've got to catch the ball.' " Tim McCarver, *Baseball for Brain Surgeons*

**bogus** "The mayor denied his proposed change in the election law was a *bogus* attempt to seize more power." *New York Times*, 9/25/99

**bona fide** "Milosevic, a *bona fide* villain, will pay for his war crimes—we can be sure of that." Editorial, *Washington Post*, 5/28/99

**brash** "Baker's *brash* manner quickly antagonized the other warehouse workers." Seymour Broock, *Labor Meets Its Match*

**brigands** "The history of motion pictures shows that, from the earliest silent films, stories about western *brigands* would capture a large audience." John Simon, *Reverse Angle*

**bristle** "No sooner had the dog caught sight of him, however, than it began to *bristle* and growl savagely." H. G. Wells, *The Invisible Man*

**buff** "Grandpa was a stock market *buff*, hanging around the Dreyfus office most every weekday and following the yo-yo Dow Jones averages." Eloise Ryan Abernethy, *One Family's Finances* [adapted]

**bulwark** "That England, hedged in with the main, That water-walled *bulwark*, still secure And confidant from foreign purposes." William Shakespeare, *King John*

**burgeoned** "In recent years programs on AM, FM, shortwave and low-powered stations have *burgeoned*." Carlos Johnston, "Intelligence Report" Summer 1998

**cache** "Fagin drew from his *cache* the box which he had unintentionally disclosed to Oliver." Charles Dickens, *Oliver Twist*

**cacophony** "At his side he had a battery run radio blasting forth a sickening *cacophony* of noise." Freeman Tilden, *The National Parks*

**cajole** "We had to *cajole* tonight's guest to come on the program because he's something of a hermit." Larry King on his CNN TV program, 8/25/99

**callous** "The movie industry was *callous* in the way it treated writers who came from New York." Alex Ross, *New Yorker*, 2/23/98

**callow** "A group of newly arrived *callow* students followed nervously at the director's heels." Aldous Huxley, *Crome Yellow*

**calumny** "Overwhelmed by the *calumny* heaped upon him for his prejudice, he quickly resigned." Jewell Bellush and Dick Netzer, *Urban Politics*

**canard** "It's a *canard* to say I want to be a millionaire: I just want to live like one." Toots Shor, quoted in *Life* Magazine, 10/12/69

**candid** "Sweepstakes companies must be more *candid* about the chances of winning a prize." *AARP Bulletin*, 9/99

**candor** "He was struck by the *candor* and self-reliance of the women in these islands." "Pacific Paradise," *New York Times*, 8/9/99

**cant** "Although we hear much *cant* about loving one's neighbor, life provides endless examples of just the opposite." Paula Love, *The Will Rogers Book*

**capitulate** "The embattled leader refused to *capitulate* to demands for his resignation." *Newsweek*, 8/19/99

# PANORAMA OF WORDS

**capricious** "The snow removal equipment is always ready to face the *capricious* weather changes during the winter." *Newsday*, 12/24/98

**carnage** "Amid the *carnage* resulting from the earthquake, many acts of courage can be seen." *New York Times*, 9/20/99

**castigates** "Here is Holofernes commenting upon Armando, a mad wordman who *castigates* another while himself vocalizes into a fine frenzy." Harold Bloom, *Shakespeare*

**catastrophic** "Romeo changes enormously under Juliet's influence, remains subject to anger and despair, and is as responsible as Mercutio and Tybalt for the *catastrophic* event." Harold Bloom, *Shakespeare*

**caustic** "His habitual sullenness, stern disposition and *caustic* tongue produced a deep impression upon our young minds." Aleksandr Pushkin, "The Shot"

**celerity** "The human mind acts at times with amazing *celerity*." Benjamin Cardozo, *The Growth of the Law*

**cessation** "The evolutions of the waltzers were quieted, there was an uneasy *cessation* of all things as before." Edgar Allan Poe, "The Masque of the Red Death"

**chagrin** "He spent great energy and achieved, to our *chagrin*, no small amount of success in keeping us away from the people who surrounded us." James Baldwin, *Notes of a Native Son*

**charisma** "Yali radiated *charisma* and energy as he led his people." Jared Diamond, *Guns, Germs, and Steel*

**charlatan** "Many of my friends believe in fortune tellers; I think they are *charlatans*." Letter to "Dear Abby," *New York Daily News*, 5/16/99

**chicanery** "As a profession, lawyers have become associated with *chicanery* and confusion." *People*, 2/4/99

**chimerical** "His utopia is not a *chimerical* commonwealth but a practicable improvement on what already exists." George Santayana, *The Sense of Beauty*

**clandestine** "Mr. DeLay's plan for another 'independent' group is nothing less than a proposal to create a *clandestine* and corrupt slush fund." Editorial, *New York Times*, 6/1/99

**cliché** "The *cliché* 'Politics makes strange bedfellows' certainly applies in this situation." *Newsweek*, 9/20/99

**cliques** "The tragic event points out the danger of forming *cliques* in school that shut out many." *Newsday*, 5/15/99

**coerce** "The loan sharks sometimes have to *coerce* people in order to collect the debt." Peter Kilborn, "Lenders Thrive on Workers in Need," *New York Times*, 6/18/99

**cogent** "This article paints a clear and *cogent* picture of how to handle blowouts." *Car and Travel*, 9/99

**cognizant** "I am *cognizant* of the interrelatedness of all communities and states." Martin Luther King, Jr., "Letter From Birmingham Jail"

**comely** "An island peopled by the most *comely* women to be seen anywhere, Bora Bora is a must." *Travel*, 11/99

**commodious** "The new baseball stadium offered a more *commodious* arena for the fans and players." *Sports Illustrated*, 5/11/99

**compassionate** "In addition to professional skills, patients want a physician who is *com-*

# PANORAMA OF WORDS

*passionate.*" Advertisement for Maimonides Medical Center, 9/25/95

**compatible** "The policies of the party are not *compatible* with his conservative beliefs." *U.S. News and World Report,* 8/25/99

**compensatory** "The *compensatory* factor was a new arrival; Anukul had a son born to him." Rabindramath Tagore, "My Lord, the Baby"

**complacent** "Weather experts warn not to be *complacent* about the possibility of a dangerous hurricane." *New York,* 9/18/95

**complicity** "After 1945, Hitler's Germans replaced *complicity* with denial." Lance Morrow, "Done in the Name of Evil," *TIME,* 6/14/99

**component** "The F.B.I. did, in fact, develop a racial *component,* the profile of serial killers as predominantly white, male loners." Jeffrey Goldberg, "The Color of Suspicion," *New York Times,* 6/20/99

**compounded** "The match between England and Argentina, always a blood feud, was *compounded* by the memory of the Falklands crisis." Henry Kissinger, "Pele," *TIME,* 6/14/99

**comprehensive** "Lecter was built up as a superman, embodying absolute yet *comprehensive* evil." Christopher Lehmann-Haupt, "Hannibal Lecter Returns," *New York Times Book Review,* 6/10/99

**concocting** "I am *concocting* a seduction; I do not require a pastry chef." Ben Brantley, *New York Times,* 6/15/99

**concomitant** "The doses of the drug were increased with the *concomitant* result that he quickly became an addict." Otto Friedrich, *Before the Deluge*

**concur** "Dr. Fishbein did not *concur* with his colleague's diagnosis and urged the Harper family to seek an opinion from the head of the Urology Department at Columbia Presbyterian." "Prostate Update," *Prostate Digest,* 9/99

**condescending** "The reviewer treated this important book in the most *condescending* and dismissing manner." Letter to *New York Times Book Review,* 7/25/99

**condolence** "Words of *condolence* seem very poor things and yet they are all one can use to tell of one's sympathy." Maisie Ward, *Father Maturin*

**condone** "He does not *condone* the actions of any of the participants in the impeachment hearings." *New York Times Book Review,* 9/26/99

**conducive** "The quiet calm of this garden is *conducive* to romance or repose." "The Sophisticated Traveler," 9/26/99

**confidant** "Lecter rents a lavish house not terribly far from the modest duplex of FBI agent Starling, his antagonist/*confidant* during the period seven years earlier." Paul Gray, "Dessert Anyone?," *TIME,* 6/21/99

**conflagration** "Did the firing of incendiary tear gas canisters cause or contribute to the *conflagration*?" *New York Times,* 9/3/99

**confronts** "When we gaze into a seeming infinity of tomorrows, we face the challenge that any generation *confronts* when it looks ahead." Editorial, "2000 and Beyond," *New York Times,* 1/1/00

**congenial** "Susan's *congenial* manner made her a favorite in the rodeo." Lacey Fosburgh, "All-Girls Rodeos," *New York Times,* 8/17/99

**conjecture** "We read to understand how to take care of ourselves, to prepare for the

# PANORAMA OF WORDS

unexpected, to *conjecture* what we would do in similar situations." Annie Proulx, "They Lived to Tell the Tale"

**conjugal** Hillary is Our Lady of Perpetual *Conjugal* Suffering; the patron saint of every woman who's every been wronged." Maureen Dowd, "Rudy in Reverse," *New York Times*, 6/6/99

**connoisseur** "This is the car for the *connoisseur* who doesn't have to think about cost." *Car and Driver*, 10/99

**connubial** "I never could imagine *connubial* bliss until after tea." W. Somerset Maugham, *Cakes and Ale*

**consternation** "Father and son stared at each other in *consternation* and neither knew what to do." Pearl Buck, *The Good Earth*

**constricted** "He grew up in slightly less *constricted* circumstances than his teammates." Darcy Frey, *The Last Shot*

**construed** "Hemingway's simple approach was *construed* as mysticism." Robert Ruark, "Ernest Was Very Simple"

**consummate** "Arnold Zweig, a writer of *consummate* artistry, presents a picture of delicacy and charm that hovers on the brink of disaster." Roger Goodman, *World-Wide Stories*

**contemptuous** "It is not difficult to feel *contemptuous* when studying the ugly behavior of some of the powerful figures of motion pictures." Pauline Kael, *I Lost It at the Movies*

**contort** "He is an actor who can *contort* his face into any number of shapes." *People*, 4/15/99

**controversial** "His three-year tenure was *controversial* and contained charges of

racism." Monte Williams, "Roosevelt Island Chief," *New York Times*, 6/10/99

**cope** "Every single muscle in the body was strained to the uttermost throughout the watch to *cope* with the steering." Thor Heyerdahl, *Kon Tiki*

**copious** "The wedding reception featured *copious* amounts of food, drink, and music." *New York Times*, 9/26/99

**corpulent** "When he squeezed his *corpulent* body into a chair he seemed to be stuck there forever." Charles W. Thompson, *Presidents I Have Known*

**corroborated** "Bill *corroborated* the captain's statement, hurried back down the glistening ladders to his duty." Hanson W. Baldwin, "R.M.S. Titanic"

**coterie** "The aristocratic *coterie* finally got the upper hand." Edith Hamilton, *The Greek Way*

**countenance** "Behind a most pleasant *countenance*, this dictator has maintained a most brutal regime." *Newsweek*, 2/21/98

**coup** "Newt Gingrich was nearly toppled in a *coup* attempt in the House." Michael Duffy, "Who Chose George?," *TIME*, 6/21/99

**covert** "In a *covert* manner, Knute traveled abroad that night." Sinclair Lewis, "Young Man Axelbrod"

**coveted** "The moment has arrived for our annual *coveted* 'Bloopie' Awards." William Safire, *New York Times*, 7/18/99

**crave** "It's the perfect way for the Clintons to hang on to the power, glamour and excitement they both *crave*." Bob Herbert, "It Could Happen," *New York Times*, 6/6/99

# PANORAMA OF WORDS

**criterion** "This new product is useful, but the major *criterion* is its safety." *Car and Travel*, 10/99

**cryptic** "Ms. Bogart, an iconoclastic director known for her *cryptic* reworkings of everything, turns out to be an ideal interpreter for Gertrude Stein." Ben Brantley, "Gertrude and Alice," *New York Times*, 6/14/99

**culminated** "The years of physical and mental training *culminated* in the fulfillment of a lifelong dream." *Vim & Vigor*, Summer 1998

**culpable** "When the jury found Stacy *culpable*, she collapsed in a state of shock." Eloise R. Baxter, "Judgment Day"

**culprit** "We pointed out the tender age and physical slightness of the little *culprit*." Thomas Mann, "Mario and the Magician"

**cumbersome** "Grizzly bears may look *cumbersome* and awkward, but don't be deceived." *Nature*, 2/97

**cumulative** "There can be an extraordinary *cumulative* strength in Mr. Foote's plays." Ben Brantley, *New York Times*, 6/18/99

**cupidity** "There is little real humor in this picture of cunning and *cupidity* as revealed by a petty contest for a paltry sum." Liam O'Flaherty, "A Shilling"

**curry** "The candidates are visiting many senior centers in an attempt to *curry* support among the elderly." *AARP Bulletin*, 9/99

**cursory** "Even a *cursory* glance at the text of the peace agreement shows that the Yugoslav leader has accepted NATO's demands in full." Tim Judah, "What Do We Do With Serbia Now?," *New York Times*, 6/4/99

**curtail** "A court decision to a freeze on regulations to *curtail* cross-state pollution was unpopular." "EPA's Reduced Standards," *Newsday*, 6/15/99

**cynical** "A *cynical* view of phone calls or mail offering free merchandise or membership is the safest approach." *Newsweek*, 6/7/98

**dearth** "There was no *dearth* of criticism of his work." H. L. Mencken, "The Case of Dreiser"

**debacle** "After leading the league for most of the season, September brought the *debacle* that ruined their hopes." Roger Kahn, *The Boys of Summer*

**debilitating** "Exercise can help people overcome *debilitating* illnesses." *Vim & Vigor*, Summer 1998

**debris** "They continued their support for earthquake victims in the *debris* of collapsed houses." *New York Daily News*, 8/7/99

**decade** "Clearly, the first *decade* of the 21st century will be the 'e-decade,' as all forms of e-commerce and e-ways of life continue to grow." Letter to the editor, *New York Times*, 1/1/00

**decadence** "I said earlier that the *decadence* of our language is probably curable." George Orwell, *Politics and the English Language*

**decapitate** "The FBI hoped that the arrest of the drug lord would *decapitate* the illegal organization." David Denby, *Beyond Rangoon*

**declaimed** "Some of the province's most illustrious men visited the courthouse and *declaimed* within its four walls." Hazel Grinnell, *Travel Journal*

# PANORAMA OF WORDS

**decorum**  "My father's sense of *decorum* was shattered by his son's bad behavior in the restaurant." Peter Balakian, *Black Dog of Fate*

**decrepit**  "Some schools are in such *decrepit* condition that students will be transferred to safer schools until repairs can be made." NYC Schools Chancellor Rudy Crew, *Newsday*, 7/6/99

**deem**  "You shall stay here as long as the proper authorities *deem* necessary." Bernard Malamud, *The Fixer*

**defamatory**  "His *defamatory* remarks about minorities are transmitted on the Internet." *TIME*, 8/30/99

**degraded**  "The world is weary of statesmen who have become *degraded* into politicians." Benjamin Disraeli

**deleterious**  "These statutes will have a *deleterious* effect on the public interest." Supreme Court Justice Tom Clark, speech, 1960

**delineation**  "There is no need for an exact *delineation* of a standard for a permit to hold a street meeting." Supreme Court Justice Felix Frankfurter, decision, 1951

**deluded**  "Mrs. Barrows had *deluded* herself that you visited her last evening and behaved in an unseemly manner." James Thurber, "The Catbird Seat"

**deluge**  "The art exhibit brought a *deluge* of criticism because of its subject matter." *New York Daily News*, 9/28/99

**delve**  "We can help you *delve* deeper into your destination and take you places most travel companies miss." *Grand Circle Travel Booklet*

**demeanor**  "You could tell by her *demeanor* that she was more than a bit upset by the unexpected news." *New York Times*, 9/7/99

**demur**  "At first the Crown Prince would *demur*, but after being prodded, he would generally choose dictation, which he liked least." Elizabeth Gray Vining, *Windows for the Crown Prince*

**denote**  "The origins of the letters 'O.K.' to *denote* 'all right' are not clear." Bill Bryson, *Mother Tongue*

**depict**  "How can one *depict* the beauty and impact of Grand Canyon in words or pictures?" Freeman Tilden, *The National Parks*

**deplorable**  "The troops were amazed at the *deplorable* conditions in the refugee camp." *Newsweek*, 5/12/97

**deploy**  "Eisenhower expressed the hope that the United States would not be the first to *deploy* a weapon so horrible." David McCullough, *Truman*

**deprecate**  "Why do they always *deprecate* the efforts of a woman press secretary, but rarely a man doing the same job?" *New York*, 9/25/95

**derided**  "He made his living in a vocation so *derided* it has become a gag phrase: wedding singer." Joyce Wadler, "Public Lives," *New York Times*, 6/15/99

**derived**  "His political success is *derived* mainly from the public awareness of his prominent family." *TIME*, 2/16/98

**derogatory**  "When a communist father noticed a religious program on TV, he uttered a *derogatory* statement and turned off the program." J. Edgar Hoover, "Why Do People Become Communists?"

**desist**  "My husband kicked me under the table and warned me to *desist*." Phyllis

Krasilovsky, "Pumpernickel in My Purse," *New York Times*, 6/12/99

**destitute** "Our Supreme Court has said that any citizen has a Constitutional right to have counsel, and that the court must appoint a lawyer to defend the *destitute*." Joseph Welch, "Should a Lawyer Defend a Guilty Man?"

**desultory** "Mortimer enters and, distracted by what his aunts are doing, plants a *desultory* kiss upon Elaine's cheek." Joseph Kesselring, *Arsenic and Old Lace*

**deter** "Concern for his job did not *deter* him from making public the dangers of smoking." "Brave Politician," *New York Times*, 4/12/99

**detriment** "The New York City Board of Education voted not to renew the chancellor's contract as the majority viewed him as a *detriment* to improvements in education." *New York Newsday*, 1/4/00

**devout** "This author has a *devout* following among young readers." *New York Times Book Review*, 7/25/98

**dexterity** "Ali built his career based on his *dexterity*, both in the ring and in the use of colorful language." *Boxing*, 3/95

**diatribe** "Rebecca Gilman's new play could easily have been an easy *diatribe* against racism." *TIME*, 6/7/99

**dilettante** "This art exhibit is not for the *dilettante*; the subject matter is too shocking." *New York Daily News*, 10/3/99

**diminutive** "A giant of a chef, he is a *diminutive*, modest man." *New York Post*, 10/10/99

**discern** "He could not see that the Justice's face was kindly nor *discern* that his voice was troubled." William Faulkner, "Barn Burning"

**disciples** "Rick and his *disciples* dominated the entire summer scene, making it unpleasant for those who were not part of the inner circle." Ellis R. Sloane, *Catskill Idyll* [adapted]

**discreet** "When questioned about her husband's illegal activities, she kept a *discreet* silence." *Newsday*, 5/16/99

**disdain** "Hillary shows *disdain* for the idea that matters other than policy are anyone's business." Margaret Carlson, "Uh-Oh, the Real First Lady Shows Up," *TIME*, 6/7/99

**disgruntled** "The police believe the damage was done by a *disgruntled* ex-employee." *Newsday*, 5/16/99

**disheveled** "The wind tugged at and *disheveled* her hair." William Cowper, *The Task*

**dismantle** "Wayne Huizenga's move to *dismantle* the World Series Marlin squad has hurt the Florida team at the box office." Ralph Kiner, baseball announcer, Fox Sports [adapted]

**disparage** "It (government control) has been called crackpot, but that doesn't *disparage* it for me." E. B. White, *One Man's Meat*

**disparate** "At the moment standardized tests have a *disparate* racial and ethnic impact." Abigail Thernstrom, "Testing, the Easy Target," *New York Times*, 6/10/99

**dispersed** "The police waded in and *dispersed* the protesting crowd." *New York Post*, 10/23/99

**disseminate** "In the history of the world, no other tool has allowed us to *disseminate*

# PANORAMA OF WORDS

more information than the Internet." *Computer World*, 5/99

**dissent** "In the totalitarian state that utopianism produced, *dissent* could not be tolerated." Anthony Lewis, "Abroad at Home," *New York Times*, 12/31/99

**distraught** "On the veranda of Banker White's house Helen was restless and *distraught*." Sherwood Anderson, "Sophistication"

**diversity** "Mr. Oates said this rare document belonged in Queens because it is the center of ethnic *diversity* for this country." *New York Times*, 1/5/00

**divulged** "The DNA tests *divulged* enough evidence to free him from death row." *Newsweek*, 2/17/98

**docile** "How long can they remain *docile*, living under such terrible oppression?" *Business Week*, 6/16/98

**doddering** "The image of the aged as suffering from memory loss and *doddering* mobility is far from accurate." *AARP Magazine*, 9/99

**doleful** "The patients were left in *doleful* plight, as the whole country resounded with the consequent cry of 'hard times'." Washington Irving, "The Devil and Tom Walker"

**domicile** "At night he returned peaceably enough to his lonesome *domicile*." Theodore Dreiser, "The Lost Phoebe"

**dormant** "The disease may lie *dormant* for years before becoming active and dangerous." *Johns Hopkins Health Letter*, 5/97

**dregs** "Some certain *dregs* of conscience are yet within me." William Shakespeare, *Richard III*

**drudgery** "And then she came to find the paralytic aunt—housework—janitor's *drudgery*." Anzia Yezierska, "Hunger"

**dubious** "Many scientists say its experimental merits are *dubious*." Margaret Wente, "Fifth Column," *Globe and Mail*, Toronto, 5/27/99

**dulcet** "Her *dulcet* tones and intelligent reading of the story captivated the hearers." "Our Town," *New York Times*, 10/7/99

**duped** "Barnum knew the American public loved to be *duped*." W. L. Phelps, *American Entrepreneurs*

**duplicity** "The *duplicity* of which he had been guilty weighed on his spirit." H. C. Bunner, "Our Aromatic Uncle"

**duress** "Under *duress* she was forced to admit having lied during a 1994 deposition in her breach of contract law suit." Associated Press report, *Newsday*, 6/24/99

**edifice** "My love was like a fair house built on another man's ground so that I have lost my *edifice* by mistaking the place where I erected it." William Shakespeare, *The Merry Wives of Windsor*

**efficacy** "He runs his office with the greatest *efficacy*." Sally Quinn, *Chicago Sun Times*, 12/9/79

**effigy** "ANGRY SERBS HANG UNCLE SAM IN *EFFIGY*" Headline over Associated Press photo, *New York Times*, 8/23/99

**effrontery** "In view of his personal background, we were astonished at his *effrontery* in attacking the morals of the candidate." Jewell Bellush and Dick Netzer, *Urban Politics*

**egotist** "It takes an *egotist* to believe that nature has provided these beauties as a special act on his behalf." Freeman Tilden, *The National Parks*

**egregious** "It is mystifying why some women still stick with Bill through so many *egregious* episodes." Maureen Dowd, *New York Times*, 6/2/99

**elapsed** "True, a decent time had *elapsed*, and it was not even suggested that Waythorn had supplanted his predecessor." Edith Wharton, *The Descent of Man* [adapted]

**elicit** "The experimental animal obviously hoped to *elicit* a reproduction of the pleasurable sensations he had experienced under laboratory conditions." Loren Eiseley, "Man and Porpoise"

**elucidate** "The Secretary of State tried to *elucidate* the government's policies in the troubled Middle East." *New York Times*, 5/7/98

**elusive** "In his appearance there was something attractive and *elusive* which allured women and disposed them in his favour." Anton Chekhov, "The Lady with the Dog"

**emaciated** "Twiggy, whose fame was related to her *emaciated* look, is now better known for her singing and dramatic talent." Play review, *New Jersey Star Ledger*, 5/12/99

**embellished** "The prioress may not have told the correct story in all its details and she may even have *embellished* the story a little bit to make it more attractive." Lin Yutang, "The Jade Goddess"

**eminent** "It was unbelievable that a man so *eminent* would actually sit in our dining room and eat our food." V.S. Pritchett, "The Saint"

**emissary** "The mayor sent an *emissary* to the striking teachers in the hope of starting negotiations." Jewell Bellush and Dick Netzer, *Urban Politics*

**emitted** "The smoke that was *emitted* when the bomb went off made some think it was a firecracker but I thought it was a revolver shot." *Journal of Andre Gide*, Vol. I

**emulate** "Her companions she loved and admired but could not *emulate* for they knew things she did not." Rose Macaulay, *The World My Wilderness*

**encomiums** "Isn't it sad that we receive our highest *encomiums* after we are gone and unable to enjoy them?" James Farley, quoted in *Ruffles and Flourishes*

**encumbrance** "Maxim decided to dispose of the *encumbrance* of a whining wife and three disrespectful teenagers by leaving silently in the dead of the night." Everett Dodds, *Greener Pastures* [adapted]

**engrossed** "The wasp was *engrossed* utterly in her task." Alan Devoe, "The Mad Dauber"

**enhance** "Her breadth of experience and determination to *enhance* her knowledge have increased her value to Con Edison." Con Edison Report, *Producing Excellence*, 1998

**enigma** "He was an *enigma*—by this I mean that he did not look soldierly nor financial nor artistic nor anything definite at all." Max Beerbohm, "A.V. Laider"

**ennui** "The *ennui* and utter emptiness of a life of pleasure is fast urging fashionable women to something better." Elizabeth Cady Stanton, *The Newport Convention*

**entourage** "Sinatra was the greatest but I was never a part of his *entourage*, his rat pack." Comedian Buddy Hackett to New York Mayor Rudy Giuliani, *New York Daily News*, 7/14/99

# PANORAMA OF WORDS

**entreaty** "The police captain made one more *entreaty* for the unruly crowd to leave." *New York Post*, 10/23/99

**enunciated** "At his press conference, Jerry Springer *enunciated* his qualifications for a Senate seat in Ohio." Francis X. Clines, "Springer Considers Race for Senate," *New York Times*, 8/4/99

**epithets** "Four scowling men sat in the dinghy and surpassed records in the invention of *epithets*." Stephen Crane, "The Open Boat"

**epitome** "My community considers a man in uniform to be the living *epitome* of heroism." Lucius Garvin, *Collected Essays*

**equanimity** "We have to call upon our whole people to stand up with *equanimity* to the fire of the enemy." Winston Churchill, speech, 1942

**eradicate** "The urologist said that prostate cancer patients shouldn't hang their hopes on having the vaccine *eradicate* the disease in the near future." Associated Press, "Vaccine Fights Prostate Cancer," *Newsday*, 10/21/99

**erudite** "The *erudite* historian, Prof. Garrett Clark, will speak on 'Evaluating Democracy' at our April meeting." Lancaster Library Bulletin, Spring 2000

**eruption** "We have learned about this ancient city, frozen in time by the *eruption* of Mt. Vesuvius in 79 A.D." *Grand Circle Travel Booklet*, 1999

**escalation** "There is a dangerous *escalation* in Kashmir as India and Pakistan are engaged in the worst fighting in decades." Editorial, *New York Times*, 6/22/99

**eschew** "When in Rome, we decided to *eschew* Arithmetic." Ruth McKinney, "Proof in Nine"

**ethics** "The vast majority of employees perform in a highly satisfactory manner because good work *ethics* exist in their kitchens." Manual for School Food Service Managers in N.Y.C. Public Schools [adapted]

**euphemism** "But now he was merely an elder statesman, the *euphemism* for a politician who no longer has any influence." Robert Wallace, "Not Him"

**evaluate** "Mr. Gooding hopes to find the answer if his mentor gives him the chance to *evaluate* the prisoner." Lawrence Van Gelder, *New York Times*, 6/4/99

**evanescent** "The incidents which give excellence to biography are of a volatile and *evanescent* kind." Samuel Johnson, "The Rambler" No. 30

**eventuated** "Her illness following the chemotherapy *eventuated* in death." Terrence Foy, *St. Louis Blues*

**evince** "The vote on Roe vs. Wade will show whether enough senators *evince* an interest in overturning the 1973 Supreme Court decision." Elaine Povich, "Abortion Politics," *Newsday*, 10/22/99

**exacerbated** "Jason Isringhausen's injuries were *exacerbated* by his immaturity." Howie Rose, Mets Baseball Announcer, Fox Sports, 6/8/99 [adapted]

**excoriate** "Senator Bradley refused to *excoriate* his opponent, preferring to take the high road in the campaign." *ABC Eyewitness T.V. News*, 10/21/99

**excruciating** "An almost *excruciating* agitation results when a leaf falls into still water." Jack London, "To Build a Fire"

**exhort** "There was no reason for me to *exhort* the guys to play hard because they were already giving me 110%." Mets

# PANORAMA OF WORDS

Baseball Manager Bobby Valentine on Radio Talk Show WFAN, 10/21/99

**exonerate** "There is no reason to *exonerate* him from the ordinary duties of a citizen." Oliver Wendell Holmes, *Collected Legal Papers*

**expatriate** "For months she lived the nocturnal life of an *expatriate* American tango bum." Jimmy Scott, "Flirting with the Tango," *New York Times*, 6/11/99

**expedient** "There exists the age old choice between a moral action and an *expedient* one." Arthur Koestler, *Darkness at Noon*

**expedite** "There was a pressing need to *expedite* assistance to those suffering after the earthquake." *Newsday*, 8/15/99

**exploit** "He has not wanted to *exploit* his fame as a basketball star for political advantage." *Boston Globe*, 7/27/99

**expunge** "If the offender made it to adulthood without further problems, everything would be *expunged*." James Kilpatrick, "Boy Learns Constitution—the Hard Way," *Burlington Vermont Free Press*, 6/12/99

**expurgate** "Lenny resisted any attempt by the law to *expurgate* his language dealing with personal and private behavior." "Lenny Bruce, Voice of Shock," *Atlantic Monthly*, 5/86

**extant** "Rumors are *extant* that the Federal Reserve members are greatly concerned about the irrational exuberance of investors." Bloomberg Financial News, 4/12/98

**extinct** "There are many warnings that loss of habitat will make many species *extinct* in the near future." "The Rotunda," Publication of the American Museum of Natural History, 5/5/98

**extol** "They *extol* the largely nonexistent virtues of bygone eras." Artemus Abruzzi, *Commonsense*

**extortion** "To the prince who goes forth with his army, supporting it by pillage and *extortion*, this open-handedness is necessary." Niccolo Machiavelli, *The Prince*

**extraneous** "The ballet struck me as *extraneous* and out of keeping with the rest of the play." Wolcott Gibbs, *More in Sorrow*

**extrinsic** "Disdaining contributions from *extrinsic* lobbying groups, the candidate won my admiration and my vote." Lawrence Burton, "Inside the Polls"

**exult** "YANKEES *EXULT* OVER PETTITTE'S PERFORMANCE" Headline, Sports Section, *Newsday*, 6/19/99

**exultation** "We face the year 2000 with a combination of concern and *exultation*." *Newsweek*, 12/15/99

**fabricate** "Perhaps the dialogues that you *fabricate* are nothing more than monologues." Miguel Unamuno, "Mist"

**façade** "He hid behind the *façade* of public servant to work at a private agenda." H. L. Woods

**facet** "As soon as one becomes computer-literate, a new technical *facet* is introduced that challenges us once again." *New York Times*, 10/25/99

**facetious** "Politicians must be careful about any *facetious* comment that can be turned into an opponent's advantage." Jewell Bellush and Dick Netzer, *Urban Politics*

**facile** "We are usually more *facile* with words we read than with words we use to write or speak." Charlton Laird, *The Miracle of Language*

# PANORAMA OF WORDS

**factitious** "The opposition was challenged by a *factitious* outpouring of what appeared to be popular support for the government." Robert Kaplan, *Balkan Tragedy*

**fallacious** "The demand was plausible, but the more I thought about it, the more *fallacious* it seemed." A. D. White, *Scams and Schemes* [adapted]

**falter** "Should we *falter* in our determination to pursue an honorable solution to the problems of the Middle-East, and face unthinkable consequences?" I. F. Stone, "The Weekly Reader"

**fastidious** "A single small elephant tusk took no less than two months of *fastidious* work to excavate." Brian Fagan, *Time Detectives*

**fatal** "What caused him to lose the election was his *fatal* mistake of not raising sufficient funds to publicize himself." Jewell Bellush and Dick Netzer, *Urban Politics*

**fatuous** "After only a few seconds of silence, speakers of English seem obligated to say something, even making a *fatuous* comment about the weather." Bill Bryson, *The Mother Tongue*

**feasible** "Everyone who has looked at the smart guns said there is no quick, *feasible* way of doing this." Leslie Wayne, "Smart Guns," *New York Times*, 6/15/99

**feint** "Young as Oliver was, he had sense enough to make a *feint* of feeling great regret at going away." Charles Dickens, *Oliver Twist*

**felicitous** "The evening of hypnotism was not a *felicitous* one; we were frightened that we would lose our will or enter into unpleasant acts." *Diary of Anais Nin*

**felon** "I was surprised to see this notorious *felon* become a regular at our bible discus-sion classes." Rabbi Myron David, *A Chaplain's Jail Tales* [adapted]

**ferment** "She herself yearned for calm, but lived in a neighborhood of *ferment* and daily chaos." Alan Lelchuk, *American Mischief*

**fervid** "I'm a mixture of my mother's determination and my father's *fervid* optimism." Gwen Robyns, *Light of A Star*

**fetish** "Today the automobile has become a *fetish* for one's standing and accomplishments." Mark Twain, *Autobiography*

**fetters** "The cruel *fetters* of the galley slaves were wet with blood." Alex Haley, *Roots*

**fiasco** "Your $25 contribution to our fund will bring you an hilarious tape of the *fiasco* of an elementary school's production of 'Peter Pan.'" Public Broadcasting Announcement, 12/25/98

**fiat** "Pitching Coach Bob Apodaca's *fiat* to Met hurlers was simple: pitch fast, change speeds, throw strikes." Howie Rose, baseball announcer, Fox Sports, 7/8/99

**flabbergasted** "The President was *flabbergasted* when his private office recorded conversations were made public." Herbert Brucker, *Journalist*

**flagrant** "Gene Savoy's *flagrant* name dropping doesn't seem to bother any of the visitors on board." Brad Wetzler, "Crazy for Adventure," *New York Times*, 6/6/99

**flamboyant** "Dame Judi Dench is not as *flamboyant* as the other British theatrical Dames such as Vanessa Redgrave or Maggie Smith." *Playbill*, Vol. 9, No. 55

**flay** "There is no shortage of critics who *flay* the journalists for being sensation seekers rather than news gatherers." Herbert Brucker, *Journalist*

**fledgling** "Women's professional basketball, recently a *fledgling* sport, has taken root and grown into a major spectator event." *Sports*, 9/14/99

**flout** "His ideas frightened the farmers, for he would *flout* and ridicule their traditional beliefs with a mocking logic that they could not answer." S. Raja Ratnam, "Drought"

**fluctuated** "He *fluctuated* between mindless talk and endless silence." Alix Shulman, "Memoirs of an Ex-Prom Queen"

**foist** "Eventually, advertisements began to *foist* off the use of perfume as a way to snare a man." E. S. Turner, *The Shocking History of Advertising* [adapted]

**foment** "The petitioners were not attempting to *foment* violence by their peaceful actions." Supreme Court Justice Hugo Black, decision, 1960

**forthwith** "Get down to your Toyota dealer *forthwith* and take advantage of our holiday saleabration." Toyota advertisement, CBS TV

**fortuitous** "Representative Foley resumed a corridor interview, making a point about the *fortuitous* beauty of bipartisanship." Francis X. Clines, "Gun Control Debate," *New York Times*, 6/18/99

**fracas** "Once the will was read, there followed a *fracas* that involved numerous law suits and lasted years." *Fortune*, 2/16/91

**fractious** "The *fractious* couple received a tongue lashing from Judge Judy." Arnold Feigenbaum, "Television Justice?"

**frail** "This *frail* woman has the strength to work where the strong turn away." "Mother Teresa," *New Republic*, 10/16/97

**fraught** "Ev'ry sigh comes forth so *fraught* with sweets, 'Tis incense to be offered to a god." Nathaniel Lee, *The Rival Queens*

**fray** "To the latter end of a *fray* and the beginning of a feast, Fits a dull fighter and a keen guest." William Shakespeare, *Henry IV*

**frenetic** "There is no place more *frenetic* than a newspaper office when a major story is breaking." Herbert Brucker, *Journalist*

**frenzy** "They had a sense of the wildest adventure, which mounted to *frenzy*, when some men rose on the shore and shouted to them, 'Hello, there! What are you doing with that boat?' " William Dean Howells, *A Boy's Town*

**fretful** "When Mike Nichols directed 'Who's Afraid of Virginia Woolf?' Warner Bros. was *fretful*, worrying about the Legion of Decency." Liz Smith, "Century's Choice," *New York Post*, 6/23/99

**frugal** "He was famously *frugal*—'so tight he damn near squeaked' says a colleague." Eric Pooley, "How George Got His Groove," *TIME*, 6/21/99

**fruitless** "Since launching a diplomatic shuttle, the Russian envoy had spent dozens of *fruitless* hours with the Yugoslav dictator." Johanna McGeary, "Why He Blinked," *TIME*, 6/14/99

**frustrated** "I will not be *frustrated* by reality." Ray Bradbury, *Forever and the Earth*

**fulsome** "I was appreciative of his sincere and *fulsome* praise." Ruth McKinney, "A Loud Sneer for Our Feathered Friends"

**furtive** "Hogan directed a *furtive* glance up and down the alley." John Steinbeck, "How Mr. Hogan Robbed a Bank"

# PANORAMA OF WORDS

**futility** "Resistance to changes in English language rules often ends in *futility*." Bill Bryson, *Mother Tongue*

**galvanize** "While he could not *galvanize* an audience, he could make them think." George Jean Nathan, *House of Satan*

**gamut** "At one end of the *gamut* of slang's humor is what Oliver Wendell Holmes called 'the blank checks of a bankrupt mind.'" Bergen Evans, "Now Everyone is Hip About Slang"

**garbled** "A *garbled* account of the matter that had reached his colleagues led to some gentle ribbing." H. G. Wells, "The Man Who Could Work Miracles"

**garrulous** "The more he drank, the more *garrulous* he became, until he suddenly seemed to fade out." Lawrence O'Brien, *W. C. Fields*

**gaudy** "This computer drawing program permits children to express themselves in the most *gaudy* art they can imagine." *Working Mother*, 5/96

**gaunt** "Her *gaunt* expression was mistaken for weakness of spirit, whereas it told the sad story of her life." George Eliot, *Middle March*

**genocide** "Accounts of the destruction of masses of people recall that *genocide* is an ancient practice." Otto Friedrich, *Before the Deluge*

**genre** "There is a certain difference between a work called a romance and the *genre* known as the novel." Nathaniel Hawthorne

**germane** "In assigning ratings to films, is it not *germane* to consider the nature and extent of violence shown?" *The Hollywood Reporter*, 5/19/97

**gesticulating** "'Three times' was still all he could say, in his thick, angry voice, *gesticulating* at the commissaire and glaring at me." Francis Steegmuller, "The Foreigner"

**gist** "The *gist* of it is . . . love is a great beautifier." Louisa May Alcott, *Little Women*

**gleaned** "I *gleaned* what I could from college, but independent reading soon broadened my horizons." I. F. Stone, *Weekly Reader*

**glib** "It is not *glib* to maintain that truth can never be contained in one creed." Mary Augusta Ward, *Robert Elsmere*

**gratuity** "What form of *gratuity* would compensate his informer's key bit of information?" Dashiell Hammett, *Red Harvest*

**gregariousness** "We will take with us one thing alone that exists among porpoises as among men; an ingrained *gregariousness*." Loren Eiseley, "Man and Porpoise"

**grimace** "When informed of the death of his best friend, he was unemotional, not a *grimace* marred his face." James Jones, *The Thin Red Line*

**grotesque** "Nowadays, men have to work, and women to marry for money; it's a dreadfully *grotesque* world." Louisa May Alcott, *Little Women*

**guise** "Freedom is not worth fighting for, if, under its *guise*, one tries to get as much as he can for himself." Dorothy Canfield Fisher, *Seasoned Timber*

**gullible** "'Charles the horse was wonderful!' cried a *gullible* goose." James Thurber, "What Happened to Charles"

**gusto** "Ali faced each fight with supreme confidence and challenged his opponents with wit and *gusto*." "His Greatest Challenge," *Sports Illustrated*, 5/5/97

**habitat** "Billy begins to be happy about life only in an artificial but cozy *habitat* on another planet." William Bly, *Barron's Book Notes*, *Slaughterhouse Five* by Kurt Vonnegut

**halcyon** "The *halcyon* days we recall with pleasure had many clouded moments." Wolcott Gibbs, *New Yorker*, 4/8/49

**hapless** "Parents, too, have an almost irresistible impulse to mold their children in their own image or at least graft a few of their own ambitions onto their *hapless* offspring." Arthur Gordon, "The Neglected Art of Being Different"

**harassing** "Over the next weeks came more amendments and *harassing* tactics including a motion to postpone selection of a new capital." Carl Sandburg, *Abraham Lincoln: The Prairie Years*

**harbingers** "It is easy enough to find *harbingers* of the episode in the early coverage of Mrs. Dole's candidacy." *TIME*, 5/24/99

**haven** "The desire to escape the city has filtered down into every other economic group, and as a result of the suburb's popularity, that *haven* of refuge is itself filling up." Lewis Mumford, "The Roaring Traffic's Boom"

**havoc** "Excessive sensitiveness plays *havoc* with children's nerves." Guy De Maupassant, "Looking Back"

**heinous** "All crimes against a whole people are measured by the *heinous* ones carried out by Hitler." *Civilization*, 12/99

**heresy** "Calvin had written that *heresy* was not an evil, deserving death." Herbert Brucker, *Journalist*

**heterogeneous** "The family is *heterogeneous* enough to make quite a good party in itself." Rose Macauley, *The World My Wilderness*

**hirsute** "The difference between this rock concert and one 10 years earlier is the marked decrease in *hirsute* young men." *TIME*, 8/8/99

**histrionics** "Bobby Valentine's *histrionics* will be irrelevant, because Rule 51 states that any manager who is ejected must remain in the clubhouse until the game is over." Jack Curry, "Valentine is Suspended and Fined," *New York Times*, 6/11/99

**hoard** "Many people give freely of their affections while you *hoard* yours." Joseph Conrad, *Victory*

**hoax** "Frank Spencer, an anthropologist who rummaged through the bones of controversy to theorize about the identity of the mastermind behind the Piltdown Man *hoax* of 1912, died on Sunday." Obituary notice, *New York Times*, 6/12/99

**homogeneous** "Archaeologists have unearthed evidence showing that the people of ancient Egypt were far from a *homogeneous* civilization." Brian Fagan, *Time Detective*

**hostile** "He might commit some *hostile* act, attempt to strike me or choke me." Jack London, *White Fang*

**humility** "Early in life I had to choose between arrogance and *humility*; I chose arrogance." Frank Lloyd Wright

**hyperbole** "It is not *hyperbole* to state that, most terribly, justice and judgment lie often a world apart." Emmeline Pankhurst, *My Own Story*

**iconoclast** "He was an *iconoclast* about everything, except his love of money." Garry Wills, syndicated newspaper column, 3/8/79

# PANORAMA OF WORDS

**idyllic** "The brilliant Hawaiian sunrise beckons you to a great breakfast as your tour of the *idyllic* islands begins." Brochure for Perillo Tours

**ignominious** "Henry Clay had ambition to become president, but he faced an *ignominious* series of setbacks." H. Foner, *Failed Candidates*

**ilk** "'That's the standard line,' Ron said, 'as promoted by some Japanese businessmen and American spokesmen of their *ilk*.'" Michael Crichton, *Rising Sun*

**imbibe** "I got up and went downstairs and into the kitchen to *imbibe* my first cup of coffee before going to the barn." Glenway Wescott, *The Breath of Bulls*

**imminent** "I admired the easy confidence with which my chief loped from side to side of his wheel and trimmed the ship so closely that disaster seemed ceaselessly *imminent*." Mark Twain, *Life on the Mississippi*

**impeccable** "That is why the so-called 'better' juvenile books, skillfully constructed, morally sanitary, psychologically *impeccable*—don't really make much of a dent on the child's consciousness." Clifton Fadiman, "My Life is an Open Book"

**impede** "Judge Jones has become known for her anger at defense lawyers who try to *impede* executions through legal maneuvers." David Firestone, "Death Penalty Conference," *New York Times*, 8/19/99

**imperative** "But unlike the others, Mrs. Hassan had yet another *imperative*: her son Huseyin has leukemia and needs blood." Edmund L. Andrews, "I Cannot Die," *New York Times*, 8/19/99

**imperceptibly** "In the two decades since W. Ugams had come to Boston, his status had *imperceptibly* shifted." John Updike, *New Yorker*, 10/22/60

**imperturbable** "The Prince de Ligne had given the Empress Catherine the name of *imperturbable*, or immoveable." Walter Tooke, *The Life of Catherine*

**impetuous** "He displayed the *impetuous* vivacity of youth." Samuel Johnson, "The Rambler" No. 27

**impious** "The Sunis regard the Shias as *impious* heretics." Matthew Arnold, *Essays in Criticism*

**implacable** "It seemed folly for this young man to hope to create a self-supporting farm in such an *implacable* environment." Leland Stowe, *Crusoe of Lonesome Lake*

**implored** "No beggars *implored* Scrooge to bestow a trifle, no children asked him what it was o'clock." Charles Dickens, *A Christmas Carol*

**importuned** "Many businessmen were *importuned* to come to Washington." John McDonald, *On Capitol Hill*

**impresario** "He was an egregious *impresario* of letters who kept a squad of writers churning out copy marketed under his signature." C. J. Rolo, *No Business Like Show Business* [adapted]

**impromptu** "At an *impromptu* airport news conference, Gov. Bush declined to respond directly to questions about his experience with drugs." Associated Press Report, "Next Question, Please," 6/5/99

**imprudent** "We are not so *imprudent* as to destroy the bees that work for us." Robert Tanner, *Principles of Agriculture*

**impunity** "Swaraj means that not a single Hindu or Mussulman shall for a moment crush with *impunity* meek Hindus or

Mussulmans." Mohandas K. Gandhi, "The Untouchables"

**inadvertently** "In our report on NASCAR RACING, we *inadvertently* attributed a quote to Doris O'Bryant." Correction made by *TIME* editors, 6/21/99

**inane** "When left with nothing to talk about, people resort to *inane* remarks about the weather." Lawrence Kaminer, "A World of Strangers"

**inanimate** "We assumed that the *inanimate* body in the rubble was dead but the dog, trained to distinguish between live and dead bodies, knew better." Stephen Kinzer, "Turkish Earthquake Relief," *New York Times*, 8/21/99

**incapacitated** "His searing empathy for the parents of *incapacitated* clients is a product of the still-raw pain over the 1980 suicide of his younger brother." Jan Hoffman, "Public Lives," *New York Times*, 6/18/99

**inchoate** "The general plan is *inchoate* and incoherent and the particular treatments disconnected." Hillary Corke, *Global Economy*

**incipient** "As columnist Jack Anderson was about to write about the Secretary of State's *incipient* departure, Al Haig panicked." William Safire, "On Language," *New York Times*, 6/20/99

**incisive** "Your hands are keen, your mind *incisive*, your sensitivity deep, your vision well honed." Thomas A. Dooley, "To a Young Doctor"

**inclement** "The *inclement* weather that has given us fits recently is over, and I'm looking for blue skies for all of next week." Weather forecast from ABC's Sam Champion, Eyewitness News, 6/23/99

**incoherent** "So seldom do editors get what they think they want that they tend to become *incoherent* in their insistent repetition of their needs." Jerome Weidman, "Back Talk"

**incompatible** "Once men tried to reach heaven by building a tower, and I made their formats *incompatible*." Garrison Keillor, "Faith at the Speed of Light," *TIME*, 6/14/99

**incongruous** "He was clothed with tatters of old ship's canvas: and this extraordinary patchwork was held together by a system of various and *incongruous* fastenings." Robert Louis Stevenson, *Treasure Island*

**incontrovertible** "The Wilsons lived in a universe of words linked into an *incontrovertible* firmament by two centuries of Calvinist divines." John Dos Passos, *U.S.A.*

**incredulous** "The Nazi war on cancer?—other readers may be as *incredulous* as I was when this book came to my attention." Michael Sherry, *New York Times*, 5/23/99

**incumbent** "As a Muslim, the Director of Interfaith Affairs for the Islamic Center said that it is *incumbent* on him to actively engage others in the service of Allah." Jioni Palmer, "Vigil to Address Growing Violence," *Newsday*, 10/10/99

**indict** "You can't *indict* a whole nation, particularly on such vague grounds as these were." Robert M. Coates, "The Law"

**indifference** "David sees Ham who, although now shows *indifference* to life, swims out to save people from a shipwreck." Holly Hughes, *Barron's Book Notes*, *David Copperfield* by Charles Dickens

**indigenous** "A MacArthur Foundation grant was given to Dennis A. Moore for helping to preserve the language and culture of *indigenous* groups in Brazil." Announcement of MacArthur Grants, 6/23/99

# PANORAMA OF WORDS

**indigent** "The bill would make modest improvements in the way that counsel is provided for *indigent* defendants." Bob Herbert, "Defending the Status Quo," *New York Times*, 6/17/99

**indiscriminate** "The *indiscriminate* spraying of pesticides add a new chapter, a new kind of havoc." Rachel Carson, *Silent Spring*

**indoctrinated** "Teachers have *indoctrinated* students in practical subjects like home ec." Jodie Morse, "Hitched in Home Room," *TIME*, 6/21/99

**indolent** "This *indolent* weather turns a student's thoughts toward last-minute truancy." Darcy Frey, "The Last Shot"

**inebriated** "Red Skelton's *inebriated* clown who was guzzling Smuggler's Gin is one of the all-time great comedy sketches." Paul De Simone, "They Made Us Laugh" [adapted]

**ineffectual** "Medicare officials told the White House that the proposed drug plan is unrealistic and would be *ineffectual*." Robert Pear, "Drug Plan Worries Democrats," *New York Times*, 6/25/99

**inert** "The Japanese drifted *inert* in his life jacket watching 449 approach until the bow crossed in front of him." Robert J. Donovan, *PT 109*

**inevitable** "The 'High Occupancy Vehicle' lanes were an attempt to avoid the otherwise *inevitable* traffic delays on the Expressway." *Newsday*, 9/23/99

**inexorably** "Note that it is all in one long sentence, developing *inexorably* like the slow decay of our lives." Clifton Fadiman, "They Have Their Exits and Their Entrances"

**infallible** "He had an *infallible* ear for the way people spoke, and he imitated them in his writing." *Reader's Encyclopedia*

**infamous** "The unsubstantiated computer rumors for which the Internet is *infamous* began flowing within hours of the arrival of Jan. 1 in Asia." Barnaby Feder, "Internet's Cheering Squad Nervously Watches Clock," *New York Times*, 1/1/00

**infraction** "Order cannot be secured through fear of punishment for an *infraction* against a political entity." Supreme Court Justice William Brennan, decision,10/64

**ingratiate** "This tax was abolished by Richard III to *ingratiate* himself with the people." Sir Francis Bacon, *Henry VII*

**inherent** "Harvey lacked graduate degrees but his *inherent* knowledge of human nature enabled him to be successful as a personnel manager." "Rungs on the Corporate Ladder," American Management Association brochure

**inhibition** "With all this '*inhibition*' stuff and Freudian approach and 'group play,' you get the distinct impression that people are actually afraid of their kids." William Michelfelder, *The Fun of Doing Nothing*

**iniquity** "I lack *iniquity* Sometime to do me service." William Shakespeare, *Othello*

**initiate** "The Russian army seems ready to *initiate* a new offensive against the defenders of the capital of Chechnya." *New York Post*, 1/10/00

**innate** "Nothing makes the weak strong or the fearful brave as much as our bodies' *innate* drive to stay alive." William Safire, "Why Die?," *New York Times*, 1/1/00

**innocuous** "Howell's seemingly *innocuous* remark about Tanya's footware led to a torrent of curses from the petite brunette." George Sokolsky, "Very Thin Ice"

**inordinate** "Was it, perhaps, because his back had broken under his *inordinate* burden?" I. L. Peretz, "Buntcheh the Silent"

**insatiable** "One needs an *insatiable* curiosity to succeed in the new technical worldwide spread of information." Jared Diamond, "Guns, Germs, and Steel"

**insidious** "For them, civilization is an *insidious* but no less sure and deadly poison." Hernando Bates, *Central America*

**integral** "Let Office 2000 be an *integral* part of your productivity tools." Newspaper ad for Microsoft Office 2000

**interjected** "The accountant *interjected*, saying that you can buy a better house in New Jersey than on Long Island for the same money." Ken Moritsugu, "Nowhere to Build," *Newsday*, 6/25/99

**interlopers** "Indeed, the magazine managers are treated as foreign *interlopers*." Michael Woolf, "Tribune and Tribulation," *New York*, 7/5/99

**interminably** "In his clean white shirt and blue jeans, with one hand resting carelessly on the black box, he seemed very proper and important as he talked *interminably* to Mr. Graves and the Martins." Shirley Jackson, "The Lottery"

**internecine** "Eight thousand zealots stabbed each other in *internecine* massacre." L. H. Farrar, *Early Christians*

**interrogate** "The District Attorney of Nassau County is set to *interrogate* a Malverne police officer who was arrested on shoplifting charges." Associated Press report, *New York Times*, 8/20/99

**intimidate** "New language could target loiterers with no apparent purpose other than to *intimidate* others from entering those areas." Margaret Hornblower, "Ending the Roundups," *TIME*, 6/21/99

**intrepid** "Scientists and support staff began celebrating the new year along with a planeload of tourists and seven *intrepid* skiers." Malcolm Browne, "Absence of Midnight Doesn't Darken Spirits," *New York Times*, 1/1/00

**intrinsic** "We appear to have lost the belief that honesty is an *intrinsic* aspect of political leadership." Editorial, *Christian Science Monitor*, 5/17/98

**introspective** "All had the thin, narrow faces and large, wide-open eyes—*introspective* eyes." Ivan Cankar, "Children and Old Folk"

**inundated** "We do know that the moon's surface has not been eroded by wind or rain or ice or snow and has not been *inundated* by oceans, lakes or rivers." Lee A. DuBridge, "Sense and Nonsense About Space"

**invalidate** "Some Reagan and Bush appointees have proved far too willing to *invalidate* decisions made by Congress and the Executive branch." Cass R. Sunstein, *New York Times*, 6/2/99

**invective** "I watched him walk into the clubhouse, kick a bench and break a toe, never once stopping the flow of *invective*." Jack Altshul, "Why Should the Other Guy Beat Me?"

**inveighed** "The County Executive *inveighed* against scofflaws who owe a total of $60 million." Television news broadcast, CBS, 6/23/99

**inveterate** "The *inveterate* Boston Red Sox fan faces seemingly endless disappointment." Peter Balakian, "Black Dogs of Fate"

# PANORAMA OF WORDS

**inviolable** "The coach broke an *inviolable* rule by striking one of his players." Don DeLillo, *End Zone*

**irascible** "He became so *irascible* that within six months he lost his wife and half of his office staff." Herman Wouk, *Don't Stop the Carnival*

**irate** "I got *irate* because people have been yelling at me my whole life." Olivia Winslow, "Cop Tells of a Confession," *Newsday*, 6/23/99

**irrational** "He became *irrational* and threatened to commit suicide." Darcy Frey, "The Last Shot"

**irrelevant** "What has existed in the past seems to him not only not authoritative, but *irrelevant*, inferior, and outworn." George Santayana, *Character and Opinion in the United States*

**itinerant** "Hamlet greeted the group of *itinerant* actors and made them part of a plan to trap Claudius." *Barron's Educational Series, Book Notes*

**jaunty** "The cadet was very trim in his red breeches and blue tunic, his white gloves spotless, his white cockade *jaunty*, his heart in his mouth." Alexander Woolcott, "Entrance Fee"

**jeopardized** "Cancellation of the event would have *jeopardized* the financial survival of the organization." Nat Hentoff, "Picket Lines are Labor's Free Speech," *Village Voice*, 6/15/99

**jettison** "He refused to *jettison* any of the manners and behavior that made him seem so odd." William Connor, *Daily Mirror*, London, 1956

**jocose** "He caught the sound of *jocose* talk and ringing laughter from behind the hedges." George Eliot, *Adam Bede*

**jostled** "When the squeege man *jostled* him, the police officer said that he feared for his life." Kit Roane, "Squeege Man Scared Him," *New York Times*, 6/25/99

**jubilant** "When he finally reached Boston, he received a *jubilant* welcome." Keith Ayling, "Race Around the World"

**jurisdiction** "Lee's *jurisdiction* included the monitoring of boxing within New Jersey." Timothy Smith, "A Sport's Credibility," *New York Times*, 6/20/99

**juxtaposed** "Theatrical vignettes are *juxtaposed* through alternating verses in clever boy-girl counterpoint." "Hot 'N Cole," *Newsday*, 6/4/99

**labyrinth** "He himself was so lost in the *labyrinth* of his own unquiet thoughts that I did not exist." Daphne Du Maurier, *Rebecca*

**lacerations** "He pressed only the already tired horse at such speed that his spurs made *lacerations* in its sides, and at last the poor animal died." Honore De Balzac, *A Passion in the Desert*

**lackluster** "The major reason for the *lackluster* look in their eyes was their discovery it is now possible to drive across the face of the nation without feeling you've been anywhere or that you've done anything." John Keats, "The Call of the Open Road"

**laconic** "The dialogue is clipped, *laconic*, understated to convey simmering underneath." John Simon, "The Worst Noël," *New York*, 6/21/99

**lampoon** "Many new TV shows succeed because they *lampoon* the behavior of teenagers." John Leonard, *New York*, 10/15/97

**landmarks** "The remarkable trees formed good *landmarks* by which the place might easily be found again." Washington Irving, "The Devil and Tom Walker"

**largess** "A *largess* universal like the sun, His liberal eye doth give to every one." William Shakespeare, *Henry IV*

**lassitude** "To poets it's vernal *lassitude* but to us it's simply spring fever." Brochure, Fort Lauderdale Chamber of Commerce

**latent** "All our *latent* strength was now alive." Winston Churchill, *Their Finest Hour*

**laudable** "American historians, in their eagerness to present facts and their *laudable* anxiety to tell the truth, have neglected the literary aspects of their craft." Samuel Eliot Morrison, *By Land and by Sea*

**lax** "The fact that his employer was *lax* on this score was one of many things that he had to condone." Henry James, "Brooksmith"

**legerdemain** "Federal investigators pursuing money-laundering schemes are concerned with alleged acts of *legerdemain* by Russian banks." Tim L. O'Brien, "Bank in Laundering Inquiry," *New York Times*, 8/20/99

**legion** "Though not Hollywood handsome, Tommy's success with the fair sex was *legion*." Janet Murphy, "Babylon on the Hudson"

**lethal** "By evening we couldn't even get any more people indoors where they would have had some protection from the *lethal* fallout." Florence Moog, "The Bombing of St. Louis"

**lethargic** "Ricky Henderson's *lethargic* stroll toward second base led the sports reporters to blast him in yesterday's papers." Ralph Kiner, baseball announcer, Fox Sports News, 10/4/99

**levity** "There was something about the company's president that made *levity* seem out of place." Lloyd Sperling, *A Boiler Room Operation*

**libel** "Issues such as freedom of speech and *libel* are going to have to be rethought as the Internet makes everyone a potential publisher in cyberspace." Thomas L. Friedman, "Boston E-Party," *New York Times*, 1/1/00

**liquidation** "Hiding the forty-six comrades who were scheduled for *liquidation* became much easier." David Hackett, *The Buchenwald Report*

**lithe** "Tasteless headlines screamed 'Newtie's Cutie' to describe the *lithe* hymn-singing young staff member who inexplicably fell for her portly Newt." Robert Reno, "Political Garbage," *Newsday*, 8/19/99

**livid** "*Livid* with anger, the poster boy for road rage jumped out of his red convertible and came running toward us." Letter to the Editor, "Big Road Hazard," *Newsday*, 8/19/99

**loath** "Still I am *loath* simply to join the conspiracy." "The Happy-Parents Conspiracy," *New York Times*, 5/23/99

**loathing** "He had braced himself not to become entangled in her *loathing* for him." Phillip Roth, *American Pastoral*

**longevity** "The *longevity* of metal parts is increased by this new process." Report, General Motors Corporation

**lucrative** "Very quickly it became a surprisingly *lucrative* property." David McCullough, *The Great Bridge*

**lugubrious** "*Lugubrious* notices on the passing of old friends were a feature of the local paper." *TIME*, 8/20/99

# PANORAMA OF WORDS

**lurid** "We thought the rookie's tale was too *lurid* to be believed, but it turned out to be true." Chuck Cavanna, *Life in the Minors*

**lush** "Can one run for political office without the promise of *lush* campaign contributions from many sources?" "Steve Forbes; In His Own Debt," *Parade*, 9/15/99

**Machiavellian** "Is there any clearer example of *Machiavellian* plotting than that of Iago in 'Othello'?" John Simon, *Reverse Angle*

**magnanimous** "There was no way he was going to be *magnanimous* and share this prized baseball with anyone who claimed a share of the glory." Don DeLillo, *Underworld*

**maimed** "Films in which characters are *maimed* or destroyed seem to be most popular with today's youngsters." Harold Owen, Jr., "The Motion Picture"

**maladjusted** "The natural assumption is that the teenage killers at Columbine H.S. were *maladjusted* youngsters but some neighbors denied that." Letters to the Editor, *Washington Post*, 7/14/99

**malady** "Homesickness can be a disease as trivial as a slight cold or it can be a deadly *malady*." Z. Libin, "A Sign of Summer"

**malevolent** "Our military action against the *malevolent* head of the Serbian government has finally ended." *Newsweek*, 4/8/99

**malign** "His chosen weapon is the verbal hand grenade by which he can outrage and *malign*." Kenneth Tynan, "On Don Rickles," *New Yorker*, 2/20/78

**malignant** "The wailing chorus turned into a *malignant* clamor that swirled into my ears like an icy breeze." Kenneth Roberts, *Oliver Wiswell*

**malleable** "Is the mayor able to change from an apparently rigid personality to one more *malleable* to differences?" Alec Kuczynski, "The Mayor's Makeover," *New York Times Magazine*, 8/1/99

**malnutrition** "The children of the Albanian refugees are suffering from *malnutrition*, and they need our help." Red Cross Appeal for Funds

**mammoth** "She began to repair the ravages made by generosity added to love—a tremendous task, dear friends—a *mammoth* task." O. Henry, "The Gift of the Magi"

**mandate** "With a federal *mandate* to convert to digital broadcasting by 2003, public TV stations are facing large capital expenditures." Ellis Bromberg, "Federal Money Vital to Progress of PBS," *The News Gazette*, Champaign-Urbana, 10/21/99

**manifest** "English is one of the great borrowing languages, more *manifest* in the origin of so many of our words." Bill Bryson, *Mother Tongue*

**manifold** "China's Xinhua News Agency treated *manifold* claims of procedural error with disbelief." "Trying to Build Bridges in China," *TIME*, 6/28/99

**martinet** "The prospect of having to talk to Sheila's principal, a real *martinet*, made him nervous, but he steeled himself to do it." John Yount, "The Trapper's Last Shot"

**masticate** "Trying to *masticate* a huge hamburger with an open mouth is a no-no." Advice from Ms. Manners, syndicated columnist, 6/4/98

**mastiffs** "That island of England breeds very valiant creatures; their *mastiffs* are of unmatchable courage." William Shakespeare, *Henry V*

**materialism** "Democracy always makes for *materialism*, because the only kind of equality that you can guarantee to a whole people is physical." Katherine F. Gerould, *Modes and Morals*

**matrons** "For ladies they had the family of the American consul and a nice bevy of English girls and *matrons*, perhaps Lady Hamilton herself." Edward Everett Hale, *The Man Without a Country*

**maudlin** "Uncle Billy passed rapidly into a state of stupor, the Duchess became *maudlin*, and Mother Shipton snored." Bret Harte, "The Outcasts of Poker Flat"

**megalomania** "Charlie desperately wanted Armaxco to lease space in what so far was the worst mistake of his career, the soaring monster that his *megalomania* led him to call Croker Concourse." Tom Wolfe, *A Man in Full*

**mendacious** "Hillary joined in efforts to dismiss as *mendacious* tarts all the women who claimed to have been involved with her husband." Maureen Dowd, "The Boy Can't Help It," *New York Times*, 8/4/99

**menial** "It is difficult to visualize the numbers of *menial* laborers required to build the famous Egyptian pyramids." E. A. Wallis Budge, *The Mummy*

**mentor** "To break into the political life of South Africa, one needed a highly placed *mentor*." Nadine Gordimer, *Face to Face*

**mercenary** "We all like money . . . but Dickens surpassed most in a *mercenary* approach to his writings." G. K. Chesterton, *Charles Dickens*

**metamorphosis** "For nearly a year, the dauber, undergoing *metamorphosis*, inhabits its silken dung-stoppered cocoon inside the mud cell." Alan Devoe, "The Mad Dauber"

**meticulous** "Even later, in 1992, Barnstead's *meticulous* records allowed

researchers to put names on six previously unidentified Titanic survivors." "Titanic and Halifax," The Nova Scotia Museum

**mien** "He had the *mien* of a man who has been everywhere and through everything." Arnold Bennett, *The Old Wives Tale*

**milieu** "In the *milieu* of a heated baseball championship contest, tickets are being sold at highly inflated prices." *New York Post*, 10/10/99

**modified** "Some schools claimed that the standard test was a lot harder than a *modified* version." Ching-Cheng Ni, "Fewer Rumbles on Earth Test," *Newsday*, 6/23/99

**mollify** "The mayor attempted to *mollify* his critics by pointing to the increased safety in the city." *New York Daily News*, 8/15/99

**monolithic** "Gertrude Stein was a stolid, heavy presence, *monolithic*, unladylike." Liz Smith, "When Love Was the Adventure," *TIME*, 6/14/99

**moribund** "After being *moribund* for years, interest in electric automobiles has revived." *Car and Driver*, 6/97

**mortality** "Socrates loves talk of fundamental things, of justice and virtue and wisdom and love and *mortality*." Hermann Hagedorn, *Socrates—His Life*

**mortify** "The comparisons between her sister's beauty and her own no longer would *mortify* her." Jane Austen, *Pride and Prejudice*

**motivate** "The loss of our star quarterback seemed to *motivate* the team to play even harder." Bill Parcells quoted in *Sports Illustrated*, 9/12/98

**mundane** "Why bother with *mundane* musings when you can sit on the lawn and build

# PANORAMA OF WORDS

cities out of grass clippings?" Enid Nemy, "The World is Her Cloister," *New York Times*, 6/20/99

**munificent** "His *munificent* gift will enable us to place computers in all the elementary schools." *Newsday*, 6/20/98

**murky** "Mud dumping from the bottom of Long Island has created a *murky* picture." "Fishermen's Woes," *Newsday*, 6/22/99

**myriad** "Genius is not born with sight, but blind: it is influenced by a *myriad* of stimulating exterior circumstances." Mark Twain, "Saint Joan of Arc"

**nadir** "He knew he had reached the *nadir* of his baseball career when they sent him to a minor league team." Roger Kahn, *The Boys of Summer*

**naïve** "Woodrow Wilson was *naïve* to believe Yugoslavia could be formed after World War I." Letter to the Editor, *New Yorker*, 6/26/99

**nascent** "The once *nascent* Women's National Basketball Association has arrived and is healthy and prosperous." *New York Times*, 7/17/99

**nebulous** "There is a *nebulous* line between confidence and over-confidence." Editorial, *Wall Street Journal*, 4/8/99

**nefarious** "A *nefarious* employee can still download secret weapons information to a tape, put it in his pocket and walk out the door." William Safire, "Culture of Arrogance," *New York Times*, 6/17/99

**negligible** "These politicians have voted themselves a big pay raise for the *negligible* amount of work they do." *The Queens Tribune*, 8/6/98

**nepotism** "Political allies and family members filled government jobs as *nepotism* flourished." Paul Alter, *This Windy City*

**nettled** "He was pretty well *nettled* by this time, and he stood in front of a bureau mirror, brushing his hair with a pair of military brushes." James Thurber, "More Alarms at Night"

**neurotic** "We shall lose all our power to cope with our problem if we allow ourselves to become a stagnant, *neurotic*, frightened and suspicious people." Walter Lippmann, "The Nuclear Age"

**neutralize** "The quinine that can *neutralize* his venom is called courage." Elmer Davis, *But We Were Born Free*

**nirvana** "*Nirvana* is in putting your child to sleep, and in writing the last line of your poem." Kahlil Gilbran, *Sand and Foam*

**noisome** "The *noisome* conditions in the refugee camps were a disgrace and a danger." *Newsday*, 8/7/99

**nomadic** After buying the big trailer, they spent a *nomadic* year visiting national parks out west." "On the Road Again," *Travel Ideas International*

**nominal** "As the *nominal* head of his party, the governor was courted by all the Sunday morning talk shows." Archer Karnes, "Politics and Poker"

**nondescript** "Jane Austen can picture ordinary, commonplace and *nondescript* characters in ways denied to me." Walter Scott, *Journal, 1826*

**nonentity** "With sufficient financial backing, almost any political *nonentity* could become a national contender." *Washington Post*, 6/15/98

**nostalgia** "The various objects one picks up just before leaving a foreign country are apt to acquire an extraordinary souvenir-value, giving one a foretaste of distance and *nostalgia*." Corrado Alvaro, "The Ruby"

**nuance** "With Minnie Driver adroitly mining each *nuance* of social primness, Jane is the first Disney cartoon heroine to provide her own comic relief." Richard Corliss, "Him Tarzan, Him Great," *TIME*, 6/14/99

**nullify** "Allowing our parks to decay is a sure way to *nullify* the beauty given to us by nature." Freeman Tilden, *The National Parks*

**nurtured** "The Telecommunications Act of 1996 introduced competition that has *nurtured* demand for communications generally and for Internet service specifically." Seth Schessel, "A Chance to Become Really Big," *New York Times*, 6/15/99

**nutritive** "They searched for anything that had *nutritive* value, but often found nothing." "The Irish Famine," *Harpers*, 5/73

**obese** "The rush to lose weight by unproven methods often leads to complications for *obese* people." *Johns Hopkins Health Letter*, Summer 1997

**obliterate** "They went out to survey the land for a possible railroad, but met with Indians on the warpath and were *obliterated*." Freeman Tilden, *The National Parks* [adapted]

**obloquy** "Hitler and his Nazis showed how evil a conspiracy could be which was aimed at destroying a race by exposing it to contempt, derision, and *obloquy*." Supreme Court Justice William O. Douglas, decision, 10/52

**obscure** "This book has serious purpose even if many will find that purpose *obscure*." Decision of Supreme Judicial Court of Massachusetts, 11/62

**obsequious** "and the survivor bound In filial obligation for some term To do *obsequious* sorrow." William Shakespeare, *Hamlet*

**obsess** "To *obsess* over acquisitions is especially damaging to human felicity." Llewelyn Powys, *Earth Memories*

**obsolescence** "After five centuries of *obsolescence*, Roman numerals still exert a peculiar fascination over the inquiring mind." Isaac Asimov, "Nothing Counts"

**obviate** "Modest pre-emptive acting can *obviate* the need for more drastic actions at a later date that could destabilize the economy." Alan Greenspan, quoted in *New Jersey Star Ledger*, 5/6/99

**occult** "Somehow, horror films have changed from one main figure who threatens a town or young women, to *occult* spirits that take over a normal human for unknown reasons." Pauline Kael, *I Lost It at the Movies*

**octogenarian** "*Octogenarian* film and stage director Elia Kazan received a mixed reception when he came up to collect his Lifetime Achievement Award." Associated Press report, 4/7/98

**ominous** "There was a Sabbath lull in the air, which, in a settlement unused to Sabbath influences, looked *ominous*." Bret Harte, "The Outcasts of Poker Flat"

**omnipotent** "In those comic strips there was always a cruel and *omnipotent* villain." Letter, *New York Times*, 9/13/99

**omnivorous** "He became an *omnivorous* reader of the classics." T. S. Lovering, *Child Prodigies*

**opprobrium** "General Sherman is still viewed with *opprobrium* in these parts of the South he once destroyed." Edmund Wilson, *Patriotic Gore*

**opulent** "Poirot followed him, looking with appreciation at such works of art as were of

# PANORAMA OF WORDS

an *opulent* and florid nature." Agatha Christie, "The Dream"

**originated** "The early Egyptian rulers, in order to stop the practice of cannibalism, *originated* the method that protected the dead—mummification." E. A. Wallis Budge, *The Mummy*

**ostensibly** "The race was *ostensibly* to test the reliability of the automobiles." Keith Ayling, *The Race Around the World*

**ostentatious** "He affected simplicity, partly because he was ugly, but more because being *ostentatious* might have irritated those of whom he always spoke of as 'my fellow citizens.' " Emil Ludwig, *Michelangelo*

**oust** "Politics will still exist as in the Republican campaign to *oust* Bill Clinton." James Pinkerton, "Mediocre Pols," *Newsday*, 6/17/99

**overt** "It is peculiarly shocking that Brutus practices *overt* self-deception." Harold Bloom, *Shakespeare*

**pall** "A *pall* had descended upon Mr. Timberlake, and I understood why he did not talk to me about the origin of evil." V. S. Pritchett, "The Saint"

**palliate** "Reducing the testosterone would *palliate* the cancer, the oncologist believed, but it wouldn't be a cure." Dr. Mervyn Elliot, "Medicine in the News"

**paltry** "Marvin was baffled by the *paltry* amount of money the widow was asking for her husband's elegant Rolls Royce." Barnett Lesser, "One Man's Will"

**panaceas** "Mrs. Clinton said that she was in Rochester to listen and learn not to offer *panaceas* for all civic problems." Associated Press report, "Pre-Campaign Strategy," 9/9/99

**pandemonium** "Then, summoning the wild courage of despair, in *pandemonium*, a throng of revellers at once threw themselves into the black apartment." Edgar Allan Poe, "The Masque of the Red Death"

**parable** "When I had trouble keeping the kindergarten class quiet, I found that telling them a *parable* (the tortoise and the hare, for example) would get their undivided attention." Lana L. Grossberg, *A Teacher's True Confessions*

**paradox** "Here was a *paradox* like the stellar universe that fitted one's mental faults." Henry Adams, *The Education of Henry Adams*

**paragon** "An angel! or, if not An earthly *paragon!*" William Shakespeare, *Cymbeline*

**paramount** "For him, winning was *paramount*; coming in second meant he had swum a poor race." Len Sussman, "Born to Swim"

**pariahs** "Apart from the other castes were the outcasts: India's untouchables, or *pariahs*." Barbara Walker, *Women's Encyclopedia*

**paroxysms** "The coughing did not even come out in *paroxysms*, but was just a feeble, dreadful welling up of the juices of organic dissolution." Thomas Mann, *The Magic Mountain*

**parsimonious** "His *parsimonious* thrift was relieved by a few generous impulses." V. L. Parrington, *Main Currents in American Thought*

**passé** "Everything old is new again is the theme for the designer's adoption of *passé* styles and making them fashionable again." Sophia Leguizamo, "New From Milan"

**pathetic** "He is the latest loser trying to solve his *pathetic* life behind a gun." Editorial, *New York Post*, 7/30/99

**paucity** "In the dictator's best-case scenario, he can hope for continuing control, thanks to a *paucity* of opponents." Massimo Calabresi, "Is This the End for Milosevic?," *TIME*, 6/21/99

**pecuniary** "The most unpleasant thing of all was that his *pecuniary* interests should enter into the question of his reconciliation with his wife." Leo Tolstoy, *Anna Karenina*

**pedagogue** "He is neither bandit nor *pedagogue*, but, like myself a broken soldier, retired on half pay for some years." Stephen Vincent Benet, "The Curfew Tolls"

**penance** "I have done *penance* for condemning Love, Whose high imperious thoughts have punished me With bitter fasts, with penitential groans." William Shakespeare, *The Two Gentlemen of Verona*

**penchant** "Annabel had a *penchant* for silver fox coats but Midge said they were common." Dorothy Parker, "The Standard of Living"

**penitent** "When father strode into the coal and ice office, he came out, the *penitent* clerk with him, promising to deliver a block of ice in time for dinner." Clarence Day, *Life with Father*

**pensive** "It was only when he found himself alone in his bedroom in a *pensive* mood that he was able to grapple seriously with his memories of the occurrence." H. G. Wells, *The Man Who Could Work Miracles*

**penury** "Afflicted by *penury*, it appeared that Putois had joined a gang of thieves who were prowling the countryside." Anatole France, "Putois"

**perceive** "The subjects, as you *perceive*, were alarming but very agreeable." Anton Chekhov, "A Slander"

**peregrination** "Each step he took represented an inward *peregrination*." Gretel Ehrlich, "On the Road With God's Fool"

**peremptory** "Mr. Greenspan encouraged his fellow Federal Reserve Board members today to undertake a *peremptory* attack against inflation." Reuters, "Financial News Letter," 3/99

**perfidious** "Alfred E. Ricks was the *perfidious* toad's designation who sold worthless shares in the Blue Gopher Mine." O. Henry, "The Man Higher Up"

**perfunctory** "Doc Martindale made a *perfunctory* examination and told Eli there was nothing to worry about." MacKinlay Kantor, "The Grave Grass Quivers"

**permeated** "The play is *permeated* with scriptural imagery, notably a Last Supper." Robert Brustein, *New Republic*, 6/7/99

**pernicious** "This chapter exposes a *pernicious* obstacle to students and teachers engaging in serious work together." Robert L. Fried, *The Passionate Teacher*

**perpetrated** "Thanks to Mr. DeLay, we learn that violence *perpetrated* by gun owners is really the product of larger forces." Editorial, "Mr. DeLay's Power Play," *New York Times*, 6/20/99

**perpetuate** "The laws would often do no more than *perpetuate* a legislator's acts of injustice." Jean-Jacques Rousseau, *The Social Contract*

**persevered** "The Knicks *persevered* as first Patrick Ewing and then Johnson went down with injuries." George Vecsey, "Sports of the Times," *New York Times*, 6/22/99

# PANORAMA OF WORDS

**perspicacious** "Nobody deserves the Lifetime Achievement Award more than Army Archerd, who is not only *perspicacious*, but a gentleman as well." Liz Smith, *Newsday*, 6/2/99

**pertinent** "What seems *pertinent* is to observe that jazz gravitated toward a particular kind of environment in which its existence was probable." Arnold Sungaard, *Jazz, Hot and Cold*

**peruse** "Stopping to *peruse* her mail, Raven didn't notice that the front door was ajar." Dolores Kent, *Instant Gratification*

**perverse** "There is something contemptible in the prospect of a number of petty states with the appearance only of union, jarring, jealous, and *perverse*." Alexander Hamilton, speech, 1782

**pesky** "Oranges down there is like a young man's whiskers; you enjoy them at first, but they get to be a *pesky* nuisance." Ring W. Lardner, "The Golden Honeymoon"

**phenomenon** "This *phenomenon* is characterized by a temporary reversal of the normal atmospheric conditions, in which the air near the earth is warmer than the air higher up." Berton Roueché, "The Fog"

**phlegmatic** "Duncan had a *phlegmatic* fourth quarter, dooming the Spurs' opportunity to humble the New York Knicks." TV announcer, NBA Finals, 6/22/99

**phobia** "My *phobia* was such that the slightest touch produced twinges of pain." Guy De Maupassant, "Looking Back"

**pinnacle** "Their little barber-shop quartet reached the *pinnacle* of their career with a first-place finish on Major Bowes' 'Amateur Hour.'" David and Marge Buchanan, "No Business Like You Know What"

**pique** "In a fit of *pique* he raised his pistol to take aim at me but Masha threw herself at his feet." Aleksandr Pushkin, "The Shot"

**pittance** "To be paid a mere *pittance* and yet to be suspected of theft; never in her life had she been subjected to such an outrage." Anton Chekhov, "An Upheaval"

**placards** "Yet a mile away at the ultra-orthodox Mea Shearim neighborhood, wall *placards* now warn residents not to have Internet-linked computers in their homes." Thomas Friedman, "All in the Family," *New York Times*, 6/22/99

**plaintiff** "When the attorney for the palsied *plaintiff* finished, there wasn't a dry eye in the courtroom." Rose Axelsohn, "The Defense Rests" [adapted]

**platitudes** "The topic was, 'What Is Life?' and the students labored at it busily with their *platitudes*." Philip Roth, *American Pastoral*

**plethora** "SUFFERERS CONFRONT A *PLETHORA* OF POLLEN" Headline, *New York Times*, 6/5/99

**plight** "I had the sense that his loneliness was not merely the result of his personal *plight*." Edith Wharton, *Ethan Frome*

**poignant** "Keen, *poignant* agonies seemed to shoot from his neck downward through every fiber of his body and limbs." Ambrose Bierce, "An Occurrence at Owl Creek Bridge"

**pondered** "As I made my way back, I *pondered* the significance of what I'd seen." Nicholas Kristof, "1492: The Prequel"

**potent** "Those huge differences in income found in our society must have *potent* causes." Jared Diamond, *Guns, Germs, and Steel*

# PANORAMA OF WORDS

**potentates** "The racing season at Saratoga invited all manner of society—from *potentates* to paupers." Lanny Richards, "They're Off!"

**potential** "We realized that this system had worked because the *potential* targets were so many that the Germans could not get a definite idea of where we would strike." Ewen Montagu, *The Man Who Never Was*

**potpourri** "A *potpourri* of fresh fruits and cool cottage cheese make for a delicious lunch treat when the temperatures rise into the high 90s." Martha Stewart, CBS News, 5/23/98

**pragmatic** "His conservative approach to investing has made millions of dollars for those who share Warren Buffet's *pragmatic* philosophy." "Master of Berkshire-Hathaway," Profile of Warren Buffet, *New York Times*

**precedent** "One can imagine a time when the voters ignore *precedent* and elect a woman to the office of President of the United States." Barbara Walker, *The Women's Encyclopedia*

**precipitate** "The weight of a finger might *precipitate* the tragedy, hurl him at once into the dim, gray unknown." Stephen Crane, "An Episode of War"

**precluded** "I would be avenged; this was a point definitely settled—but the very definitiveness with which it was resolved *precluded* the idea of risk." Edgar Allan Poe, "The Cask of Amontillado"

**precocious** "Pediatricians interviewed this week were somewhat divided on the value of TV viewing by *precocious* children." Lawrie Miflin, "Tough Rules for TV," *New York Times*, 8/4/99

**prelude** "Bounderby's *prelude* to his main point was very well received by Mrs. Sparsit

who said, 'Very sagacious indeed, sir.'" Charles Dickens, *Hard Times*

**premise** "That train of reasoning has all the various parts and terms—its major *premise* and its conclusion." T. H. Huxley, "We Are All Scientists"

**premonition** "There seemed to be a gentle stir arising over everything—a very *premonition* of rest and hush and night." Mary Wilkens Freeman, "The New England Nun"

**prerogative** "Governor Pataki exercised his *prerogative* as titular head of the party to endorse Mayor Rudolph Giuliani." Editorial, "Truce Among New York Republicans," *New York Times*, 8/7/99

**prestigious** "He had finally reached his present *prestigious* position of wealth and security, and he felt he was entitled to sit back and enjoy his happiness." Ronald Byron, "Happy Days for Harrison Gumedi"

**pretext** "Our mother had been expressly enjoined by her husband to give Madame Cornouiller some plausible *pretext* for refusing." Anatole France, "Putois"

**prevalent** "On the all-news channels the most *prevalent* images were from a helicopter pursuing the police chase." *New York Post*, 7/30/99

**prevarication** "They must honestly swear to this oath without *prevarication* or reservation." Supreme Court Justice Byron White, speech, 12/1/64

**privations** "It aroused a strong response in our hearts when he told about their sufferings and *privations*." Selma Lagerlöf, *Harvest*

**procrastinated** "Mr. Brooksmith *procrastinated* for several days before accepting my offer." Henry James, "Brooksmith"

357

# PANORAMA OF WORDS

**prodigious** "He knew from the moment he left the ground that it was a *prodigious* jump." Joseph N. Bell, "The Olympics Biggest Winner"

**prodigy** "I grant you Clive—Clive was a *prodigy*, a genius and met the fate of geniuses." Stephen Vincent Benet, "The Curfew Tolls"

**proffer** "Orin came to *proffer* his condolences when, wonder of wonder, he fell in love with the grieving widow." Terence Cavanaugh, "An Ill Wind"

**profligate** "Her innocent appearance had a peculiar attraction for a vicious *profligate*, who had hitherto admired only the coarser types of feminine beauty." Fyodor Dostoyevsky, *The Brothers Käramazov*

**profound** "So why no *profound* works on the need for $660 million in tax credits for companies that burn chicken droppings?" Editorial, "Tax-Cut Favors," *New York Times*, 8/7/99

**profuse** "He offered *profuse* apologies for his show of exasperation, and he volunteered to read to her, something in French." Aldous Huxley, "The Giaconda Smile"

**progeny** "First, let me tell you whom you have condemn'd: Not me begotten of a shepherd swain, But issued from the *progeny* of kings." William Shakespeare, *Henry IV*

**prognostication** "Nay, if an oily palm be not a fruitful *prognostication* I cannot scratch my ear." William Shakespeare, *Antony and Cleopatra*

**prohibition** "The U.S. public is slowly coming around to accepting the idea that a *prohibition* against the easy access to hand guns is inevitable." Roger Rosenblatt, "Get Rid of the Damned Things," *TIME*, 8/9/99

**prolific** "Isaac Asimov was a truly *prolific* writer, seemingly able to complete a book every two weeks." Art Nichols, *Selling Your Manuscript*

**promulgated** "The rules and regulations are *promulgated* for the guidance of administrative employees, bureau heads, and supervisors." "Rules and Regulations for Administrative Employees," NYC Board of Education

**propagate** "The Republican leadership planned to *propagate* their philosophy for a huge tax cut during the summer recess." Wolf Blitzer, CNN Nightly News, 7/14/99

**propensity** "You had a *propensity* for telling simple and professional tales before the war." Joseph Conrad, "The Tale"

**propinquity** "It occurred to him that Varick might be talking at random to relieve the strain of their *propinquity*." Edith Wharton, *The Desert of Man*

**propitious** "Sometime later, I will find a *propitious* ground and bury you there in the same grave." Shen Chunlieh, "In Memory of a Child," 1619

**propriety** "There is a *propriety* and necessity of preventing interference with the course of justice." Supreme Court Justice Oliver Wendell Holmes, decision, 10/28

**proximity** "Stryker had built a small cannery in close *proximity* to the house where the turtles were raised in shallow tanks." Edmund Wilson, "The Man Who Shot Snapping Turtles"

**prudent** "Those who thought the *prudent* thing to do at the end of 1999 was to stay away from flying resulted in the slowest day of the year for every airline." *TIME*, 1/12/00

**pugnacious** "Two *pugnacious* guard dogs in the railyard eliminated the nightly vandalism in a hurry." Lewis Tumulty, "Civic Pride"

**puissant** "The combination of the drugs has become a *puissant* cocktail in the fight against AIDS." Medical report, CBS News, 9/20/98

**pungent** "The *pungent* aroma of the cream puffs told Sadie that the man from Goobers had arrived." Katherine Mansfield, "The Garden Party"

**puny** "I have said that I am a weak and *puny* man, and you will have proof of that directly." Max Beerbohm, "A. V. Laidler"

**qualms** "The manager had *qualms* about allowing him to continue playing with an injured hand." *Sports Illustrated*, 6/16/98

**quandary** "New Year's Eve presented a *quandary* for people in China, a country where the observance of non-political Western celebrations is a relatively recent phenomenon." Elizabeth Rosenthal, "Party? What Party?," *New York Times*, 1/1/00

**quarry** "The state troopers had tracked their *quarry* to the thickly wooded area near the crime scene." *Newsday*, 4/10/98

**quell** "He also did not *quell* the speculation surrounding Van Gundy's status as coach." Mike Wise, *New York Times*, 5/25/99

**quip** "The audience screamed and applauded hysterically at every musical number, every *quip*, every little movement on the stage." Liz Smith, *Newsday*, 6/2/99

**rabid** "Politicians avoid the appearance of being *rabid* on issues that seem to be evenly viewed by the voters." Arthur Willner, "Taking Sides"

**raconteur** "As a popular *raconteur*, George Jessel was prized as a speaker at award ceremonies." *The Hollywood Reporter*, 7/18/96

**railed** "He cursed and *railed*, and finally declared he was going to trail the raiders." Zane Grey, *Raiders of the Purple Sage*

**raiment** "No matter what her *raiment*, Marilyn Monroe looked absolutely fabulous on the screen." Billy Wilder quoted by Earl Wilson, *Chicago Tribune*, 2/28/76

**rampant** "What's more curious about the determination to end social promotions is that the practice is far from *rampant*." Romesh Ratnesar, "Held Back," *TIME*, 6/14/99

**rash** "Thou art as *rash* as fire to say That she was false." William Shakespeare, *Othello*

**rationalize** "It is the task of the scientist to *rationalize* the remains of extinct civilizations to discover their histories." Brian Fagan, *Time Detective*

**raucous** "The 1968 Democratic nominating convention in Chicago was the scene of *raucous* confrontations." I. F. Stone, *Weekly Reader*

**razed** "In the gorge, continually *razed* by the clawing wind, he would probably find his other dog." Francisco Coloane, "Cururo . . . Sheep Dog"

**realm** "In all the churches of the *realm* the Blessed Sacrament is exposed night and day, and tall candles are burning for the recovery of the royal child." Alphonse Daudet, "The Death of the Dauphin"

**rebuke** "The defeat of the charter revision was viewed as a *rebuke* of his policies." Editorial, *New York Times*, 11/7/99

**recanted** "The government's key witness in the case *recanted* her testimony, claiming she had been intimidated by prosecutors." Rob Polner, "Set Back for Prosecutors," *New York Post*, 6/23/99

# PANORAMA OF WORDS

**recoil** "It is a gesture of response to my remarks, and it always makes me *recoil* with a laugh." Thomas Mann, "A Man and His Dog"

**recondite** "If it seems too *recondite* for anyone but dwellers in the groves of Academe, one must consider rhyming slang which originated in the underworld." Bergen Evans, "Now Everyone Is Hip About Slang"

**redolent** "The scene—a decrepit classroom, *redolent* of moldy books, and the pencil shavings of generations of boys being ground into the hardwood floor." Jon Robin Baitz, *The Film Society*

**redress** "There has been much discussion about the fairest way to *redress* centuries of discrimination." "A Time to Begin," *Readers Digest*, 5/92

**refute** "The tobacco industry has stopped trying to *refute* the charge that smoking is both dangerous and addictive." *U.S. News and World Report*, 2/3/98

**relegated** "They were to be *relegated* to the outer circle of my life." Van Wyck Brooks, *Helen Keller*

**remiss** "If the mayor thought that one of his commissioners had been *remiss* in following instructions, he would fly into a rage and throw his glasses at him." David Rockefeller on Mayor LaGuardia, *New York Times*, 10/10/99

**remote** "The pull of the *remote* stars is so slight as to be obliterated in the vaster moments by which the ocean yields to the moon and sun." Rachel Carson, *The Sea Around Us*

**remuneration** "Please mail your resume along with your expected *remuneration* to our Director of Personnel." Want ad, *New York Times*, 7/7/99

**repented** "At his court martial, the officer admitted to the charges and *repented*." "General Demoted," *Washington Post*, 9/2/99

**repertoire** "He led a secret life as a forger of paintings, with the most famous as part of his *repertoire*." Peter Landesman, *New York Times*, 7/18/99

**replenish** "We'll dip down into our farm system to *replenish* our stock of left-handed pitchers." Bobby Valentine, *ABC-TV Sports Interview*

**replete** "When a composition is so *replete* with errors, I call attention to only a few, the most important ones." Fran Weinberg, English teacher, NYC High Schools

**repose** "Good night, good night! as sweet *repose* and rest Come to thy heart as that within my breast." William Shakespeare, *Romeo and Juliet*

**reprehensible** "She thought that the prisoners, no matter how morally *reprehensible* their crimes, still should have the benefit of pretrial representation." Jimmy Breslin's syndicated column, *Newsday*, 6/15/99

**repressed** "General McClellan *repressed* his feelings about President Lincoln but he expressed his private anger in letters to his wife." David Herbert Donald, *Lincoln*

**reprimand** "The difficulty lay in the fact the man had previously received a *reprimand* from his employer regarding his easy-going ways with the men under him in his department." James Thurber, "Let Your Mind Alone"

**reproached** "When reminded that he knew little history, Henry Ford *reproached* his critics by reminding them that history would know him." Quoted in *The Will Rogers Book*, Paula Love, editor, 1961

**repudiate** "If upheld, the decision would *repudiate* one of the Administration's environmental achievements." Editorial, *New York Times*, 5/19/99

**repugnant** "The behavior of the few rioters at the rock concert was *repugnant* to the huge, peaceful crowd." "Woodstock Revisited," *TIME*, 6/7/99

**repulse** "The cannons were set up to *repulse* a possible invasion but none was ever attempted." Col. F. X. Prescott, "History as Our Teacher"

**reputed** "The language of Iceland has changed so little that modern Icelanders are *reputed* to be able to read sagas written thousands of years ago." Bill Bryson, *Mother Tongue*

**requisite** "Secrecy is more *requisite* than ever during the sensitive negotiations over the release of our prisoners." I. F. Stone, *Weekly Reader*

**resourceful** "The crew of the $20 million independent film had to be very *resourceful* to hold down costs." Beth L. Kiel, "Allen in Hollywood," *New York*, 6/21/99

**respite** "The plan enabled the oiler and the correspondent to set *respite* together." Stephen Crane, "The Open Boat"

**restrictive** "Mr. el Hage said that the law was too *restrictive*, claiming that he had nothing to do with violent acts." Benjamin Weiser, "Terrorism Suspect," *New York Times*, 6/23/99

**reticent** "He was as inquisitive about the country as he was *reticent* about his business there." Frances Gilchrist Woods, "Turkey Red"

**retort** "There is no need to *retort* to an employee who has written a critique of your original warning letter." NYC Board of Education's Food Service Division, *Guide for Managers*

**retrospect** "I shivered in *retrospect* when I thought of that afternoon meeting in the freezing hall." Anna L. Strong, *The Chinese Conquer China*

**reverberated** "When that putt plunked into the hole yesterday, the 40,000 people exploded in a roar that *reverberated* through more than a century of U.S. Open history." Dave Anderson, "Longest Final Putt," *New York Times*, 6/21/99

**revere** "Paul McCartney and other celebrities who yet *revere* the name of rock-and-roll great Buddy Holly will host a tribute to him at the Roseland Ballroom." Letta Taylor, "Tribute to Buddy," *Newsday*, 9/3/99

**reverts** "She dreamily *reverts* to the hour when old age will throw down his frosts upon her head." Walt Whitman, "Dreams"

**reviled** "Former Haitian President Aristede was *reviled* by orphanage graduates who claimed that he had lied to them about the promise of jobs." Associated Press story, "Haiti Gunmen Confront Police," *New York Times*, 6/25/99

**rhetoric** "Nothing good can come out of the *rhetoric* of hatred that will be heard at the rally." New York Congressman Charles Rangel, ABC TV News, 9/2/99

**rife** "Cyberspace is *rife* with sweatshops but very few people realize it." Karl Taro Greenfield, "Living the Late Shift," *TIME*, 6/28/99

**rift** "The 1993 tear gas assault on the Branch Dividian cult has created a *rift* between the FBI and the Attorney General's office." Associated Press report, "FBI Video Released," *Newsday*, 9/3/99

# PANORAMA OF WORDS

**romp** "She was expected to win the governor's race in a *romp*." Wolf Blitzer, CNN News, 2/2/98

**roster** "The *roster* of stars for our gala celebration includes Cher, Meatloaf, and Lyle Lovett." Las Vegas hotel ad

**rudimentary** "Some of them were singing, some talking, some engaged in gardening, hay-making, or other *rudimentary* industries." "The Other Side of the Hedge," E. M. Forster

**rue** "When they make a mistake they will *rue* it." Randi Feigenbaum, "Realtors' Deal Irks Lawyers," *Newsday*, 9/3/99

**ruminated** "Lou Gehrig, the great N.Y. Yankee star, *ruminated* on his career as he left because of an incurable illness: 'I consider myself the luckiest man on the face of the earth.'" Speech, 7/4/39

**rustic** "This week a *rustic* setting in the Berkshire Hills was a gathering place for a group that is dedicated to preserving the Yiddish language." Tina Rosenberg, "Living an American Life in Yiddish," *New York Times*, 9/3/99

**saga** "The *saga* of the Kennedy family has enthralled and saddened us." Barbara Walters, quoted in *New York Times*, 7/10/99

**sage** "I am not a visionary, nor am I a *sage*—I claim to be a practical idealist." Mohandas Gandhi quoted by John Gunther, *Procession*, 1965

**salient** "The *salient* feature of the Americans With Disabilities Act of 1990 is that it prohibits discrimination against the disabled." Robert McFadden, "Court Ruling on Disabled Teacher Is Annulled," *New York Times*, 6/25/99

**sally** "The next morning we decided to *sally* forth to try to find a site for our new home." Stephen Leacock, "How My Wife and I Built Our Home for $4.90"

**salubrious** "For my later years there remains the *salubrious* effects of work: stimulation and satisfaction." Kathe Kollwitz, *Diaries and Letters*, 1955

**salvation** "Maybe it is connected with some terrible sin, with the loss of eternal *salvation*, with some bargain with the devil." Aleksandr Pushkin, "The Queen of Spades"

**sanctimonious** "There has never been a shortage of *sanctimonious* arguments for starting a war." Peter Finley Dunne, *Mr. Dooley Remembers*

**sanction** "He received his father's *sanction* and authority." George Meredith, *Diana of the Crossways*

**sanctuary** "The identity of Rinehart may be a temporary *sanctuary* for the narrator, but it is another identity he must reject if he is to find himself as a person." Anthony Abbott, *Invisible Man*

**sanguine** "I'm not *sanguine* about the Knicks' chances to upset the San Antonio Spurs." Telephone caller to WFAN Sports Radio Program, 6/8/99

**satiety** "One of the soldiers was given leave to be drunk six weeks, in hopes of curing him by *satiety*." William Cowper, *Selected Letters*

**saturate** "Vanilla sweetens the air, ginger spices it; melting nose-tingling odors *saturate* the kitchen." Truman Capote, "A Christmas Memory"

**schism** "The *schism* between the manager and his best pitcher spilled over from the locker room onto the field." Bob Klapisch, *The Worst Team That Money Could Buy*

**scion** "Al Gore is the Good Son, the early achieving *scion* from Harvard and Tennessee who always thought he would be President." Maureen Dowd, "Freudian Face-Off," *New York Times*, 6/15/99

**scoffed** "No one was injured except the woman who had *scoffed* at the belief." Leonard Fineberg, "Fire Walking in Ceylon"

**scrutinized** "The jockey waited with his back to the wall and *scrutinized* the room with pinched, creepy eyes." Carson McCullers, "The Jockey"

**scurrilous** "They were infuriated by the *scurrilous* articles about them that started to crop up in the tabloids." Charles Blauvelt, *Edward and Wally*

**scurry** "Some small night-bird, flitting noiselessly near the ground on its soft wings, almost flapped against me, only to *scurry* away in alarm." Ivan Turgenev, "Bezhin Meadows"

**sedate** "Few public places maintain a *sedate* atmosphere equal to the majestic chambers of the Supreme Court." Milton Konvitz, editor, *Bill of Rights Reader*

**sedentary** "Seeger had seen him relapsing gradually into the small-town hardware merchant he had been before the war, *sedentary* and a little shy." Irwin Shaw, "Act of Faith"

**senile** "Being on golf's Senior Tour doesn't mean that we're *senile*." Leon Jaroff, "Those Rich Old Pros," *TIME*, 9/27/99

**serenity** "At the top, they planted the crucifix and gathered round, moved by the *serenity*." Sontag Orme, "Solemnity and Flash in the Land of Jesus," *New York Times*, 1/1/00

**servile** "Uriah Heep, so physically repulsive and hypocritically *servile*, fascinated David

at first but later revolted him." Holly Hughes, *Barron's Book Notes*, *David Copperfield* by Charles Dickens

**shibboleths** Dialects are sometimes used as *shibboleths* to signal the ethnic or social status of the speaker." Bill Bryson, *Mother Tongue*

**sinecure** "Matthew Arnold's job was a *sinecure*, allowing him plenty of time to travel and write lyrics." Nicholas Jenkins, "A Gift Improvised," *New York Times*, 6/20/99

**singular** "The fate that rules in matters of love is often *singular*, and its ways are inscrutable, as this story will show." Meyer Goldschmidt, "Henrik and Rosalie"

**sinister** "The man had a cordially *sinister* air." Hernando Tellez, "Ashes for the Wind"

**site** "The *site* of the bison herd's destruction was a tall cliff over which they were driven." Brian Fagan, *Time Detectives*

**skirmish** "They never meet but there's a *skirmish* of wit between them." William Shakespeare, *Much Ado About Nothing*

**slovenly** "The twenty-six year old's *slovenly* appearance belied the fact that he was one of the Silicon Valley's brightest stars." Reuben Cowan, "Today Dot-Com"

**sojourn** "He returned from a long *sojourn* in Europe." Alan McCulloch, *Encyclopedia of Australian Art*

**solace** "He read in a Bible that he had neglected for years, but he could gain little *solace* from it." Theodore Dreiser, "The Lost Phoebe"

**solicited** "The police chief said that Commissioner Safir had not yet *solicited* his opinion on the question." "Police Chief Says Officers Deserve Raise," *New York Times*, 6/15/99

# PANORAMA OF WORDS

**somber** "There was a *somber* and moving tribute for his last game at Yankee Stadium." John Updike, *New Yorker*, 10/22/94

**sophistry** "No amount of *sophistry* could disguise the obvious fact that the legislation was biased against one particular office holder." *New York Times*, 9/2/99

**sordid** "The workmen used revolting language; it was disgusting and *sordid*." Katherine Mansfield, "The Garden Party"

**spate** "There has been a *spate* of tell-all memoirs, destroying the organization's special status." *Jewish Monthly*, 9/99

**spew** "It was obvious as the miles of electronic tape began to *spew* out the new patterns of American life that the census was to be of historic dimension." Theodore H. White, *The Making of the President*

**spontaneous** "Professor Einstein burst out in *spontaneous* candidness." Thomas Lee Bucky, "Einstein: An Intimate Memoir"

**sporadic** "TROOPS ENCOUNTER *SPORADIC* VIOLENCE" Headline, *Newsday*, 6/14/99

**spurious** "The only known picture, albeit a *spurious* one, had been printed some years earlier." James Monaghan, *Diplomat in Carpet Slippers*

**squeamish** "My brother, who voted for Mr. Mbeki and who has faith in his leadership, is not *squeamish*." Mark Mathabane, "South Africa's Lost Generation"

**stagnant** "The place was small and close, and the long disuse had made the air *stagnant* and foul." T. E. Lawrence, *The Desert of the Stars*

**staunch** "Known as a *staunch* supporter of the Republican agenda, the young politician astounded us all by his defection." Monte Halperin, "Party Turncoat?"

**steeped** "Edward Francis had *steeped* himself in the internal mystery of the guinea pig." Paul De Kruif, *Hunger Fighters*

**stentorian** "He proclaimed the fact in *stentorian* tones that were easily heard throughout the auditorium." A. A. Berle, *The 20th Century Capitalist Revolution*

**stereotypes** "Treating the most respected leader in the land that way confirms the worst *stereotypes* and that really hurts us." Alessandra Stanley, "Asking a Favor of the Pope," *New York Times*, 6/12/99

**stigmatized** "People who so much as whisper during a performance are *stigmatized* as barbarians." Joseph Wechsberg, *The Best Things in Life*

**stipulated** "I shall come out from here five minutes before the *stipulated* term, and thus shall violate the agreement." Anton Chekhov, "The Bet"

**strident** "No matter how *strident* or insulting he became, he was not interrupted by the police." *New York Daily News*, 9/5/99

**strife** "Either there is a civil *strife*, Or else the world, too saucy with the gods, Incenses them to send destruction." William Shakespeare, *Julius Caesar*

**stunted** "Their physical and mental development became *stunted* during childhood." Roger Pineles, *Shame of the Cities*

**stupor** "If your child watches late night television and comes home from school in a *stupor*, she's not getting enough sleep." "Getting Enough Sleep," *Working Mother*, 5/98

**stymied** "The family has been *stymied* in its attempt to remove a dead relative from the juror rolls." Associated Press story, "Jury Duty Summonses Don't Stop Despite Death," *New York Times*, 6/25/99

**subjugated** "The country had been bitterly divided, so ruthless in its determination to keep the black majority *subjugated*." Sheryl McCarthy, "Mandela Was South Africa's Perfect Choice," *Newsday*, 6/17/99

**subservient** "From the earliest times, including the Bible, women have been counseled to be *subservient* to men." Barbara G. Walker, *The Women's Encyclopedia*

**substantiate** "The Queens District Attorney said that there were not enough facts to *substantiate* the charges against the tour operator so no prosecution would take place." *Queens Courier*, 1/18/00

**subterfuge** "He was a free-will agent and he chose to do careful work, and if he failed, he took the responsibility without *subterfuge*." Marjorie Kinnan Rawlings, "A Mother in Mannville"

**subterranean** "Another celebrity expected during the three games at Madison Square Garden is Ed Norton—the actor, not the *subterranean* sanitation professional." Richard Sandomir, "N.B.A. Finals," *New York Times*, 6/21/99

**succinct** "In clear and *succinct* tones, our division head proceeded to tear me to shreds in front of the entire staff." Elleyn Falk, "They Promised Me a Rose Garden"

**succulent** "Use this coupon to get $1 off on a *succulent* holiday turkey." Advertisement, Waldbaum's Supermarket, 11/99

**succumbed** "This young gentleman was of an excellent family but had been reduced to such poverty that the energy of his character *succumbed* beneath it." Edgar Allan Poe, "The Murders in the Rue Morgue"

**sullen** "My decision to leave put her into a *sullen* silence, broken only by a mumble under her breath." Alan Lelchuk, "American Mischief"

**sultry** "The sun would shine up there in the lengthening spring day and pleasant breezes blow in *sultry* summer." Maurice Walsh, *The Quiet Man*

**sumptuous** "In the summer the table was set, and the *sumptuous* meals—well, it makes me cry to think of them." Mark Twain, *Autobiography*

**superficial** "His teachings had only a *superficial* relationship to the orthodox religion he advocated." Carl Dreyer, "The Roots of Anti-Semitism"

**superfluous** "He drove through the beautiful countryside in silence; conversation would have been *superfluous*." *Travel and Leisure*, 10/94

**supine** "The clergy as a whole were therefore obedient and *supine*." G. M. Trevelyan, *Carlyle*

**supplication** "The last *supplication* I make of you is that you will believe this of me." Charles Dickens, *A Tale of Two Cities*

**surfeit** "A *surfeit* of the sweetest things The deepest loathing to the stomach brings." William Shakespeare, *A Midsummer Night's Dream*

**surge** "In one wild *surge* they stormed into a police station, where the bewildered officers tried to maintain order." James Michener, "The Bridge at Andau"

**surmised** "The commanding officer *surmised* that the other ship in the cove was a coaster." Joseph Conrad, *Tales of Hearsay*

**surreptitiously** "He was *surreptitiously* negotiating to have 70 percent of the pay-

# PANORAMA OF WORDS

ments turned over to himself." David C. Johnson, "Tax Evasion Scheme," *New York Times*, 1/1/00

**susceptible** "Wrestling matches are *susceptible* to being heavily scripted, as ardent fans know." Edward Wyatt, "Pinning Down a Share Value," *New York Times*, 8/4/99

**symptomatic** "The widespread dislocation and downsizing in hospitals is *symptomatic* of relentless cost pressures." Carol Eisenberg, "Nurses Contend With System's Ills," *Newsday*, 6/22/99

**taboo** "The modern motion pictures have shown so much that once was considered *taboo*." Harold H. Owen, Jr., *The Motion Picture*

**tacit** "There is a *tacit* agreement in a civil conversation that each avoid making of it a monologue." Rebecca West, "There Is No Conversation"

**tainted** "The defense argued that poor police procedures had *tainted* the evidence." *Newsday*, 6/19/98

**tangible** "I hated it, not because of our one overcrowded closet, but because of intrusions and discomforts of a far less *tangible* nature." Mary Ellen Chase, "A Room of My Own"

**tantalized** "We were *tantalized* by a glimpse of a brown bear and her cubs in the wood." *Travel and Leisure*, 10/97

**tantamount** "Opponents of the proposed agreement claim it is *tantamount* to a surrender of holy land." *USA. Today*, 1/13/00

**taut** "His face grew *taut* as he was questioned about his use of illegal drugs in his youth." *New York Post*, 8/19/99

**technology** "Mr. Greenspan noted that 'history is strewn' with miscalculations about

*technology* developments." Richard Stevenson, "Fed Chief on New-Age Economy," *New York Times*, 6/15/99

**temerity** "In the first month of his service in the House, the young Congressman had the *temerity* to challenge his party's Speaker; it was a mistake." Blanche Kassell, *Up on the Hill*

**tenable** "He took the *tenable* position that lawyers should never cross examine a witness without knowing the answer before asking the question." Harper Lee, *To Kill a Mockingbird*

**tenacious** "Their talent and *tenacious* actions on the court will at last reward them." Darcy Frey, *The Last Shot*

**termagant** "This book deals with the matrimonial adventures of an extremely rich and bullying *termagant*." *Saturday Review*, 11/99

**terminate** "A continuation of such chronic lateness may lead us to *terminate* your employment." Regulations of the NYC Board of Education's Office of School Food & Nutrition Services

**terse** "The mayor sent a *terse* letter to the school's chancellor over his cancellation of a meeting." *New York Times*, 8/5/99

**therapy** "He will have to undergo long-term *therapy* before considering playing baseball again." *The Washington Post*, 7/9/99

**throng** "When the *throng* had mostly streamed into the porch, the sexton began to toll the bell." Nathaniel Hawthorne, "The Minister's Black Veil"

**thwarted** "The man who made up the name for flies must have been *thwarted* in a lifelong desire to have children, and at last found that outlet for his suppressed baby-talk." Robert Benchley, "The Lure of the Road"

**timorous** "He was a *timorous* incompetent who was lucky to have good men under him." W. A. Swanberg, *Citizen Hearst*

**tinged** "The sermon was *tinged*, rather more darkly than usual, with the gentle gloom of Mr. Hooper's temperament." Nathaniel Hawthorne, "The Minister's Black Veil"

**tolerated** "They despise anyone who hasn't had the luck to be born Masai, but for one reason and another, they *tolerated* me." Robert W. Krepps, "Pride of Seven"

**tortuous** "The *tortuous* descent down the mountain resulted in one additional fatality, this time a sure-footed Sherpa guide." Winston Adair, "Everest Takes Its Toll"

**tradition** "The town had a century-old *tradition*—an eight-hour canoe race." Brenda Flock, "The Race"

**tranquil** "Over this house, most *tranquil* and complete, Where no storm ever beat, She was sole mistress." Phyllis McGinley, "The Doll House"

**transient** "City championships and national tournaments, however thrilling, are *transient* moments." Darcy Frey, *The Last Shot*

**tremulous** "'Will Pa get hurt?' asked Jane in a *tremulous* voice." Jessamyn West, "Yes, We'll Gather at the River"

**trenchant** "Mr. Salinger's views on celebrity are often funny and *trenchant*." Clyde Haberman, "A Recluse Meets His Match," *New York Times*, 6/18/99

**trend** "We should make every effort to reverse the *trend* in popular music towards violent lyrics." *Portland Oregonian*, 8/12/99

**trivial** "In the study of past civilizations, nothing is considered as a *trivial* discovery." Brian Fagan, *Time Detectives*

**truncated** "It will be much harder if their state (Palestine) is so *truncated*, so cut up, that it is not viable." Anthony Lewis, "The Irrelevance of a Palestinian State," *New York Times*, 6/20/99

**turbulent** "Up to the *turbulent* surface came a peculiar-looking craft, risen from the calm but dangerous depth of the ocean." Lt. Don Walsh, "Our Seven-Mile Dive to the Bottom"

**turpitude** "The government must be held responsible for these acts of moral *turpitude* resulting in so many civilian casualties." *TIME*, 8/25/98

**tussle** "It often doesn't pay to *tussle* with your child to take music lessons." *Working Mother*, 5/96

**tyro** "The computer training center will soon turn a *tyro* into a successful user." *Senior News*, 9/99

**ubiquitous** "Che Guevera has become *ubiquitous*; his figure stares out at us from coffee mugs and posters, pops up in rock songs and operas." Ariel Dorfman, "Che," *TIME*, 6/14/99

**ultimate** "The *ultimate* possibility for hero and chorus alike is stated in Father Mapple's sermon, and it is to become a saint." W. H. Auden, "The Christian Tragic Hero"

**umbrage** "I do not take *umbrage* when I'm looked over, I do when I'm overlooked." Mae West, *The Wit and Wisdom of Mae West*, Joseph Weintraub, Editor

**unabated** "The summer list of auto fatalities continues *unabated* as three more Southampton teens are killed in a Sunday

# PANORAMA OF WORDS

crash." W. Mariano, "A Final Farewell," *Newsday*, 6/25/99

**unconscionable** "Viewers of TV's coverage of disasters find it *unconscionable* for mourning family members to be shown and interviewed so close up we can see the tears." John Stephens, *New York*, 4/16/98

**unctuous** "Today's car salesmen are a far cry from the high-pressured and *unctuous* ones of the past." *Car and Travel*, 9/99

**underwrite** "We are pleased to feature those local businesses who help to *underwrite* our programs." *Patterns*, monthly magazine of WILL, Champaign, Illinois

**universal** "With the approach of the new millennium we see an almost *universal* fear of major disruptions." *TIME*, 9/19/99

**unkempt** "Budget cuts have resulted in overcrowded and *unkempt* camping sites in our parks." Freeman Tilden, *The National Parks*

**unmitigated** "The crossword puzzle is the *unmitigated* sedentary hobby of Americans." Bill Bryson, *Mother Tongue*

**unsavory** "Punishing students by assigning them more work, has made education *unsavory* and unappealing to the average student." H. C. McKown, "The Three R's Today"

**unwieldy** "Today's light weight, compact cameras are a far cry from the *unwieldy* ones used by early photographers." *Popular Photography*, 9/96

**urbane** "Their prose is less ornate, their *urbane* satire more muted." Book review, *New York Times*

**usurp** "There is a constant struggle as one branch of government attempts to *usurp* some of the powers of the other." Milton Konvitz, editor, *Bill of Rights Reader*

**utopia** "I was held spellbound by the middle-class *utopia*, without a blot, without a tear." William James, "What Makes Life Significant"

**vacillated** "In planning for the book I *vacillated* between a selective, but deeper approach or a general, more limited approach." Milton Konvitz, editor, *Bill of Rights Reader*

**valor** "Thrice have the Mexicans before us fled, Their armies broken, their prince in triumph led; Both to thy *valor*, brave young man, we owe." Sir Robert Howard & John Dryden, *The Indian Queen*

**vapid** "The new James Bond movie lacks the excitement of the many before and is a *vapid* copy." *Newsday*, 10/25/98

**vehemently** "The President spoke *vehemently* against any large tax cut." *New York Times*, 9/16/99

**veneer** "Since then, she has frequently tried to crack the *veneer* of role, surface, and pose." Mark Stevens, "Spice Girls," *New York*, 6/21/99

**venerable** "Despite their huge popularity the most *venerable* papers refused to accept crossword puzzles as more than a passing fad." Bill Bryson, *Mother Tongue*

**venial** "The coach tried to overlook the *venial* errors of his players and concentrated on the serious ones." *Sports Illustrated*, 5/12/99

**venom** "The point envenom'd too! Then, *venom*, do thy work." William Shakespeare, *Hamlet*

**vertigo** "Iron workers on beams, hundreds of feet above Broadway, were immune to periods of *vertigo*." *Architectural Digest*, 1/93

**vestige** "They kept at the rescue efforts as long as there was a *vestige* of hope for the earthquake victims." *TIME*, 8/30/99

**vexatious** "This *vexatious* law suit dragged on interminably, becoming a legend in the process." Charles Dickens, *Bleak House*

**viable** "The organism remains *viable* in the soil for years." Rachel Carson, *Silent Spring*

**vicissitudes** "Her husband was not only faithful but patient in the face of remarkable *vicissitudes*." Eliza Jane Berman, *Noble Minds*

**vigil** "The U.N. peacekeeping troops are keeping a *vigil* over the disputed area." *New York Times*, 9/21/99

**vigilant** "I deny not but that it is of great concernment in the church and commonwealth to have a *vigilant* eye how looks demean themselves." John Milton, "Aereopagitica"

**vilified** "One who belongs to the most *vilified* minority in history is not likely to be unaware of the freedoms guaranteed by our constitutions." Supreme Court Justice Felix Frankfurter, decision, October 1943

**vindicated** "His family was certain that his actions would be *vindicated* when all of the facts became available." "Pilot Blamed in Crash," *New York Post*, 11/26/99

**virile** "The danger to our *virile* economy from weaknesses in the Far East should not be overlooked." *Wall Street Journal*, 5/16/98

**virtuosity** "Employing his *virtuosity* as an orchestrator of suspense, the author puts Lector in Florence, Italy, speaking impeccable Italian." Paul Grey, "Dessert, Anyone?," *TIME*, 6/21/99

**virulently** "Another part of my hope was for communities of people of colour that, for the most part, have been *virulently* homophobic." Mark Haslam, "When Bigotry Kills," *Globe and Mail*, Toronto, 3/5/99

**vitiate** "This act is an attempt to *vitiate* the separation of powers upon which our democracy is founded." Justice Earl Warren, *Bill of Rights Reader*, 1957

**vitriolic** "The speaker's *vitriolic* comments about ethnic and religious groups brought condemnation from the mayor." *New York Daily News*, 9/5/98

**vituperation** "To justify his action he used *vituperation*, calling his enemies 'detestable pests.'" Barbara G. Walker, *The Women's Encyclopedia*

**vivacious** "The performance of this *vivacious* leading lady made the play a delight." *New York Post*, 10/15/98

**vogue** "Examining the private lives of our political leaders is in *vogue* this election period." *New York*, 9/4/99

**volition** "To prove her innocence, she took a lie detector test of her own *volition*." *New York Times*, 9/21/99

**voluble** "He came to hate Ray Gribble and his *voluble* companions of the submerged tenth of the class." Sinclair Lewis, "Young Man Axelbrod"

**voluminous** "The testimony in the case relating to the President's actions has become *voluminous*." *Washington Post*, 5/15/99

**voracious** "We spent a good number of our waking hours feeding *voracious* stoves." Jean Stafford, "New England Winter"

# PANORAMA OF WORDS

**vulnerable** "Any *vulnerable* area in an otherwise strong person or structure is known as an Achilles heel." Barbara G. Walker, *The Women's Encyclopedia*

**wan** "Why so pale and *wan*, fond lover? Prithee, why so pale?" John Suckling, "Encouragement to a Lover"

**wane** "Japan, once an economic power, has seen its influence *wane*." *New York Times*, 8/1/99

**wary** "These figures were *wary* in their movements and perfectly silent afoot." Joseph Conrad, *Lord Jim*

**wheedle** "The first step of a politician is to *wheedle* the editorial backing of a newspaper." Frederick Nebel, *A Free Press*

**whet** "The accepted purpose of coming attractions in movie theatres is to *whet* the viewers' desire to see the film." John Simon, *Reverse Angle*

**whimsical** "This is not a *whimsical* idea—it is a serious plan." Calvin Klein, *New York Magazine*, 9/15/95

**wince** "He took the cruel blow without a *wince* or a cry." A. Conan Doyle, *The Last Book of Sherlock Holmes*

**wistful** "I am sad when I see those *wistful* ads placed by the lovelorn in the classified columns." E. B. White, *The Essays of E. B. White*

**wrest** "Their attempt to *wrest* control of the company was thwarted by the Colonel and his three supporters on the board." Edmund Ward, Jr., "Bulls and Bears" [adapted]

**yen** "She could not resist the *yen* to see how her classmates had progressed so she agreed to attend the class reunion." *Woman's Home Companion*, 9/94

**zealous** "James I was *zealous* in prosecuting Scottish sorcerers." George Lyman Kittredge, *Witchcraft in Old and New England*

**zenith** "At the *zenith* of her fame as a musical star, she was assassinated by a crazed fan." H. Hudson, *People*, 7/21/97

# BONUS Week **A** ❖ Day **1**

## NEW WORDS

**impregnanble**
im preg´ nə bəl

**toxic**
tok´ sik

**patriarch**
pā trē ark´

**neophyte**
ne´ ə f ī t

**extenuating**
ik sten´ yoo āt ing

## *TITANIC* MYSTERY

On April 14, 1912, an incident took place that became a front page story in newspapers all over the world. It is a tale that has continued to capture the attention of movie and theatre goers, of opera and television audiences, of novelists and playwrights—it's the story of the allegedly *impregnable Titanic*, the unsinkable majestic ocean liner that tumbled to the bottom of the icy Atlantic waters with 1600 passengers still aboard.

How could such a *toxic* tragedy have occurred? Could it have been avoided? How could the naval *patriarch*, Captain Edward Smith, no *neophyte* he, have allowed the disaster to happen? What were the *extenuating* circumstances that led to the death of that glorious White Star queen?

In September 1985, the hulk of the *Titanic* was found on the ocean's floor, providing many answers to the questions that seamen and landlubbers had wrestled with over the years.

**Sample Sentences**  Insert the new words in the following sentences.

1. Coal miners are often subject to _____ fumes.

2. Robert's defense lawyer pointed out the _____ conditions of the case.

3. Although Sarah was skillful at math, she was a _____ at computers.

4. A company of marines was unable to penetrate the seemingly _____ fortress.

5. Grandfather is the recognized _____ of our family.

**Definitions**  Match the new words with their meanings.

6. impregnable  _____   **a.** harmful

7. toxic  _____   **b.** elder

8. extenuating  _____   **c.** incapable of being entered

9. neophyte  _____   **d.** beginner

10. patriarch  _____   **e.** excusable

---
### TODAY'S IDIOM
---

*a dry run*—trial, test, exercise
Before opening night, the actors had several *dry runs.*

**forebodings**
for bo´ dings

**emanting**
em´ ə nā ting

**miscreant**
mis´ krē ənt

**protocol**
prō´ tə kol

**circuitous**
sar kyoo´ i təs

## WHAT WENT WRONG?

Investigators found that a series of mistakes led to the sinking of the *Titanic*. A wireless message had come in from a French liner, warning of ice ahead, but that was a thousand miles away, and so, no need to worry. On April 13, the vessel *Rapphannock* also warned the *Titanic* of dangerous ice ahead. On the following day, there came a spate* of other warnings from a Cunard ship, a Dutch liner, and the White Star *Baltic*—all telling of icebergs about 250 miles from the *Titanic*'s current position. Next came the German *Amerika*, echoing the same *forebodings*, followed by the *California*, cautioning the *Titanic* about the field ice. Finally, the *Mesaba* called attention to an enormous belt of ice stretching directly across the *Titanic*'s path. All the messages *emanating* from sister ships should have had a profound* effect on Smith and company.

No one *miscreant* could be fingered, but a host of crew members were certainly blameworthy. Why didn't Captain Smith's officers react to those messages? Notations were indeed made on slips of paper but largely ignored and forgotten. There was no standard *protocol* for the handling of such messages; if there had been, Captain Smith would certainly have taken a *circuitous* route so as to avoid the dangerous icebergs.

**Sample Sentences** Insert the new words in the following sentences.

1. Cindy took a _____ route home to avoid the class bullies.

2. Caesar's wife had _____ about danger facing her husband.

3. The rulings _____ from the local court were cheered by the conservatives.

4. The class _____ was made to remain after school.

5. Failing to follow _____ got Sophia into trouble at the office.

**Definitions** Match the new words with their meanings.

6. forebordings _____ a. one who behaves badly

7. emanating _____ b. forms of ceremony

8. miscreant _____ c. premonitions, evil omens

9. protocol _____ d. roundabout

10. circuitous _____ e. coming from

---

## TODAY'S IDIOM

***to throw someone a curve*—to do the unexpected**

When I least expected it, Helen *threw me a curve.*

---

ANSWERS ARE ON PAGE 397

**NEW WORDS**

knell
nel

macabre
mə kaˊ brə

ramifications
ramˊ ə fi kā shəns

rapacious
ra pāˊ shəs

insurgent
in surˊ jənt

## DEATH *KNELL* FOR THE *TITANIC*

And then it happened. White in its innocence, a monstrous iceberg smashed into the luxury liner, ripping an ugly gash of 250 feet along the starboard and causing a fatal wound. Within seconds, thousands of cubic feet of water had penetrated the shattered hull. One after another, dominolike, the watertight compartments and bulkhead were flooded. The unthinkable had happened despite the absolute guarantees of the shipbuilders, Harland & Woolf.

There followed a *macabre* scene as the ship's band, clad in their tuxedos, continued to play show tunes while hordes of terrified passengers, many in nightclothes, rushed toward the lifeboats. The crew called out, "Women and children first," but their lack of an orderly plan for loading would have profound* *ramifications.* In fact, some boats that could hold 30 were sent into the Atlantic with only a handful of people—generally first-class passengers.

As panic began to take hold, the realization that there weren't enough lifeboats exacerbated* the situation, bringing out the worst in a *rapacious* few. Several *insurgent* males ignored the crew and jumped into descending lifeboats. It was an act of shame they would have to live with for the rest of their lives.

**Sample Sentences** Insert the new words in the following sentences.

1. The _____ dictator used mustard gas against his enemies.

2. Additional troops were dispatched to deal with the _____ threat.

3. When the _____ sounded, the students closed their books and their minds.

4. Some critics were unhappy about the bloody _____ scenes in the movie.

5. Heidi was concerned about the _____ of her employer's new policy.

**Definitions** Match the new words with their meanings.

6. knell        _____   **a.** complications

7. macabre      _____   **b.** greedy, taking by force

8. ramifications _____  **c.** gruesome

9. rapacious    _____   **d.** rebellious

10. insurgent   _____   **e.** sound of a bell

--- **TODAY'S IDIOM** ---

*to cross the Rubicon*—a limit that allows for no return (The Rubicon was a river in Italy that Julius Caesar's army crossed, knowing there was no retreat.)

When I *crossed the Rubicon* by signing the contract,
I knew I could never go back on my commitment.

ANSWERS ARE ON PAGE 397

## NEW WORDS

**glut**
glut

**risible**
riz´ ə bəl

**dilatory**
dil´ ə tor ē

**specious**
spē shəs

**denouement**
dā noō man´

# BONUS WEEK **A** ❖ DAY **4**

## THE LAWYERS' TURN

As one might have expected, manifold* law suits against the White Star Line began to crop up within weeks of the sinking and rescue. The *glut* of billionaires on board (Astors, Wideners, Guggenheims, Strausses, et al.) did not file any claims, but other cases went all the way to the Supreme Court and kept lawyers and judges busy for the next four years. The average claim had been for a modest $1500, and the average award, paid by the White Star Line, was a *risible* $1000. White Star's top notch legal staff was accused of using *dilatory* tactics, tiring the claimants until they agreed to settle for a mere pittance*. Their lawyers called many claims *specious* and rejected them out of hand.

The *denouement* of the story is rather sad. American and British maritime law had long given special protection to ship owners on the grounds that their business was such a risky one. And so there was a limit to the amount of money that White Star could be assessed. In the end, they paid only 4% of the $16 million originally demanded by the survivors and were happy to close the books on the ocean disaster. We can imagine that if a similar tragedy were to take place today, the settlements would be in the hundreds of millions.

**Sample Sentences** Insert the new words in the following sentences.

1. The play's _____ came with three dead bodies on the stage.

2. Umpires do not like pitchers who use _____ styles.

3. In debating, _____ arguments are rarely effective.

4. What Harry felt was _____, Sally thought was pathetic.

5. Our choir has a _____ of tenors and a shortage of sopranos.

**Definitions** Match the new words with their meanings.

6. glut _____ a. delaying

7. risible _____ b. laughable

8. dilatory _____ c. oversupply

9. specious _____ d. deceptively attractive

10. denouement _____ e. outcome

---
### TODAY'S IDIOM
---

***to brave the elements***—to go out in bad weather

Despite the freezing rain, Cynthia decided to *brave the elements*.

ANSWERS ARE ON PAGE 397

## REVIEW WORDS

**DEFINITIONS**

| | REVIEW WORDS | | DEFINITIONS |
|---|---|---|---|
| _____ | 1. circuitous | a. | coming from |
| _____ | 2. denouement | b. | a rebel |
| _____ | 3. dilatory | c. | aged male family leader |
| _____ | 4. emanating | d. | gruesome |
| _____ | 5. extenuating | e. | roundabout |
| _____ | 6. forebodings | f. | complications |
| _____ | 7. glut | g. | tending to delay |
| _____ | 8. impregnable | h. | forms of ceremony |
| _____ | 9. insurgent | i. | lessening the seriousness |
| _____ | 10. knell | j. | sound of a bell |
| _____ | 11. macabre | k. | premonitions, evil omens |
| _____ | 12. miscreant | l. | greedy, taking by force |
| _____ | 13. neophyte | m. | harmful, destructive |
| _____ | 14. patriarch | n. | oversupply |
| _____ | 15. protocol | o. | deceptively attractive |
| _____ | 16. ramifications | p. | cannot be entered by force |
| _____ | 17. rapacious | q. | laughable, ludicrous |
| _____ | 18. risible | r. | one who behaves badly |
| _____ | 19. specious | s. | beginner, novice |
| _____ | 20. toxic | t. | outcome |

## IDIOMS

| | IDIOMS | | |
|---|---|---|---|
| _____ | 21. a dry run | u. | a limit that allows for no return |
| _____ | 22. to throw someone a curve | v. | trial exercise |
| _____ | 23. to cross the Rubicon | w. | do the unexpected |
| _____ | 24. to brave the elements | x. | go out in bad weather |

Check your answers on page 397. Make a record of those words you missed.

**WORDS FOR FURTHER STUDY**    **MEANINGS**

1. _____   _____

2. _____   _____

3. _____   _____

4. _____   _____

5. _____   _____

# SENSIBLE SENTENCES?
## (From Week A)

❖ Underline the word that makes sense in each of the sentences below.

1. When the *(ramifications, knell)* of his action were explained, Roger apologized.

2. There is no known antidote for the *(specious, toxic)* poison.

3. Following *(forebodings, protocol)*, Ben bowed before the emperor.

4. The young *(patriarch, miscreant)* was brought before the judge.

5. Seeking his prey, the lion took a *(circuitous, dilatory)* route on the trail of the deer.

6. Victor's weak explanation elicited* a *(risible, rapacious)* reaction from his teacher.

7. The *(insurgent, neophyte)* forces launched a successful attack.

8. We thought the *(knell, denouement)* of the play was ridiculous.

9. Harmful fumes were *(emanating, extenuating)* from the laboratory.

10. Critics rated the *(impregnable, macabre)* play to be the season's best.

ANSWERS ARE ON PAGE 397

❖ Using the clues listed below, fill in each blank in the following story with one of the new words you learned this week.

## *An Unusual Perk*

A study ①_____ from the Department of Health and Mental Hygiene declared that one in eight adults in our major cities has diabetes, a ②_____ disease. Many, however, are not aware that they have it or how ③_____ it can be. There is a ④_____ of evidence revealing that the high blood sugar that affects diabetics is more characteristic of Asian Americans, African-Americans, and Hispanics than of the white population.

Unfortunately, many of the victims of diabetes do not take immediate steps to deal with the disease. New York City's health commissioner has warned of the ⑤_____ of a failure to control the high blood sugar: blindness, amputations, and heart disease. In fact, diabetes is the nation's fastest growing major disease.

**Clues**

① 2nd Day

② 1st Day

③ 5th Day

④ 4th Day

⑤ 3rd Day

## NEW WORDS

**dolorous**
dō la rəs

**enervated**
en´ ər vā tid

**suffrage**
suf´ rij

**cabal**
ka bal´

**odious**
o´ dē əs

## GOOD NEWS—AND BAD

On Palm Sunday, April 9, 1865, General Ulysses S. Grant sent a terse* dispatch to Secretary of War Edwin Stanton. It contained the long-awaited sentence that the Confederate General Robert E. Lee had surrendered. The *dolorous* Civil War that had crippled the young nation was finally over.

President Lincoln was only 56 at the time, but he looked twenty years older. The burden of being a wartime president had so *enervated* Lincoln that Surgeon General Barnes feared an imminent* nervous breakdown. When Grant's news reached Lincoln, he went to the front windows of the White House and waved to the crowd below. He proceeded to make a brief speech about the problems of Reconstruction and advocated* the granting of *suffrage* to Negro soldiers.

Among the listeners was a Southern patriot, the popular actor John Wilkes Booth, almost as famous in the theater as his father, Junius. "That's the last speech he will ever make," said Booth to a fellow member of his *cabal* of conspirators. Booth's *odious* plan was to assassinate Lincoln whom he hated passionately, while an associate, George Atzerodt, would do the same to Vice-President Andrew Johnson.

**Sample Sentences** Insert the new words in the following sentences.

1. The dictator lied when he claimed he favored _____ for women.

2. We were surprised when Ted's happy expression turned into a _____ one.

3. The members of the revolutionary _____ were arrested and jailed.

4. Sylvia's _____ remarks caused the audience to turn against her.

5. _____ by his long walk, Jose took to his bed.

**Definitions** Match the new words with their meanings.

6. dolorous _____ a. right to vote

7. enervated _____ b. secret group of plotters

8. suffrage _____ c. worn out

9. cabal _____ d. sad

10. odious _____ e. despicable

---

### TODAY'S IDIOM

*to kill the goose that laid the golden egg*—to spoil a good deal

By being greedy, the accountant *killed the goose that laid the golden egg.*

---

ANSWERS ARE ON PAGE 397

# BONUS WEEK B ❖ DAY 2

NEW WORDS

**prescient**
pre´ shē ənt

**verbatim**
vər bā´ tim

**reverie**
rev´ ər ē

**thespian**
thes pē ən

**despot**
des´ pət

## THE DREAMS OF LINCOLN AND BOOTH

Lincoln's family and friends remembered that the President had a *prescient* dream in March, several weeks before the fatal day, and provided them with a *verbatim* account. He told of entering the East Room in the White House where a throng* of people were gathered around an open coffin. In his *reverie*, Lincoln asked a soldier, "Who is dead in the White House?" "The President," was the reply. "He was killed by an assassin."

Mrs. Lincoln said, "I'm glad I don't believe in dreams or I should be in terror from this time forth." Lincoln's was the calming voice, "Let's try to forget it. I think the Lord in His own good time and way will work this out all right."

Of course, all who loved Abe Lincoln would have been deeply agitated if they had known what John Wilkes Booth was planning. As a Southern secessionist, he despised the President. As a *thespian*, he romanticized the action that he could take to rid the nation of a cruel warmonger. Although he had not taken an active part in the Civil War, he was convinced that he could contribute to the Confederate cause by kidnapping the bearded *despot*. It wasn't exactly clear in his mind whether he would "capture" Lincoln and take him to Richmond where he could be exchanged for Confederate prisoners of war—or whether he would just put a bullet in the President's head.

**Sample Sentences**  Insert the new words in the following sentences.

1. Yearning to be a _____ , Roger took lessons from a dramatic coach.

2. When he lost control of the militia, the _____ was forced to flee.

3. Claiming to be _____ , the fortune teller took advantage of the gullible* woman.

4. With remarkable talent, the reporter was able to quote speeches _____ .

5. In her _____ , Ellen saw herself as the next U.S. President.

**Definitions**  Match the new words with their meanings.

6. prescient      _____    **a.** dream

7. verbatim       _____    **b.** actor

8. reverie        _____    **c.** able to predict

9. thespian       _____    **d.** word for word

10. despot        _____    **e.** tyrant

---

### TODAY'S IDIOM

***to carry coals to Newcastle*—a waste of time**
**(since Newcastle had a great deal of coal)**

Telling the racing car driver how to drive is like *carrying coals to Newcastle*.

---

ANSWERS ARE ON PAGE 397

## BONUS WEEK **B** ❖ DAY **3**

**pathological**
path´ ə loj i kal

**articulate**
ar tik´ yə lit

**grandeur**
gran´ jər

**polemic**
pə lem´ ik

**impasse**
im´ pas

### THE ASSASSINS MAKE READY

The *pathological* yet *articulate* Booth had rounded up several co-conspirators and shared his delusions of *grandeur* with them. He had produced a *polemic* that convinced his crew that it would be a patriotic thing to capture the President. One of them was assigned to shut off the master gas valve at Ford's Theatre when Mr. and Mrs Lincoln were seated there at the play. With all the lights out, Booth would bind and gag the President. Two men would lower Lincoln onto the stage, and then carry him out the rear door to a covered wagon waiting in the alley. They would head for Port Tobacco and then ferry across the Potomac to their ultimate* destination, Richmond, Virginia.

Several dry runs* had not worked out for the cabalists* who were about to reach an *impasse* when Booth learned that Lincoln would be celebrating General Grant's victories with a party at Ford's Theater on the night of April 14. He promised the small group that destiny was at hand; their bold act, he said, would make their names famous forever in the annals of U.S. history.

In the late afternoon of April 14, Booth watched a rehearsal of the play that would be performed that evening. He had reviewed his action plan and the escape route, and he believed it to be foolproof. He mouthed the phrase he would use after killing Lincoln, "Sic Semper Tyrannis" ("Thus always to tyrants").

The curtain was about to go up on one of the darkest days in the country's history.

**Sample Sentences**  Insert the new words in the following sentences.

1. The _____ was broken when the union agreed to management's offer.

2. In history class, we studied the _____ of Greece and the glory of Rome.

3. Hal was surprisingly _____ for a high school freshman.

4. The defense lawyer admitted that his client was a _____ liar.

5. The team captain's _____ led to a fist fight in the locker room.

**Definitions**  Match the new words with their meanings.

6. pathological _____    **a.** well-spoken

7. articulate _____    **b.** magnificence

8. grandeur _____    **c.** disordered in behavior

9. polemic _____    **d.** deadlock

10. impasse _____    **e.** controversial argument

---
**TODAY'S IDIOM**

*an axe to grind*—to pursue a selfish aim

Senator Smith was in favor of the bill, but we knew that he had *an axe to grind*.

---

ANSWERS ARE ON PAGE 397

# BONUS WEEK **B** ❖ DAY **4**

**NEW WORDS**

**regimen**
rej´ ə mən

**denigrated**
den´ i grāt ed

**guile**
gīl

**mortal**
mor´ tl

**inflicted**
in flikt´ ed

## "NOW HE BELONGS TO THE AGES"

At 8:25 the Lincolns arrived at the theater. When they entered Booths 7 & 8, as *regimen* dictated, the band played "Hail to the Chief." The 1675 members of the audience stood to honor the great man, and then the play commenced. It is reported that Booth said to a drunk who had *denigrated* his acting skill, "When I leave the stage, I will be the most famous man in America."

At about 10 P.M., with extreme *guile*, Booth had managed to be behind Box 7 in the darkness of the hallway. He saw the silhouette of a head above the horsehair rocker. Derringer in his hand, he aimed it between the President's left ear and his spine. The shot was drowned out by laughter on the stage. Shouting "Revenge for the South," Booth climbed over the ledge of the box and jumped onto the stage, breaking his leg in the process.

In pain, Booth limped out the stage door where his horse was waiting and made his getaway. Days later, however, he was cornered in a Virginia barn and shot. Three of the cabal* members were arrested and hanged.

At the theater, a 23-year-old doctor attended to the wounded President. He found that the lead shot had lodged in Lincoln's brain, a bad sign. Several soldiers carried Mr. Lincoln across the street to a private house. His family physician came and so did the Surgeon General. The President struggled throughout the long night, but it was apparent that a *mortal* wound had been *inflicted*, and he could not be saved.

At 7:22 A.M. it was over; two silver coins were placed on the assassinated President's eyes. Then Secretary Stanton uttered the famous words, "Now he belongs to the ages."

**Sample Sentences** Insert the new words in the following sentences.

1. The blow to the boxer's jaw turned out to be a _____ one.

2. Using _____ , the magician pulled the wool over the spectators' eyes.

3. Aunt Ethel's morning _____ called for three cups of coffee.

4. When her boss _____ Martha's stenographic ability, she quit.

5. The prison guards _____ torture on some of the inmates.

**Definitions** Match the new words with their meanings.

6. regimen _____ a. leading to death

7. denigrated _____ b. defamed

8. guile _____ c. a system of control

9. mortal _____ d. trickery

10. inflicted _____ e. imposed upon

### ——— TODAY'S IDIOM ———

***to throw one's hat in the ring*—to run for political office**

Before a gathering of the party's faithful, the local congressman
*threw his hat in the ring* for the position of senator.

## REVIEW WORDS

_____ 1. articulate
_____ 2. cabal
_____ 3. denigrated
_____ 4. despot
_____ 5. dolorous
_____ 6. enervated
_____ 7. grandeur
_____ 8. guile
_____ 9. impasse
_____ 10. inflicted
_____ 11. mortal
_____ 12. odious
_____ 13. pathological
_____ 14. polemic
_____ 15. prescient
_____ 16. regimen
_____ 17. reverie
_____ 18. suffrage
_____ 19. thespian
_____ 20. verbatim

## DEFINITIONS

a. absolute ruler
b. hateful, despicable
c. secret group of plotters
d. actor
e. disordered in behavior
f. defamed one's character
g. a controversial argument
h. able to speak clearly
i. able to know beforehand
j. greatness of character, magnificence
k. word for word
l. worn out
m. a system of control
n. to impose something painful
o. deadlock
p. a daydream
q. subject to death
r. the right to vote
s. sorrowful
t. trickery, deceit

## IDIOMS

_____ 21. an axe to grind
_____ 22. to carry coals to Newcastle
_____ 23. to throw one's hat in the ring
_____ 24. to kill the goose that laid the golden egg

u. a waste of time
v. to spoil a good deal
w. to pursue a selfish aim
x. to run for office

## WORDS FOR FURTHER STUDY    MEANINGS

Check your answers on page 397. Study the words you missed.

1. _____    _____

2. _____    _____

3. _____    _____

4. _____    _____

5. _____    _____

❖ Using the clues listed below, fill in each blank in the following story with one of the new words you learned this week.

## Perks Are In

Do you know what a "perk" is? Simply put, it's an extra reward, a special benefit given to sweeten the job for an employee. Now an ①_____ staffer at Serus, a software maker in California's Silicon Valley, has skillfully described an incredible perk given to him and his fellow workers—a thrill-packed parachute plunge as they jumped from a plane 14,000 feet above the ground.

"Our employees work hard and can become ②_____ ," said a Serus executive, "and we want to invigorate them with sky dives, as well as cruises, beauty treatments at spas, birthday parties, maid services, and other creative perks that our ③_____ might conjure up."

Of course, company executives are deeply interested in keeping productive staff members from quitting and going to work for competitors. And so, the host of perks they offer reflect the ④_____ behind their generosity. "Cash bonuses won't have the same effect," a CEO said. In a ⑤_____ remark he declared, "It's like a parent who throws money at his child when what the youngster really wants is attention."

### Clues

① 3rd Day

② 1st Day

③ 1st Day

④ 4th Day

⑤ 2nd Day

# SENTENCE COMPLETIONS
## (From Weeks A and B)

❖ Each sentence below has two blanks, indicating that something has been omitted. Beneath the sentence are five sets of words labeled A through E. Choose the set of words that, when inserted, *best* fits the meaning of the sentence as a whole.

1. The _____ dictator used _____ to achieve his goals.

    a. rapacious...guile
    b. articulate...protocol
    c. odious...regimen
    d. dilatory...ramifications
    e. prescient...polemics

2. Having overcome the _____ _____, the executive had high hopes for the future.

    a. specious...cabal
    b. circuitous...knells
    c. dolorous...forebodings
    d. mortal...reverie
    e. toxic...insurgents

3. The _____ _____ fled the country with the millions he had stolen from the treasury.

    a. impregnable...neophyte
    b. pathological...despot
    c. dilatory...miscreant
    d. risible...insurgent
    e. articulate...patriarch

4. The _____ circumstances were clearly explained by the play's _____ .

    a. extenuating...denouement
    b. prescient...knell
    c. macabare...forebodings
    d. circuitous...protocol
    e. odious...polemic

5. "We have had a _____ of _____ tactics," the judge declared, "and I will not put up with it."

    a. regimen...toxic
    b. glut...dilatory
    c. cabal...odious
    d. grandeur...verbatim
    e. impassse...suffrage

ANSWERS ARE ON PAGE 397

# VOC/QUOTE

❖ Select the best word from the five choices to fit in the blanks below.

1. "There are no political _____ except in the imagination of political quacks."
                                                    —Francis Parkman

   **a.** compounds     **b.** panaceas     **c.** milieus     **d.** ethics     **e.** diatribes

2. "The effect of my _____ is that always busy with the preliminaries and antecedents, I am never able to begin the produce."
                                                    —Henri Amiel

   **a.** genre     **b.** expedient     **c.** iniquity     **d.** bias     **e.** prognostication

3. "Once philosophers have written their principal works, they not infrequently simply become their own _____ ."
                                                    —Theodore Haecker

   **a.** accomplices     **b.** disciples     **c.** cynics     **d.** arbiters     **e.** badgers

4. "I hate the aesthetic game of the eye and the mind, played by those _____ who 'appreciate' beauty."
                                                    —Pablo Picasso

   **a.** connoisseurs     **b.** charlatans     **c.** rustics     **d.** stentorian     **e.** paragons

5. "Anglo-Saxon _____ takes such very good care that its prophecies of woe to the erring person shall find fulfillment."
                                                    —George Gissing

   **a.** foreboding     **b.** morality     **c.** protocol     **d.** polemic     **e.** guile

6. "The universe is not friendly to _____ and they all perish sooner or later."
                                                    —Don Marquis

   **a.** icons     **b.** patriarchs     **c.** despots     **d.** insurgents     **e.** perennials

7. "_____ means influence."
                                                    —Jack London

   **a.** Affluence     **b.** Cupidity     **c.** Complicity     **d.** Decorum     **e.** Proximity

8. "No one wants advice—only _____ ."
                                                    —John Steinbeck

   **a.** corroboration     **b.** alacrity     **c.** delineation     **d.** dissent     **e.** jurisdiction

ANSWERS ARE ON PAGE 397                                                    **385**

# VOC/QUOTE

9. "If by the time we're sixty, we haven't learned what a knot of _____ and contradiction life is, we haven't grown old to much purpose."

   —John Cowper Powys

   **a.** vertigo    **b.** surmise    **c.** sophistry    **d.** privation    **e.** paradox

10. "The concept of 'Momism' is male nonsense. It is the refuge of a man seeking excuses for his own lack of _____ ."

    —Pearl Buck

    **a.** regimen    **b.** virility    **c.** grandeur    **d.** temerity    **e.** satiety

11. "_____ is the dabbling within a serious field by persons who are ill equipped to meet even the minimum standards of that field, or study, or practice."

    —Ben Shahn

    **a.** Amnesty    **b.** Artifice    **c.** Decadence    **d.** Propriety    **e.** Dilettantism

12. "Accustomed to the _____ of noise, public relations, and market research, society is suspicious of those who value silence."

    —John Lahr

    **a.** realm    **b.** veneer    **c.** surfeit    **d.** diatribe    **e.** cacophony

13. "In almost every act of our lives we are so clothed in _____ and dissemblance that we can recognize but dimly the deep primal impulses that motivate us."

    —James Ramsey Ullman

    **a.** volition    **b.** rationalization    **c.** sophistry    **d.** impunity    **e.** heresy

14. "When men talk honestly about themselves, one of the themes that crops up is a _____ for the old days, at least for an idealized version of them."

    —Myron Brenton

    **a.** pretext    **b.** landmark    **c.** nostalgia    **d.** fetish    **e.** candor

15. "We love a congenial _____ because by sympathy we can and do expand our spirit to the measure of his."

    —Charles H. Cooley

    **a.** egotist    **b.** nonentity    **c.** iconclast    **d.** ascetic    **e.** disciple

16. "Man is certainly a _____ animal. A never sees B in distress without thinking C ought to relieve him directly."

    —Sydney Smith

    **a.** discreet    **b.** benevolent    **c.** banal    **d.** whimsical    **e.** somber

17. "I cannot tolerate _____ . They are all so obstinate, so opinionated."

—Joseph McCarthy

    **a.** arbiters      **b.** culprits      **c.** dregs      **d.** expatriates      **e.** bigots

18. "We look upon _____ as degrading. Our mothers' voices still ring in our ears: 'Have you done your homework?'"

—Wilhelm Stekhel

    **a.** indolence      **b.** opulence      **c.** levity      **d.** invective      **e.** histrionics

19. "By far the most dangerous foe we have to fight is _____ —indifference from carelessness, from absorption in other pursuits."

—Sir William Osler

    **a.** umbrage      **b.** apathy      **c.** repose      **d.** nepotism      **e.** histrionics

20. "One who sees the _____ everywhere has occasion to remember it pretty often."

—Oliver Wendell Holmes

    **a.** inevitable      **b.** precedent      **c.** efficacy      **d.** idyllic      **e.** mundane

21. "There's life for a _____ in the characters he plays. It's such a beautiful physical escape. I enjoy the transformation of personality."

—Sir John Gielgud

    **a.** thespian      **b.** miscreant      **c.** termagant      **d.** tyro      **e.** sage

22. "The writing of a biography is no _____ task; it is the strenuous achievement of a lifetime, only to be accomplished in the face of endless obstacles."

—Havelock Ellis

    **a.** paltry      **b.** facile      **c.** lucrative      **d.** impious      **e.** egregious

23. "Cleanliness, said some _____ man, is next to godliness. It may be, but how it came to sit so near is the marvel."

—Charles Lamb

    **a.** abstemious      **b.** banal      **c.** comely      **d.** sage      **e.** devout

24. "I should like most candid friends to be anonymous. They would then be saved the painful necessity of making themselves _____ ."

—J. A. Spender

    **a.** venial      **b.** odious      **c.** sanctimonious      **d.** fractious      **e.** benevolent

ANSWERS ARE ON PAGE 397     

# VOC/QUOTE

25. "A stricken tree is beautiful, so dignified, so admirable in its _____ longevity; it is, next to man, the most touching of wounded objects."

    —Edna Ferber

    **a.** rash    **b.** vulnerable    **c.** potential    **d.** singular    **e.** omnipotent

26. "Grandparents are frequently more _____ with their grandchildren than with their children. A grandparent cannot run with his son but can totter with his grandson."

    —Andre Maurois

    **a.** raucous    **b.** congenial    **c.** sedate    **d.** tenacious    **e.** vexatious

27. "It is unjust to the child to be born and reared as the 'creation' of the parents. He is himself, and it is within reason that he may be the very _____ of them both."

    —Ruth Benedict

    **a.** veneer    **b.** requisite    **c.** antithesis    **d.** profuse    **e.** anathema

28. "This, indeed, is one of the eternal _____ of both life and literature—that without passion little gets done; yet without control of that passion, its effects are largely ill or null."

    —F. L. Lucas

    **a.** trends    **b.** subterfuges    **c.** harbingers    **d.** fiats    **e.** paradoxes

29. "What has maintained the human race if not faith in new possibilities and courage to _____ them."

    —Jane Addams

    **a.** divulge    **b.** flout    **c.** advocate    **d.** initiate    **e.** mandate

30. "No sooner do we take steps out of our customary routine than a strange world _____ about us."

    —J. B. Priestly

    **a.** surges    **b.** wanes    **c.** recants    **d.** juxtaposes    **e.** galvanizes

31. "As the two _____ cultures began to mingle, they encountered some revealing and shocking truths."

    —Nelson DeMille

    **a.** venerable    **b.** transient    **c.** sedentary    **d.** disparate    **e.** servile

32. "Nothing is so exhausting as indecision, and nothing is so mired in _____ ."

    —Bertrand Russell

    **a.** futility    **b.** vituperation    **c.** subterfuge    **d.** foment    **e.** iniquity

ANSWERS ARE ON PAGE 397

33. "Most quarrels are _____ at the time, incredible afterwards."

—E. M. Forster

**a.** rash    **b.** salient    **c.** trenchant    **d.** inevitable    **e.** whimsical

34. "We live at the mercy of a _____ word. A sound, a mere disturbance of the air sinks into our very soul sometimes."

—Joseph Conrad

**a.** reviled    **b.** malevolent    **c.** vexatious    **d.** innocuous    **e.** evanescent

35. "There must be some good in the cocktail party to account for its immense _____ among otherwise sane people."

—Evelyn Waugh

**a.** vogue    **b.** cupidity    **c.** calumny    **d.** audacity    **e.** asperity

36. "One drifting yellow leaf on a windowsill can be a city dweller's fall, _____ and melancholy as any hillside in New England."

—E. B. White

**a.** somber    **b.** cryptic    **c.** pungent    **d.** aloof    **e.** doleful

37. "For generations of German plutocrats, duelling was a bastion against weakness, effeminacy, and _____ ."

—Arthur Krystal

**a.** redress    **b.** sophistry    **c.** decadence    **d.** temerity    **e.** vituperation

38. "No one weeps more _____ than the hardened scoundrel as was proved when a sentimental play was performed before an audience of gangsters whose eyes were seen to be red and swollen."

—Hesketh Pearson

**a.** copiously    **b.** vapidly    **c.** raucously    **d.** nominally    **e.** laudably

39. "My greatest problem is my dislike of _____ , of battle. I do not like wrestling matches or arguments. I seek harmony. If it is not there, I move away."

—Anais Nin

**a.** artifice    **b.** avarice    **c.** celerity    **d.** belligerence    **e.** diversity

40. "The only agreeable existence is one of idleness, and that is not, unfortunately, always _____ with continuing to exist at all."

—Rose Macauley

**a.** bogus    **b.** compatible    **c.** culpable    **d.** felicitous    **e.** inviolable

# VOC/QUOTE

41. "Diaries are sometimes meant to be a _____ record of one's daily waking hours. Sometimes they are an unconscious relief from the day's tensions."

    —Edna Ferber

    **a.** zealous    **b.** tacit    **c.** terse    **d.** supine    **e.** prudent

42. "Was there ever a wider and more loving conspiracy than that which keeps the _____ figure of Santa Claus from slipping away into the forsaken wonderland of the past?"

    —Hamilton Mabie

    **a.** vigilant    **b.** venerable    **c.** sedate    **d.** frenetic    **e.** factitious

43. "For him who has no concentration, there is no _____ ."

    —Bhagavad Gita

    **a.** tranquility    **b.** respite    **c.** solace    **d.** equanimity    **e.** humility

44. "Real excellence and _____ are not incompatible; on the contrary, they are twin sisters."

    —Jean Lacordiare

    **a.** potential    **b.** inhibition    **c.** propinquity    **d.** equanimity    **e.** humility

45. "Children are cunning enough behind their innocent faces, though _____ might be a kinder word to describe them."

    —Nan Fairbrother

    **a.** recondite    **b.** prudent    **c.** fatuous    **d.** incisive    **e.** inexorable

46. "It is not easy to _____ of anything that has given us truer insight."

    —John Spalding

    **a.** repent    **b.** rue    **c.** recant    **d.** eschew    **e.** cant

47. "There is no diplomacy like _____ . You may lose by it now and then, but it will be a loss well gained if you do. Nothing is so boring as having to keep up a deception."

    —E. V. Lucas

    **a.** hyperbole    **b.** chicanery    **c.** serenity    **d.** candor    **e.** opprobrium

48. "In America I was constantly being introduced to _____ persons by people who were unmistakably superior to those notables and most modestly unaware of it."

    —John Ayscough

    **a.** eminent    **b.** ostentatious    **c.** mendacious    **d.** intrepid    **e.** garrulous

**49.** "It is because nature made me a _____ man, going hither and thither for conversation that I love proud and lonely things."

—W. B. Yeats

    **a.** magnanimous    **b.** fastidious    **c.** doleful    **d.** banal    **e.** gregarious

**50.** "My greatest problem here, in a _____-loving America, is my dislike of polemics, of belligerence, of battle."

—Anais Nin

    **a.** docile    **b.** polemic    **c.** fastidious    **d.** implacable    **e.** nebulous

ANSWERS ARE ON PAGE 397

# THE LIGHTER TOUCH 100

The following jokes contain some of the words you have been taught in this book. Even the humorists know how to make use of a challenging vocabulary.

1. Henry joined Alcoholics Anonymous. He still **imbibes**, but under an assumed name.

2. A **hapless** man was run over by a steamroller. He's in the hospital, in Rooms 36-42.

3. My father's accountant treats people with **compassion**. His office has a recovery room.

4. Samson must have been quite a **thespian**, because he brought down the house.

5. **Inanimate** owls don't give a hoot.

6. You're probably an **octogenarian** if dialing long distance wears you out.

7. You have a right to be **wary** on a cheap airline if the oxygen mask has a meter on it.

8. The **magnanimous** husband bought his wife a clothes dryer—50 feet of clothesline.

9. He's so proud of his **longevity**, he has an autographed Bible.

10. Victor has a **voracious** appetite; his favorite food is seconds.

11. With a **pugnacious** wife, it's always better to give than to receive.

12. Henry Ford had millions, and yet he never had a **yen** for a Cadillac.

13. A woman in Tibet looked at her stove and **quipped**, "Oh, my baking yaks."

14. The rabbit's **progeny** consisted of ten bunnies. It beat the record by a hare.

15. My **astute** fish swims backwards. It keeps the water out of his eyes.

16. He made a **bogus** claim about the surgery to remove an ingrown cell phone.

17. The **intrepid** paratrooper spent three years climbing down trees he never climbed up.

18. Van Gogh had a **voluminous** output. As of today, Americans own 423 of his 72 paintings.

19. The **frugal** man complained about the cost of raising a baby. The nurse said, "Sure, but look how long they last."

20. The **maladjusted** baby just started to eat solids—his crib, blanket, pillows.

21. My old neighborhood **bristled** with trouble; even the candy store had a bouncer.

22. Uncle Eddie is not **bereft** of curly locks. He's just taller than his hair.

23. Today's financial **phenomenon**—a dollar saved is a quarter earned.

24. "What is the name of your bank?" I asked the **timorous** investor. "Piggy," he replied.

25. I don't like my **garrulous** barber, because he talks behind my back.

26. The **prudent** girl found the key to looking beautiful—she hangs out with real ugly people.

27. The pigeons in our neighborhood are quite **prescient**, because they always know when my Dad has polished our car.

28. "Do boats sink often?" I asked the **laconic** sailor. "Only once," he replied.

29. I'm such a **dilatory** reader that it takes me six weeks to read the Book of the Month.

30. Some make **sporadic** payments when their bills are due, some when overdue, some never do.

31. I asked the literary **dilettante**, "Have you read all of Shakespeare?" "I think so," he replied, "unless he's written something lately."

32. A flying goose in a **quandary** asked, "Why do we always follow the same leader?" The goose next to him answered, "Because he's got the map."

33. A bore is the guy who, when you ask him how he feels, he tells you so with **gusto**.

34. The **pertinent** advice my father was given was to buy a used car when it was new.

35. A **trenchant** remark: a cat has nine lives, but a bullfrog croaks every night.

36. My family had to **jettison** our car. It had low mileage, but most of it from being towed.

37. The charity was **reputed** to have raised three million dollars. Now they are going out in search of a disease.

38. **Squeamish** about paying a restaurant check, he reached for it as though it were a subpoena.

39. He's so **parsimonious** he tosses money around like manhole covers.

40. Han's parents weren't too thrilled with him. His mother had a **penchant** for wrapping his lunch in a road map.

41. The pompous actor ran the **gamut** from A to B.

42. Our **glib** doctor is a humorist. He said my uncle has the body of a 20-year-old—a twenty-year-old Chevy.

43. We call our **vigilant** dog Rolex, because he's a watchdog.

44. My **artless** neighbor lost her dog but refused to put an ad in the newspaper—he said his dog can't read.

45. Our doctor has a **lucrative** practice; he just bought a cemetery.

46. We heard of the **asinine** chicken who sat on an ax, trying to hatchet.

47. Mark asked his **sage** waiter, "What do you call two thousand pounds of Chinese soup?" The answer was, "Won ton."

48. Last Christmas I told Santa what I wanted. His **retort** was, "Me, too."

49. The **abstemious** young man boasted that he had finally given up trying to quit smoking.

50. P.T. Barnum's **grotesque** two-headed man asked him for a raise. "After all," he said, "I have two mouths to feed."

51. Eddie is a **paragon** of style. He has a suit for every day of the year—and this is it.

52. It was so cold that, when the thermometer plunged to its **nadir**, I sneezed and broke my Kleenex.

53. My **profligate** brother was a two-letter man in college. Monday and Friday he wrote home for money.

54. She comes from a confused family. During the Civil War they were **fervid** supporters of the East.

55. Aunt Helen underwent plastic surgery after Uncle Ted, the **martinet**, cut up her credit cards.

56. Dr. Grill gave me an **infallible** cure for insomnia: "Get lots of sleep."

57. My **inebriated** uncle stopped drinking recently. Two bars sued him for nonsupport.

58. The teenage driver is **alleged** to have received a ticket for making a U-turn in the Lincoln Tunnel.

59. The new miracle drug is a **hoax**. It keeps you alive only until your bill is paid.

60. What a **fiasco** was his attempt to raise eggplants by burying a chicken!

61. When I **scrutinize** the obituary column, it seems that everybody dies in alphabetical order.

62. I enjoyed the **levity** of the bumper sticker: DYSLEXICS OF THE WORLD UNTIE!

63. You know that bad times are **rampant** when couples get married because they need the rice.

64. An **egotist** is a man who doesn't go around talking about other people.

65. Cousin Randy was in the sixth grade so long, they thought he was the **pedagogue**.

66. I've got a lot of frozen **assets**—ten T.V. dinners.

67. The English complain about **nepotism**, but the Queen got her job through family.

68. I caught a fish so **mammoth** that the picture required two cameras.

69. Jerry was **frustrated** trying to find his glasses without his glasses.

70. Never make an undertaker your **adversary**. Sooner or later he'll have you dead to rights.

71. My **affluent** uncle always gives me cash for Christmas because it always will be the right size.

72. There was an **awesome** mishap at the circus yesterday. The lion tamer needs a tamer lion.

73. Did you hear of the **plight** of the new human cannonball? He was hired and fired the same night.

74. My brother made his first income since college. He had the **audacity** to sell the car my father gave him for graduation.

75. A conscience is that **ominous** inner voice that warns you someone is watching.

76. There's no need to **revere** Jeff as a speaker; he never opens his mouth unless he has nothing to say.

77. The judge asked, "What **bizarre** reason can you have for freeing this defendant?" A juror replied, "Insanity." The judge asked, "All twelve of you?"

78. In our neighborhood we don't worry about crime in the street. The **felons** make house calls.

79. My parents went on an **opulent** cruise. The smokestacks had filter tips.

80. You can **expedite** your weight loss by giving up only two things: a knife and a fork.

81. Roger is so **phlegmatic** that he puts more people to sleep than ether.

82. She's such a **dupe** that she put a zip code on the Gettysburg Address.

83. My **erudite** neighbor has a B.A., an M.A., a Ph.D., but no J.O.B.

84. We flew on a **pecuniary** airline. To save money, they use student drivers.

85. Our cuckoo clock is old and **decrepit**. All it does now is come out and shrug.

86. Eloise is a child **prodigy**; she can describe how an accordion works without using her hands.

87. Our neighbor had the **temerity** to borrow our car and then say, "Your air bag works."

88. Dad's birthday gift to Mom was not **conducive** to connubial bliss. She expected a Mercedes but got a toaster.

89. I read about the **corpulent** jockey who kept putting a la carte before the horse.

90. On our vacation, my father asked the **imperturbable** hotel clerk, "Do you take children?" "No," the clerk answered, "only cash and credit cards."

91. He had **universal** bad luck. He spent years paying off a funeral plot, and then he died at sea.

92. My grandfather used to suffer from **senility**, but he forgot all about it.

93. Now I know why we could never keep up with our neighbors. The Joneses were just **indicted** for tax evasion.

94. In all **candor**, the movie was so bad that people were waiting in line to get out.

95. Aunt Minnie is so **fastidious** that when she's having guests, she runs around putting in fresh lightbulbs.

96. There was such a **paucity** of money in his family that they couldn't give his sister a sweet sixteen until she was twenty-eight.

97. **Procrastination** has its good side—you always have something to do tomorrow.

98. We went sightseeing until our eyes were sore. Then they took us to an **idyllic** sight for sore eyes.

99. Uncle Arthur **acknowledged** that Aunt Blanche must be descended from Noah because whenever they went anywhere, she took two of everything.

100. I know it's a **cliché**, but on a trip whatever you want is in the other valise.

# ANSWERS

## ❖ WEEK A

| Day 1 | | Day 2 | | Day 3 | | Day 4 | |
|---|---|---|---|---|---|---|---|
| 1. toxic | 6. c | 1. circuitous | 6. c | 1. rapacious | 6. e | 1. denouement | 6. c |
| 2. extenuating | 7. a | 2. foreboding | 7. e | 2. insurgent | 7. c | 2. dilatory | 7. b |
| 3. neophyte | 8. e | 3. emanating | 8. a | 3. knell | 8. a | 3. specious | 8. a |
| 4. impregnable | 9. d | 4. miscreant | 9. b | 4. macabre | 9. b | 4. risible | 9. d |
| 5. patriarch | 10. b | 5. protocol | 10. d | 5. ramifications | 10. d | 5. glut | 10. e |

### Day 5

| REVIEW | | | | SENSIBLE SENTENCES? | WORDSEARCH A |
|---|---|---|---|---|---|
| 1. e | 7. n | 13. s | 19. o | 1. ramifications | 1. emanating |
| 2. t | 8. p | 14. c | 20. m | 2. toxic | 2. toxic |
| 3. g | 9. b | 15. h | 21. v | 3. protocol | 3. rapacious |
| 4. a | 10. j | 16. f | 22. w | 4. miscreant | 4. glut |
| 5. i | 11. d | 17. l | 23. u | 5. circuitous | 5. ramifications |
| 6. k | 12. r | 18. q | 24. x | 6. risible | |
| | | | | 7. insurgent | |
| | | | | 8. denouement | |
| | | | | 9. emanating | |
| | | | | 10. macabre | |

## ❖ WEEK B

| Day 1 | | Day 2 | | Day 3 | | Day 4 | |
|---|---|---|---|---|---|---|---|
| 1. suffrage | 6. d | 1. thespian | 6. c | 1. impasse | 6. c | 1. mortal | 6. c |
| 2. dolorous | 7. c | 2. despot | 7. d | 2. grandeur | 7. a | 2. guile | 7. b |
| 3. cabal | 8. a | 3. prescient | 8. a | 3. articulate | 8. b | 3. regimen | 8. d |
| 4. odious | 9. b | 4. verbatim | 9. b | 4. pathological | 9. e | 4. denigrated | 9. a |
| 5. enervated | 10. e | 5. reverie | 10. e | 5. polemic | 10. d | 5. inflicted | 10. e |

### Day 5

| REVIEW | | | | WORDSEARCH B | SENTENCE COMPLETION |
|---|---|---|---|---|---|
| 1. h | 7. j | 13. e | 19. d | 1. articulate | 1. a |
| 2. c | 8. t | 14. g | 20. k | 2. enervated | 2. c |
| 3. f | 9. o | 15. i | 21. w | 3. reverie | 3. b |
| 4. a | 10. n | 16. m | 22. u | 4. guile | 4. a |
| 5. s | 11. q | 17. p | 23. x | 5. prescient | 5. b |
| 6. l | 12. b | 18. r | 24. v | | |

## ❖ VOC/QUOTES

| | | | | | | | | | |
|---|---|---|---|---|---|---|---|---|---|
| 1. b | 6. c | 11. e | 16. b | 21. a | 26. b | 31. d | 36. c | 41. c | 46. a |
| 2. e | 7. a | 12. b | 17. e | 22. b | 27. c | 32. a | 37. c | 42. b | 47. d |
| 3. b | 8. a | 13. b | 18. a | 23. d | 28. e | 33. d | 38. a | 43. a | 48. a |
| 4. a | 9. e | 14. c | 19. b | 24. b | 29. c | 34. b | 39. d | 44. e | 49. e |
| 5. b | 10. b | 15. a | 20. a | 25. c | 30. a | 35. a | 40. b | 45. b | 50. b |

# PANORAMA OF WORDS

**articulate** "The senator's supporters were upset by the adjectives used to describe him: clean and *articulate.*" Editorial, *The New York Times*

**cabal** "If a *cabal's* secrets are revealed to the wind, you should not blame the wind for revealing them to the trees." Kahlil Gibran

**circuitous** "Although it took a *circuitous* route, the curveball finally reached the catcher's mitt." Red Smith

**denigrated** "Napoleon's henchmen *denigrated* the memory of Voltaire whose name the Emperor abhorred." Christopher Morley

**denouement** "We all sat awaiting the *denouement* of the play in silence." Mayne Reid

**despot** "The universe is not freindly to *despots*, and they all perish sooner or later." Don Marquis, *The Almost Perfect State*

**dilatory** "Between *dilatory* payment and bankruptcy there is a great distance." Samuel Johnson

**dolorous** "Diabetic patients are constantly tormented by *dolorous* sensations." William Roberts

**emanating** "The feudal idea viewed all rights as *emanating* from a head landlord." John Stuart Mill

**enervated** "I have had one of my many spasms which has almost *enervated* me." Lord Nelson, *Letters*

**extenuating** "In Clive's case there were many *extenuating* circumstances." Dame Rose Macaulay

**foreboding** "We are more disturbed by *forebodings* of a calamity which threatens us than by one which has befallen us." John Lancaster Spalding

**glut** "The world in that age had a *glut* rather than a famine of saints." R. S. Fuller, *Holy War*

**grandeur** "I have studied the glories of Greece but am more impressed by the *grandeur* of Rome." Rainer Maria Rilke

**guile** "Oh, that deceit should steal such gentle shapes, And with a virtuous vizard hide foul *guile.*" Shakespeare, *Richard III*

**impasse** "We expect the *impasse* between Britain and Iran to be resolved this weekend." United Nations Press Release

**impregnable** "The Maginot Line, a French system of fortifications, was considered *impregnable* at the start of World War II. *The Columbia Encyclopedia*

**inflicted** "Many of the cares that we are *inflicted* with are but a morbid way of looking at our privileges." Sir Walter Scott

**insurgent** "The *insurgents'* improvised explosive devices killed six more American soldiers yesterday." Michael Ware, CNN TV Broadcast

**knell** "Hear it not, Duncan; for it is a *knell* / That summons thee to heaven or to hell." Shakespeare, *Macbeth*

**macabre** "The Mardi Gras parade featured rowdy celebrants wearing *macabre* masks and colorful costumes." Eliza Berman, *Let the Good Times Roll*

**miscreant** "This is the basic measure of damages, and it's owed by the *miscreants* to the company and shareholders." Ben Stein, *State of the Union*

**mortal** "All is *mortal* in nature, so is all nature in love mortal in folly." Shakespeare, *As You Like It*

# PANORAMA OF WORDS

**neophyte** "The elaborate masked ritual of the courtroom holds attraction only for the *neophyte* and layman." David Riesman

**odious** "You told a lie, an *odious* damned lie." Shakespeare, *Othello*

**pathological** "A *pathological* liar is one whose lies are suggestive of a mental disorder." *Webster's Medical Dictionary*

**patriarch** "If a *patriarch* wants to put his foot down, the only safe place to do it in these days is in a note-book." Florida Scott-Maxwell

**polemic** "My greatest problem here, in a *polemic*-loving America, is my dislike of polemics, of belligerence, of battle." Anais Nin, *The Diaries of Anais Nin*

**prescient** "The Spanish Republic fell in April 1939, and World War II began soon after because those prescient fighters had not been heeded." Edward Rothstein, *Spanish Civil War*

**protocol** "The most advantageous *protocol* is very rarely the one I did follow." Andre Gide

**ramifications** "I don't live in a laboratory; I have no way of knowing what *ramifications* my actions will have." Hugh Prather

**rapacious** "Charles V levied fines with *rapacious* exactness." James Robertson

**regimen** "I guarantee weight loss when my *regimen* is followed strictly." Dr. Robert Atkins

**reverie** "All through the ages, people have regarded their *reveries* as sources of wisdom." Rollo May

**risible** "He is the most *risible* misanthrope I ever met with." Tobias Smollett, *Humphrey Clinker*

**specious** "It was a *specious* argument but delivered so effectively that it was convincing." Murray Bromberg, *Wagers of Sin*

**suffrage** "My successor was chosen by general *suffrage*." John Marsden

**thespian** "I regard Liev Schreiber as the outstanding *thespian* of our times." Ben Brantley, Theatre Critic, *The New York Times*

**toxic** "A hope, if it is not big enough, can prove *toxic*; for hope is more essentially an irritant than a soporific." William Bolitho

**verbatim** "Court reporters have to be able to take 250 words a minute in their *verbatim* accounts." *Court Reporters' Association Guide*

# INDEX

## A

abhor, 147, 324
abjure, 204, 324
abortive, 108, 324
abound, 2, 324
abrogate, 91, 324
abstemious, 121, 324
absurd, 147, 324
access, 91, 324
accommodate, 108, 324
accomplice, 90, 324
accost, 8, 324
acknowledged, 136, 324
acme, 222, 324
acrimonious, 29, 324
acute, 161, 324
adamant, 167, 324
adherent, 177, 324
admonish, 28, 324
adroit, 10, 324
advent, 254, 324
adversary, 178, 325
adverse, 53, 325
advocate, 55, 325
aegis, 154, 325
afflict, 46, 325
affluent, 33, 325
alacrity, 20, 325
allay, 205, 325
alleged, 91, 325
alleviate, 195, 325
allude, 253, 325
aloof, 267, 325
altruistic, 98, 325
ambiguous, 196, 325
ameliorate, 264, 325
amicable, 56, 325
amnesty, 115, 325
amorous, 99, 325
analogous, 139, 325
anathema, 73, 325
annals, 3, 326
anomaly, 190, 326
anthropologist, 145, 326
antipathy, 227, 326
antiquated, 209, 326
antithesis, 97, 326
apathy, 178, 326
appalled, 280, 326
appellation, 134, 326
arbiter, 192, 326
arbitrary, 40, 326
archaic, 198, 326
ardent, 164, 326
array, 164, 326
articulate, 376, 398
artifact, 145, 326
artifice, 259, 326
artless, 260, 326
ascend, 45, 326
ascertain, 283, 326
ascetic, 129, 326

asinine, 210, 327
asperity, 93, 327
aspirant, 23, 327
aspire, 84, 327
asset, 53, 327
assiduous, 103, 327
astute, 55, 327
atrophy, 264, 327
attenuated, 192, 327
attest, 105, 327
atypical, 180, 327
au courant, 211, 327
audacity, 235, 327
augment, 248, 327
austere, 228, 327
automaton, 2, 327
avarice, 173, 327
aversion, 159, 327
avid, 11, 327
awesome, 152, 328

## B

badger, 4, 328
bagatelle, 279, 328
balk, 117, 328
banal, 179, 328
barometer, 111, 328
bedlam, 170, 328
begrudge, 260, 328
belated, 239, 328
belittle, 21, 328
belligerent, 20, 328
benevolent, 265, 328
bereft, 165, 328
besiege, 46, 328
besmirch, 166, 328
bias, 87, 328
bigot, 53, 147, 328
bizarre, 145, 196, 328
blasé, 258, 328
blatant, 54, 328
bliss, 177, 329
blunt, 117, 329
bogus, 255, 329
bona fide, 130, 329
brash, 21, 329
brigand, 277, 329
bristle, 16, 329
buff, 110, 329
bulwark, 97, 329
burgeoned, 283, 329

## C

cabal, 374, 398
cache, 98, 329
cacophony, 170, 329
cajole, 11, 329
callous, 242, 258, 329
callow, 280, 329
calumny, 210, 329
canard, 271, 329
candid, 220, 329
candor, 184, 329
cant, 246, 329
capitulate, 235, 329
capricious, 261, 330
carnage, 270, 330

castigate, 22, 330
catastrophic, 142, 330
caustic, 14, 330
celerity, 195, 330
cessation, 16, 330
chagrin, 34, 330
charisma, 286, 330
charlatan, 186, 330
chicanery, 236, 330
chimerical, 136, 330
circuitous, 368, 398
clandestine, 27, 330
cliché, 217, 330
clique, 245, 330
coerce, 66, 330
cogent, 161, 330
cognizant, 41, 330
comely, 259, 330
commodious, 209, 330
compassion, 221, 330
compatible, 172, 331
compensatory, 142, 331
complacent, 202, 331
complicity, 90, 331
component, 104, 331
compound, 3, 331
comprehensive, 66, 331
concoct, 102, 331
concomitant, 191, 331
concur, 27, 331
condescend, 184, 331
condolence, 17, 331
condone, 196, 331
conducive, 230, 331
confidant(e), 36, 331
conflagration, 153, 331
confront, 227, 331
congenial, 154, 331
conjecture, 68, 331
conjugal, 111, 332
connoisseur, 205, 332
connubial, 134, 332
consternation, 33, 332
constrict, 165, 332
construe, 30, 332
consummate, 102, 332
contemptuous, 147, 332
contort, 248, 332
controversial, 93, 332
cope, 133, 332
copious, 222, 332
corpulent, 277, 332
corroborate, 66, 332
coterie, 98, 332
countenance, 214, 332
coup, 114, 332
covert, 133, 332
covet, 223, 332
crave, 109, 332
criterion, 266, 333
cryptic, 81, 333
culminate, 164, 333
culpable, 90, 333
culprit, 28, 333
cumbersome, 208, 333
cumulative, 135, 333
cupidity, 98, 333

curry, 252, 333
cursory, 96, 333
curtail, 81, 333
cynic, 265, 333

**D**
dearth, 284, 333
debacle, 215, 333
debilitate, 202, 333
debris, 152, 333
decade, 140, 333
decadence, 128, 333
decapitate, 280, 333
declaim, 92, 333
decorum, 186, 334
decrepit, 239, 334
deem, 110, 334
defamatory, 271, 334
degrade, 220, 334
deleterious, 191, 334
delineation, 241, 334
delude, 136, 334
deluge, 270, 334
delve, 261, 334
demeanor, 241, 334
demur, 134, 334
denigrated, 377, 398
denote, 253, 334
denouement, 370, 398
depict, 222, 334
deplorable, 153, 334
deploy, 105, 334
deprecate, 271, 334
deride, 34, 334
derived, 284, 334
derogatory, 334, 334
desist, 59, 334
despot, 375, 398
destitution, 128, 335
desultory, 129, 335
deter, 205, 335
detriment, 154, 335
devout, 272, 335
dexterity, 221, 335
diatribe, 71, 335
dilatory, 370, 398
dilettante, 180, 335
diminutive, 273, 335
discern, 33, 335
disciple, 129, 335
discreet, 203, 335
disdain, 20, 335
disgruntled, 171, 335
disheveled, 209, 335
dismantle, 116, 335
disparage, 35, 335
disparate, 121, 335
dispersed, 152, 335
disseminate, 283, 335
dissent, 192, 336
distraught, 29, 336
diversity, 259, 336
divulge, 208, 336
docile, 236, 336
doddering, 155, 336
doleful, 60, 336
dolorous, 374, 398

domicile, 67, 336
dormant, 283, 336
dregs, 23, 336
drudgery, 4, 336
dubious, 36, 336
dulcet, 273, 336
dupe, 15, 336
duplicity, 29, 336
duress, 28, 336

**E**
edifice, 122, 336
efficacy, 191, 336
effigy, 41, 336
effrontery, 215, 336
egotist, 167, 336
egregious, 29, 337
elapse, 67, 337
elicit, 30, 337
elucidate, 246, 337
elusive, 61, 337
emaciated, 45, 337
embellish, 98, 337
emanating, 368, 398
eminent, 1, 337
emissary, 278, 337
emit, 79, 337
emulate, 198, 337
encomium, 285, 337
encumbrance, 183, 337
enervated, 374, 398
engrossed, 62, 337
enhance, 11, 337
enigma, 105, 337
ennui, 259, 337
entourage, 54, 337
entreaty, 148, 338
enunciate, 141, 338
epithet, 93, 338
epitome, 221, 338
equanimity, 172, 215, 338
eradicate, 171, 338
erudite, 230, 338
eruption, 152, 338
escalation, 135, 338
eschew, 35, 338
ethics, 27, 338
euphemism, 17, 338
evaluate, 104, 338
evanescent, 204, 338
eventuate, 79, 338
evince, 159, 338
exacerbate, 42, 338
excoriate, 272, 338
excruciating, 48, 338
exhort, 178, 338
exonerate, 115, 339
expatriate, 115, 339
expedient, 258, 339
expedite, 195, 339
exploit, 170, 339
expunge, 73, 339
expurgate, 260, 339
extant, 122, 339
extenuating, 367, 398
extinct, 183, 339
extol, 245, 339

extortion, 53, 339
extraneous, 196, 339
extrinsic, 92, 339
exult, 105, 339
exultation, 165, 339

**F**
fabricate, 10, 134, 339
façade, 210, 339
facet, 234, 339
facetious, 198, 339
facile, 245, 339
factitious, 285, 340
fallacious, 102, 340
falter, 165, 340
fastidious, 211, 340
fatal, 234, 340
fatuous, 248, 340
feasible, 33, 340
feint, 20, 340
felicitous, 228, 340
felon, 9, 340
ferment, 192, 340
fervid, 189, 340
fetish, 145, 340
fetter, 92, 340
fiasco, 35, 340
fiat, 115, 340
flabbergasted, 215, 340
flagrant, 28, 340
flamboyant, 73, 340
flay, 241, 340
fledgling, 185, 341
flout, 41, 341
fluctuate, 209, 341
foist, 235, 341
foment, 203, 341
foreboding, 368, 398
forthwith, 42, 341
fortuitous, 71, 341
fracas, 178, 341
fractious, 74, 341
frail, 272, 341
fraught, 103, 341
fray, 40, 341
frenetic, 259, 341
frenzy, 23, 341
fretful, 48, 341
frugal, 97, 341
fruitless, 65, 341
frustrate, 61, 341
fulsome, 127, 341
furtive, 9, 341
futility, 270, 342

**G**
galvanize, 183, 342
gamut, 139, 342
garbled, 65, 342
garrulous, 179, 342
gaudy, 183, 342
gaunt, 216, 342
genocide, 286, 342
genre, 220, 342
germane, 230, 342
gesticulate, 10, 342
gist, 161, 342

glean, 203, 342
glib, 233, 342
glut, 370, 398
grandeur, 376, 398
gratuity, 260, 342
gregarious, 96, 342
grimace, 210, 342
grotesque, 221, 342
guile, 377, 398
guise, 267, 342
gullible, 105, 342
gusto, 179, 342

**H**
habitat, 96, 343
halcyon, 228, 343
hapless, 9, 343
harass, 40, 343
harbinger, 47, 343
haven, 78, 343
havoc, 85, 343
heinous, 241, 343
heresy, 189, 343
heterogeneous, 139, 343
hirsute, 216, 343
histrionics, 61, 343
hoard, 154, 343
hoax, 104, 343
homogeneous, 233, 343
hostile, 158, 343
humility, 167, 343
hyperbole, 286, 343

**I**
iconoclast, 229, 343
idyllic, 183, 344
ignominious, 223, 344
ilk, 71, 344
imbibe, 155, 344
imminent, 62, 344
impasse, 376, 398
impeccable, 103, 344
impede, 171, 344
imperative, 146, 344
imperceptible, 248, 344
imperturbable, 239, 344
impetuous, 202, 344
impious, 254, 344
implacable, 39, 344
implore, 4, 344
importune, 78, 344
impregnable, 367, 398
impresario, 53, 344
impromptu, 273, 344
imprudent, 146, 344
impunity, 30, 344
inadvertent, 15, 345
inane, 27, 345
inanimate, 145, 345
incapacitated, 134, 345
inchoate, 81, 345
incipient, 15, 345
incisive, 86, 345
inclement, 59, 345
incoherent, 71, 345
incompatibility, 133, 345
incongruous, 17, 345
incontrovertible, 78, 345

incredulous, 80, 345
incumbent, 192, 345
indict, 120, 345
indifference, 135, 345
indigenous, 96, 345
indigent, 40, 346
indiscriminate, 1, 346
indoctrinate, 127, 346
indolent, 179, 346
inebriated, 178, 346
ineffectual, 55, 346
inert, 62, 346
inevitable, 160, 346
inexorable, 28, 346
infallible, 171, 346
infamous, 15, 346
inflicted, 377, 398
infraction, 242, 346
ingratiate, 223, 346
inherent, 110, 346
inhibition, 71, 346
iniquity, 265, 346
initiate, 153, 346
innate, 108, 346
innocuous, 190, 346
inordinate, 141, 347
insatiable, 173, 347
insidious, 253, 347
insurgent, 369, 398
integral, 72, 347
interject, 61, 347
interloper, 96, 347
interminable, 4, 347
internecine, 284, 347
interrogate, 208, 347
intimidate, 20, 347
intrepid, 8, 347
intrinsic, 160, 252, 347
introspective, 141, 347
inundate, 65, 347
invalidate, 91, 347
invective, 166, 347
inveigh, 84, 347
inveterate, 167, 347
inviolable, 148, 348
irascible, 141, 348
irate, 9, 348
irrational, 173, 348
irrelevant, 109, 348
itinerant, 111, 348

**J**
jaunty, 74, 348
jeopardize, 80, 348
jettison, 160, 348
jocose, 184, 348
jostle, 15, 348
jubilant, 186, 348
jurisdiction, 39, 348
juxtapose, 133, 348

**K**
knell, 369, 398

**L**
labyrinth, 104, 348
laceration, 22, 348
lackluster, 14, 348

laconic, 8, 348
lampoon, 214, 348
landmark, 92, 348
largess, 266, 349
lassitude, 191, 247, 349
latent, 110, 349
laudable, 35, 349
lax, 67, 349
legerdemain, 233, 349
legion, 114, 349
lethal, 86, 349
lethargic, 158, 349
levity, 123, 349
libel, 271, 349
liquidation, 90, 349
lithe, 177, 349
livid, 279, 349
loath, 55, 349
loathe, 14, 349
longevity, 155, 349
lucrative, 160, 349
lugubrious, 123, 349
lurid, 68, 350
lush, 128, 350

**M**
macabre, 369, 398
Machiavellian, 240, 350
magnanimous, 246, 350
maim, 264, 350
maladjusted, 139, 350
malady, 56, 350
malevolent, 273, 350
malign, 184, 350
malignant, 47, 350
malleable, 233, 350
malnutrition, 46, 350
mammoth, 85, 350
mandate, 142, 350
manifest, 261, 350
manifold, 103, 350
martinet, 279, 350
masticate, 35, 350
mastiff, 60, 350
materialism, 130, 350
matron, 2, 351
maudlin, 123, 351
megalomania, 114, 351
mendacious, 115, 351
menial, 196, 351
mentor, 245, 351
mercenary, 266, 351
metamorphosis, 129, 351
meticulous, 67, 351
mien, 216, 351
milieu, 190, 351
miscreant, 368, 398
modify, 108, 351
mollify, 266, 351
monolithic, 40, 351
moribund, 173, 351
mortal, 377, 399
mortality, 140, 351
mortify, 184, 351
motivate, 229, 351
mundane, 17, 351
munificent, 286, 352

murky, 104, 352
myriad, 109, 352

**N**
nadir, 173, 352
naive, 222, 352
nascent, 229, 352
nebulous, 120, 352
nefarious, 56, 352
negligible, 258, 352
neophyte, 367, 399
nepotism, 284, 352
nettle, 84, 352
neurotic, 140, 352
neutralize, 142, 352
nirvana, 130, 352
noisome, 211, 352
nomadic, 93, 352
nominal, 72, 352
nondescript, 180, 352
nonentity, 215, 352
nostalgia, 117, 352
nuance, 11, 353
nullify, 270, 353
nurture, 130, 353
nutritive, 255, 353

**O**
obese, 177, 353
obliterate, 153, 353
obloquy, 285, 353
obscure, 165, 353
obsequious, 127, 353
obsess, 60, 353
obsolescence, 36, 353
obviate, 68, 353
occult, 202, 353
octogenarian, 22, 353
odious, 374, 399
ominous, 16, 353
omnipotent, 185, 353
omnivorous, 121, 353
opprobrium, 240, 353
opulence, 127, 353
originate, 148, 354
ostensible, 189, 354
ostentatious, 74, 354
oust, 42, 354
overt, 84, 354

**P**
pall, 252, 354
palliate, 136, 354
paltry, 196, 354
panacea, 171, 354
pandemonium, 240, 354
parable, 214, 354
paradox, 3, 354
paragon, 93, 354
paramount, 158, 354
pariah, 267, 354
paroxysm, 39, 354
parsimonious, 116, 354
passé, 234, 354
pathetic, 177, 355
pathological, 376, 399
patriarch, 367, 399
paucity, 29, 355

pecuniary, 116, 355
pedagogue, 141, 355
penance, 129, 355
penchant, 280, 355
penitent, 204, 355
pensive, 217, 355
penury, 223, 355
perceive, 4, 355
peregrination, 111, 355
peremptory, 185, 355
perfidious, 223, 355
perfunctory, 34, 355
permeate, 80, 355
pernicious, 30, 355
perpetrate, 102, 355
perpetuate, 142, 355
persevere, 92, 355
perspicacious, 139, 356
pertinent, 60, 356
peruse, 59, 356
perverse, 34, 356
pesky, 120, 356
phenomenon, 140, 356
phlegmatic, 65, 356
phobia, 230, 356
pinnacle, 164, 356
pique, 180, 356
pittance, 211, 356
placard, 72, 356
plaintiff, 271, 356
platitude, 179, 356
plethora, 9, 356
plight, 133, 356
poignant, 66, 356
polemic, 376, 399
ponder, 128, 356
potent, 272, 356
potentate, 283, 357
potential, 135, 357
potpourri, 253, 357
pragmatic, 267, 357
precedent, 185, 357
precipitate, 86, 357
preclude, 91, 357
precocious, 34, 357
prelude, 136, 357
premise, 80, 357
premonition, 59, 357
prerogative, 284, 357
prescient, 375, 399
prestigious, 72, 357
pretext, 10, 357
prevalent, 158, 357
prevarication, 286, 357
privation, 46, 357
procrastinate, 234, 357
prodigious, 195, 358
prodigy, 165, 358
proffer, 254, 358
profligate, 114, 358
profound, 195, 358
profuse, 273, 358
progeny, 99, 358
prognosticate, 2, 358
prohibition, 146, 358
prolific, 97, 358
promulgate, 21, 358
propagate, 190, 358

propensity, 205, 358
propinquity, 170, 358
propitious, 80, 358
propriety, 254, 358
protocol, 368, 399
proximity, 247, 358
prudent, 189, 358
pugnacious, 21, 358
puissant, 123, 359
pungent, 167, 359
puny, 152, 359

**Q**
qualm, 260, 359
quandary, 258, 359
quarry, 203, 359
quell, 36, 359
quip, 68, 359

**R**
rabid, 198, 359
raconteur, 278, 359
rail, 277, 359
raiment, 277, 359
ramifications, 369, 399
rampant, 27, 359
rapacious, 369, 399
rash, 68, 359
rationalize, 229, 359
raucous, 255, 359
raze, 85, 359
realm, 3, 359
rebuke, 159, 359
recant, 90, 359
recoil, 59, 360
recondite, 135, 360
redolent, 121, 360
redress, 242, 360
refute, 216, 360
regimen, 377, 399
relegate, 84, 360
remiss, 158, 360
remote, 47, 360
remuneration, 72, 360
repent, 266, 360
repertoire, 248, 360
replenish, 261, 360
replete, 1, 360
repose, 121, 360
reprehensible, 39, 360
repress, 81, 360
reprimand, 14, 360
reproach, 204, 360
repudiate, 16, 361
repugnant, 221, 361
repulse, 85, 361
reputed, 272, 361
requisite, 261, 361
resourceful, 103, 361
respite, 48, 361
restrictive, 117, 361
reticent, 8, 236, 361
retort, 236, 361
retrospect, 166, 361
reverberating, 48, 361
revere, 172, 361
reverie, 375, 399
revert, 42, 361

reviled, 120, 361
rhetoric, 245, 361
rife, 117, 361
rift, 278, 361
risible, 370, 399
romp, 110, 362
roster, 264, 362
rudimentary, 11, 362
rue, 153, 362
ruminate, 278, 362
rustic, 186, 362

S

saga, 239, 362
sage, 154, 362
salient, 62, 362
sally, 33, 362
salubrious, 198, 362
salvation, 130, 362
sanctimonious, 214, 362
sanction, 253, 362
sanctuary, 45, 362
sanguine, 65, 362
satiety, 252, 362
saturate, 99, 362
schism, 73, 362
scion, 127, 363
scoff, 21, 363
scrutinize, 56, 363
scurrilous, 23, 363
scurry, 86, 363
sedate, 172, 363
sedentary, 97, 363
senile, 155, 363
serenity, 172, 363
servile, 227, 363
shibboleth, 255, 363
sinecure, 87, 363
singular, 87, 363
sinister, 46, 363
site, 208, 363
skirmish, 39, 363
slovenly, 203, 363
sojourn, 227, 363
solace, 23, 363
solicit, 55, 363
somber, 202, 364
sophistry, 285, 364
sordid, 22, 364
spate, 254, 364
specious, 370, 399
spew, 54, 364
spontaneous, 108, 364
sporadic, 67, 364
spurious, 189, 364
squeamish, 62, 364
stagnant, 234, 364
staunch, 240, 364
steeped, 1, 364
stentorian, 87, 364
stereotype, 86, 364
stigmatize, 235, 364
stipulate, 17, 364
strident, 191, 364
strife, 114, 364
stunted, 264, 364
stupor, 217, 364
stymie, 41, 364

subjugate, 78, 365
subservient, 265, 365
substantiate, 255, 365
subterfuge, 102, 365
subterranean, 79, 365
succinct, 196, 365
succulent, 252, 365
succumb, 48, 365
suffrage, 374, 399
sullen, 278, 365
sultry, 122, 365
sumptuous, 116, 365
superficial, 159, 365
superfluous, 228, 365
supine, 85, 365
supplication, 128, 365
surfeit, 190, 365
surge, 45, 365
surmise, 81, 365
surreptitious, 78, 365
susceptible, 140, 366
symptomatic, 61, 366

T

taboo, 146, 366
tacit, 236, 366
taint, 146, 366
tangible, 22, 366
tantalize, 235, 366
tantamount, 204, 366
taut, 279, 366
technology, 2, 270, 366
temerity, 99, 366
tenable, 228, 366
tenacious, 210, 366
termagant, 280, 366
terminate, 42, 366
terse, 161, 366
therapy, 229, 366
thespian, 375, 399
throng, 8, 366
thwart, 47, 366
timorous, 74, 367
tinge, 3, 367
tolerate, 30, 367
tortuous, 111, 367
toxic, 367, 399
tradition, 148, 367
tranquil, 45, 367
transient, 161, 367
tremulous, 16, 367
trenchant, 122, 367
trend, 233, 367
trivial, 196, 367
truncated, 74, 367
turbulent, 41, 367
turpitude, 242, 367
tussle, 160, 367
tyro, 285, 367

U

ubiquitous, 47, 367
ultimate, 79, 367
umbrage, 246, 367
unabated, 123, 367
unconscionable, 240, 368
unctuous, 265, 368
underwrite, 116, 368

universal, 147, 368
unkempt, 211, 368
unmitigated, 209, 368
unsavory, 220, 368
unwieldy, 247, 368
urbane, 109, 368
usurp, 196, 368
utopia, 73, 368

V

vacillate, 239, 368
valor, 87, 368
vapid, 247, 368
vehemently, 222, 368
veneer, 109, 368
venerable, 197, 368
venial, 220, 368
venom, 54, 368
verbatim, 375, 399
vertigo, 230, 368
vestige, 267, 369
vexatious, 56, 369
viable, 79, 369
vicissitudes, 122, 369
vigil, 208, 369
vigilant, 10, 369
vilify, 246, 369
vindicate, 241, 369
virile, 155, 369
virtuosity, 99, 369
virulent, 54, 369
vitiate, 247, 369
vitriolic, 166, 369
vituperation, 242, 369
vivacious, 216, 369
vogue, 159, 369
volition, 227, 369
voluble, 36, 369
voluminous, 166, 369
voracious, 1, 369
vulnerable, 148, 170, 370

W

wan, 60, 370
wane, 180, 370
wary, 205, 370
wheedle, 186, 370
whet, 217, 370
whimsical, 214, 370
wince, 217, 370
wistful, 277, 370
wrest, 14, 370

Y

yen, 279, 370

Z

zealous, 66, 370
zenith, 185, 370